ALL ABOARD!

ALL ABOARD!

THE STORY OF JOSHUA LIONEL COWEN & HIS LIONEL TRAIN COMPANY

RON HOLLANDER

WORKMAN PUBLISHING
NEW YORK

To my parents and Virginia Cornue, my co-engineer, with great love.

While the author has had the full and extremely generous cooperation of the family of Joshua Lionel Cowen, The Lionel Corporation, and the Lionel Division of Fundimensions, the author is solely responsible for the contents of *All Aboard!*

Lionel is a registered trademark of The Lionel Corporation.

Copies of Lionel material are made with the permission of Fundimensions, manufacturers of Lionel trains. Fundimensions has an exclusive license from The Lionel Corporation.

Library of Congress Cataloging in Publication Data

Hollander, Ron.
All aboard!

1. Cowen, Joshua Lionel, 1877-1965. 2. Lionel Corporation—History
3. Railroads—Models—Biography. I. Title. TF140.C65H64
338.7′62519′0973 81-40506 ISBN 0-89480-184-8 AACR2

Book design: Wendy Palitz

Workman Publishing Company, Inc.
708 Broadway
New York, NY 10003

Manufactured in the United States of America
First printing October 1981

15 14 13 12 11 10 9 8 7 6 5 4

CONTENTS

TIMETABLE

LIONEL TRAINS
APPROVED SERVICE

BUYING YOUR TICKET

I have become a man in the thirty-five years since my first electric train Christmas, but the lure of that December morning is with me still. The apartment where first I ogled Joshua Lionel Cowen's toy trains has long been inhabited by strangers. But so fantastic was the train layout my father built for me, I think surely some trace of it must still exist in that Brooklyn living room. Despite decades of sweeping, there must be a piece of wire, a lump of miniature coal, a forgotten white smoke pellet in some corner of that apartment. Soon I will go back and ask the present tenants to indulge me while I crawl around their floor, searching (maybe under the radiator?) for something tangible from those days that now run round and round in my head like my Lionel trains.

In the beginning, Joshua Lionel Cowen had nothing to do with my trains... at least not directly. If I ever linked a name with them other than Santa Claus, it was probably Lionel Barrymore (who along with Ronald Coleman was my favorite actor, solely on the basis of distinguished first names). In the beginning, the trains were something special between my father and me. My mother and sister were there, but in the background, just as women were in the Lionel train catalogs.

Actually, my Uncle Herbie's gray *Commodore Vanderbilt* engine, pulling its orange Shell oil tank car, was the first Lionel I ever saw. The *Commodore* had no whistle, nor did it puff smoke like later models, but it did have a headlight and wonderfully busy driving rods that churned furiously. I don't remember how, but I inherited Herbie's *Commodore Vanderbilt* without that orange Shell tank car with its silver wheels. But a few years ago, like a benign Ghost of Christmas Past, one like it surfaced in the back room of a train shop. The distinctive orange of the tank car recalled more powerfully than the widest-screen Panavision those days in 1944 when I rocked myself to sleep singing a song to end the war: "When Johnny comes marching home again, hoorah, hoorah..." I bought the car for five dollars. Uncle Herbie's train, my first Lionel, had been made whole.

Besides the *Commodore,* one other hand-me-down train preceded the great Christmas layout built by my father: a prewar silver and red metal steamliner. I never knew where it came from—a great-uncle, perhaps. The silver, fluted sides of the passenger cars and the bright red front of the engine fascinated me as it scooted around its temporary circle of track.

One day some people came to visit. They had a boy my age with them. Who were they? Friends of my parents? Distant cousins? In any case, my silver and red streamliner was given to this wretched unknown boy.

"You have another train," someone told me with disgusting adult logic. "So what!" I wanted to shout and stamp. "So what. I can have more than one train. I can have a lot of trains, a hundred." But I said none of this. I didn't want to appear selfish. So it was carried off, and for years I had no passenger train on my railroad.

Then came the end of the war.The grown-ups strung Chinese lanterns from the chestnut trees and danced in the street. There were parades of homecoming soldiers, just like my little lead ones. Unknown to me at the time, a sprawling brick factory across the Hudson River in Irvington, New Jersey, was converting from the wartime manufacture of compasses to the production of electric trains. It was time to make up for years of sacrifice. It was time to go for drives in the country, to compete for that dream house in something called the suburbs. It was time to celebrate the family reunited. It was time to buy electric trains.

I had a burgeoning awareness in those wonderful, seemingly endless days after the war that my father was somehow better than the other dads. Neighbors came to borrow tools. They sought his opinion, and he gave advice about repairs. He had a wise air about him, and it was clear to me that he was someone special.

Hadn't he been one of the first to string street decorations for the armistice party? While other men parked their cars on the street, didn't he rent a wooden garage with its own lock whose combination he taught me? Didn't he then build me a brown and yellow garage for the locomotive he had made for me of scrap lumber? And finally, didn't he build me the best Lionel railroad ever for Christmas?

We all had electric trains, and my friends all had Lionels. (Some less fortunate children had American Flyers. They were alright—the engines made a nice chuffing sound and there was a passenger car that picked up a mailbag while the train was moving—but they ran on flimsy track and were smaller than our mighty Lionels.) Mitchell, my best friend, had a black steam locomotive that pulled an orange box car lettered "Baby Ruth." When the doors slid open, we put the round, wooden knobs from Tinker Toys inside.

Mitchell's trains ran on his blue living room rug. They were there only by temporary fiat, and we had to be careful not to get anything dirty. He had no operating accessories like coal loaders. But his little train fascinated us for hours. When the locomotive chugged past Mitchell got so excited he stuck his tongue out and made wild, fluttering motions with his hands.

Joseph, who lived two floors below, had even less. While he had no steam engine, he did eventually have a black diesel switching engine with a bell that rang continuously. It had couplers at both ends for pulling or pushing freight cars. Behind this engine (I thought it had something to do with Christmas, for it was lettered *Santa Fe*) came a red metal dump car that, at the touch of a button, plopped tiny, artificial coal into a plastic bin beside the track. A small lever on the side of the car allowed the bin to tilt by hand. When I mischievously pushed it, the coal spilled on the carpet. There was also a bright red and yellow metal derrick car with a dangling hook. The hook went up and down on a pulley.

When my layout magically appeared Christmas morning, with track mounted on boards and two complete trains, it was so superior to anything we had seen outside of the Lionel catalog that I immediately became—as Joshua Cowen would have put it—the chief railroad engineer in my neighborhood.

I don't remember lobbying for a train that Christmas. The genesis of my railroad probably lay more with my father. I don't think it had so much to do with his attraction to the trains as with the image Lionel created of a happy father and son together around the family train set. After all, Lionel came right out and said electric trains were "The Perfect Instrument Of Father-Son Relationship."

I think my father wanted to belong, wanted us to become the perfect all-American family, a myth that imprisoned and encapsulated the country for years. Trains were the gift you got your boy on Christmas if you were a regular dad, a pal. Such a relationship was totally different from the one my father must have had with his own father, an immigrant tailor from Poland. In that dignified, European-shaped generation, fathers did not need to prove their love, least of all by abandoning their club chairs and newspapers to crawl on the floor with their sons in pursuit of a small, motorized locomotive.

My father had just survived the Depression and a war and it was time for a new beginning, a postwar celebration with something at once as extravagant and as frivolous as electric trains. So it was not merely the trains, it was what they symbolized, what they said to us and to the rest of the world. They were both a reassurance and an advertisement: "Lionel's in the home, all's right with the world." And if a simple circle of track on the linty living room carpet said all that, how much more convincing was it if my father built a whole railroad empire for me, just as the Lionel catalog urged him to do?

The trains came as an amazing surprise. The layout covered my mother's normally inviolate living room rug from breakfront to love seat. And it was my very own, laid out before me in my apartment, a feast to rival a department store's but with no clerk or glass partition to keep me away from it. Every object was unique. No one, anywhere, had the railroad I had: a red and green station with soft lights and real billboards on its picket fence; a silver girder bridge emblazoned "Lionel"; a semaphore that went up and down and changed colors as the train passed; a man in blue who came out of his gatekeeper's shack waving a lighted lantern; a red coal loader with a conveyor belt that endlessly carried artificial coal; a village of wooden houses with little chimneys and painted vines growing up their sides (my mother liked them best); a highway flasher whose red lights twinkled as the train passed.

All this was fastened to green plywood boards

on which I could already imagine roads, lakes, and budding mountain ranges. Two lines of track curved off toward the mirror around our artificial fireplace. In the middle of the railroad, two switches showed red or green lights as the track setting changed. On the outside track was my old friend, Uncle Herbie's *Commodore Vanderbilt,* with its familiar string of cars. But on the inside track was something new and startling. A black steam locomotive with so many wheels there seemed no room for any motor stood waiting, smoke drifting from its stack. The tender, coal heaped high, had silver letters proclaiming "Lionel Lines." Then came a silver coal dumping car, a flatcar with big iron pipes between its stakes, a hulking gray crane car that seemed real and powerful, and a work caboose with a tiny spotlight that lit up and swiveled. The train sat at the station awaiting my orders.

The transformer that ran the railroad was so heavy I couldn't lift it, with two levers and two dials to run four trains at once, reverse them, and even blow their whistles. Beside the transformer there were buttons and switches to run the coal loader, dump the coal car, and uncouple trains while they were moving. I sat on the carpet in my pajamas in front of this console. I looked up, and there was my father beaming down at me. "Why, what is all this and how did it get here?" his twinkly smile seemed to say. His skinny shins (which I have inherited) stuck out of his blue night shirt. I knew then I had the best father there was.

At the time I sincerely thought my father had arranged with Santa to have the railroad delivered. At most, I thought perhaps he and Santa had collaborated on the harder parts. It was only years later that I realized the months of planning that had gone into building my railroad. My father must have assembled it in the basement of our apartment building, or perhaps next door at Mitchell's. Thinking of the nights when he laid out the track, soldered the wires, made difficult choices between the purchase of a coal loader or a lumber conveyor (which I eventually also got), I loved him all the more.

The railroad occupied the living room for probably two weeks at most. Basking in its glory, I brought boys home from school, doling out brief turns at the uncoupling button, the whistle lever, and—for a favored few—the throttle of the *Commodore.* I was the only one to run my smoking Pennsy twenty-wheel steam turbine. The railroad was put away in the middle of January. The trains went back into their orange, white, and blue boxes, colors as important in my mind as red, white, and blue must have been for Betsy Ross. Once stored, the railroad did not come down until next year. Part of its majesty was that it was not a toy to be set up on the spur of the moment, like a mere circle of track. I linked it with Christmas, and that was the time it should reappear. I understood it did not belong in the living room in July.

For many years, thinking back on that railroad—the trains themselves sit on the shelves above me now, the hook from the gray crane car dangling over my desk as I write—I assumed it was the trains and the layout I valued and prized. But Cowen understood he was selling more than a toy, even if the boys and fathers of America did not. The Lionel catalog for 1946 featured a color photograph of a father and son: A shining-faced little boy with a pompadour and his dad, in checked sports jacket, arm around his son, beamed over a train layout. The father asked his boy, "Which LIONEL do you want, son?" Seeing me, rapt, before this tableau, absorbing every detail of locomotive and water tower, my wife, Virginia, observed, "It's not the trains you want; it's your father's arm around you."

She was right, of course. Cowen was selling the perfect family, and the nation was buying. As with all myths, it was a seller's market. And though we boys did not know it then, the dream would stay with us long after the trains were gone. My father had given me a perfect gift of his love, and nothing would ever be as simple again... not for me, and not for America.

The author with his first Lionel.

SEYMOUR HOLLANDER

1

IN THE STATION

1877-1900

WARD KIMBALL

A *mellow fifteenth of June in New York City in the bustling year of 1902: Teddy Roosevelt is in the White House, the Spanish have been humbled in Cuba and the Philippines, and the country is riding high. Horses clop past on the street; only a few of the wealthy own automobiles, driven by specially-trained "engineers." There are already twenty million incandescent lamps in the country, but electricity is still unusual and somewhat frightening. There are toy trains, but most are pull toys or, at best, are driven by springs or fueled by burning alcohol.*

In a cramped third floor loft at 24 Murray Street, just west of City Hall, Joshua Cowen is in his second year of electric toy train manufacture, the profit from his first year's labor being eight hundred dollars. The battery-powered flat car going in circles on steel track before him is primarily a novelty item, designed to attract attention to store window displays.

Fifty blocks uptown, at the open, steam-shrouded train sheds of the New York Central and Hudson River Railroad's Grand Central Depot, a new passenger train is leaving for Chicago from Track 20, its advertised running time an eyebrow-raising twenty hours. Park Avenue north of the depot is a smoky maze of exposed tracks and overhead pedestrian walks. Fresh from Delmonico's if they are with Hearst's Journal, *or from the depot's quick-lunch counter's fried oysters if they are not, reporters scribble in their notebooks as the four-car train departs at 2:45* P.M.

The electric train is called a Lionel, after the middle name of its inventor. The passenger train is named The Twentieth Century Limited, *after the new century whose speed and progress it will symbolize. For the next sixty-five years, each will be synonymous with excellence and preeminence. They will pace each other, Lionel and* The Twentieth Century, *growing and prospering with America, reflecting the style and times through which they travel. Finally, when their day has passed, they will depart at almost the same time: Joshua Lionel Cowen in retirement in Palm Beach in 1965,* The Twentieth Century *hours off schedule in Harbor Creek, Pennsylvania, in 1967.*

Though *The Twentieth Century* made daily runs between Chicago and New York, the Cohens (Cowen's forebears) made the longer journey—and the miles of dirt roads and turbulent sea crossing were only the beginning. The transition from a sheltered nineteenth-century Eastern European shtetl to a New World where hurtling passenger trains opened up Indian territory must have been, at the very least, unsettling. Not even Horatio Alger could claim to have traveled farther.

Joshua Cowen's grandparents came from Suvalk, a small town in the Eastern Pale of Settlement—that area in which Jews could legally settle—near the murky, fought-over border between modern Poland and Russian Lithuania. In many ways, they were typical of the hundreds of thousands of shtetl Jews who eventually emigrated to the United States, escaping persecution and seeking the fabled good life for their children. Cowen's maternal grandfather, Joshua Kantrowitz, after whom he was presumably named, was a leather craftsman, perhaps tooling his more elaborate work with gold or embellishing an occasional bookbinding for a wealthy patron. His maternal grandmother, Ida, was born in 1802. She and Joshua were married young, as was traditional at the time, in a match probably arranged by the local marriage broker.

Ida and Joshua had six children by the time fighting broke out in another border dispute. The Kantrowitz house was near the battlefield, and each night the day's dead were brought through the town. The stench was terrible; Ida and Joshua would close their shutters in a vain attempt to keep out the smell. Inevitably, with the unburied dead lying in the streets, cholera broke out. The oldest son, Michael, sixteen and newly married, contracted the disease, as did his father. With no effective medical care available, they died within an hour of each other. Joshua Lionel's mother, Rebecca, was only eight at the time.

The family and neighbors were at the double funeral when soldiers came through the village, looting and pillaging. Prospects were as bleak as the war-scarred countryside for Ida and her remaining five children. But an improbable turn of events changed things for the better. Ida had been friendly with a Polish baroness who had broken with her family and was running a bakery. As befitted its noble ownership, the bakery offered goods produced with white flour, a great luxury in that poor area. The baroness took Ida in and taught her the business. Then, in fairy tale fashion, the baroness became re-

The Twentieth Century Limited *steaming for Chicago on the New York Central's four-track mainline.*

HYMAN NATHAN COHEN
c. 1836-1912

REBECCA KANTROWITZ COHEN
c. 1841-1934

RACHEL COHEN MARCUS
Roy Cohn's grandmother

SARAH COHEN KAPLAN
Born about 1871

LEAH COHEN HYMAN
Son managed Lionel office

BENJAMIN COHEN
Sold millinery goods

ROSE COHEN GOODMAN
Artist son sold his paintings to Cowen

JOSHUA LIONEL COWEN
Founded Lionel

ISIDORE COHEN
Worked for Knickerbocker Toys

ESTELLE NEWMAN

The Hyman Cohen family, in order of birth. Missing are first-born Abraham, who died young, and Jennie, who came after Rachel and was the first born in America.

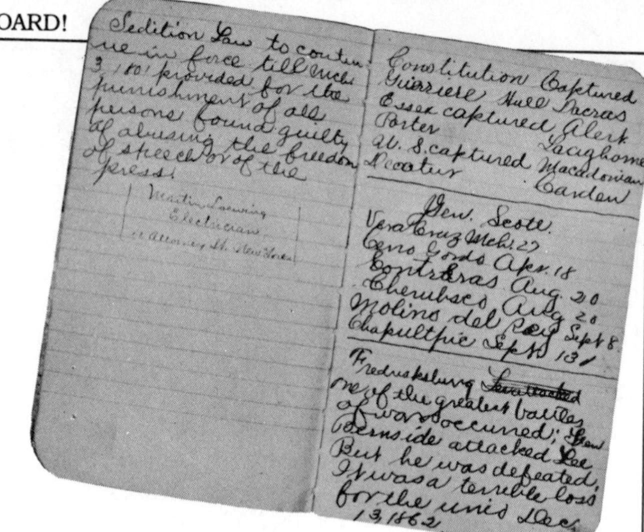

Cowen's school notebook contains this tantalizing entry—an electrician's address.

united with her family and turned the bakery over to Ida. Little Rebecca helped in the shop and made deliveries, while her brothers acquired the education expected of Jewish boys.

Cowen's paternal grandparents died when their son, Hyman Nathan Cohen, was a young boy, and the promising yeshiva student was raised by an uncle. Hyman excelled in languages and mathematics and was already well known and respected in the village when he married Rebecca in about 1859. Shortly after this, they went to England, where Hyman started a cap manufacturing business, producing cloth and fur hats.

The Cohens stayed in London for about five years (long enough for Rebecca to learn English—with a Cockney accent). Two of their children were born there: Abraham, who would die at age twenty-six, and Rachel, future maternal grandmother of McCarthy-era lawyer Roy Cohn, who became chairman of Lionel in 1960. Hyman was eminently practical and ambitious, and his cap business flourished. But the damp London weather did not agree with him. His doctor advised him to return to his home (now inside the Russian border); instead, Hyman decided to explore business opportunities in America. According to family tales, he made two exploratory trips to the United States by himself, supposedly going as far west as Denver, Colorado, perhaps to investigate the beaver and fur hat trade. Apparently he liked what he saw, for shortly after the Civil War had ended and President Lincoln was assassinated, Hyman and his family arrived on New York's Lower East Side.

His was not the typically helpless immigrant family of American folklore. The great waves of pogrom-inspired immigration from Eastern Europe had not yet begun. Hyman had a trade, business contacts, spoke English, and brought with him the then-considerable sum of one thousand dollars. The Cohens settled first on East Broadway, one of the main thoroughfares of what eventually would be one of the largest Jewish neighborhoods in the world. As Hyman's cap business grew and the family expanded, they moved one street south to Henry Street, four blocks from the East River. Four more daughters and a son had already been born to Hyman and Rebecca in this comfortable brownstone house when on August 25, 1877, Joshua Lionel came into the world. (In later years Cowen always gave 1880 as the year of his birth—probably out of vanity.)

The eighth of nine children (a brother would come after him), Joshua Cowen was an intelligent, curious boy with more than a bit of the devil in him. Intrigued by the moving eyes of his sisters' bisque dolls and determined to learn how they worked, little Joshua held the dolls by their feet and cracked their fine heads open on the front steps of the house. One child of many in a large family, Cowen seems to have gone his own way, occasionally skipping school or spending his time carving toys out of wood. According to a tale he was fond of telling interviewers in later years, at the age of seven he singlehandedly carved a steam-powered toy locomotive that subsequently blew up, removing much of the kitchen wallpaper. Although it is unlikely that he actually constructed such an intricate toy, he certainly could have had an actual steam-operated locomotive. Many toy trains available at the time did in fact manufacture their own steam in miniature boilers fired by alcohol; the flame underneath the boiler produced the steam

WHY LIONEL?

Joshua Cowen's middle name came down to him through his family. At least one ancestor was named Lionel, Cowen's descendants believe, but they are not sure who. Asked at the peak of his fame why he named the company Lionel, Cowen replied rather bluntly, "Well, I had to name it something."

DRIVING THE GOLDEN SPIKE

Cowen was a child of the American railroad age, born only eight years after the country was at last linked by rail on May 10, 1869. The driving of the golden spike at Promontory, Utah, west of Ogden, created a unified nation, joining crusty old Boston to gold-fevered Sacramento.

Irish and Chinese laborers chipped rock by hand at the rate of inches a day. They built thirty-seven miles of protective snowsheds so the trains would be able to get through in winter (the snows of the Sierras were too deep for even locomotive plows to clear). They hung over cliffs in baskets, drilling holes for dynamite. All the while military escorts kept the Indians at bay while hunters like Buffalo Bill Cody shot the still free-ranging bison to feed the brawling track crews.

The Union Pacific, laying track west from Council Bluffs, Iowa, and the Central Pacific (later the Southern Pacific), working east from Sacramento, raced toward one another (they were paid by the mile), until Washington put an end to the competition by setting Promontory as the place where the railroads would join each other.

Polished and gleaming, the Central's locomotive, *Jupiter*, faced the UP's No. 119, while the last rail was put in place on a sunny afternoon. The nation waited by its telegraph offices for the big news. California Governor Leland Stanford swung his silver hammer at the ceremonial golden spike... and missed. The crowd of railroad workers roared in laughter. Dr. Thomas Durant, the Union Pacific representative, also missed, perhaps tactfully. Impatient with the dignitaries' foolishness, General Grenville Dodge, chief engineer for the UP, stepped forward and drove home the polished steel spike that actually secured the last rail. The *Jupiter* and No. 119 eased forward until their cowcatchers touched. The country was one.

AAR

The country celebrated with bell-ringing, parades, and banners ("California Annexes The United States," read San Francisco's) when the golden spike was driven on May 10, 1869.

Grand Central Depot launched the first Twentieth Century Limited.

BETTMANN

Lower Manhattan (above) *was a crowded neighborhood even when Cowen was growing up, before massive immigration had begun. The elevated subway* (right) *was powered by small steam locomotives whose sparks were a hazard to horse and man alike.*

that turned the wheels. When they fell over—as they often did—they might well set the living room rug on fire. And if their safety valves were held closed by mischievous boys, they could conceivably explode, doing substantial damage to both their young engineers and the kitchen wallpaper.

Cowen attended Elementary School Number One in lower Manhattan, walking together with his brothers and sisters for protection against a neighbor's goat, which would sometimes get loose and chase the children. While they apparently made no lasting impression, violin lessons were imposed on young Joshua so that he might acquire the "culture" so dear to Jewish hearts. He performed no doubt restless duets with his older sister, Rose, who played the piano.

Cowen's childhood was full of simple pleasures. Sundays offered the excitement of horse-drawn coach trips up Fifth Avenue, past Fourteenth Street to the reservoir at Forty-Second Street, where families enjoyed weekly promenades, exchanging decorous greetings. Or they would go to Central Park to admire the sedate broughams or sporty one-horse traps of the wealthy. On summer evenings, the family strolled along the paths watching young men catch fireflies and fasten them with stick pins to their cravats. The flies glowed softly while the men strutted and preened.

But most activities centered around the home in which Cowen was raised. Rebecca, quiet and retiring, "a little bit of a thing" as she was remembered years later, kept a Kosher home and lit the Sabbath candles on Friday night. Hyman, tall and robust, was preoccupied with the somber affairs of men: business, religion (he was president of the local synagogue), politics, and debating Talmudic philosophy around the dining room table with his cronies. There was a religious atmosphere in the house and strong Jewish ties. But when Rebecca and Hyman wanted to speak between themselves without the children understanding, they spoke Polish, not Yiddish. (When Ida, Rebecca's mother, arrived in New York to join the family some years later, she was horrified that the children didn't speak Yiddish and excoriated her daughter for raising "a bunch of infidels.")

And this was not the only way in which the Cohens differed from the norm. Superficially, they fulfilled the stereotype of the classic Jewish family: the scholarly philosopher/father, somewhat distant from his children, and the efficient

TRAINS IN A BOY'S LIFE

To grow up in the last third of the nineteenth century was to be surrounded by trains. The steam locomotive was the symbol of the new age in America. Children were almost constantly exposed to railroads in one form or another.

They learned their ABCs from books embellished with pictures of locomotives, and when they did well in their studies, they received certificates decorated with trains from their teachers. There were train puzzles and train building blocks. Paint books for "young artists" contained pictures of locomotives from different railroads. Especially, there were story books with exciting titles like *The Lightning Express.*

WARD KIMBALL

The ABC primer (above) *was sedate compared to the tale of* The Lightning Express (left), *in which a magical locomotive leaped a bridgeless chasm.*

SMITHSONIAN

A wood-burning locomotive adorned a school boy's certificate of merit .

COWEN'S BOYHOOD TRAINS

The earliest toy trains were pulled by a string across ornately-patterned rugs in Victorian parlors. They were made of iron coated with tin to prevent rust and to enable the parts to be soldered together easily. Though they had no motors and no tracks, they were as gorgeously colored as real locomotives, which puffed flamboyantly on the less than five thousand miles of railroad track in existence.

By about 1856, a wind-up, clockwork motor was added to the tin trains by the Connecticut company of George W. Brown, one of the most famous American toy makers. The trains could be set to go either in straight or curved paths. There was no track as yet, and most clockwork locomotives were not powerful enough to pull any cars. As wind-ups became more sophisticated, however, the Ives Company added a whistle, provisions for putting a lit cigarette in the smokestack so the engine puffed smoke, and even an explosive cap that went *bang!* when the locomotive struck a wall.

Toy engines that actually were powered by steam became popular in the 1870s, shortly before Cowen's birth. Their great appeal was that they duplicated the motive power of real locomotives. The engines, which often ran on tracks, were usually fired by alcohol (imported versions burned the more expensive coal).

Wooden trains covered with brilliantly-colored paper on which was printed the details of the engine and cars were also in vogue during Cowen's childhood. These had neither power nor track, but they did come with several cars.

The use of cast iron was the next innovation in toy trains. Some of these came with clockwork motors, but because iron was so heavy, most were child-powered. None of them had track.

Electric trains became commercially available in the United States in about 1896, when the Cincinnati firm of Carlisle & Finch offered a polished brass trolley car with track and battery for three dollars.

In 1901 Ives combined wind-up trains with workable track. These clockwork trains sold well, and would continue to do so for years. But they were already outdated. Cowen had begun to offer his first electric trains, and the age of Lionel was here.

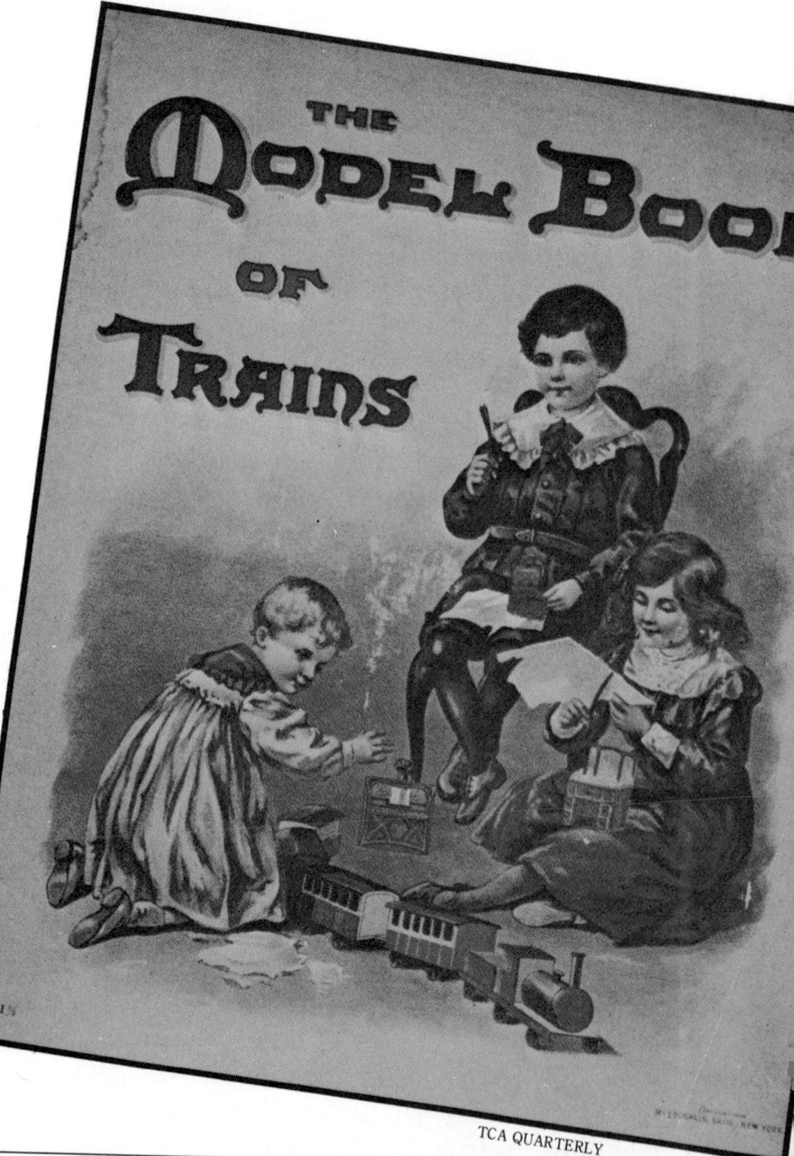

The earliest toy trains were homemade, cut from paper and played with on the floor. By the 1880s, heavy cast-iron trains were being advertised in boys' magazines.

TCA QUARTERLY

ALLEN LEVY

HERE COME THE CARS!

BY CY WARMAN

How often at night, when I'm rocked o'er the
rail,
And the little stars shine overhead,
My mind wanders back, over memory's trail,
And I think of the days that are dead.
The red locomotives we had for our toys,
The coaches so gaudy and gay:
How we played together, Bill, when we were
boys,
And again I can hear you say:
"Chuchu!! Chuchu!! here comes the railroad!
I'll be the brakeman and open the bars."
Big bell a-ringing,
Somebody singing:
"Chuchu!! Chuchu!! here come the cars!"

EDWIN ALEXANDER

BETTMANN

Wind-up, or clockwork, trains ran on the floor or on track (top) *and made charming table-top railroads. In the 1870s, a miniature steam-powered train* (above) *attracted a fascinated and varied audience in a New York toy shop.*

COWEN'S BOYHOOD

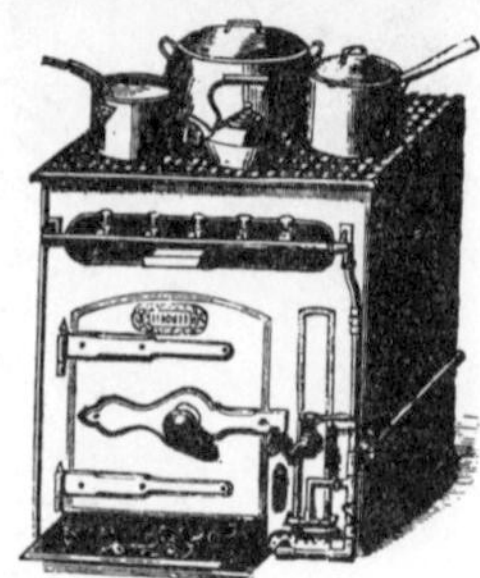

During Cowen's boyhood, Manhattan was a different world than it is today. Gas lights and ranges were so new that the Cohens were paid three dollars a year by the gas company to try a modern gas stove. (The children were happy to see gas come in, for it relieved them of the duty of trimming the wicks and cleaning the mantles on the oil lamps. The coal stove in the front parlor still needed polishing, however.) When the family lived downtown, Cowen played in the back yard, where castor beans and sunflowers grew. He made make-believe umbrellas of the large sunflower leaves or went swimming in the East River. There were steam locomotives on the elevated subway tracks, horses in the streets, and masted vessels at the river's wharves. It was an exciting time to grow up.

mother taking care of both the family and household matters. Yet neither Hyman nor Rebecca exactly fit the pattern. Hyman's main interests were the synagogue and his charitable works, but he was far from an impractical dreamer. He was a successful businessman; in addition to his cap business, in which he employed several workers, he branched out into real estate and even dabbled in jewelry. Rebecca, while creating the proper family atmosphere, was not a self-effacing stay-at-home. She was independent enough to have discarded the wig Orthodox Jewish women are supposed to wear and was spoken of with respect as "a good businesswoman" in the successful piece goods shop she opened on Hester Street. It was Rebecca, however, who was closer to the children, reflecting both Judaism's traditionally distant patriarchy and Victorian mores, which emphasized that anything relating to the home was women's work. Fathers were not then the "pals" Cowen tried so hard to make them in his train catalogs, as if to create something he felt he had missed.

Hyman was relaxed and generous with his family. When he came home with the rents he had collected from the stores and apartments he was managing, he and Rebecca would play a little game. When they counted out the rental money together on the kitchen table, Hyman would always come up short. Shaking his head in mock consternation, he would wonder where the rest of the money had gone. Then, from the deep pockets of her apron, Rebecca would produce the balance. They were an affectionate couple, and Hyman was always bringing her surprises—a piece of jewelry, a new dress—especially when he had closed a good real estate deal. (Years later, Cowen would exhibit the same generous nature.)

The Cohens were comfortable, but not wealthy; still, Hyman was always taking people in, giving them a place to stay until they could establish themselves. When a young, struggling couple married, he could be counted on to contribute a piece of furniture to their new home. He was one of the founders of the local synagogue, where he had a pew, and was an organizer of charity balls in the Jewish community to raise money for land for an expanded Beth Israel Hospital. (The hospital, which started in a brownstone, was later one of Joshua Cowen's favorite charities.) Hyman would frequently allow new businesses several months rent-free in his buildings until they got established. "When you're making money, then you'll pay me," he would say. He was well-known in the community, and strangers sought him out for help. Years later, many of them would attend his funeral, paying their respects for kindnesses shown about which he had said nothing.

Like most immigrant families, the Cohens did not forget their relatives on the other side of the Atlantic. They wrote and sent money, especially to Rebecca's mother, Ida. Yet nothing in their correspondence prepared Hyman for the notice he received in 1892 from immigration authorities downtown that someone was waiting for him at Castle Garden, the processing center at the foot of Manhattan Island overlooking the harbor. Hyman arrived to find Ida, now eighty-five, sitting patiently on her steamer trunks, hands clasped over a small bundle on her knees. In the trunks were the family heirlooms: linens, silver, and precious religious books and scrolls.

And on her knees, tied in a big kerchief, was a pile of gold coins. In her typically adventurous way, Ida had decided it was time for her to be with her daughter and had simply booked passage without bothering to write to anyone.

In 1889, when Cowen was twelve, the family moved uptown to 104th Street and Madison Avenue. At that time, the area was so rural the Cohens were only a block from McNally's farm at Central Park, a dairy that supplied milk to many Manhattan neighborhoods. More importantly for young Cowen, one block east on what eventually would be Park but was then still Fourth Avenue, the tracks and steam locomotives of both the New York and Harlem and the New York and New Haven Railroads ran on a huge stone viaduct under which carriage traffic passed. There was a major elevated open-platform station at 110th Street, and the locomotives, cinders flying, whistled as they passed in either direction. The exciting sound carried easily to the Cohen residence and to a restless boy who found mechanical devices far more

ON THE JOB

"My real first job was one I got when I was about fourteen. I was hired to do odd jobs in a trade-magazine office. I was paid three and a half dollars a week, and I can't tell you the long hours I put in.

"The office was on the fifth floor, in a building that had no elevators. I ran up and down those stairs five hundred times a day, or so it seemed. When my boss suggested he would have to cut my salary, I said I would be willing to work longer hours, if he would just keep my wages the same.

"You know, the unions are asking for a thirty-hour week now [in 1957]. Why, when I was a kid, thirty hours would have been only two days' work. But times change."

—Joshua Lionel Cowen
as told to Lawrence Johnson

The athletic young Cowen posed in a photographer's studio on his bicycle.

interesting than the three Rs.

In the few comments he made about his childhood in later years, Cowen gave the impression of having spent a good deal of unsupervised time on his own. He made cryptic references to his truancy from public school and his distaste for formal education. Besides fiddling around with toy steam locomotives and other inventions, Cowen liked being outside, playing ball in the street, bicycling, or hiking (he belonged to a local outing group called the Fifty Mile Club). Despite these activities, he was not very athletic and had weak ankles all his life. Once, wanting to impress a girl in the neighborhood, he roller-skated past her stoop, did a fancy turn, and fell on his face. But he was a good sport. They both laughed, and in later years he told the story with no trace of embarrassment.

Notwithstanding his lackadaisical attitude, Cowen was enrolled at Peter Cooper Institute high school, for Jewish families placed too much value on education to allow him to drop out of school. Peter Cooper afforded him a good opportunity to do what he would enjoy doing all his life: tinkering. He was fascinated with electricity and with the then-developing concept of storing it in batteries. While at the school, Cowen invented what he later claimed to have been the first electric doorbell, using storage batteries for power. However, he was discouraged by an instructor who pompously advised him nothing would ever replace the knuckles for announcing one's arrival.

Cowen did well enough in his technical classes at Peter Cooper, and at age sixteen, in September 1893, he entered the College of the City of New York. But wherever Cowen's future lay, it was not within the confines of formal education. In quick succession, he dropped out of City College, returned, dropped out again, enrolled at Columbia University, and quit after one semester to apprentice at the electrical firm Henner & Anderson, which manufactured one of the first dry cell batteries in the United States. He then took a job at the Acme Electric Lamp Company at 1659 Broadway in midtown Manhattan. At this small electrical shop, Cowen would develop the skills that would eventually enable him to launch Lionel.

Cowen's apprentice position at Acme involved assembling battery lamps. His job also gave him the resources to conduct his own experiments after work, usually involving batteries. It was during this period that he claimed to have in-

STEVENS INSTITUTE OF TECHNOLOGY

This painting depicts the first locomotive in America, which ran at Hoboken, New Jersey, in 1825.

vented the dry cell battery.

At that time, batteries were made of containers of sulfuric acid, which was highly caustic. "I put together one of the first dry cell batteries ever seen in this country," Cowen later said in his characteristically immodest, no-nonsense style, "but I couldn't make it last for more than thirty days. The materials were lousy. I let it slide." It was not the last invention Cowen would "let slide" out of impatience and a desire to go on to something new.

These must have been good days for young Cowen, working in a new field, bounded only by his own creativity. Always extroverted, Cowen exhibited his ebullient spirits in a bubbling, mock-epic poem he wrote for a social club to which he belonged. Full of "moon/June" rhymes, the poem sings the praises of Cowen's fellow members with a humor on the level of a college fraternity. Whatever Cowen would accomplish in years to come, however effective his catalog copy would be, his strengths were not as a poet.

Cowen's time at Acme was apparently well spent. On June 6, 1899, he filed his first patent, a device for igniting photographers' flash powder using dry cell batteries to heat a wire fuse. The patent, number 636,492, was granted in November. Cowen described his invention in the official four-page document as "a flash-light apparatus which can be held in the hand in use, can be conveniently manipulated, and can be packed up into a small compass when not in use." It was quite simple, consisting of a slim tube about twelve inches long containing dry cell batteries, with a switch on the side. At one end was a socket "corresponding in general character with the Edison type of socket for incandescent lamps." A long pole screwed into this socket, making electrical contact. At the end of the pole was a horizontal trough for holding the flash powder, which exploded with a *poof!* and a cloud of smoke when the button was pressed that closed the circuit, heating a wire in the trough.

Mechanically, the apparatus was no more than clever, exhibiting good design rather than any new principle or invention. It was the idea of using dry cell batteries to ignite an explosive charge electrically that was new. Yet Cowen devoted much of the space in the patent to a description of how the individual components folded and clipped to each other, making it easily portable, and was curiously unenlightening about the electrical circuitry. He gave no an-

THE FIRST ELECTRIC TRAIN

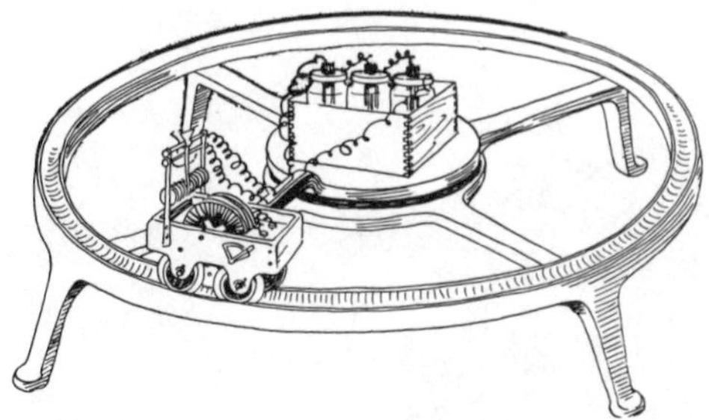

A sulfuric acid wet-cell battery powered the first electric train.

The first electric train in the United States was not designed as a toy but as a means of demonstrating that electricity could, in fact, be used to run a real railroad.

The age of steam-powered locomotives had hardly begun when, on October 14, 1835, a poor upstate New York blacksmith, Thomas Davenport, tried to convince a scientific convention in Troy, New York, that it was electricity that could best run the country's railroads. The sceptical scientists laughed as Davenport, assisted by an apprentice, set up his ungainly model railroad on a table in the Troy Courthouse.

The clumsy-looking engine ran on a circle of track three feet in diameter, powered by wet cell batteries attached directly to the locomotive. "Impractical!" judged the scientists, who were still assimilating the new steam engine. (The *Tom Thumb* and *Best Friend of Charleston* were both less than five years old.)

Davenport was too far ahead of his time. Electricity was in its infancy, and in any case the scientific world was obsessed with developing a perpetual motion machine, not with running electric railroads. Batteries and the storage of electricity (which would fascinate Joshua Cowen) were understood even less than the mysterious new force itself.

Davenport demonstrated his invention for other groups but was unable to get any financial backing. Eventually, even his helper gave up on the electric railroad. Davenport retired the device to his blacksmith shop, where he ran it for his own amusement. He was long dead when the first electric trolley began operating in 1887 in Richmond, Virginia.

Cowen was young and full of confidence when he filed his first patent for a photographer's lighting device on June 16, 1899.

swers at all to the obvious questions. What was the composition of the new dry cell batteries? How could the batteries produce enough current to heat a wire red hot while still retaining enough charge for repeated use? What kind of wire was used that could be heated repeatedly without quickly deteriorating? The patent answered none of these. Its design—a tube with a screw-on cap at one end, and a switch in between—presaged the flashlight, which Cowen later claimed to have invented and then given away in a moment of impatience.

Patenting what Cowen described as the "Flash Lamp" soon brought him an invitation to Washington to talk with the Navy. The scene is described in a long profile by Robert Lewis Taylor that appeared in *The New Yorker* in December, 1947. As narrated by Cowen to Taylor, the episode is probably typically colored by Cowen's flair for the dramatic and by his sense of self-importance (he apparently told the interviewer he was only eighteen at the time of the Navy meeting, when in fact he was probably closer to twenty-two). But even with Taylor's own creative embellishments, it is a good story:

> "When Cowen . . . walked into a room full of admirals in Washington, they took him for a messenger. His Sunday suit was badly rumpled, as a consequence of having slept in it on the train, and under one arm he had a ratty old shoe box containing his materials. 'You the gentlemen interested in photography fuses?' he asked, with no trace of awe that he can recall, and the conference got down to business. The Navy, he learned, was interested not in photography but in a foolproof detonator for mines. The admirals were convinced that Cowen had the answer in the box, and he was given a contract to equip 24,000 mines. He returned to New York, hired an even younger employee from the Acme Company, and set up shop in a downtown loft. The job proved to be ticklish. The principal ingredient they worked with was mercuric fulminate, which was delivered in a tightly closed case resembling a coffin by two men from the Pompton Lakes Power Company. When they set the box down, gingerly, one of them said, 'You sure you know how to use this stuff, sonny?' Although he had never seen any mercuric fulminate, Cowen replied that he did. 'Well,' the man added, 'the company said you should always keep a good deal around. It's better to be dead than maimed.' Cowen thanked him, tossed him a fifteen-cent tip, and started on the fuses. The Navy had set a strict deadline—a Saturday noon—for delivery at the Brooklyn Navy Yard, and the boys had to work fast to make it. The morning of the day in question, they hired a wagon, loaded it with the finished products, and headed at a gallop for the Navy Yard. 'Gangway!' Cowen kept shouting at the public from the driver's seat. 'You want to get blown up?' He was, he says, halfway convinced that the fuses *were* going to explode, and he wanted to keep the casualties as low as possible. 'We had enough on that wagon,' he says, 'to blow off the entire lower end of Manhattan.' Despite his worries, they made it all right, and the Navy was much pleased."

The profile is illuminating—even with its obvious exaggerations—because it shows how Cowen enjoyed presenting himself: devil-may-care, impulsive, even reckless: full steam ahead and damn the torpedoes. He liked the article. It fed the irrepressible showman in him, and it nurtured his self-image as a rugged, confident, even irascible individualist.

Cowen claimed he realized the then huge sum of twelve thousand dollars from the contract, more than enough to enable him to go into business on his own. He filed a second patent in January, 1900, for "improvements in Electric Explosive Fuses." His simple fuse consisted of a cardboard or other combustible tube packed with a flammable chemical like sulfur or phosphorous, through which wires were passed that would heat up and ignite the chemicals. The patent again omitted any details about the type of wire used, amount of current required, or the various other technical specifications.

With the stake from the Navy contract and two patents to his credit, Cowen opened his own establishment. On September 5, 1900, Cowen and a colleague from Acme, Harry C. Grant, filed to conduct business in New York at 24 Murray Street in Lower Manhattan. The firm would engage in "the manufacture of electrical novelties." It would be known as the Lionel Manufacturing Company, and neither childhood nor Christmas in America would ever be the same.

COND
NGINEER

2

PULLING OUT

1900-1910

The early years of famous men are transformed by time, their own egos, press agents, and a public that yearns for mythic heroes. Their beginnings become ever humbler (or more well-to-do, if they aspire to refinement). As interviews multiply, their early accomplishments become more dazzling and varied, achieved at progressively earlier ages with the help of fewer and fewer partners. Joshua Cowen, salesman extraordinaire, was not immune to spinning a few yarns himself, and in his later years, he claimed a potpourri of inventions dating from those exuberant days around the turn of the century. It's not clear how much was fact and how much was the flowing narrative of a colorful raconteur with an eager audience. In any case, sometime around 1901, just before the train business began meaningful production, Cowen claimed to have invented—and abandoned—the flashlight, the dry cell battery, and the electric fan.

In his inimitable way, Cowen told the story about the fan a number of times. It was a hot, humid day, typical of summer in Manhattan. Cowen was in his loft office, wistfully hoping for both a breeze and a new business idea, when the solution to both problems struck him simultaneously. He would invent a battery-powered fan! He assembled a small electric motor, attached blades to a shaft, and—just like that!—created the world's first portable electric fan. The fan would later become a souce of wry humor for the mature Cowen. "It was the most beautiful thing you ever saw," he would say. "It ran like a dream and it had only one thing wrong with it. You could stand a foot away from the thing and not feel any breeze." And that wasn't the only problem. The weather soon cooled—

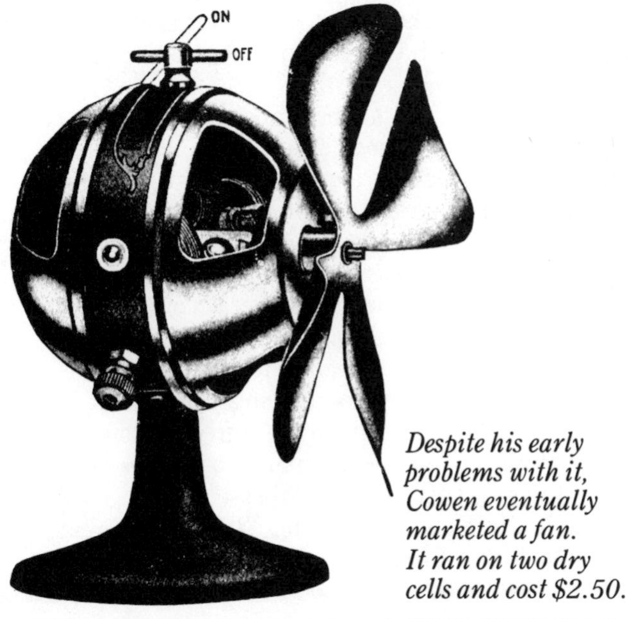

Despite his early problems with it, Cowen eventually marketed a fan. It ran on two dry cells and cost $2.50.

COWEN AND THE FLASHLIGHT

Cowen claimed he invented the flashlight, but his stories were contradictory. "I first went into business with a restaurateur by the name of Conrad Hubert," Cowen recounted in the fifties. "I'd made a table decoration he liked that had a recirculating fountain in the middle with lights that played on it. I was intrigued with lights and pumps in those days. While Hubert and I were together, I invented the flashlight; it was shaped like a pistol. It lighted when you pulled the trigger and worked with a cylindrical dry cell battery." In other accounts, Cowen described his flashlight as having the conventional cylindrical shape he depicted in his 1899 patent for the photographer's flash lamp.

Whatever the truth was, Cowen in later years said he failed to realize the immense potential of a portable, lightweight source of light at a time when gas lamps were still used in most homes. Instead of seeing the flashlight for what it was, he thought of it solely as a decorating tool, just the thing to stick in the base of a potted palm to create a dramatic lighting effect. In one version of the story, Hubert tried one in his restaurant; it worked so well that he subsequently went on the road selling them while Cowen tended to production. In another version, Cowen said he and Hubert hired a salesman to do the selling for them.

"Patents got all overlapped," Cowen once said, "and it seemed every day Conrad Hubert and I were suing four people and having four people sue us for patent infringements. I got disgusted with the whole thing. Hubert took the flashlight part of the business and we split up." But according to another account, Cowen said he gave the flashlight to Hubert when the invention continued to malfunction.

Cowen enjoyed portraying himself as impulsive and not given to regrets. "You may have heard of the company that grew out of Hubert's part of the business," Cowen would tell interviewers, grinning. "It's the Eveready Flashlight Company.

and so did the public's interest in his new device.

So there he was, a young man with his own business but no product. He had his stake from the completed Navy contract, he had two patents to his name, he had a partner, but Cowen and his Lionel Manufacturing Company had no direction, no reason for being. The first decade of the twentieth century in America, however, was hardly a time for despair, nor was Cowen a man overly given to hand-wringing. Opportunity was all around if only you had the spirit to grab it. It was, after all, a time for getting ahead, for building empires and fortunes, for rising from obscurity into the limelight. Cowen had done it once with the Navy mine contract; there was no reason he couldn't do it again.

The small motor he had used in the fan had worked well enough. The problem was what to do with it. Cowen never actually described the grand moment of creation, when childhood was forever changed for millions; it is lost along with most of Cowen's earliest hand-built *Electric Express* wooden gondola cars. But if the precise moment of invention is unknown, the surrounding details are no mystery. The scene is easily imagined.

The new century has just begun and the country is obsessed with railroads. Speed records, new passenger runs, and train wrecks are topics of avid interest. Trains are all around Cowen. Their coal smoke hangs over Fourth Avenue down to Grand Central Terminal. Cinders fly from the steam engines on the elevated trains. Like most other Americans, he always stops to wave at trains, having grown up listening to their rumblings over the viaduct at 104th Street.

In lower Manhattan, an already-balding Cowen strolls the narrow, shop-crammed streets around City Hall, musing on what to do with his idle fan motor. As always, he examines the display windows with interest. Cowen likes special effects and presentations. They are a major component of good merchandising, though one of America's premier merchandisers-to-be is not yet thinking in these terms. So Cowen examines not merely what is for sale but the way it is presented. He is disappointed. The displays all seem dull and static.

Cowen pauses at a toy and novelty shop a few blocks from the Hudson River on Cortlandt Street, six blocks south of his loft workshop. Here are the toys of the period: cast-iron fire engines drawn by galloping horses; balancing clowns and elephants on wheels; wind-up boats; tin locomotives with pull strings; wind- and spring-driven tradesmen. They sit, still and lifeless, although many can move in wonderful ways when activated.

Cowen squints his eyes. Despite the hurly-burly of teams of horses, metal-rimmed wagon wheels on cobblestones, and an occasional raucous, chain-driven car, he is fantasizing. In his mind he sees something moving in the window, something electrical that doesn't need constant attention. Its continual motion draws people to the window, stops their brisk, preoccupied New York pace. Whatever it is goes around and around. What is it, this elusive toy, running in the shadowy corners of his mind? A fan? A merry-go-round? A windmill with blades? What if it moved, traveled, like a . . . a . . . that's it!

Cowen rushes into the shop and explains his idea to the startled proprietor, Robert Ingersoll. No, no, not an old-fashioned wind-up train that stops after making a few circles, but a modern, up-to-date electric car on track. It'll pull 'em in like flies. Soon every store in New York will be hollering for one to put in the window, Cowen assures the sceptical Ingersoll, and off he rushes to his shop and immortality. . . .

It makes a wonderful story—even though Cowen's "original" idea had its antecedents. Electric toy trains were already in existence when Cowen strolled Cortlandt Street at the turn of the century. A toy electric streetcar running on a track was exhibited at the Columbian World's Fair in Chicago in 1893 by the German toy maker Georges Carette and Company. And the Cincinnati firm of Carlisle & Finch had introduced a similar brass car in 1896, advertising it in *Scientific American* the same year. But the laissez-faire economy of the early twentieth century always allowed for competition, especially if it involved something as new and radical as a toy driven by that barely understood force, electricity.

Because he wanted his new device to dress up a window, perhaps even to carry merchandise as it went around, Cowen didn't make his first "electric car" look much like a real train. Instead, working with Harry Grant, he slapped together something resembling an open cigar box on wheels. The corners were dovetailed; the wooden sides were stained red and bore the name *Electric Express* in gold letters. The primitive track consisted of metal strips set in wooden ties. The "fan" motor was attached to the bottom of the car and geared to the insulated metal wheels. The gauge between rails of the new train was 2⅞ inches. Dry cell batteries were wired directly to the track. There was no means of regulating the speed of the car.

"I sold my first railroad car not as a toy, mind you," Cowen later explained, "but as something to attract attention to Ingersoll's window. I guess it was the first animated advertisement in New York, outside of sandwich men and live demonstrators. I sold it for four dollars. Well, sir, the next day he was back for another. The first customer who saw it bought the advertisement instead of the goods."

Ingersoll in fact ordered half a dozen; other shops followed. Cowen and Grant were in business. They set up production in the loft on Murray Street. Parts like wheels and components for the motors were farmed out to neighborhood work shops, and the two men spent a good deal of time scurrying about lower Manhattan, picking up wheels from here, bodies from there, metal frames from a foundry. Track rails were cut from steel strips. The young manufacturers nailed the car bodies together—without such niceties as the brass cor-

FUNDIMENSIONS

This early Electric Express *car was kept by Cowen for sixty years in Lionel's showroom.*

LIONEL'S MYSTERY MAN

Who *was* Michael R. Conley, Brooklynite, whose name appears on Lionel's original incorporation papers and then is lost to toy train history? Perhaps Conley was Cowen's lawyer. In any case, will the descendants of *the* Michael R. Conley please come forward and end the suspense?

ners and step rungs that were added the next year—and rushed the new trains out to meet the unexpected demand. Cowen scratched his initials into the wooden bottoms of the cars during the first days of production, a proud craftsman signing his work, but soon gave up the practice. It took too much time.

A Providence, Rhode Island, firm ordered twenty-five cars. The order was so important that Cowen gave them the exclusive right to sell trains throughout New England. Spurred by this and other orders, the Lionel Manufacturing Company was incorporated in New York on March 13, 1902, with Cowen and Grant each holding two shares of the new company and a Michael R. Conley of Brooklyn, third member of the board of directors, holding one. The purposes of the corporation were listed as, "The manufacture of electrical, mechanical and industrial appliances, and toys, also the purchase and sale of merchandise, patents and real estate." Capital was listed at five hundred dollars (on the low side for purposes of the application) and a hundred shares of capital common stock were issued, valued at ten thousand dollars. In the space on the incorporation form that asked for *Duration,* Cowen optimistically entered, "Fifty years." He was both right and wrong, for while The Lionel Manufacturing Company was superceded in 1918 by a new corporate entity, The Lionel Corporation, this second company to bear Cowen's middle name is still thriving.

With the company incorporated, Cowen began keeping a precise ledger of his sales. Begun April 2, 1902, with the sale of two bulbs for seventy-five cents to "F. Bissell & Co., Toledo, Ohio," the immaculate handwritten ledger was kept for five years. After 1907, Cowen began to use that still-new device, the typewriter (for a long time, the word referred not to the machine but to the person operating it, as in "a lady typewriter"). Sales reached $22,322.93 that year. By the end of the decade, they would fall just short of $57,000 annually.

In June, 1902, when *The Twentieth Century Limited* was inaugurated, Cowen was well into the company's first full line for the coming season. The little *Electric Express* gondola was proving far more than a mere window display attention-getter. People were buying it to play with, despite the awkwardness of dry cell batteries or the even more clumsy sulfuric acid wet cells. What was needed now was something more exciting than the simple open gondola car. Even painted red and with the addition of steps and a freight load of six miniature barrels, the gondola was not very lifelike. People couldn't easily relate to it. But something they saw every day—maybe a passenger car from the new *Twentieth Century,* or a car from the city's elevated "subway" system, or a trolley, like Carlisle & Finch had started with—that would be something!

It was the age of the electric trolley. Trolleys

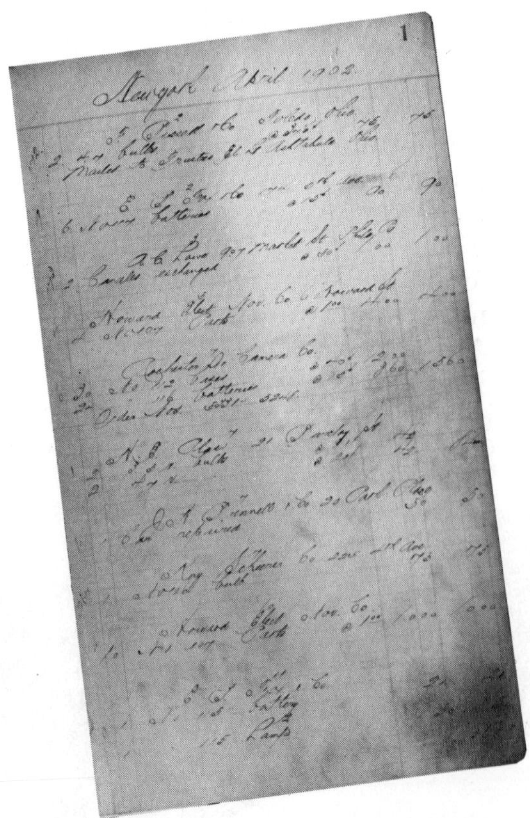

Cowen's first ledger recorded 300 pages of sales through 1907.

The Cincinnati firm of Carlisle & Finch was the first to produce electric trains in quantity in the United States. The company was founded by Robert S. Finch and Morton Carlisle in July 1893, who bought out an industrial electrical repair shop that had formerly been General Electric's Cincinnati division.

The first product was a steamboat searchlight. The firm did pioneering work in carbon arc lamps and maritime lighting devices, which it still manufactures today. Clothes dryers, marine engines, dynamos, and radio receivers were some of the diverse products of Carlisle & Finch, in addition to electric trains, cars, torpedo boats, and inclined railways.

After manufacturing its first brass trolley of 1896, Carlisle & Finch expanded its two-inch gauge train line to include everything needed for a complete layout before the line was abandoned in favor of war contracts in 1915.

Like Lionels, the company's first trains ran on metal strips placed on edge in slotted wooden ties. They were powered by wet cell batteries. Carlisle & Finch recommended assembling the batteries at home using "fruit jars" to avoid breakage during shipping.

TERENCE DODSON

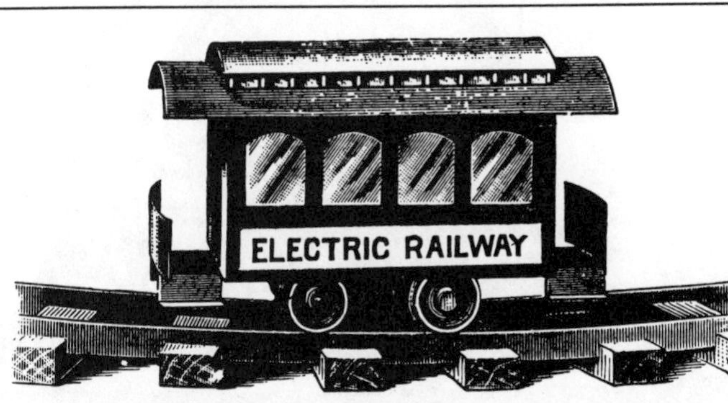

Electrical Novelties

Railway shown in cut, with Battery and Track, ready to run, price . **$3.50**

☞ Send for Catalogue of Show Window Attractions, Hand Dynamos, Water Motor Dynamos, Inclined Planes, etc.

THE CARLISLE & FINCH CO.
SIXTH STREET, CINCINNATI, O.

WARD KIMBALL

Carlisle & Finch first advertised publicly in Scientific American *in 1896. Steamers* (center) *soon joined the trolleys* (above). *The 1911 catalog* (top right) *offered a full line of trains.*

CHANGES IN MODES OF TRAVEL

RAILROADS	1900	1960
Steam Locomotives	37,463	374
Diesel Locomotives	0	30,240
Electric Locomotives	200	498
Companies	1,224	407

AUTOMOBILES	1900	1960
Miles of Paved Roads	Under 150	3,546,000
Cars	8,000	61,682,000
Trucks and Buses	0	12,213,000
Maximum Speed	65 mph	394 mph

TROLLEY CARS	1902	1960
Vehicle Miles	1.1 billion	100,700,000
Miles of Track	22,577	2,196

clanged through America's cities and between its small towns. To lure riders, trolley companies built elaborate parks on the outskirts of cities, at the ends of trolley lines. These parks, with rides and games for the children, became extremely popular. Downtown, trolleys provided swift, reliable transportation along streets clogged with wagons and horse teams. So Lionel's second "train" was not a train at all: It was a streetcar.

Cowen's office was located only two blocks from New York's City Hall and its park, and it was natural that Cowen would name the trolley *City Hall Park* in bold gold letters. In his first catalog, distributed in 1902, Cowen bragged of this new "window display." "...It will be noticed that these cars are built on the lines of the regular electric trolley cars," he wrote. "Every feature is carried out to the minutest detail." He also upped the price to six dollars per car, which included thirty feet of metal track.

The trolley was carefully modeled after its delightful open-air, turn-of-the-century prototype. Made entirely of metal and enameled with delicate gold pinstriping, it had six reversible benches so its hypothetical passengers (miniature figures were never offered for it) could

The first of many Lionel trolleys came with thirty feet of rail and cost a hefty seven dollars.

always face forward, regardless of whether the car was traveling to "City Hall Park" or "Union Depot," according to the destination boards on the roof. At the front of the car was a realistic replica of a motorman's control lever.

The trolley was an ambitious undertaking for the fledgling Lionel Manufacturing Company. While the wood-frame open gondolas could be constructed locally, the metal trolley body was manufactured by Morton E. Converse & Company of Massachusetts, a toy firm that made trolleys that ran on the floor. Converse's own cars were sometimes blue and yellow; the electric Lionel models were always maroon, pea soup green, and yellow.

The *Electric Express* gondola was also offered that year, and curiously, Cowen praised it at the expense of his new trolley. "As a toy it will afford the user greater pleasure than the trolley car," his catalog read, "as it may be loaded and unloaded. Six miniature barrels are supplied with each outfit." Perhaps Cowen still thought of the trolley as part of a window display; perhaps the gondola was easier to manufacture, making it a more remunerative product. Or perhaps he was a little sentimental about his first electric toy.

But Cowen should certainly have had a weak spot for trolleys as well, for it was on a Manhattan trolley that he met his wife, Cecelia Liberman, a short, delicately-featured secretary with a somewhat aristocratic tilt to her head. Cecelia was the image of the fashionable Gibson girl, crisp and cool, her hair carefully pinned up in the fashion of the day. Years later, Cowen still remembered how neat she had looked in her immaculate white collar. ("That was typical of Ceil," a relative noted. "If an ashtray wasn't washed the instant you used it there was an uproar in the house.") Such fastidiousness appealed to Cowen, who himself was prone to throw the Sunday papers out unread rather than have them stacked messily at home. Cowen courted Liberman with postcards from his trips on the road, selling what he described as "miniature electric cars." In 1902 he wrote from St. Louis: "To the sweetest girl in the world I send my greeting," signing the card formally, "Joshua L. Cohen." They were married two years later.

Cowen produced his first known train catalog in 1902. It was extremely modest by comparison with the elaborate, full-color "wish books" that tantalized and inspired children later in the century as Lionel picked up steam: In Cowen's hands, the electric train catalog was to become one of the most potent merchandising devices in America. But that first, sixteen-page black and white catalog did contain many of the themes that would mesmerize generations of Lionel catalog readers.

"The goods described herein," it proclaimed, "are offered for sale to the general public for the second year, although they have been in use for

Cecelia Liberman as she looked about the time Cowen met her on a crowded uptown trolley.

While on a sales trip, Cowen wrote to Cecelia.

THE CATALOGS SPEAK

The early catalogs of Lionel established the themes that would resound in Cowen's later masterpieces. Even in the first decade of the century, Cowen imbued the trains with an almost sacred mission—to prepare America's youth for the great opportunities awaiting them. By 1926, Cowen had refined the somewhat stilted phrases of the first catalogs to the following inspired prose: "Who knows but what it may be your destiny to go into fields as yet untouched and pioneer big engineering projects like Hill, Harriman and others whose names will always be identified with the railroad history of our great land."

Lionel trains' educational value, durability, and attractiveness to fathers—three of Cowen's favorite themes—were touted early on, though never again in the clever way Cowen did in the 1931 catalog: "Perhaps your dad, as well as thousands of other boys' dads, obtained his early training for the job he holds today by playing with a Lionel train."

SUSPENSION BRIDGE.

(Catalogue No. 340.)

(Actual size, 2 feet long, 10 inches high.)

This bridge is an exact reproduction of the suspension railroad bridges to be found all over the country. It is 2 feet in length and 11 inches high. The braces which form this bridge are all apart, so that the user may have the advantage of setting it up. Each brace is numbered, so that no error can be made.

This accessory adds to the attractiveness of the road. It may be elevated to any height by placing some of the ties underneath it.

Price complete, boxed.................. $1.50

13

Lionel's first known catalog was issued in 1902. Cowen wrote in its introduction: "We have on file a large number of letters of recommendation from parties who have used [our goods] heretofore, and . . . it is safe to assume that they are all we claim for them."

a long time by mechanical institutions for demonstrating purposes, as they give a thorough insight into the workings of the electric cars now so universally used. [It is highly unclear just which, if any, "mechanical institutions" had been using the trains "for a long time."] We received so many inquiries from students and their friends for duplicate outfits that we decided to manufacture them in larger quantities, thereby reducing their cost and enabling us to offer them at a popular price. Our goods should not be conflicted with any other on the market—they are in a class by themselves. They are so substantially constructed that they may be used from year to year. All parts are interchangeable, and, as we are continually adding new features, a wholly equipped miniature road may be built from time to time."

From the beginning, Cowen realized that accessories would be an important part of his business. Lionel's first bridge was offered in 1902, a two-foot-long suspension model that Cowen described as "an exact reproduction of the suspension railroad bridges to be found all over the country." The bridge was offered in kit form for $1.50 to save Lionel the expense of assembly, though the catalog made a virtue of this, noting, "The braces which form this bridge are all apart, so that the user may have the advantage of setting it up." Switch tracks that could send the trains on one of two alternate routes, a ninety-degree crossover track allowing the railroad to describe a figure eight pattern and cross back over itself, and a track bumper to stop trains at dead end sidings were also available.

The primitiveness of the trains, however, was nothing compared to the Neanderthal electrical equipment designed to run them. Thomas Edison had electrified a one-square-mile area of lower New York as early as 1881 (the first electrically-lit Christmas tree appeared in a New York home the next year), so some of Cowen's customers already had electricity. For them, the catalog offered a frightening contraption that looked more like a torture device than something that would enable them to operate the innocent *City Hall Park* trolley. In order to adapt the standard home's direct current voltage to toy train use, sinister wires were run from the parlor's electric light bulb to glass jars of sulfuric acid with lead plates, and from there to the metal track. Cautioned the catalog, "NEVER ADD WATER TO THE ACID IN ANY EVENT, BUT POUR

Curved Track

TRACK

Track is the highway on which both real and toy trains move. The wheels of engines and cars roll on thin strips of metal known as rails. The rails are rigidly held a set distance apart (their gauge) by being fastened to supporting pieces under them known as ties. The ties in turn are held in place on real railroads by being embedded in gravel known as ballast. This is not necessary on toy railroads, but ballast is often simulated to make the layout more realistic (kitty litter looks a good deal like ballast). Rails and ties taken together are known as track.

STRAIGHT TRACK is the most direct link between two points.

CURVED TRACK can have varying radii (degrees of curve). The tighter the curve, the slower the train must go. Tight curves also limit the length of individual cars and engines. Only shorter cars can negotiate these curves without derailing.

SWITCH TRACK has a movable set of rails that permit the train to continue straight or to follow a detour.

CROSSOVER allows one track to cross another on the same level.

REMOTE CONTROL TRACK (toy trains only) is a track specially wired to permit cars to uncouple or to unload at the press of a button some distance from the track.

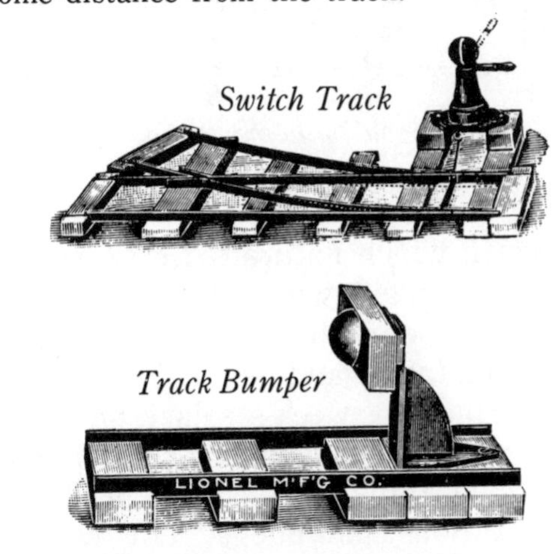

Switch Track

Track Bumper

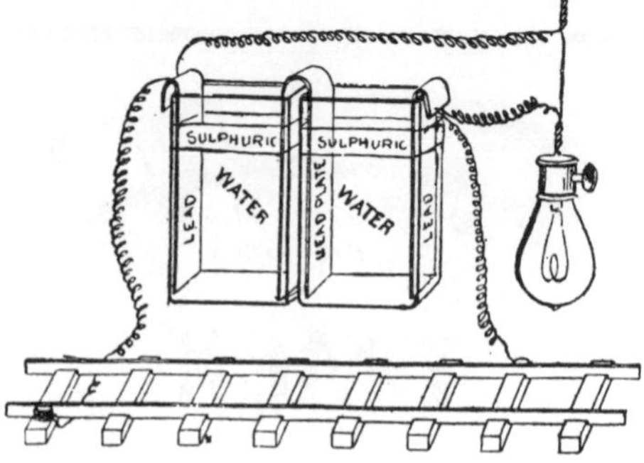

Wet-cell batteries were used in some homes by 1902.

THE ACID ON TOP OF THE WATER." The jars and lead plates were available for fifty cents. The customer supplied his own wire.

The joys of the *Electric Express* were not limited to those homes with electricity, however. If Cowen had had to rely on these for his sales—especially in the early part of the century—his market would have been severely curtailed. To expand his clientele, Cowen became a tireless champion of rural electrification. There was no reason why farmer as well as city dweller should not know the delight of finding an electric train under the Christmas tree, he felt. Until his notions caught on, he offered batteries by which to run the trains. Four large dry cells provided ten to fifteen hours of running time if used intermittently. They were wired together and then attached to the track by brass connectors. Like Cowen, the *Electric Express* operated only at full speed.

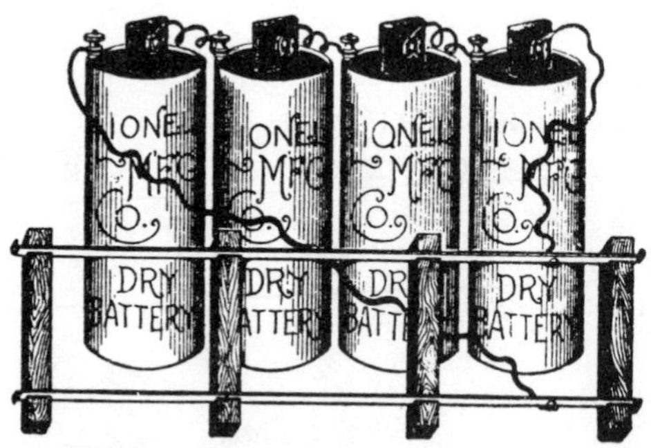

Dry-cells were sold for homes without electricity.

Electric trains were extremely expensive and very special, which naturally led to their being indissolubly linked with Christmas. Only at Christmas (or on your birthday, if you were lucky) would father and mother feel justified in spending almost a week's salary on a toy. At $6.00 a set in 1902, plus another $1.20 or so for batteries, the trains represented a healthy piece of a typical household budget. This was a time when industrial workers averaged $9.42 for a

ELECTRIC TOY TRAIN LEXICON

TOY TRAIN: Railroad car miniatures like those manufactured by Lionel, American Flyer, Ives, Marx, and others. They are intended primarily for children to play with and are mass-produced, widely distributed, and reasonably priced. Despite claims by their manufacturers, they are usually not exact models of real trains but are approximate representations that capture the major features of the real thing.

TIN-PLATE: Another term for a toy train, which refers to the fact that early electric toy trains were made of iron plated with tin to prevent rusting and to facilitate soldering the pieces together. The track was also tin-plated.

MODEL TRAIN: An exact replica of a real train. Almost every detail is reproduced in proper proportion to the whole. Model trains are generally intended for adults, who operate them according to real railroad procedures. They are made in smaller quantities than electric toy trains, use more costly materials like brass, and have more detail work.

SCALE: The size relationship between the toy train and the real one, usually expressed as a fraction. Modern Lionel trains are approximately one forty-eighth the size of their actual counterparts. Model train locomotives and cars are all "in scale," or in the proper proportion to each other. Toy/tin-plate trains are not. Lionel passenger cars, for instance, are smaller than they should be when compared with certain Lionel locomotives.

GAUGE: The width between the outside rails of the track, usually determined by the scale of a manufacturer's train line. Modern Lionel trains are O-gauge (1¼ inches between outside rails). Modern American Flyer trains are S-gauge (⅞ of an inch between rails). The most popular gauge for model trains today is HO (half O)—(⅝ of an inch between rails).

LAYOUT: A miniature train world, complete with mountains, rivers, trees, houses, and other details. Both toy and model trains lend themselves to layouts, though with differing degrees of realism.

six-day week; 1.7 million of them were children, who worked for as little as twenty-five cents a day. Office workers, paid $12.00 for a sixty hour week, fared somewhat better, but buying one of Cowen's trains still meant foregoing a new coat and vest ($7.00) or weighing it against a hundred pounds of sugar at $5.80. A new Kodak Brownie camera, by comparison, cost only $1.00.

But it was also an age of extreme opulence and conspicuous spending by such real railroad tycoons as William K. Vanderbilt and J. P. Morgan, and Cowen looked upon these barons as confirmation of one of his cherished beliefs: that hard work and imagination would surely be rewarded with success. Teddy Roosevelt typified the brash, blustering confidence of the age. For Cowen, the child of immigrants, there could be no better role model than the impetuous, straight-talking Rough Rider. All around Cowen, men were building fortunes with new inventions: the sewing machine, the telephone, the self-binding harvester, the primitive automobile. There was no reason the electric train couldn't share in the profits.

In 1903, Cowen and Grant came out with the first Lionel car based on an actual railroad engine. Rather than recreating a steam locomotive, whose romantic silhouette would come to represent the toy train just as it already did the real railroad, Cowen chose an electric engine as the prototype for his electric miniature. It was solid, durable, and probably easier to manufacture than a steam engine, which had a curved boiler and complicated wheel and gear detail.

Square and stodgy, the No. 5, as it was lettered on its side, was described in the Lionel catalog as "a faithful reproduction of the 1,800 horse power electric locomotives used by the B.&O.R.R. for hauling trains through the tunnels of Baltimore. Every line is carried out to the proper proportions. All parts are japanned and lettered in harmonious colors." [By the next year *japanned* was Americanized to *enameled.*] The catalog copy was not strictly accurate; the engine, a reproduction of the Baltimore & Ohio's Camden-Waverly tunnel engine, wasn't overly faithful to the original—in fact, it had only four wheels in place of its namesake's eight. Lionel would often take such liberties in years to come, capturing the essence of a train but indulging in poetic license (and production economies) in its construction.

Lionel's No. 5 was based on an actual electric locomotive, but the derrick car was a Cowen original.

FUNDIMENSIONS

The 2⅞-gauge boxcar had doors that opened and peculiar barred windows.

Cowen and Cecelia sent this postcard home during a first-anniversary trip to Lakewood, New Jersey.

The open gondolas were still in the catalog, now made of metal instead of wood. And there was a brand new car, a cast-iron, motorized derrick with a heavy hook for picking up freight loads and swinging them into the gondola. At seven dollars "complete with thirty feet of rail and sixty ties," the derrick—with its lovely crank mechanism for raising and lowering the hook—epitomized a new Cowen concept in toy manufacture. "Play value" would come to be the hallmark of Lionel trains. Children could actually do something with them besides running them around in hypnotizing circles. "A few minutes of that," Cowen explained "and the little nippers will wander off and squeeze out some toothpaste or set fire to the curtains. They've got to be *in* on it." Over the years, many other derricks, railroad cranes, and other "operable" equipment would be produced, all designed to get children "in on it."

By 1904, Cowen had become a man of means. When his father suffered a stroke while going to the synagogue, Cowen arranged for the medical care that Hyman would need for the last eleven years of his life. Although other brothers and sisters helped, Cowen became the main source of support for his parents. That year, too, on February 2, he married Cecelia Liberman, and set up housekeeping at 114th Street, just north of Central Park. He also moved his shop nine blocks uptown to 4-6 White Street, west of Chinatown.

As the company expanded, Cowen turned his attention to hiring more employees. While Grant was mechanically skilled, contributing many patentable inventions to Lionel, he was a poor administrator. Cowen was constantly on the road opening new markets; he needed a reliable supervisor in New York. Grant never finished any job he started, going from one thing to another in haphazard fashion. So when a young Sicilian named Mario Caruso was recommended to Cowen in 1904 by the distinguished William Davenport of the Italian Settlement House in Brooklyn, Cowen took him on.

Caruso, eighteen, had arrived in Staten Island the year before from Messina, Italy. A slim, intense apprentice marine engineer, Caruso had jumped ship and made his way to the settlement house where Davenport, a descendant of an old, respected Connecticut family, helped him learn English and find work suited to his mechanical abilities and training. Caruso came to Lionel as a solderer. However, when Cowen returned from a selling trip to find the line only half ready and Grant trying to repair an automobile instead of attending to business, Caruso stepped forward. "Put it in my hands and it will be ready," he quietly told Cowen. It was the beginning of a relationship that would make Lionel the leading toy train manufacturer in the world.

In Caruso, Cowen found his ideal counterpart: a brilliant manufacturing supervisor who would balance Cowen's own genius for merchandising. Stern, unsmiling, a severe taskmaster who rose before dawn for a vigorous fencing session with a younger protégé, Caruso ran the factory with an iron hand and left Cowen free to attend to selling. Caruso's serious demeanor permitted Cowen to assume the role he most favored—that of the genial, smiling, warm-hearted father who took a personal interest in each of his employees. Lionel's chief engineer, Joseph Bonanno, would later describe the difference between Cowen and Caruso: "When the workers saw Mr. Cowen coming they came out to say hello to him. When they saw Mr. Caruso coming, they hid."

In the mature years of the company, Cowen ran the business and selling from New York, while Caruso—now secretary/treasurer—managed the sprawling factory in New Jersey. Cowen would come out to the factory at least once a week and shake hands all around; Caruso bore the burden of day-to-day administration, including disciplining and firing employees. Caruso insulated Cowen from these more distasteful chores, enabling him to remain the beloved papa.

While "electric cars" were becoming extremely popular as toys, Cowen did not want to abandon his strategy of also marketing them as displays. In 1904 he offered a spectacular set for store window use. He used a regular Baltimore & Ohio engine with gondola in tow, but instead of being the normal maroon and black, the trains were nickel plated and housed a special motor designed to run eight or ten hours a day with no maintenance other than a drop of lubri-

ELIZABETH BONANNO

Mario Caruso (center) *and Cowen* (left) *enjoying a leisurely lunch in a gazebo outside the plant in the 1930s.*

cating oil. The set ran on eight-inch-high elevated columns and included the suspension bridge. The lucky shop owner could have it for thirty dollars.

"There is nothing so attractive as a moving window display," Cowen wrote, "but heretofore this has been very expensive for it was either a steam railway that was dangerous and needed constant care, or an attraction with a clock movement [wind-up motor] that also required considerable attention. An electrical arrangement therefore that is properly constructed is the only outfit that can be depended upon that is inexpensive and requires little attention. Our outfits are conceded by those who have used them to be superior to any show piece brought before their notice, for the track may be laid around the edges of the window leaving the center open for the display of goods, and the open trailer supplied with the outfit may be loaded with small articles which puts them prominently before the public."

The set sounded wonderful, but thirty dollars was a steep price for an electric train, even a polished nickel one, in a day when a roast beef dinner could be had for fifteen cents and chicken fricassee for twenty. Although the "Special Show Window Display" set occupied a full page in the catalog, there were apparently few orders for the elaborate outfit, and it is doubtful any were produced.

The 1906 catalog announced the three-rail track.

Cowen always kept an eye on the competition. In addition to Carlisle & Finch, several other firms including Knapp, the Howard Miniature Lamp Company, and Voltamp soon began making electric trains. Although most lasted only a short time, Cowen thundered against them in 1905: "UNSCRUPULOUS MANUFACTURERS have endeavored to duplicate our outfits and sell the goods at lower prices, but the fact remains: If you want an electric miniature train to work satisfactorily and for all time, 'YOU MUST GET A LIONEL.'" This was the first time Cowen clearly identified the trains with his own name. It was the genesis of a merchandising strategy that would end with *Lionel* becoming synonymous with *electric train,* not only in the United States but in export markets around the world. At the end of 1905, sales were eight thousand dollars, ten times what they were approximately four years earlier.

Cowen's first trains ran on two-rail tracks with a wide gauge of 2⅞ inches, much wider than the standard 2-inch width used by other manufacturers. This proved awkward in two respects. For the trains to look even reasonably proportioned, they had to be fairly tall, which gave them a somewhat bulky appearance. And while two-rail track was realistic looking, it was complicated electrically. Because one rail was positive and the other negative, the wheels of the cars had to be insulated from each other. The positive and negative rails also had to be kept separate from each other when the track curved back on itself in complex track patterns. Two-rail track was, of course, traditionally used by real railroads with steam locomotives. But in New York City and other urban areas, where railroads were relying on powerful electric engines, an outside third rail was added to carry current. This rail was sheathed in wood to protect pedestrians and railroad workers from being electrocuted and was marked with large warning signs: DO NOT STEP ON THIRD RAIL.

What worked for real railroads would surely work for toy ones, Cowen reasoned. In 1906, the Lionel line was completely revamped. The new catalog cover announced, "Look Out For The Third Rail." Current was carried in the insulated center rail, the outside rails acting as the negative, or ground, rails. Other manufacturers also adopted three-rail track, but it became Lionel's hallmark, especially during the great railroad war of the fifties, when American Flyer trains went to two rails while Lionel stayed with three.

Along with three-rail track came a new look for Lionel trains. Gone were the bulky 2⅞-gauge trains, the boxy look of the Baltimore & Ohio tunnel engine, clumsy gondolas, tinny trolleys perched on four flimsy-looking wheels. In their place were the beginnings of a dazzling variety of trains that would tempt and confuse gener-

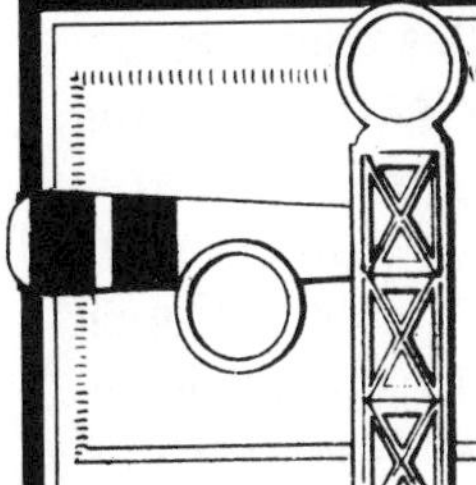

IVES PIONEERS TOY TRAINS

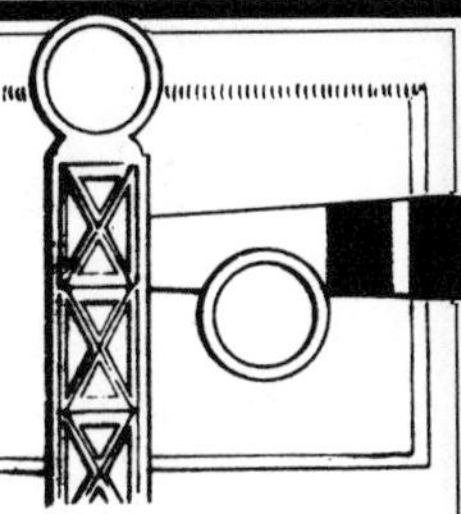

Although it never achieved the success of Lionel, the Ives Company of Bridgeport, Connecticut played a historic role in the toy train industry. The company was founded in 1868 by Edward Ives, a descendant of Massachusetts' Colonial Governor Bradford. By 1874, Ives was offering tin wind-up trains: Cast-iron, live steam and electric trains would follow during its sixty years of production.

In the 1880s, the company manufactured and exported a diverse line of toys. Cast-iron fire engines, horse and carriages, animated fiddle players, and fur-covered bears were offered in its 190-page catalog. A wind-up suffragette or "Woman's Rights Advocate" was one of the firm's most popular toys.

Ives took the lead in creating a complete line of stations, tunnels, and other accessories for its trains. In 1907 it trademarked the term *toy railroads,* indicating it was offering more than merely individual trains. Because it was so successful with wind-up trains, Ives didn't start manufacturing electric trains until 1910. Its tardy entry into the field allowed Lionel to establish an unbeatable lead.

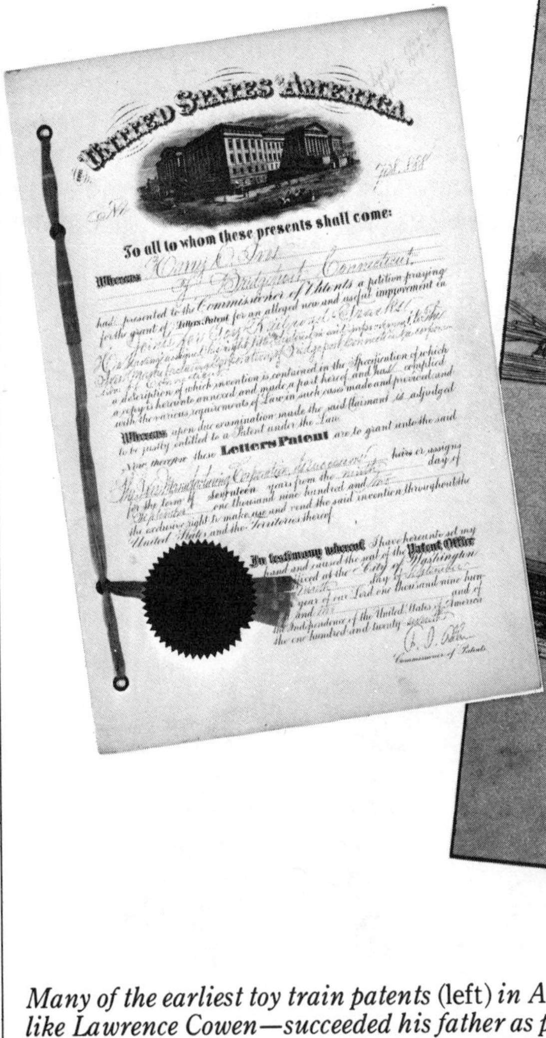

Many of the earliest toy train patents (left) *in America belonged to Edward Ives and his son, Harry, who—like Lawrence Cowen—succeeded his father as president of a toy train company. Ives specialized in lithography—(which Cowen despised). Its 1906 catalog* (right) *offered only wind-up trains.*

THE SOURCE

Electric trains operate by picking up positive (+) current from one track rail, passing it through their motors, then returning it to the other negative (-) track rail. From that rail it flows back to the transformer or battery to complete the circuit.

When Lionel used two-rail track, the engine took up positive current through the wheels on one side, fed it to the motor, then returned it via the wheels on the other side of the engine. To prevent the current from taking a short cut through the axle (short-circuiting) and bypassing the motor altogether, the axle was insulated.

Lionel's later three-rail track eliminated this problem. The new center rail was the positive rail. A roller on the bottom of the engine picked up current from the rail and carried it to the motor. Current then flowed out through the wheels (both outside rails were now negative).

ations of children, producing endless debates on the merits of *this* engine (with extra driving wheels and a whistle) and *that* (not as many drivers, but just look at that cream-colored stripe on the running boards!). The 1906 Lionel line included three trolleys, two steam locomotives (a switcher and a road engine), a Pullman sleeper, a baggage car, and seven different freight cars, including a caboose with seats and a sliding roof.

The young engineer was no longer limited to being president and general manager of only the Baltimore & Ohio. Now he could command steam engines lettered "N.Y.C. & H.R.R.R." for New York Central and Harlem River Rail Road, the cornerstones of Vanderbilt's New York Central system. He could oversee passenger cars with "Pennsylvania R.R." markings, or switch freight cars of the "Chicago, Minneapolis & St. Paul" or "Lake Shore" railroads. If he were of a more urban frame of mind, he could dispatch trolleys of the "Electric Rapid Transit." Lionel's ties with real railroads were forged in this catalog. Eventually, railroad companies would submit blueprints of their newest engines and cars to Lionel in hopes of popularizing them.

But the greatest changes in the trains were electrical. The track was now preassembled in straights and curves, rigidly kept in gauge by

DAVID EISENDRATH

Steam switching engine was a best-seller for Lionel although it carried coal in a bunker rather than in a tender.

FUN FACTORY

"COME ON BOYS"—I'LL TAKE YOU FOR A TRIP THRU MY FACTORY—YOU'LL SEE THEN WHY LIONEL TRAINS ARE BETTER

J. LIONEL COWEN

When in 1910 the New Haven Chamber of Commerce offered tax breaks to lure new industries to Connecticut, Cowen decided to move the manufacturing end of the business to New Haven under Mario Caruso. The move emphasized the division between manufacturing and sales that would come to characterize the company. The New Haven plant developed as a separate fiefdom under Caruso. Manufacturing was Caruso's domain.

The four-story, large-windowed factory on Winchester Avenue was a boy's dream. Pullman cars were stacked three high, coated with the rich, baked-on enamel paint for which Lionel was known. (Ives, Lionel's competitor, specialized in beautiful lithography on its cars, but Cowen hated the thinner metal of their bodies. "That stuff, that's cheesy," he said with loathing. "It's so sharp you can shave yourself with it.")

Joseph Bonanno, who became Lionel's chief engineer, recalls going to the factory when he was seven to visit his uncle Caruso. "My mother dressed me in a beautiful white suit to take the train from New York," he says. "But with the steam engine blowing coal dust and the windows open I was gray by the time I reached New Haven.

"I was very curious about everything. A workman was soldering wires on commutators for train motors. I asked him if I could help. First he let me put the flux on the commutators. When I did that well he let me solder. I did a whole tray. My uncle came by and the workman said, 'Look, your nephew soldered all these.' But Mr. Caruso was angry. 'Don't do it again,' he scolded the man. 'They might not be up to standards.'"

Caruso gave Bonanno a red and black No. 5 steam locomotive. ("It didn't have a tender," he recalls somewhat wistfully.) Bonanno didn't meet Cowen during his visit to the factory. But when he went to work for Lionel in the late twenties and reminded Cowen of the New Haven days, Cowen, speaking of his weekly trips to the factory with the payroll, jokingly remarked, "I had to hock my watch every week to pay people."

THOMAS PAGANO

In July 1923, young Thomas Pagano (front row, right) *stood with his father, Jack* (back row, far left) *and others at Lionel plant.*

Thomas Pagano, who became assistant superintendent in charge of parts production, literally grew up in Lionel's Irvington, New Jersey, plant, accompanying his father, Jack, on his Sunday inspection rounds. Pagano senior was responsible for assembling cars, but to earn extra money he served as weekend watchman.

Young Tom skipped along in his knickers in the echoing factory as his father punched in on his watchman's clock. "I played with whatever was being made," Pagano recalls. "While my father did his rounds, I'd roll cars back and forth on the work benches. I felt comfortable in the plant. When the factory grew bigger, my father made his rounds on a fork lift truck. In between his watches, I'd read aloud to him from newspapers and magazines. I learned to read by practicing in the factory."

During the week, on his way to school, Pagano dropped off lunch for his father. At the end of the day, if his father were working late, Pagano brought him a hot dinner plate wrapped in a napkin or shawl. "For me the factory was always a special place," he says fondly. "It was tremendously exciting, with all the machines going and new products coming out. I have happy memories of it."

metal ties. Pins in the end of one piece fit into grooves in the next, ensuring a tighter fit than the primitive interlocking hook method provided on the 2⅞ track. The width was narrowed to 2⅛ inches, although Cowen advertised his new track as "2-inch gauge." Also introduced was a transformer that could reduce regular house current to a voltage suitable for toy trains. The transformer was packaged in a marble box and designed to be fastened to the wall.

Cowen made a special point of reassuring the buyer that electrical toys were safe. "The word 'electric' does not always stand for power dangerous to handle," the catalog noted. "It is true of current sufficiently powerful to operate large street cars... but as applied to our models it is totally impossible to experience the slightest shock.... Now that we have brought these goods to a state of perfection and the schools throughout the country teach the scholars the principles of electricity, the tendency of the boy is to get anything electrically operated. His elders who continually see electrical machinery, trolley cars and hundreds of other electrical devices will naturally want the young one to become familiar with toys operated by this mysterious power especially as they are SAFER than any mechanical toy on the market. There is nothing so educating to the scholar as a working model.... They will get the user to thinking and aid him in bringing out ideas that may be very ingenious and profitable to him."

Cowen was exaggerating slightly when he claimed that electrical toys were safer than mechanical wind-up ones, especially since Lionel's early transformers had a tendency to heat up quickly until they almost glowed. The problem was soon corrected, however, and Lionel trains rolled around store windows and on parlor floors in ever mounting numbers. Never one to be humble, by 1909 Cowen had adopted as his slogan the immodest claim that Lionel trains were the "Standard of the World." "As superior to any on the market as the telephone is to the speaking tube," the 1909 catalog pointed out. In a clever promotional stroke, Cowen applied the slogan to Lionel's track, calling it standard gauge. In fact, at 2⅛ inches, it was wider than most other toy tracks and could more appropriately have been called odd gauge. But Cowen clung both to his eccentric track width and to its description as standard gauge, and eventually, other manufacturers changed their track to match Lionel's.

THE TRANSFORMER

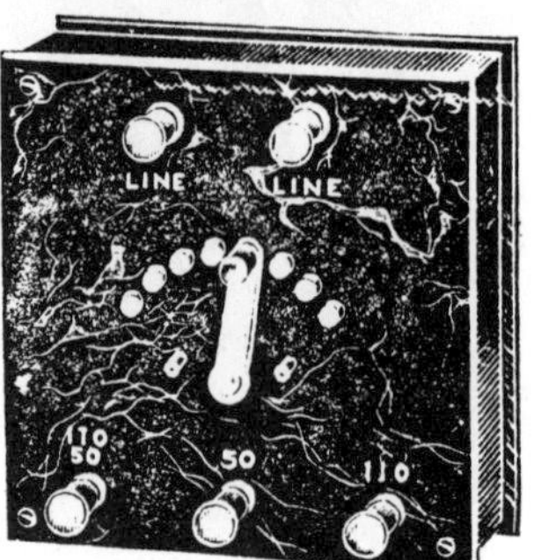

1906 wall transformer

A transformer reduces 110-volt house current to the safer levels of 20 to 30 volts comonly used by electric trains. Lionel's first transformers got their power from electric light bulb sockets; later, as electricity became more common, they plugged into wall outlets. If a house did not have electricity, its occupants had to rely on batteries to run the trains. But if the house was already wired, then the transformer became the most important piece of electrical equipment in the toy train set. Lionel's early transformers got hot too quickly, but they were eventually perfected.

From the lamp socket or wall outlet, 110-volt current entered the soft metal core of the transformer. Wire wound around the core enabled the transformer to reduce that current to a safe level. A lever on the outside of the transformer allowed the train operator to choose the amount of current needed for a particular train. Moving the lever increased the voltage (up to the transformer's limit of 20 to 30 volts). Increasing the voltage increased the speed of the train. In this way the transformer acted as the throttle of the toy train.

Transformers were a great advance over batteries because they allowed the Lionel engineer to control the speed of his train. Other accessories, like street lamps, could also be wired to the transformer. Eventually, in addition to controlling a train's speed, the transformer could change the direction in which it was traveling and even make its whistle blow. And the operator never had to actually touch the train.

CLANG, CLANG, CLANG GOES THE TROLLEY

Trolleys became the mainstay of Lionel's catalog after the company shifted to production of standard gauge sets in 1906. At their peak in about 1910, thirteen different trolleys were offered. There were powered and "trailer" units, four- and eight-wheel versions, and lighted and unlit models. Duplicating those that clanged on America's streets, Lionel's early trolleys were completely open, but later cars had windows and closed-in fronts to protect the motorman.

Trolleys ranged in price from four dollars for simple, unlit units to seventeen dollars for twin-motored, eight-wheel cars. Like their real counterparts, some of the trolleys came with odd-looking front fenders or bumpers. These were designed to scoop up any pedestrian in the trolley's path and cradle him safely in the basket of the bumper.

As it did in later years, Lionel made up specially-lettered versions of its trolleys for important dealers. For a Baltimore firm, the Maryland Electric Supply Company, Lionel manufactured trolleys named after popular Baltimore trolley routes, including *Linden Avenue, Bay Shore,* and *Washington, Baltimore and Annapolis.*

Trolleys were dropped from the Lionel catalog in the mid-teens. Trains could be used in elaborate layouts, while trolleys rarely had more than one trailing car in tow. And, from a merchandising standpoint, trolleys did not lend themselves to signals, switch towers, bridges, freight loaders, and the other accessories that eventually constituted 35 to 40 percent of Lionel's sales.

Binghamton R. R. Co.
TRANSFER.
Good only for this current trip, from point of transfer, on next car over the line punched after time canceled. Subject to Rules of Company.
PICTURE PUNCHED INDICATES TYPE OF PASSENGER.
Issued by Conductor No. 47
IF BLACK PORTION PUNCHED TIME IS P. M.
GLOBE TICKET COMPANY, PHILA., PA.

Early trolley ticket.

BETTMANN

For many cities, trolleys were the major means of mass transit at the turn of the century.

FUNDIMENSIONS

Lionel's No. 3 trolley of 1906 came in motorized and trailer versions in cream, olive green, or orange.

Cowen's brashness, his driving desire to make Lionel a success, helped him sweep most of the competition before him. "Today we stand foremost in the manufacture of Miniature Electric Cars and Motors," he proclaimed in 1909, "not only in the United States, but in the world—quite a statement to make but we can prove it." It was a questionable boast that would have embarrassed a more reflective man, especially given the primacy of German train manufacturers like Bing or Marklin. But Cowen was just beginning to hit his stride. "Can you conceive of any toy that will delight the heart of a youngster to a greater extent than one that has REAL LIFE and POWER, that will respond to the commands of start, stop, reverse, slow and fast without the operator even coming in contact with the model?" the 1909 catalog demanded. This emphasis on power and control would serve Lionel well in coming years. What could be more appealing to a small child—powerless in real life—than to acquire control, at least in miniature, over that most mighty of machines, the steam locomotive?

Lawrence Cowen was less than three months old when Cecelia posed with him for this picture postcard.

Cowen also continued to harp on electricity: "What real-live-wide-awake boy is not interested in electricity? What boy and his elders are not anxious to know more about this wonderful study? Is there any better way than to have a perfect model as an instructor? Knowledge of electricity is valuable, not only as a profession, but as an education, whether one is an electrical engineer or a bell-hanger." There was no place in Lionel Land for that dreamy dunderhead of a boy more interested in things musical or artistic, say, than in things electrical. It was not a time for the aesthete, not when a series of juvenile nickel pulp magazines was entitled *Fame and Fortune Weekly—Stories of Boys That Make Money,* full of tales of precocious successes on Wall Street and of young heroes who outwitted rapscallions attempting to kidnap for ransom the lovely daughters of benevolent financiers. In later years, Cowen even implied you weren't a "real" boy unless you were fascinated with the challenge of railroading, even in toy form. This was hardly a theme he foisted on the boys of America by himself; he was merely using a prevalent obsession to help him to do business.

And if only forthright, fearless boys were addressed in the catalogs, girls were neglected entirely. It was a reflection of the sexes' respective roles in turn-of-the-century adult society that trains and electricity were for boys while dolls were for girls. It would have taken a marketing genius even greater than Cowen to have conceived of a girls' market for toy trains. Why on earth would girls be interested in trains and electricity when their place was in the home? Not only were women not allowed to vote in America, but in one-quarter of the states, wives could not own property; one-third gave wives no claim to their own earnings and four-fifths denied a wife an equal share in the guardianship of her own children. Despite an active suffragist movement, women had no real share in what railroads (and their toy counterparts) were truly about: power. Lionel's first appeal to girls was in 1930, when it offered a working electric stove to teach "sister" that "there's lots of fun in playing housewife." And it made no pitch for feminine interest in trains until 1957, when it created a misguided "Lady Lionel" train set "in fashion-right colors" with a frosted pink locomotive and lilac hopper. Understandably, it was a huge flop.

By the end of the decade Lionel trains came in many configurations. Trolleys led the catalog, supplied now with a dozen seated figures that could be removed from their hard metal benches when the metal pins they were seated on grew too uncomfortable for their wooden behinds. Trolleys and steam engines were equipped with miniature electric headlights to illuminate the three-rail track and to disclose any unexpected and mischievously-placed piles of ABC building blocks obstructing the right of way. Prices had increased greatly over the original $4.00 for Lionel's first wooden gondola; the top-of-the-line trolley cost $17.00 by 1910. But it was done in three colors, was a foot-and-a-half long, and had sliding doors and a separate motor over each set of wheels. In locomotives, Cowen outdid himself with a classic polished brass American-type steamer boasting four pilot wheels behind the cowcatcher and four big driving wheels. Designed once again as a shining window display piece, the *Electric Express* was priced at a hefty $22.50—without track.

Metal lithographed stations were offered with intricately-painted brick siding and carved doorposts. Real leaded glass dome train sheds arched over the track. These stations were made by the venerable Ives Company of Bridgeport, Connecticut. Founded in 1868, Ives manufactured cast iron toys and wind-up trains; it also introduced its own line of electric trains in 1910. It is surprising, therefore, that it made its fine lithography available to Lionel. Perhaps Edward Ives, founder of the company, and Harry, his son, did not consider the new boy on the block much of a threat. If so, they made a gross miscalculation, for within twenty years Lionel would take over their company.

As the line grew, so, too, did the rhetoric in the catalog. Cowen continued to rail against competitors who were putting out lower-priced sets. "Cheap goods are dear in the long run," he warned. To make his point, he drew a mince-no-words comparison with another popular toy of the time, the Teddy bear. "Whenever a demand is created for an article," he wrote in 1910, "a number of firms attempt to imitate it. Their object is not to improve it but to cheapen its cost and undersell the original manufacturers. For example, take the craze for 'Teddy bears.' Hundreds of firms bought the cloth and stuffing and in a short time the Teddy bear, originally beautiful in design and finish, evolved to an ugly rat."

A proud Cowen—already losing his hair—showed off the future president of Lionel.

Cowen now had two children, both of whom eventually played important roles in the corporation. Lawrence, the eldest, born in 1907, became president of the company in 1945 under his father's chairmanship. Isabel became secretary and a director of Lionel in 1959 when Cowen, then retired, sold his stock to a group headed by Roy Cohn, Cowen's great-nephew. In 1910, Cowen legally changed his name from Cohen to Cowen. The reason for this is not clear. Probably it was to avoid any anti-Semitism—the toy business was old and primarily Protestant—although there is little evidence that Cowen attempted to hide his Jewishness. He supported Jewish charities, belonged to a synagogue, and occasionally went to services on the Jewish high holy days. But besides being a business convenience, changing his name might have been an expression of his Americanism.

In one decade, Cowen had created a new company and had impressed its product on the American consciousness. He had begun with a four-dollar sale and by decade's end was making almost $57,000 a year. At the same time, he had started a family of his own and was supporting his parents. It was a good beginning to the new century.

3

PICKING UP SPEED

1910-1919

The teens were a decade of growth and of increased sophistication both for America and for Lionel. The nation's gross national product more than doubled from 1910 to 1920, while Lionel's sales grew fifteen times. The simple vitality of the turn of the century yielded to the complex reality of a war abroad and the growing assertiveness of both labor and women at home. The blustering confidence of Teddy Roosevelt was replaced by the reflective introspection of Woodrow Wilson. The new automotive and film industries matured.

By the end of the decade, Cowen was president of a corporation employing seven hundred workers. In addition to miniature trolleys and diminutive locomotives, he had produced hundreds of thousands of dollars of war goods. Sales had increased every year. They were $57,000 in 1910, $355,000 in 1916, and $839,000 by 1921, augmented by Lionel's war contracts. But Cowen never neglected his first love. By 1920, toys and electric trains had grown from being Christmas-only items to year-round successes whose sales had tripled in overall volume.

Despite the introduction of an automobile to the catalog in 1912, trolleys and trains predominated. Four different models of electric engines and two steam locomotives were available. Passenger cars, which could be lit up from the inside, came in three sizes to go with each of the locomotives. The variety of trolleys ranged from open summer cars to closed "Pay-As-You-Enter" winterized cars with vestibules and sliding doors ("A new model in keeping with trolley car progress...an exact reproduction of the new pay-as-you-enter cars which are growing so popular throughout the country"). Rheostats were offered to regulate the speed of the trains. Prior to that, speed had to be controlled by adding more cars or weights, subtracting dry cells, or by inserting dangerous resistance bulbs into the circuit. New "multi-volt" transformers were introduced for those homes having electricity. Lionel trains, "standard of the world" and "more than a toy—an electric achievement," were gathering momentum.

The "Pay-As-You-Enter" trolley was twenty inches long and cost twelve dollars when last made in 1916.

Despite its size,

RACING CARS FOR LIONEL ENGINEERS

DAVID EISENDRATH

The cars operated by means of a sliding shoe under the center of the car that picked up current from the groove in the middle of the circular track (below).

Cowen loved automobiles, the bigger and faster the better, so it was perhaps inevitable that Lionel would come out with its own racing cars. Automobiles were booming in the teens. From a rich man's diversion, the automobile rapidly became the means by which millions of Americans could obtain a freer lifestyle. Some ten million cars were bought during the decade, four million of them Henry Ford's Model T, the reliable Tin Lizzie.

There were many similarities between Henry Ford and Joshua Lionel Cowen. Both were self-made men who created industries from their tinkering. Each was a premier merchandiser, concerned with offering quality at an affordable price. Ford worked to lower the cost of a Model T; Cowen, in a letter to an inventor offering an expensive game to Lionel, wrote, "You must cater to the masses rather than the classes if you want to get the most out of any article these days."

Lionel's open "racing automobiles," introduced in 1912, went fast enough in miniature to satisfy even Cowen, who delighted in sitting in his own car's front seat even when a chauffeur was driving his Isotta-Fraschini or Rolls-Royce.

Lionel's cars were models of the open road-racing machines that were thrilling—and sometimes scandalizing—the country. "The appearance of the cars, especially when whizzing around the track at top speed, is realistic in the extreme," the catalog crowed. "To watch them racing, neck and neck, one now forging ahead, and the other striving to overtake it, is, to say the least, exciting. It is as though the spectator were suddenly transported, as if by some magic hand, to a liliputian land, and stands like a giant over some tiny sports congress. To add to the realism, the cars are controlled by a driver and mechanic, who pilot their respective cars with that tense, set attitude so characteristic of them."

Like the trains, the cars went in circles. But since they were racing each other on parallel tracks, the inside car always had the advantage. To offset this, talcum powder could be sprinkled on the outside metal roadway to increase its traction.

The racing cars—which did not sell very well—were an ironic presage of things to come. For just as the automobile and the interstate highway system eventually ended first-class passenger train travel, so the demise of the electric train in the early 1960s came at the hands of the toy racing car.

Lionel was a family company. Both Cowen and Caruso felt it was their duty to provide jobs for relatives ranging from Caruso's brothers to Cowen's nephews and brother-in-law. It was therefore not surprising that young Lawrence, Cowen's son, should become the symbol of Lionel in the teens and early twenties, the epitome of the happy Lionel boy. Lawrence's figure appeared on more than a million train boxes, flyers, and catalogs. Life-size cardboard cutouts of him stood in dealers' windows. His image adorned catalogs that were studied and treasured in boys' rooms across the country. In his neat, brown-checked suit, his high, lace-up shoes, and Eton collar, Lawrence kneeled behind an eight-wheel No. 42 electric engine on the cover of every box of Lionel Electric Toy Trains. "The Happy Lionel Boy. He represents the joyous feelings of over 550,000 boys who own Lionel outfits," a brochure said of Lawrence, though he was never identified by name. It must have been heady stuff for Joshua's young son.

The Cowen family was no different from those pictured in the catalog. It was Lawrence who had the electric trains; his sister, Isabel, was not supposed to touch them. Instead, she awoke one Christmas morning to find her room festooned with thirty-two dolls carefully arranged by her father. Lawrence, on the other hand, received a twenty-four-tube radio built by Cowen. Trains for boys, dolls for girls: It was an established pattern that Cowen did much to confirm. Yet, as in so many families, Isabel probably would have done as well or better than Lawrence at the throttle of the Lionel Express. For although Lawrence, at his father's insistence, did succeed him as president of Lionel, it was Isabel who seemed to have inherited Cowen's mechanical aptitude and skill at fixing things. (Cowen's passion for such work was so great the family accused him of breaking household items so he could have the pleasure of repairing them.) Cowen himself seems to have been conflicted about the boys-only message in his catalogs, for he apparently made no sexual distinctions when teaching his children (or grandchildren) how to repair a broken plug or solder a lamp.

In the public sphere, Cowen was the patriarchal father and husband demanded by the times. He attended to his affairs: building up his company, providing for his family, catering to the needs of his wife, shielding her from those financial matters that traditionally were not her concern. And although he extolled close father-son relationships, he was probably too busy in the early years of Lionel to be the "pal" to his son that he wrote about in his catalogs. Lawrence went to boarding school, and there were few pictures of him with his father in the family photo albums.

After four years of commuting from New York to the factory, then located in New Haven, Connecticut, Cowen wearied of the long trip and moved the plant to Newark, New Jersey, somewhat closer to home. With 150 employees, booming train sales spurred by color catalogs, and the prospect of government war contracts, Lionel soon needed still more room. Mario Caruso picked out a site in the nearby small town of Irvington. A nickel trolley ride from Newark, Irvington was a rural farming community. A series of Lionel factories was built there and one of the top-of-the-line passenger cars was even-

FIRST SALES MANAGER

Mark Harris was Lionel's first sales manager. Cowen had become impressed with Harris when he encountered him in the toy department of the Simpson-Crawford department store. Harris was selling Lionel trains, and he seemed to know what he was doing. Cowen offered him nine dollars a week to come to Lionel. Simpson-Crawford countered with an offer of ten dollars a week if Harris stayed. Back came Cowen with eleven. The store saw Cowen's eleven and raised him to twelve. The conclusion was inevitable, given Cowen's bulldog tenacity, and Harris came to work for Lionel for thirteen dollars a week.

THE BOSS'S SON

Lawrence grew up with all the Lionel trains a boy could dream of, but as in many American households, they didn't hold the same lure for him that they did for his father. Despite having posed for Lionel ads, Lawrence rarely visited the New York showroom or the New Jersey plant. "Just wasn't interested," he explained in his succinct manner after he became president of the company.

And while he was interested in business and finance, Lawrence had none of his father's passion for technical things. "I'm mechanically inept," Lawrence once admitted.

Though it was camouflaged by his urbane, cultured exterior, Lawrence did share his father's stubbornness. "I don't know where he gets it from," Cowen once joked, "but this Larry is the bull-headedest guy you ever saw."

Like any little boy, Lawrence had trains to play with. These, however, were for a promotional photograph used on a sales brochure in the teens.

Lawrence posed for this photograph at the bottom of a flight of marble steps in his home with his arms outstretched and fingers spread, but with no train before him. The photo was then used as a basis for Lionel's advertising campaign in the teens.

Lawrence became "The Happy Lionel Boy" on box covers, catalogs, flyers, and store-window cutouts (above).

In his riding outfit, complete with crop, Lawrence stands with Cecelia Cowen, who is certainly not dressed for an equestrian romp.

Cowen (left) *visiting Lawrence at camp, or perhaps boarding school. This is the only picture in the family photo albums of the teen-aged Lawrence with his father.*

Lawrence, wearing his natty golfing costume—complete with argyles—holds a cigarette in his right hand.

Lawrence at about the time he entered Cornell.

tually lettered *Irvington* in honor of the town.

Lionel drew its workers from the Italian neighborhoods of Newark. They came to Irvington on the trolley, happy in those discriminatory times for any kind of employment—especially work that was a step up from the manual labor to which they were generally relegated. Caruso spoke their language and respected their culture. Employees often remained devoted to Lionel for many years, bringing their children into the company after them. Payment was on a piecework basis, averaging about twenty-two dollars a week for the fastest workers—probably slightly lower than what other small companies paid for unskilled labor.

Among the new products rolling out of the factory were smaller, O-gauge trains, which were 1¼ inches wide. (Lionel was practically forced into manufacturing them to compete with Ives, who had introduced its own line of O-gauge electric trains in 1910.) These took up less room than standard gauge models and were cheaper to produce. The economical O-gauge eventually dominated toy train production in America.

Lionel offered passenger and freight cars in O-gauge, and engines that were modeled after real electric-powered ones. No steam locomotives were available in the new gauge until 1930, and steamers continued to be made in the wider standard gauge until 1939. This may have been because Cowen wanted to link the new O-gauge with modern trends in railroading. Electric engines were the newest thing on actual railroads, especially in the urban East, which was Lionel's largest market.

2⅞-GAUGE
1901-1905

STANDARD GAUGE
1906-1939

O-GAUGE
1915-present

Lionel faced competition not only from other American train manufacturers but from foreign competitors as well, especially the older German toy makers who had long dominated the American scene. But the outbreak of World War I in 1914 stopped the flow of German toys into the United States and gave the domestic toy industry a chance to grow. To help deal with the industry's other problems, including the shortage of materials caused by the war in Europe, the Toy Manufacturers of the U.S.A. was created in 1916. A trade association of sixty-eight manufacturers, it eventually managed the annual Toy Fair in New York at which new toy lines were displayed in late winter.

Although train manufacturers were instrumental in creating the association, Cowen was not among them. He had never been a part of the

Lionel has made electric trains in five sizes (gauges), ranging from the earliest trains, which were 2⅞ inches between rails, to the ⅝-inch HO, today's most popular size for scale model railroading. OO-gauge trains were made for both two- and three-rail track. Plastic was used to make certain cars and engines (especially diesels) in O and HO gauge.

OO-GAUGE
1938–1942

HO-GAUGE
1957–1967

ROBERT STEIN

PAUL HILZEN

LOCOMOTIVE TYPES

Locomotives are of three general types: steam, electric, or diesel. (In the earliest days of railroading, trains were pulled by horses. One impractical locomotive even had a sail to catch the wind.)

STEAM. Steam locomotives have long boilers in which water is boiled, usually by burning coal. The power of the expanding steam then turns the locomotive's wheels. Both water and coal are carried in the tender behind the steam engine and are fed to the locomotive while it is moving. Escaping steam makes the familiar chugging sound. Steam is also used to blow the whistle. Smoke from the burning coal and excess steam puff out of the locomotive's smokestack.

ELECTRIC. Electric engines are powered by electricity, which they pick up as they move. The current can be gathered from overhead wires in the manner of trolley cars, or from an outside third rail running beside the tracks, as in many subway systems. Electric engines have a squarer shape than steamers and can travel equally well in either direction.

DIESEL. Diesel locomotives burn diesel fuel oil to drive electric generators. These in turn power electric motors that turn the engine's wheels. Diesels have several advantages over steam locomotives: They require less maintenance and are easier to service, their fuel consumption is low, and their pulling power is smoother and less damaging to the tracks. Also, one engineer can control many diesel engines hooked together, while each steamer needs its own crew.

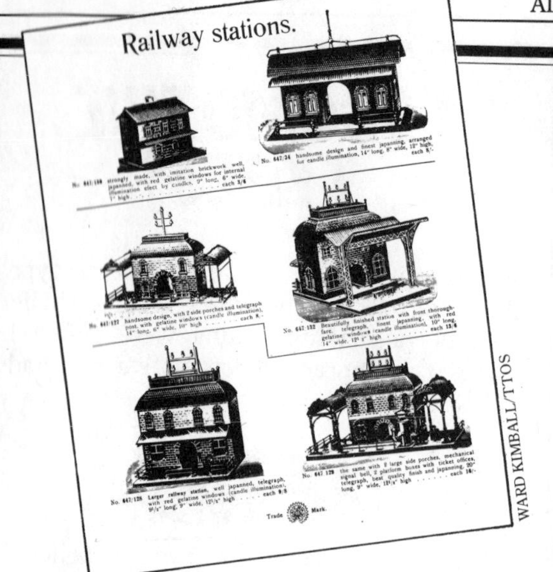

WARD KIMBALL/TTOS

The Georges Carette English export catalog for 1911.

FOREIGN COMPETITION

Until World War I, "Made in Germany" was the label most Americans expected to find on their toy trains. The tradition of toy making established in Nuremberg in the 1700s carried over into toy trains in the nineteenth and early twentieth centuries. The American toy market was dominated by imports from Germany, and in fact there was an actual prejudice against American toys, which were considered to be not as well made as their European counterparts.

The German firms of Bing and Marklin, both founded in the nineteenth century, had a clear toy train lead over American companies like Lionel. Bing, established in Nuremberg in 1865, exported seventy-five different types of railroad cars designed for the American market. Other lines were destined for Canada, England, and specific European countries, all decorated appropriately.

Marklin, dating to 1888 as a train company, is thought to have been the first to produce a miniature electric railroad in Europe. Its sectional track was usually displayed in a figure eight pattern. Marklin trains caused a sensation at the Leipzig Spring Fair of 1891, and they were soon being exported to America.

The firms of Karl Bub and Georges Carette (a Frenchman who built his business in Nuremberg) also exported cheap, wind-up trains to the United States.

old-line establishment. A. C. Gilbert, who manufactured Erector building sets and who eventually bought American Flyer, was elected president. Other founders included W. O. Coleman of Chicago, president of Flyer, and Harry Ives, who succeeded Gilbert and who served as president of the association for three years. Ironically, the Ives and Flyer trade names were eventually taken over by Lionel.

Perhaps piqued by their neglect of him, Cowen devoted several pages at the beginning of the 1917 catalog to proving rather pointedly that Lionel was superior to other manufacturers. "Come on, boys," he called, "I'll take you for a trip thru my factory—you'll see then why Lionel trains are better." A picture of an almost-bald Cowen was shown under the heading "Fun Factory." "'Fun'—that's the magic word all us boys like to hear" wrote the forty-year-old "boy." One by one, Cowen took the virtues of his (unnamed) competitors and turned them into defects. Ives's detailed lithographed finish? "This is a very cheap process. The color chips off in flakes, it cracks very easily, and soon the cars lose their attractiveness." The solid heaviness of traditional cast-iron engines? "There is no joy in getting a cast iron electric locomotive. You are always expecting it to fall to pieces or afraid you will knock it off the table with your elbow—then your locomotive body is broken, your motor is liable to be filled with pieces of iron which will short circuit it." The normal method of constructing cars of two matching pieces? "Such construction is extremely shaky, flimsy and rickety, and will easily fall apart. The floor and trucks of the car are liable to fall off, in time the side is likely to split off and separate from the roof, and the car will soon be a wreck and in the ash box."

Side-by-side comparisons were made, although the cheapest Ives item was always matched against Lionel's most expensive model. Finally, the importance of the Lawrence-adorned box was stressed. "Study this end label till you know it. Look for it on the shelf. A good many dealers buy just one Lionel Electric Train and use it for an advertisement but sell something else. They know that the Lionel Train is the most reliable—will run all day—will draw people to their windows and help sell the cheaper train. Ask if it is Lionel and look at the label 'sharp.' Get what you ask for!"

Cowen was relentless in his monitoring of the competition. Several years later, when Ives used

Assembling compass binnacles in Lionel's first Irvington, New Jersey, factory in 1918. The building is used today by a company that manufactures foam rubber pillows.

the Lionel-associated word *standard* in its price list, Cowen fired off a letter to Harry Ives, noting that *standard* was used to describe Lionel trains and track and could Ives please observe some "fair treatment" in its promotional material. The normally-reserved Ives responded in kind. Tired of seeing what were clearly Ives trains pictured as broken-down wrecks in the Lionel catalog, he accused Cowen of "illustrating competitive toys unfairly" and of "unmistakably" referring to Ives in its picture comparisons. Undaunted, Cowen responded: "We illustrate a car body made of one piece in comparison with a car of another make made in three pieces. All paint and marks of identification were removed before the illustration was made. We think you will agree with us that there is nothing distinctive about the car illustrated. There are a great many makes of foreign and domestic cars marketed of which the three-piece construction is typical." As for Ives's complaint that Lionel showed its own track supporting a weight of 110 pounds while another brand fell apart under a weight of just 20 pounds, Cowen said, "... The track is not aimed at or illustrative of any particular make, and if you will permit us to say so, has done a great deal to raise the quality demanded by the public for a better constructed toy roadbed."

Having disposed of Ives's complaints, Cowen returned to his original point. "Your use of the word 'standard,' begun about two years ago, is enlarging all the time and will ultimately cause confusion of our lines with the trade. We have spent a great deal of time and money in teaching the public to associate the word 'standard' and the expression 'standard of the world' with our product, and we feel that in the interest of fair trading you should discontinue the use of this word in connection with any of your output. We have always been very careful to avoid the employment of any of the exclusive terms as-

"PLAY WAR!"

WARD KIMBALL

Cowen's jingoist cry of "Play War!" was not an isolated call. The German toy train manufacturer, Marklin, made a train that fired caps, the smoke drifting realistically out of the muzzles and gun slits. In the thirties, Marklin's catalogs offered miniature railroad military equipment—precise to the last detail—so that German youth would be familiar with mobile antiaircraft guns, armored reconnaissance cars, and self-propelled cannon when the boys eventually joined the Third Reich's panzer divisions. Marklin's military trains gave such an accurate picture of Germany's illegal armaments that the government had some of the toys withdrawn from production. Their prototypes eventually rolled across Poland in 1939.

With the war on, boys patriotically celebrated the Fourth of July 1918 with flags and an imposing sidewalk locomotive. Lionel's O-gauge armored war train (right) *was slightly smaller. The somber gray of engine and cars was relieved by the red-spoked wheels of the turreted locomotive* (below), *whose guns looked fierce but did not shoot.*

DAVID EISENDRATH

sociated with other toy makers and expect our 'friendly competitors' to treat us the same way.

"In view of the large amount of pioneer work which both of us have accomplished in building up this industry, we feel that each of us can well afford to let the exclusive names and features originated by the other alone. As we will continue more or less to travel the same road we naturally wish to come to an understanding in these matters and would like to hear from you again."

It took over a year and the involvement of patent and trademark attorneys, but eventually Ives wrote that the word *standard* was being omitted from its price lists and that, in any case, it had only appeared in a small printing. "It is not our intention to try to put anything over as I am sure you know," Ives noted. At the same time, although it was not part of a formal agreement, Cowen dropped the pictures of the beat-up train and flimsy track from the catalog and contented himself with extolling the positive virtues of Lionels.

The government, too, was coming to appreciate the quality of Lionel workmanship. Cowen secured war contracts from the Navy and Signal Corps for compasses, binnacles, and signal and navigating equipment. Caruso developed a paint formula for coating the alcohol-filled bowls of the compasses. When Congress declared war on Germany on April 6, 1917, Lionel was in a good position to benefit from the wartime economic boom. The company had an advantage over other train manufacturers like American Flyer in Chicago and Ives in Bridgeport, Connecticut, because of its proximity to New York, main port of embarkation for Europe.

Toy train production suffered during the war as materials, machinery, and manpower were routed to the manufacture of military goods. At Lionel as elsewhere, women took over many jobs previously held by men, their slogan being, "Equal pay for equal work." All over America, people fell in to support the war that would "make the world safe for democracy." There were meatless Tuesdays and gasless Sundays. Older men got in shape at fitness classes based on Yale football coach Walter Camp's "Daily Dozen" system of exercises. Housewives in greatcoats and campaign hats held close-order drills and learned how to shoot obsolete rifles. And boys with B-B guns and whittled broomsticks added trench warfare to their games of crack the whip and Johnny on a pony. Lionel was right on the spot, producing an armored train set that made war seem like the greatest fun there was and brainwashing a future generation of self-sacrificing doughboys.

"Play War!" thundered the 1917 catalog in rhetoric as frightening in its callousness as the war itself. "Bring Up Siege Guns On Tracks! Best yet, boys! Now there's bushels of fun ahead. You can be a general just like the soldiers in Europe. These outfits are faithful copies of those new, terrifying siege guns now booming on the battlefields of Europe, brought up to the front on specially built, temporary tracks." The catalog went on to explain that "the bodies of these monsters are made of heavy sheet steel" and that "the revolving turret upon which two long miniature guns are mounted is a wonderful reproduction of the original." Every detail of "the heavy riveted plates, ventilators and doors" was captured in the model, according to the catalog. The actual outfit, however, bore no resemblance at all to the real thing. It included a strange-looking train in battleship gray that came with either two boxcars described as "ammunition" cars or two truncated baggage cars listed as "supply" cars. The engine itself looked like a cross between the flat-turreted Civil War gunship *Monitor* and an ungainly World War I tank.

NO TRAINS FOR ROCKEFELLER

One day Cowen got a call that young Nelson Rockefeller wanted to come to the Lionel showroom to pick out some trains. Would Cowen be able to show him around? Sure, send him over, Cowen said. Rockefeller arrived with a whole entourage that included a governess, bodyguard, chauffeur, and several others. He walked around and around the showroom, a formal little boy in a suit and tie, examining the wonderful trains. Finally he decided on a station. Cowen told him it was $1.50. Crestfallen, Rockefeller said he didn't have that much. While Cowen looked on in astonishment, the group turned and trooped out.

IVES FLEET OF POWER BOATS

While toy trains were making future engineers of America's youth, Ives determined that its fleet of boats would make them good sailors as well. Running the gamut from "diving submarines" to tugs, the Ives flotilla occupied young train engineers during the summer, when it was too nice to be cooped up inside playing with trains.

"It is time for American boys to play with toy ships that teach them something about our merchant marine," the catalog said, quoting a maritime official. "If they have good working models of ships, they will learn what real ships are, and where they go, and how American commerce with other nations is conducted. They will know as much about ships as they do about railroads."

Using wind-up motors similar to those in Ives's clockwork trains, the boats really worked, steering a course determined by their adjustable rudders. Motors could be removed for repairs. With the exception of the sub and the tug, the ships came in two sizes and ranged in price from one to four dollars.

Educational materials were included with the fleet so children would have something to study in between naval battles at the local swimming hole or yacht basin. For five cents in postage stamps, the Ives sailor received a copy of *Rules of the Road at Sea,* a nautical dictionary and diagram "showing names and location of all the parts of ships," and a brochure on the sailing order of the boats in the Ives fleet.

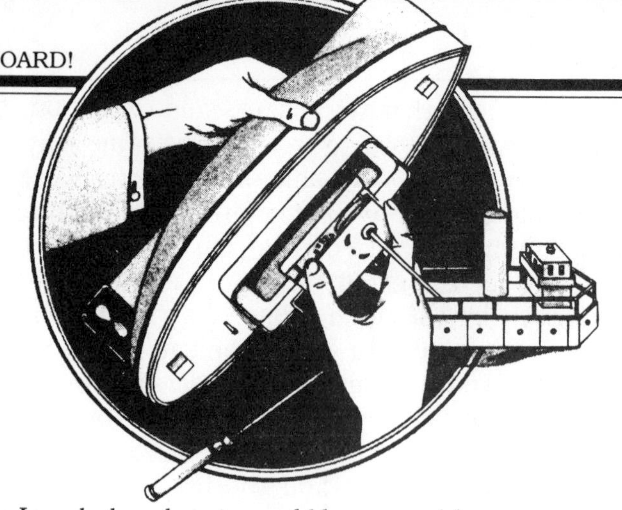

The Ives clockwork motor could be removed from the boat and returned to the Bridgeport, Connecticut, factory for repairs. However, Ives warned customers not to return the boat itself, as "we cannot repair dented or damaged hulls."

Ives Toys Make Happy Boys

The Ives Fleet of Power Boats

No. 1009 Diving Submarine 10½-inch Model.

No. 5011 Ocean Liner. 10½-inch Model.
No. 5014 Ocean Liner. 13½-inch Model.

No. 2010 Tug Boat 10½-inch Model.

No. 4011 Scout Patrol. 10½-inch Model.
No. 4014 Scout Patrol. 13½-inch Model.

No. 3009 Destroyer. 9-inch Model.
No. 3012 Destroyer. 12-inch Model.

No. 4009 Motor Boat. 9-inch Model.
No. 4012 Motor Boat. 12-inch Model.

No. 6011 Merchant Marine. 10½-inch Model.
No. 6014 Merchant Marine. 13½-inch Model.

THE ships of the Ives Fleet are built like real ships and include the famous Hog Island type of Steamships as well as Tugs, Motor Boats, Yachts, Destroyers, Submarines that dive, Motor Cruisers, etc. They are strongly made of real steel and beautifully painted and equipped to look like the real ships which were used as designs.

RUN BY IVES CLOCKWORK

These ships are run by Ives Clockwork, installed in the hull in such a way that water cannot get to it and injure it. They wind up with a key and will glide through the water under the power of their real propellers for a long while. They can be steered in any direction by means of their rudders. The Ives submarine will glide along the surface, then dive automatically, rise to the surface and dive again, just like a real submarine.

WHAT IVES SHIPS MEAN TO BOYS

With one or more of the boats of the Ives Fleet a boy can have fun outdoors all summer long, while in the winter he can sail them in the bath-tub.

REMEMBER

Boat clockworks are easily removed. If damaged they can be sent to us for repairs. Don't send the boat itself. We cannot repair dented or damaged hulls.

The 1922 Ives catalog devoted a full page to its motorized fleet of power boats.

Ives also made sailboats, though they did not have the same serious educational mission as did the power boats.

ROBERT GINGHER/TOY TRAIN MUSEUM

Ives's Grand Central Station bore no resemblance to its New York namesake. The lithographed station was also sold by Lionel and came with a leaded glass train shed that fit over the track like a tunnel.

Toy trains were supposed to prepare boys for their future roles as engineers and railroad presidents. It was merely a small jump to encourage them to become "generals" or "soldiers" (the distinction was somewhat blurred in the Lionel catalog) who would have "bushels of fun" on the gas-choked, machine gun-raked, mine-infested battlefields of Europe. Toy makers were well aware that the destinies of children could be shaped by their playthings.

In 1917, the Federal Council of National Defense suggested no Christmas gifts—including toys—be given that year to save raw materials and to remind Americans of the need for sacrifice. A delegation of the Toy Manufacturers of the U.S.A. went to Washington to plead for Christmas toys before the secretaries of war, navy, commerce, and interior. Headed by A. C. Gilbert, the group brought a selection of toys with them to the austere hearing room.

"The greatest influences in the life of a boy are his toys," Gilbert testified. "A boy wants fun, not education. Yet through the kind of toy American toy manufacturers are turning out, he gets both. The American boy is a genuine boy, and he wants genuine toys. He wants guns that really shoot and that is why we have given him air rifles from the time he was big enough to hold them. It is because of the toys they had in childhood that the American soldiers are the best marksmen on the battlefields of Europe.

"America is the home of toys that educate as well as amuse, that visualize to the boy his future occupations, that start him on the road to construction and not destruction, that as surely as public school or the Boy Scouts, exert the sort of influences that go to form right ideals and solid American character." The dignified officials were soon down on the floor playing with submarines and steam engines, and the Council subsequently rescinded its decision. Christmas was held after all, and the toy manufacturers did not miss their most profitable season.

The patriotic duty of American toy train manufacturers to prepare boys for the army and navy was epitomized by Ives's fleet of wind-up freighters, destroyers, ocean liners, and other vessels. The Connecticut toy maker began producing the ships at the urging of the chairman of the U.S. Shipping Board, Edward Hurley, who feared the boys of America would not be equipped to man the future merchant marine fleet. "Every American boy for fifty years has played with toy railroad engines," Hurley told Harry Ives, "and we Americans excel in railroading. But for many years our boys have had no play ships except old-fashioned sailboats—and America has had no real ships traveling to foreign countries." Even when the line became a drain on the company, Ives refused to drop the Ives Navy and Ives Merchant Marine, bearing in mind Hurley's conviction that "every play ship put into the hands of an American boy helps us to put real ships on the ocean."

But just as the devastation of war would disillusion the world about the nobility of combat, so Cowen would change his attitude toward military toys.

By the thirties, he had developed serious doubts about the wisdom of urging boys to do

PULLMAN DELUXE

Lionel's top-of-the-line passenger train was the Pullman Deluxe, over five feet of softly glowing coach and baggage cars pulled by the reliable No. 42 electric engine. "If you should get one of these for a present you'd be the proudest boy in seven counties," Cowen told young Lionel engineers. "It's one of the most perfect models you ever dreamed of." Engine, three cars, and track could be had for $62.50 by the end of the decade. Or, for another $12.50, engine No. 54, finished in brass and nickel, could be substituted for the more conservative No. 42.

What any boy would want for Christmas: No. 42. Curiously, this photo was used on a back page of The Lionel Corporation's annual report for 1956.

FUNDIMENSIONS

Engine No. 54—bells ringing—was a shining step up from No. 42, the workhorse of the Lionel locomotive roster.

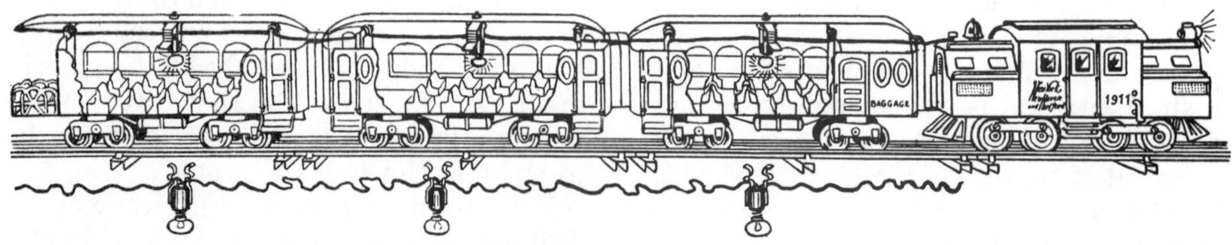

To light the Pullman Deluxe, a separate lighting kit was available for two dollars. It included five feet of wire, three bulbs and sockets, and all contacts. A wire ran from the engine through each car. Eventually, each car got its own third-rail power pickup so it could be illuminated independently of the others, and the awkward wiring kit disappeared.

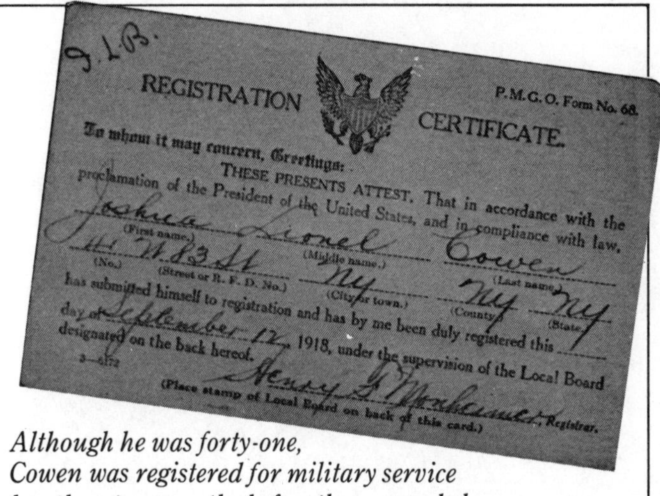

J.L.B.

REGISTRATION CERTIFICATE. P.M.G.O. Form No. 68.

To whom it may concern, Greetings:

THESE PRESENTS ATTEST, That in accordance with the proclamation of the President of the United States, and in compliance with law,

Joshua (First name.) Lionel (Middle name.) Cowen (Last name.)

141 (No.) W. 83 St (Street or R. F. D. No.) NY (City or town.) NY (County.) NY (State.)

has submitted himself to registration and has by me been duly registered this day of September 12, 1918, under the supervision of the Local Board designated on the back hereof.

3—6172

(Place stamp of Local Board on back of this card.) , Registrar.

Although he was forty-one,
Cowen was registered for military service
less than two months before the war ended.

something as contradictory as "play war." When a customer wrote Cowen suggesting Lionel make a military train "with a long range naval rifle which I saw bombard the enemy's rear positions," Cowen vetoed the idea. "We have given considerable thought to the production of a military gun mounted on a flat car," Cowen wrote the man, "but we have not placed it on the market for the reason that we are not desirous of bringing the idea of war to the minds of children. We would much prefer to devote our efforts and energy to the development of toys that are more elevating to the mind of a child."

Like the rest of the country, Lionel matured with World War I. The trolley, symbol of a more innocent America, was dropped from the catalog. It did not reappear until 1955, in the form of the "Lionelville Rapid Transit," a pale, yellow plastic ghost of the beautiful pre-World War I metal cars. Other Lionel engines and cars were available throughout the war. However, perhaps because much of Lionel's manufacturing energy went into producing war goods, the train line remained fairly static and uninspired for the last part of the decade. Several basic freight and passenger sets were offered, but the best train was still the "Pullman De Luxe" that Lawrence was pictured playing with years earlier.

Lionel had begun the decade as an intimate company manufacturing a toy still regarded with suspicion and skepticism by a public raised on wind-up trains. But, aided by war contracts and the growth of electric power, Lionel became a solidly successful concern. Its expansion necessitated a reorganization of the company. On July 22, 1918, the Lionel Manufacturing Company was succeeded by The Lionel Corporation, Joshua L. Cowen, President. Like its predecessor, The Lionel Corporation was a privately held concern. But while the common stock of the Manufacturing Company was worth $10,000 at the time of incorporation, the new corporation listed the value of its capital stock at $50,000. Initial subscribers for the filing were Cowen and two colleagues, Albert T. Scharps and Mandel Frankel. Frankel later served as a receiver of the company when it came close to failing during the Depression. The 500 shares of stock were apportioned at 225 for Cowen, 225 for Scharps, and 50 for Mario Caruso, presented in exchange for their stock in the original company.

On November 11, 1918, the war to end all wars itself ended. Lionel had prospered. At the time of the armistice, the company had some $500,000 in new government contracts, most of them secured in the last months of the war. It had been such a good year the board of directors declared a 10 percent dividend. Cowen's salary was $35,000. A West Coast representative was hired with offices in San Francisco. The board of directors voted to modernize and pay employees each Saturday by check, not in cash.

Lionel did not escape the decade without being touched by the nationwide labor unrest, with its strikes and lockouts. While Lionel's own employees were not involved, Cowen suffered from the effects of the 1919 printers' strike in New York that prevented his producing the annual color catalog. He was forced to mail an apology to those children who had written for the catalog. The flyer was headed, "An Apology from the man who makes Lionel Trains to his millions of boy friends."

"It's awful to have to disappoint you and send you these circulars instead of what was planned to be the most absorbing toy catalog ever offered," Cowen explained, "but I can't do a thing. The strike is a long way from being settled and until it is, I can't get a single catalog." But the boys were not to fear, Cowen said. "Next season I will have that catalog printed if I have to buy a printing plant and print it myself."

It never came to that. "Next season" was the start of the roaring twenties. The catalogs would be more elaborate than ever, listing trains and accessories that made the teens look like the Dark Ages. Lionel's sales would exceed $2 million and Cowen would triumph over Ives, becoming, indisputably, America's electric train king.

LIONEL TRAINS
NEW YORK, N.Y.

EARLY YEARS

1877–1929

When Joshua Lionel Cowen was a boy, toy trains were simple, pushed on the floor or powered by springs or steam. But Cowen the man changed all that. Within its first two decades, his Lionel Corporation produced the mightiest toy trains and accessories yet seen in America.

DAVID EISENDRATH

1903: Lionel's first engine was based on a B. & O. electric one. The control lever in front actually worked.

1927: The imposing 408E had twin motors, headlights, and was reversible. But it lacked a whistle, which had not yet been invented.

Early wood and cast-iron toy trains were pushed on the floor. They became a favored Christmas gift, and were featured on postcards.

1913: Both Lionel's catalog *(top)* and Ives's box cover *(above)* put boys at the throttle and girls in the audience. Lionel's new racing cars paced its trains around the room.

Joshua Lionel Cowen grew up on such pulp stories *(left)* of railroad adventure and maidens in distress.

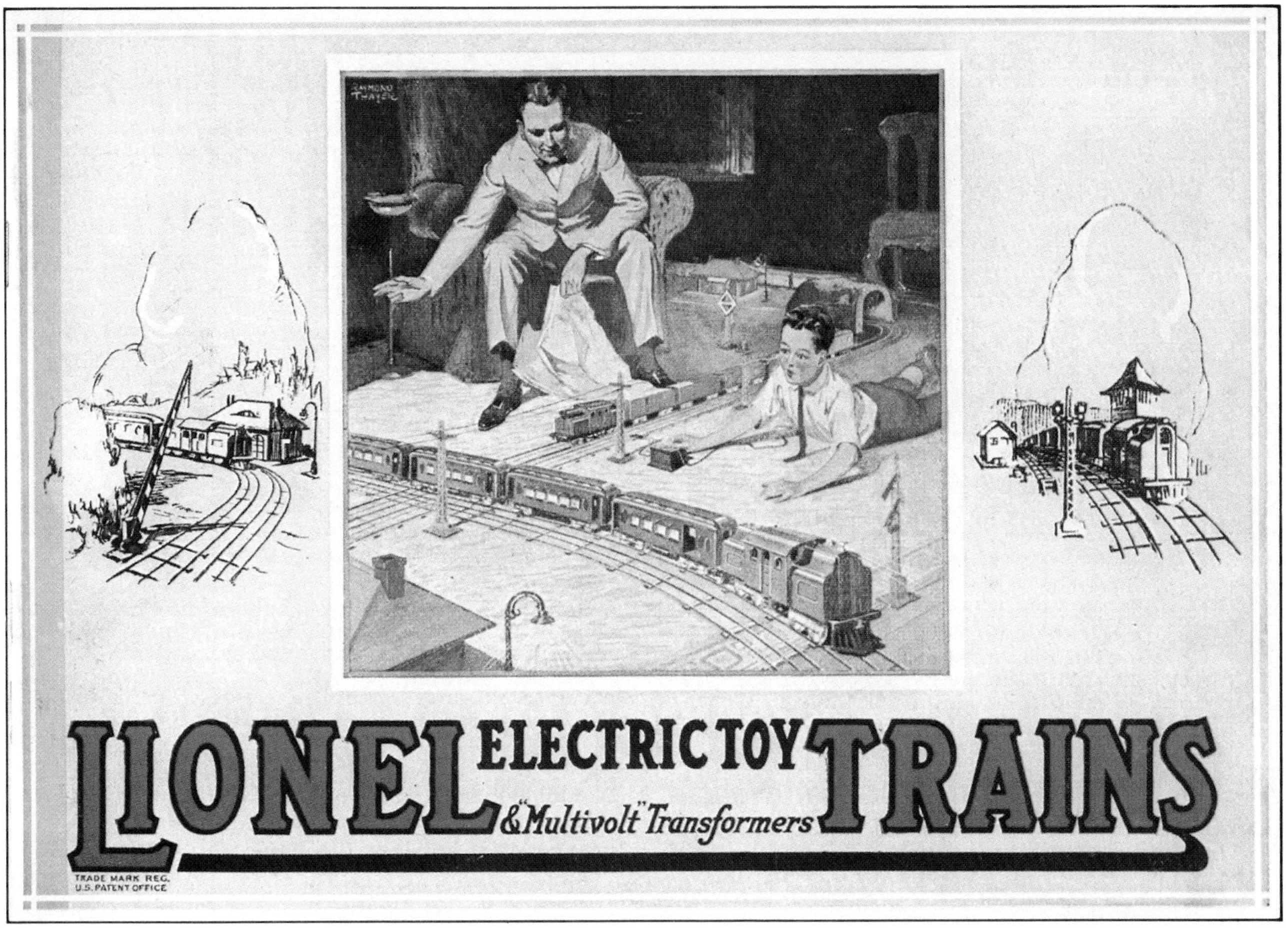

1923: For the first time, a father and son appeared on a Lionel catalog cover, introducing an enduring advertising theme for all toy train manufacturers.

1923: "The Factory That Has Made Millions Of Boys Happy" was pictured somewhat fancifully on the back of the Lionel catalog.

1927: The glory of Lionel Lines, eight feet of the Lionel Limited with lighted cars, all for only $82.50.

1928: By the late twenties, Lionel was advertising in national magazines whose combined circulation was over five million.

Cowen's son, Lawrence, appeared on Lionel train boxes in the early teens as the epitome of "The Happy Lionel Boy."

1908: Trolleys were important in Lionel's early standard gauge production. The No. 1 also came lettered *Curtis Bay,* after a trolley car line in Baltimore.

DAVID EISENDRATH

1926: A boy, his dog, and Lionel trains was the childhood trinity immortalized on the catalog covers. Lionel engines now could be reversed from a distance.

1924: Coats and ties were required even when down on the floor chasing Rover with Lionel's top-of-the-line No. 402 electric engine.

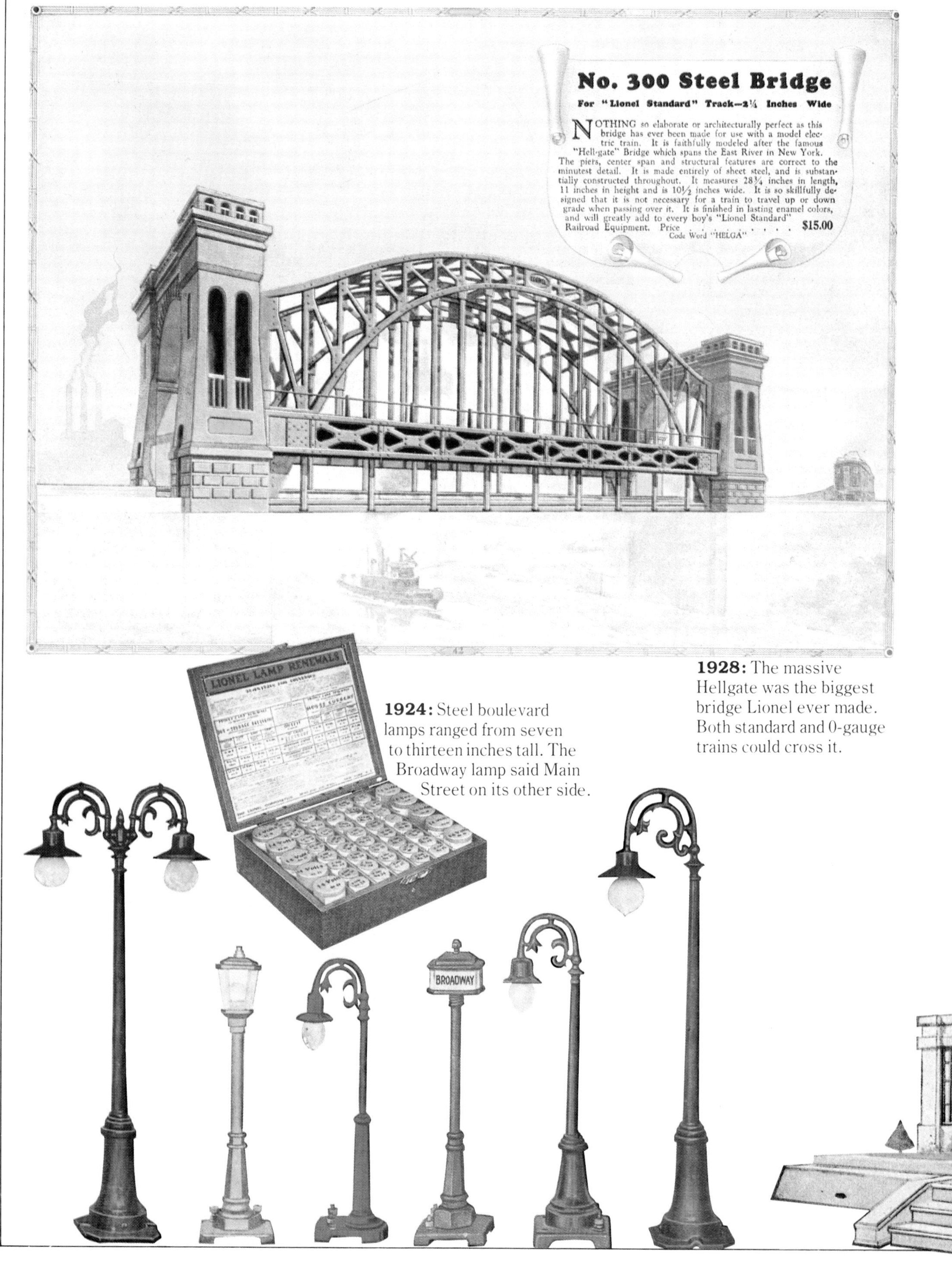

1928: The massive Hellgate was the biggest bridge Lionel ever made. Both standard and 0-gauge trains could cross it.

1924: Steel boulevard lamps ranged from seven to thirteen inches tall. The Broadway lamp said Main Street on its other side.

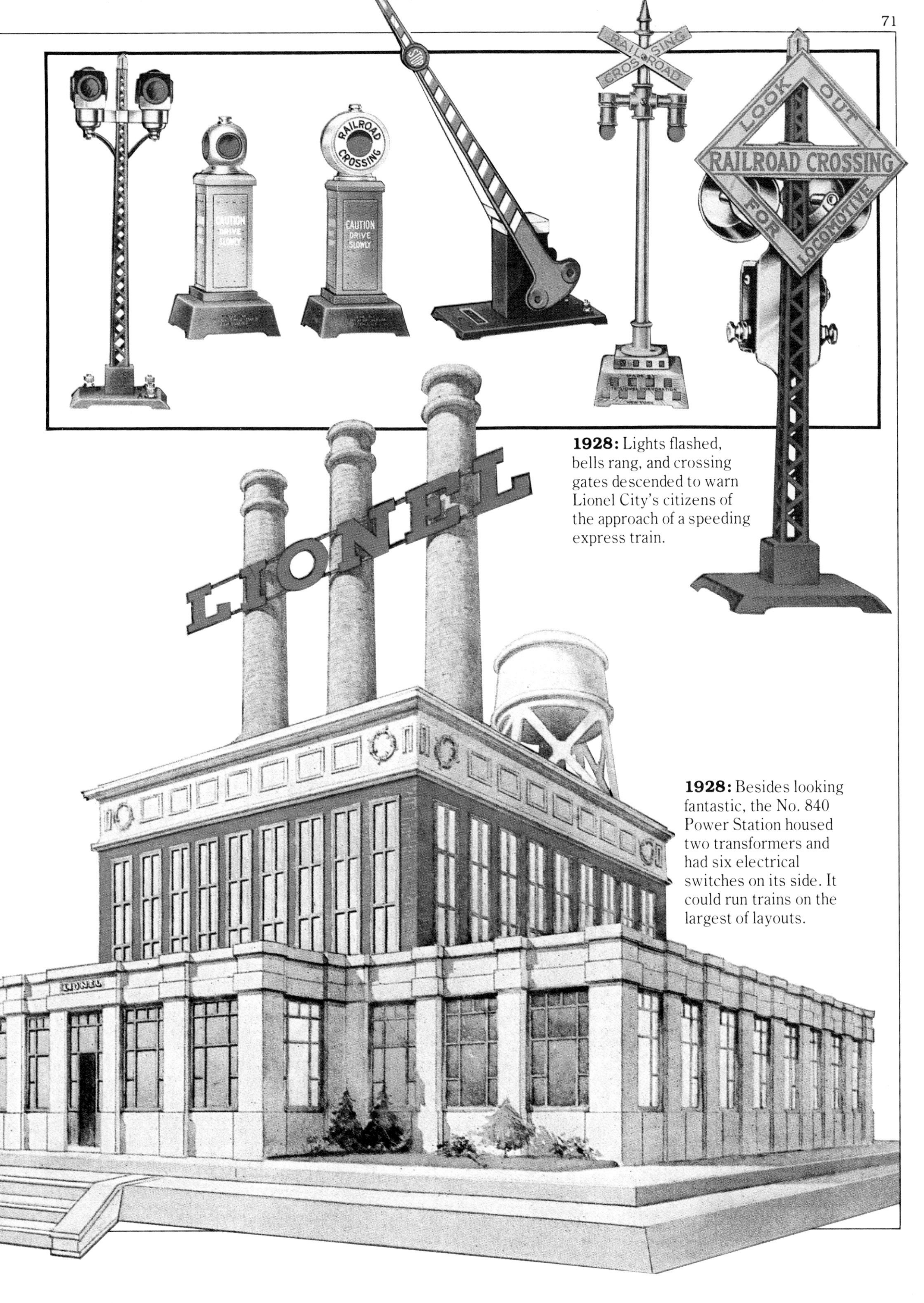

1928: Lights flashed, bells rang, and crossing gates descended to warn Lionel City's citizens of the approach of a speeding express train.

1928: Besides looking fantastic, the No. 840 Power Station housed two transformers and had six electrical switches on its side. It could run trains on the largest of layouts.

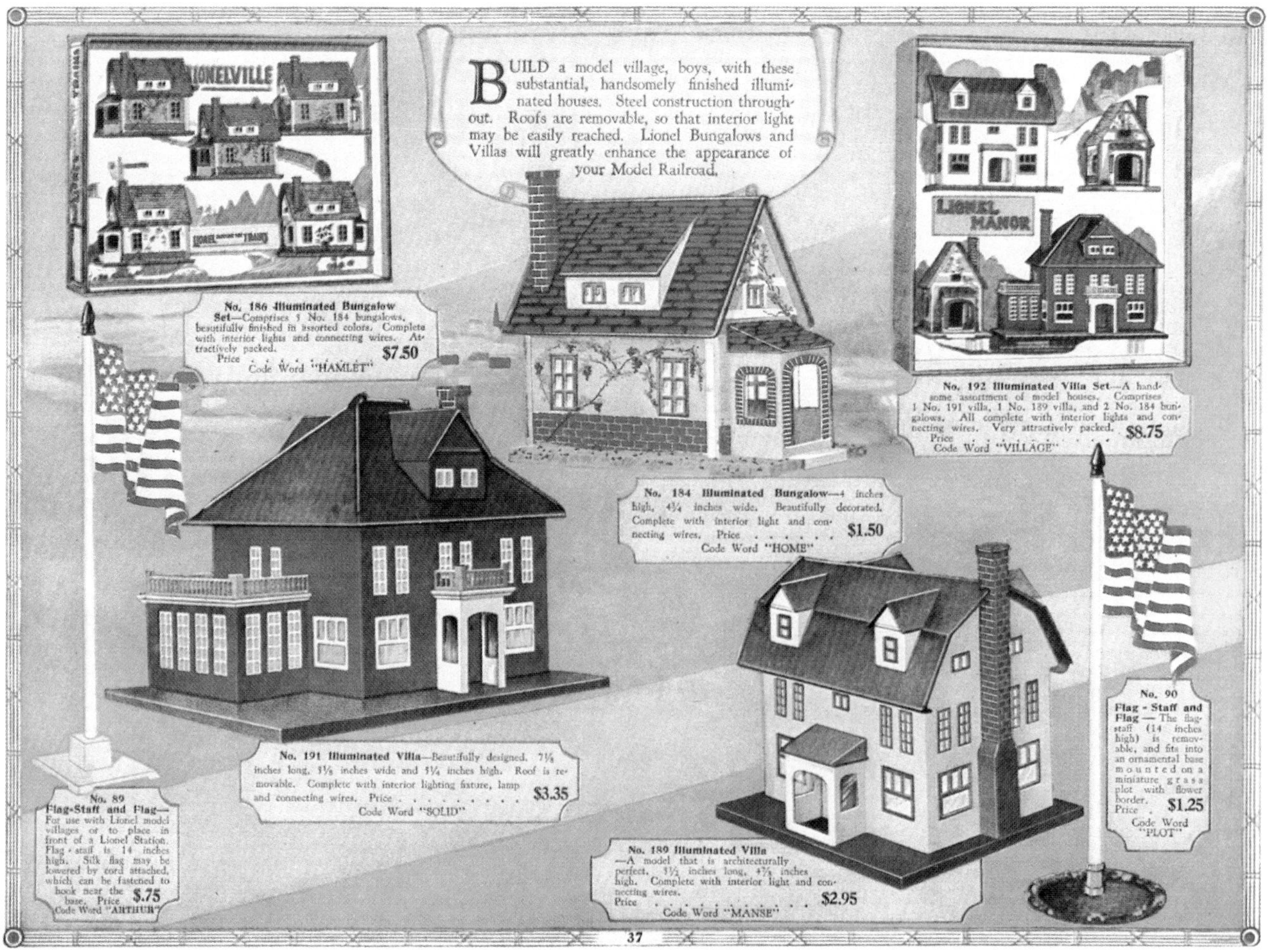
BUILD a model village, boys, with these substantial, handsomely finished illuminated houses. Steel construction throughout. Roofs are removable, so that interior light may be easily reached. Lionel Bungalows and Villas will greatly enhance the appearance of your Model Railroad.
LIONELVILLE
LIONEL MANOR
No. 186 Illuminated Bungalow Set—Comprises 5 No. 184 bungalows, beautifully finished in assorted colors. Complete with interior lights and connecting wires. Attractively packed. Price . . . . $7.50 Code Word "HAMLET"
No. 192 Illuminated Villa Set—A handsome assortment of model houses. Comprises 1 No. 191 villa, 1 No. 189 villa, and 2 No. 184 bungalows. All complete with interior lights and connecting wires. Very attractively packed. Price . . . . $8.75 Code Word "VILLAGE"
No. 184 Illuminated Bungalow—4 inches high, 4¾ inches wide. Beautifully decorated. Complete with interior light and connecting wires. Price . . . . $1.50 Code Word "HOME"
No. 191 Illuminated Villa—Beautifully designed. 7⅛ inches long, 5⅜ inches wide and 5¼ inches high. Roof is removable. Complete with interior lighting fixture, lamp and connecting wires. Price . . . . $3.35 Code Word "SOLID"
No. 89 Flag-Staff and Flag—For use with Lionel model villages or to place in front of a Lionel Station. Flag-staff is 14 inches high. Silk flag may be lowered by cord attached, which can be fastened to hook near the base. Price $.75 Code Word "ARTHUR"
No. 90 Flag-Staff and Flag—The flag-staff (14 inches high) is removable, and fits into an ornamental base mounted on a miniature grass plot with flower border. Price . $1.25 Code Word "PLOT"
No. 189 Illuminated Villa—A model that is architecturally perfect. 5½ inches long, 4⅞ inches high. Complete with interior light and connecting wires. Price . . . . $2.95 Code Word "MANSE"
37

1928: All-metal toy houses based on Lionel executives' actual homes lined the tracks, although the houses were too small in proportion to the trains.

LIONEL ELECTRIC TOY TRAINS & Multivolt Transformers

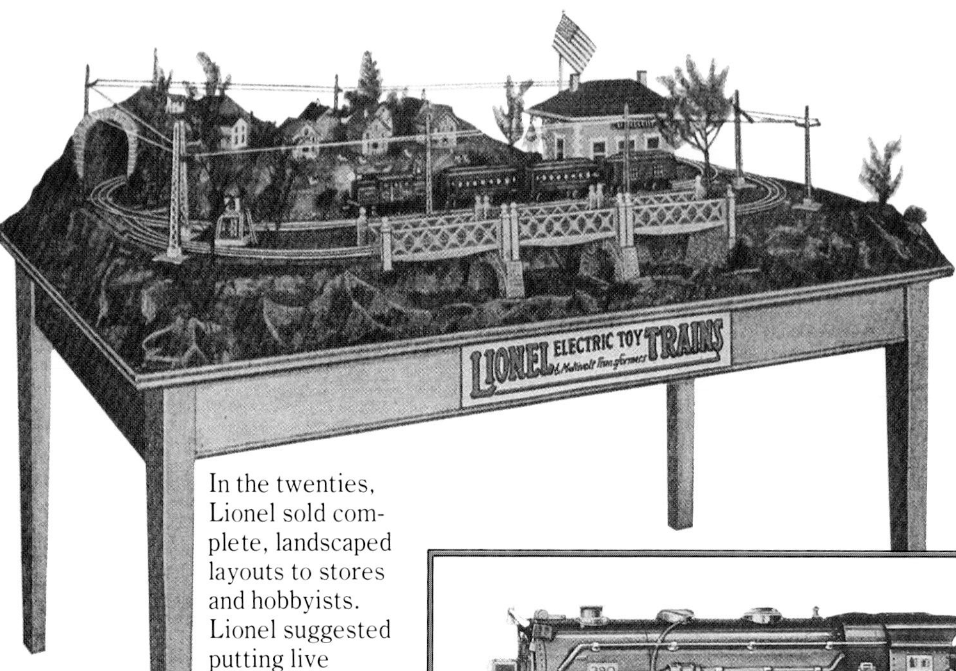

In the twenties, Lionel sold complete, landscaped layouts to stores and hobbyists. Lionel suggested putting live goldfish in the brook under the bridges.

1929: Lionel's new, more realistic standard gauge steam engines reflected the progress of America's real railroads. No. 390 had a removable motor that could power other toys.

390
LIONEL
THE LIONEL LINES

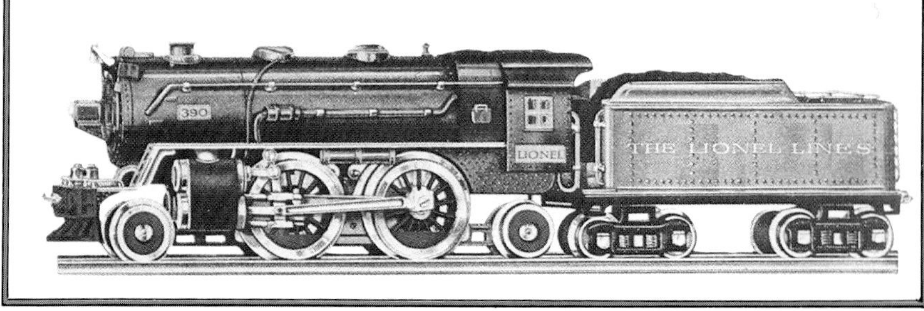

HILLEL DON LAZARUS

1930: The State Set dominates a catalog cover (*above*), in contrast to a sentimental ad (*right*) of the 1920s.

1931: Bob Butterfield claimed that the new Lionel 400 E steamer was "just like" his Hudson locomotive. However, he later acknowledged that Lionel's model was short one set of driving wheels.

GOLDEN YEARS

1930–1942

Standard gauge reached its acme in the thirties with huge steam engines and opulent terminals, despite the Depression, which required Lionel to manufacture inexpensive wind-up trains. But as America's railroads turned to streamlining, so did Lionel, producing sleek *Hiawathas* and *Zephyrs* in O-gauge. The trend toward realism culminated in the scale-model Hudson. By World War II, Lionel's remote control had revolutionized toy trains.

LIONEL ELECTRIC TRAINS

THE TRAINS THAT RAILROAD MEN BUY FOR THEIR BOYS

"Just Like Mine", SAYS BOB BUTTERFIELD, ENGINEER OF THE "20TH CENTURY LIMITED" (See Page 3)

SARASOTA LIONEL MUSEUM/JOSEPH STEINMETZ

The *Blue Comet*, in all its standard gauge grandeur, glides past the slightly smaller *Broadway Limited*. Behind them, locomotives steam out of the Lionel roundhouse, whose stalls were too short for most engines.

Freight sheds, signal towers, floodlight stanchions, and searchlight cars were part of Lionel's bustling standard gauge world in the mid-thirties.

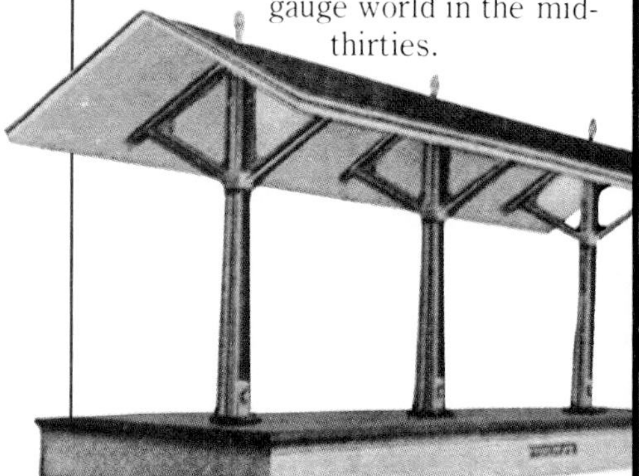

"Lionel City" first appeared on a modest rural station in the twenties (*right*), but in 1931 a metropolitan depot was produced (*below*) that had eight swinging doors and windows modeled on those in Grand Central Terminal.

SARASOTA LIONEL MUSEUM/JOSEPH STEINMETZ

1931: Lionel's biggest steamer ever, the 400E had a tender that "carried" oil instead of coal as fuel.

1932: People come to Lionelville! The first inhabitants of Lionel Land since the trolley passengers of the early teens included a European-looking engineer, redcap with detachable suitcase, and porter with removable stepstool.

1934: The Mickey and Minnie Mouse wind-up handcar ran on a circle of two-rail track. The publicity it received during the Depression helped Lionel as much as its one-dollar selling price. Lever on right was a brake.

DAVID EISENDRATH

1930: Lionel promised that its operating electric range "will initiate the little girl in the art of cookery. There's lots of fun in playing housewife."

1936: A diving plane was added to Lionel's trains and boats, but it was fragile and broke easily.

A locomotive *(above)* moves onto the standard gauge turntable under the glare of the twenty-inch-high floodlight tower. *Below left*, a hopper loaded with Lionel's sculpted metal "coal" waits at a freight shed. *Below right*, the *Hiawatha* steams through a grade crossing as the gates come down and a gateman waves his lantern.

Lionel's electric engine (*foreground*) was based on a New York Central prototype still used occasionally by the Penn Central in the 1970s.

Dump trucks and tool chests for train crews helped keep Lionel Lines' right-of-way in shape.

DUANE SKOKUT

The locomotive engineer was a hero to generations of small boys who dressed like him and ran their own (toy) trains. Lionel marketing reflected this.

1935: The Milwaukee Road's *Hiawatha* was one of the early streamlined steam locomotives. Lionel's version was realistic but had an *L* on its front instead of the engine's number.

1935: The *Hiawatha* and Lionel's new whistle both made their debuts on the same catalog cover. The engineer was Hugh McManus of the Milwaukee Road.

1934: Streamlining came to Lionel in earnest with the Union Pacific's diesel-powered *City of Portland*. The three-car train could be lengthened with extra coaches at four dollars apiece.

1938: Like the real railroads, Lionel's engine roster combined traditional steamers with streamlined diesels, all in 0-gauge as standard gauge declined.

1938: Lionel's bimonthly magazine showed young engineers how to build projects like a station platform or a newsstand.

Fold back and forth on this line, then tear out neatly. Fill in the number of the outfit you want and your name, then hand this note to Dad. Tell him it's important.

Dear Dad;

One thing I want this Christmas more than anything else is a Lionel Electric Train No. . Be sure it's a Lionel, Dad. That's the kind all the other fellows have and it's the one and only kind I want. You ought to see the way they run! Like a million dollars. And they whistle too. Real railroad whistle signals by remote control. You can couple and uncouple cars electrically, from a distance, just by touching a button; and reverse the train or speed it up or slow it down.

Please get me a Lionel, Dad. We'll have lots of fun together.

Your son,

P.S. don't forget switches. We'll need them.

1940: The detailed Hudson locomotive had moved Lionel into scale modeling for adults, while remote control kept children busy loading and uncoupling trains.

1938: A letter to dad that could be torn out of the catalog left space for sonny's choice of trains.

1936: This inexpensive Lionel Jr. streamliner was based on the Burlington *Zephyr*.

1942: During the war, Lionel's catalog resembled the American flag. As it had for the previous five years, the Hudson ruled the cover.

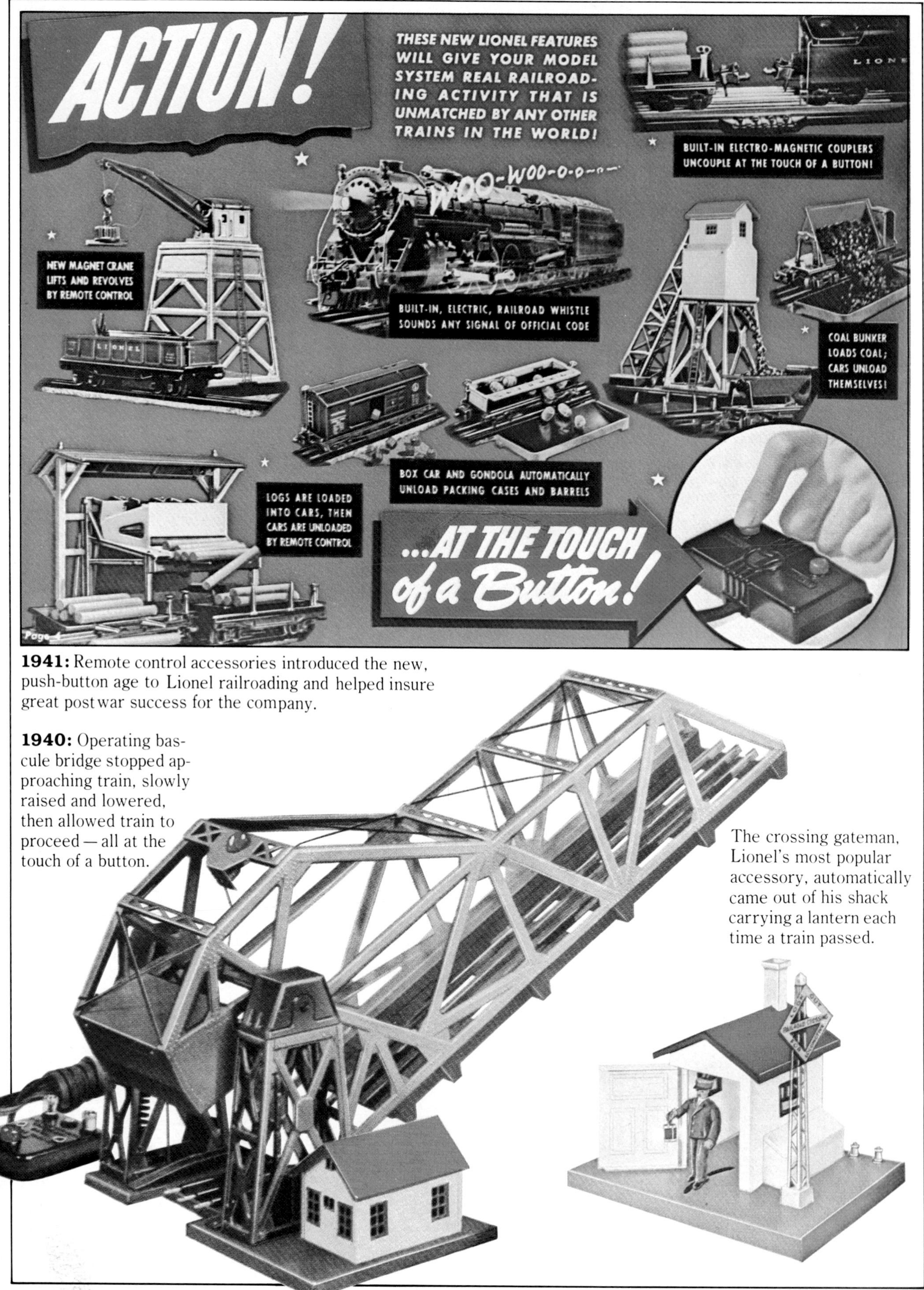

1941: Remote control accessories introduced the new, push-button age to Lionel railroading and helped insure great postwar success for the company.

1940: Operating bascule bridge stopped approaching train, slowly raised and lowered, then allowed train to proceed—all at the touch of a button.

The crossing gateman, Lionel's most popular accessory, automatically came out of his shack carrying a lantern each time a train passed.

LIONEL TRAINS
NEW YORK, N.Y.

4

FULL STEAM AHEAD

1920-1929

The twenties were a grand time for electric toy trains. Americans wanted to forget the horrors of war and to escape the confusion of the modern world. Flamboyant hedonism—or, at the very least, frivolity—became fashionable; the swelling economic boom made self-indulgence easy. Cowen followed the trend, producing trains, bridges, powerhouses, and terraced stations as gorgeous and as opulent as his pin-striped, deep red Isotta-Fraschini.

Americans sought excitement and diversion, whether atop flagpoles or on the silver screen. While adults fantasized about Rudolph Valentino or "It" girl Clara Bow, children were transported to the cabs of *The Twentieth Century* or *The Broadway Limited* through their Lionel trains. There was plenty of money for luxuries like electric trains, even among those who did not speculate in the apparently bountiful stock market. Wages for skilled laborers increased 50 percent from 1913 to 1927. And if weekly salaries weren't enough to pay for a Lionel Express, the new rage of installment buying made the most elaborate, twin-motored engine affordable. By 1929, 80 percent of all refrigerators, radios, and vacuum cleaners were bought on the installment plan. "Buy now, pay later" came to epitomize the decade.

It was a period that contributed fascinating personalities and phenomena to American legend: Charles Lindbergh, Babe Ruth, Jack Dempsey, F. Scott Fitzgerald, Sacco and Vanzetti; Prohibition, the Charleston, gangsters, the jazz age, flappers, the lost generation, the crash. The words themselves are redolent of that borrowed time between the war and the Depression. At Lionel, too, words would become legend: *State Set, Hellgate Bridge, Power Station, Blue Comet.* They spoke of the golden age of

Boy and dog are transported from 402 electric to cab of The Twentieth Century *on 1925 catalog cover.*

INSIDE LIONEL

Lionel engines were built to last, to be passed on from father to son. Locomotive bodies were of sheet steel, not brittle cast iron. Cars were heavily enameled. Wheels were nickeled steel. All engines had headlights. The major parts before electric reversing was introduced in 1926:

MOTOR FIELD (1, 2): The field is of laminated steel with insulated winding wire.

BRUSH HOLDERS AND BEARINGS (3, 4): Made of brass with detachable tops so brushes can be replaced.

BRUSHES (5, 6): Self-lubricating graphite with brass compression springs.

ARMATURE (8): Made of steel and mounted on solid shaft (11). Wound with triple-covered wire (9), then dipped in shellac and baked.

COMMUTATOR (13): Heart of the motor. Made of solid bronze, with insulators (10) placed between it and the armature shaft (11). Fiber washers (12) help keep it functioning.

THIRD RAIL SHOE (14): Picks up current from the center rail through case-hardened contactor. Spring keeps it pressed against the rail.

REVERSING CONTROLLER (15): Changes direction of travel. Can be moved by hand or by trackside trip device.

WHEEL GEARS (16): Transfer motion of motor to wheels. Made of heavy steel disks.

PINION GEARS (17): Mesh with wheel gears to make the engine move.

WHEEL BEARINGS (21): Reduce friction as the wheels turn.

CONNECTING RODS (23): As on a real locomotive, these make all wheels move together with no looseness or play.

COUPLERS (28): Connect one car to another at either end. Made of polished nickel-plated steel.

COWCATCHER (29): This is a heavy casting connected directly with locomotive's steel frame. Will stand up to a lot of bumping.

A disassembled electric engine (with cowcatchers at either end) was shown for several years in the catalog.

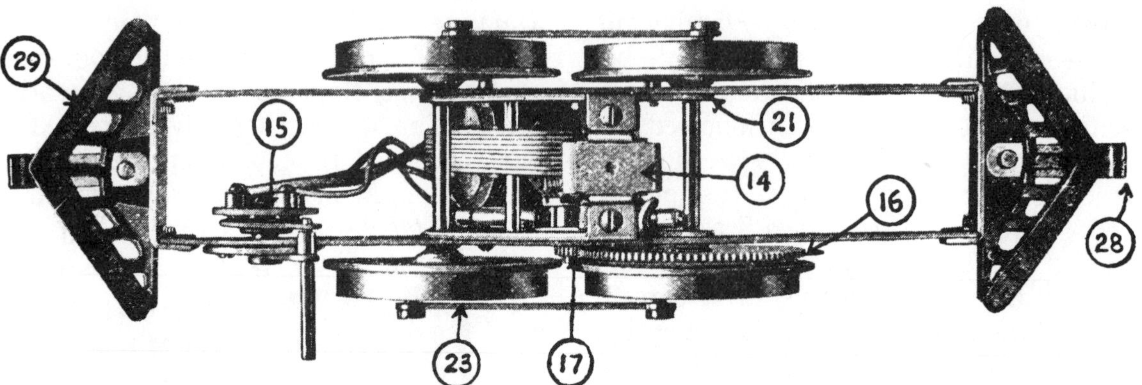

Bottom View of Locomotive Chassis

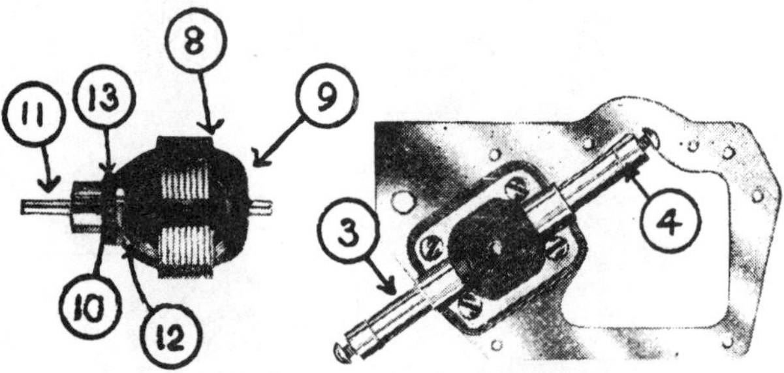

Laminated Armature *Bearings and Brush Holders*

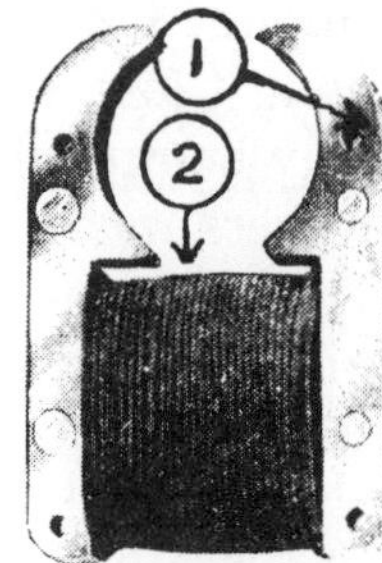

Motor Field

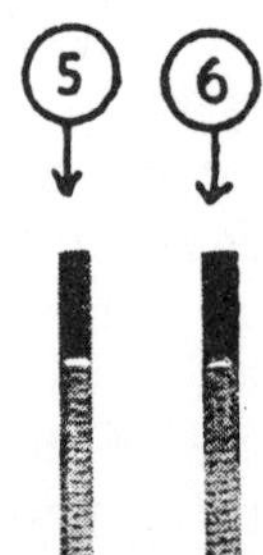

Self-Lubricating Brushes

Press proof of Lionel's first ad in the comic section of The American *in 1921.*

electric toy trains, of Pullman cars with not one but two bathrooms and of engines so massive it took two hands to lift them. They told of bridges whose latticework seemed capable of spanning New York's East River, of terminals with landscaped, terraced promenades, of ornately embellished lampposts identical to those beneath which Cowen strolled on Fifth Avenue.

It was a decade of toy train inventions. Engines could be reversed using the transformer without having to touch them. Crossing gates dipped, block signals changed colors, traffic warning bells sounded, highway flashers twinkled—all automatically as the train passed. Semaphores stopped speeding freights "as if by magic," detained them a few seconds, then allowed them to proceed. Best of all, track switches could be set for straight or curved train routes from a distance, even from the next room. It was no longer necessary to crawl along ahead of the train, throwing the switches by hand.

If the twenties encouraged the creation of extravagant toy trains, they also provided the means for selling them. It was the age of supersalesmen, marked by the emergence of the modern advertising agency. Colorful national ad campaigns were launched. Mass marketing emphasized the competitive, aggressive hard sell. Psychoanalyst Sigmund Freud revealed human motivations, and manufacturers began to utilize fear, guilt, and envy to sell their products. It was a milieu in which Cowen flourished. In a time of flashy promotions, the Lionel catalog was the flashiest. Stores received quantities of the catalogs at little or no charge when they ordered trains. The beautifully printed "wish books" were then given away free to anyone who asked for one. (Later, catalogs could be ordered directly from Lionel for a dime. The names of those who wrote for them were passed on to a Lionel dealer for follow-up.)

To many children, the catalog *was* Lionel. Unable to afford the trains themselves, they wiled away the hours studying the horizontal pages of the catalogs, creating elaborate railroads in their imagination. The catalogs were read so thoroughly that children often knew their contents as well or better than store clerks, ordering trains by their product numbers or code word rather than by name.

Cecelia and Cowen wintering in Palm Beach.

Beginning in the twenties, Cowen hired talented illustrators to create original paintings for catalog covers that resembled the work of Norman Rockwell. On the inside pages, the trains were often pictured on three-page foldouts in realistic settings, occasionally in distorted perspective to make them appear bigger than they actually were. A complete record of Lionel's production was preserved in the catalog. No other toys in America were ever catalogued as thoroughly or as lavishly. In the peak years of the 1950s, over one million Lionel catalogs were distributed annually, second only to the massive mail order houses of Sears and Roebuck and Montgomery Ward.

The catalog wasn't the only advertising tool Lionel employed. Cowen took one of the first ads in a newspaper's comic section, paying the then-huge sum of thirty-five hundred dollars to appear in *The American* under "On Our Block." He also began to secure endorsements from famous people, although in Lionel's case they were not movie stars but railroad presidents, engineers, and locomotive builders. Lionel's advertising budget grew from ten thousand to forty-five thousand dollars. The advertising paid off. Lionel actually became the "standard of the world." Sales more than doubled during the twenties, reaching a one-year high of $2.3 million. (Ives's best was $998,000). Annual profits for Lionel increased almost ten times over the prior decade, falling just short of $500,000 in 1927. Cowen's salary, excluding stock dividends paid every year, was $60,000. He invested judiciously in the stock market and lived the good life, traveling to Europe with Cecelia at least once a year. They lived in a fashionable apartment on Park Avenue, and sent the children to private schools. Everything about the roaring twenties suited Cowen and Lionel. It was even the high point of deluxe passenger service on American railroads. Were it not for the Black Tuesday of the stock market crash, it would have been a perfect decade for electric trains.

Actually, a sudden recession in the early twenties got things off to an uncertain start for Lionel and many other businesses. Lionel had had its best year ever in 1920, breaking $1 million in sales for the first time (and awarding Cowen a fifteen-thousand-dollar bonus as a result). But dealers were overstocked and orders fell off seriously in 1921. Cowen explained what had happened in a long interview in a New York paper. The article revealed what an astute businessman Cowen was, how he planned ahead and was unafraid to gamble on his prediction of future market conditions.

"Many toy makers figured that they had captured the American market for good and all [from foreign competition after the war]," Cowen told the reporter. "So they came up to 1920 with the biggest inventories in their history. We did have our biggest year, but at the beginning of 1920 it looked as though it was going to be a whole lot bigger.

"It looked like it was up to us to double our output. But it was about that time we had the first signs of the storm. Prices were way up then, you remember, and I began to notice a little cessation of buying around the country. I don't mean that our orders fell off, but there was a falling off in the retail trade. There began to be price cutting. Then, you remember, John Wanamaker [the department store] sprang his first big price slashing sale.

"I didn't feel that I needed any more signals. Things had gone far enough. We had reached the top and were ready to start on the down grade. I said, 'We won't go out for any more orders. We will be satisfied with what we have. We are going to have some cancellations of orders already on the books and we will take just enough new orders to cover the cancellations.'" In that way Lionel avoided being seriously overstocked and having to dump trains at a loss.

Cowen used the same market conditions that were slowing retail sales to help him secure the best prices on the raw materials Lionel needed. "In this business we have to buy our raw material in advance," Cowen explained. "But because retail orders were slowing I went to the people I had ordered my raw materials from and I said, 'I'll take all this stuff I have ordered from you. I won't cancel a pound. But these orders are now for future delivery, and you must give me the stuff at the future price on the date of shipment.'" Cowen felt that as retail orders were canceled and production was cut back, the cost of metals and other supplies would go down. Then he would be in a position to make a killing by buying at the depressed prices.

His judgment was confirmed. "When prices are down is the time to buy for us," Cowen said. "I figure prices are just about at the bottom now. Anyone who buys now will make money on his purchases, no matter whether prices are not quite at the bottom or whether they have begun to go up, because they are going to go up a good deal more. So the man who buys today will have the edge on the man who waits a few months and as a consequence has to pay a higher price.

"Just to prove my belief, I will tell you that a few days ago I bought 1,000 tons of brass. I don't need it today, but I will need it next year, and I will have it very close to the bottom of the market, if not exactly at the bottom." Then Cowen cautioned against being too greedy: "All you need is to buy pretty close to the bottom. It is mighty easy to overreach yourself by trying to grab the last penny."

That went for workers' salaries, too, according to Cowen. Asked if he had cut wages, as many companies did during the recession, Cowen said, "I didn't have the heart to do it. We thought we would have to make a cut. We even set the date. But when we came up to that date, we put it off and set another. We did that three times and we haven't cut wages yet and don't

SIGNALING

Signals were a big seller for Lionel Lines. The company distributed sheets describing real railroad signals and their meaning. Over the years, Lionel made all of the signals below, though often with two lights instead of three.

SEMAPHORE SIGNALS
(Lower Quadrant)

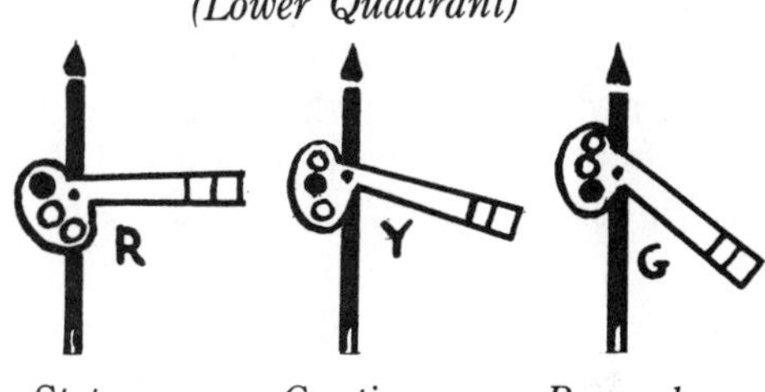

Stop *Caution* *Proceed*

SEMAPHORE SIGNALS
(Upper Quadrant)

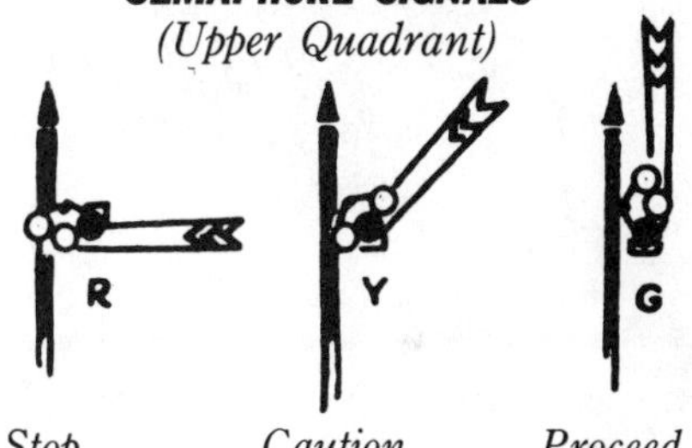

Stop *Caution* *Proceed*

COLOR LIGHT SIGNALS

Stop *Caution* *Proceed*

POSITION LIGHT SIGNALS

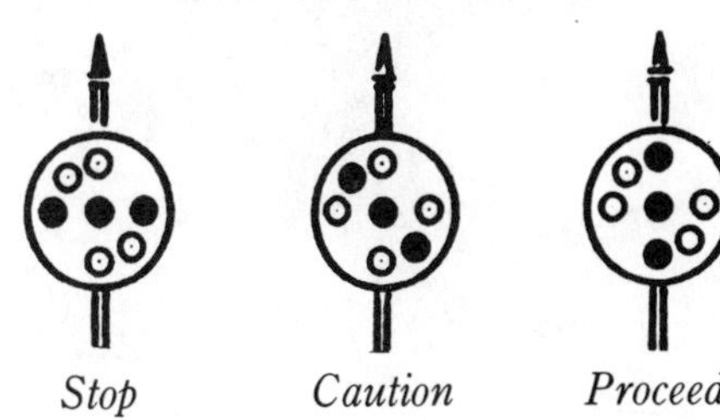

Stop *Caution* *Proceed*

"American Flyer"

Toy train companies were almost all father and son businesses. Like Lionel and Ives, American Flyer was no exception. It was founded in Chicago in 1907 by W. O. Coleman, Sr., and William Hafner, each of whom had a son who went into the business with him.

Hafner split with Coleman in 1914. He and his son formed the Hafner Manufacturing Company, which made wind-up trains until 1951. Coleman and his son, Ogden, continued with American Flyer until it was bought in 1938 by A. C. Gilbert of Erector who, with *his* son, Alfred, Jr., added it to their line of construction sets and moved Flyer to New Haven, Connecticut.

"Chicago" Flyer made wind-up trains until 1918, when it went into competition with Lionel and Ives with its own O-gauge electrics. Flyer standard gauge was added about 1925. All ran on three-rail track; it was not until after World War II that Gilbert put Flyer trains on two rails.

Flyer's 1930 catalog cover showed typical toy train merchandising magic: electric trains grown as big as their young operator, but still under his secure control.

intend to. The workingman has already lost his overtime from the years during the war and that's about all the cut he can stand. When his overtime is cut off he is pretty nearly cut in half already compared to those days and I haven't the heart to cut him any more."

With great prescience, Cowen foresaw that the boom of the twenties would have to end in depression, although when the crash came he was unprepared for its magnitude. "The way it looks to me," he said, "in the spring things will open up and from then on we will have steady progress until inflation once more goes too far, when we will have another depression. We are on the upturn now and the thing to do is to take advantage of the prosperity that is on the way to prepare for the storms the future holds."

Cowen followed his own advice, capitalizing on America's prosperity by producing elaborate trains that were worlds removed from the primitive steam engines he had had as a boy. (Not to be outdone, Ives manufactured a copper-plated passenger train actually named *The Prosperity Special,* while American Flyer offered a cadmium-plated beauty, *The Mayflower.*) By 1921, Cowen estimated he had made one million train sets. Year after year they grew increasingly extravagant, and Cowen's promotion became even more clever. "I've been a boy and I know what boys like," he asserted a bit truculently at the beginning of the decade. "Twenty years ago I started to make Lionel electric trains for you boys to play with—and NOW—over 550,000 sets are in daily use. Are you one of the lucky thousands?"

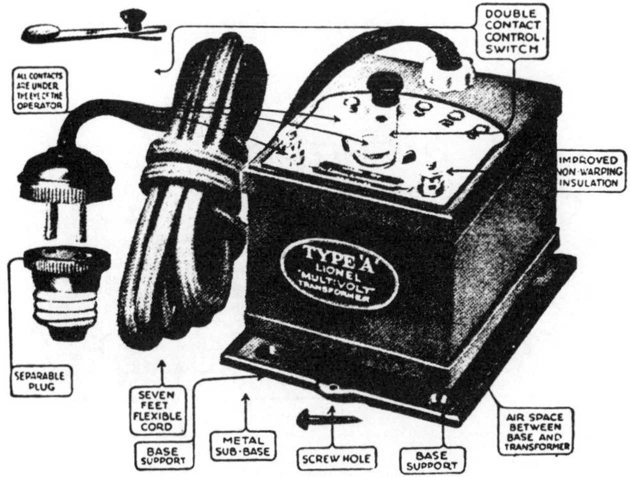

With the spread of electricity, transformers became an important part of the train set. Plugs had adapters so that the transformer could be screwed into light sockets in homes that did not yet have wall outlets.

COWEN ON COLOR

Cowen had a wonderful eye for color. Sample trains were painted in a variety of color combinations and made up with brass, nickel, and copper trim at the factory. Cowen then picked the combinations he thought would sell best, which usually looked nothing like those on actual trains. Children loved these brightly-colored cars, but adult model railroaders were sometimes upset at their lack of realism.

William K. Walthers, who later founded his own model train accessory company, went to the Lionel showroom to complain. "I called on the Lionel people in 1929 to ask them why they did not paint their toy signals in railroad colors (black and white) instead of a gaudy combination of colors that had no resemblance to real signals," Walthers said. "Mr. Lionel Cowen came out of his inner office to answer my question.

"'Young man,' he said, 'do you know who actually buys toy trains and accessories? It's the women—mothers, sisters, and aunts of the kids who play with them. Don't forget, women buy on color and don't give a damn what the thing is just as long as it is bright."

It was peculiar that Cowen attributed buying power to women, for the 1929 catalog reflected none of it. "Lionel Railroading!" it proclaimed. "Unlimited Fun For Dad And His Son. Pleasure knows no bounds for the boy and his Dad when indulging in that most fascinating of pastimes—Lionel Model Railroading."

By 1922 Cowen was selling the fantasy of both being a railroad president and having your own father work for you: "Boys, wouldn't you shout for joy and feel might happy if Dad or Mother gave you a beautiful Lionel Train? [This was one of the rare times mothers were ever mentioned in the catalogs.] You can be railroad president, station master, conductor and train dispatcher. Dad will have lots of fun too. You can make him your assistant and bring him back to his boyhood days, although he did not have such wonderful trains to play with." Two years later, Cowen decided maybe dad had enjoyed Lionels as a boy, after all: "Go through this book now with Dad and plan your Lionel

BUILT TO LAST

Cowen was truly proud of the construction of Lionel's engines and cars. Many of the structural features were innovations he himself had patented. A full page in catalogs of the twenties was usually devoted to showing Lionel's special construction techniques, giving the patent numbers that protected them.

Steel, one-piece construction and thick enamel painting were two of Cowen's special concerns. "Of utmost importance is the fact that cast iron does not enter into the manufacture of any of these bodies," the catalog said. "Heavy sheet steel is used for every model. Panels and rivets are embossed in the metal which add strength; so that Lionel Locomotives are practically indestructible."

And of Lionel painting, the catalog said, "All Lionel Cars and Locomotive Bodies are enameled in a variety of attractive colors, and baked at high temperature, which insures a permanent finish that can always be kept bright."

The 402 was Lionel's major electric engine from 1923-1927. It was made in a dull grayish tan that Lionel called mojave.

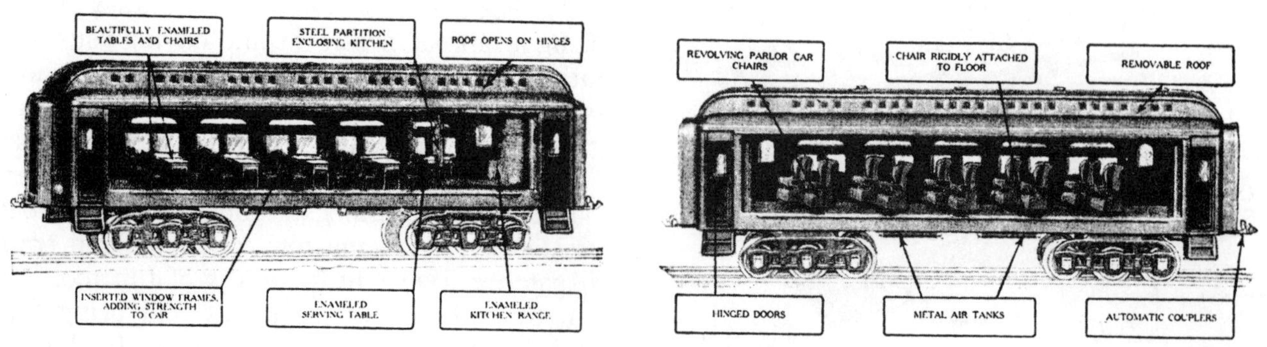

The interior detailing of diner (left) *and coach cars paled when the State Set appeared in 1929 with two full bathrooms in each car.*

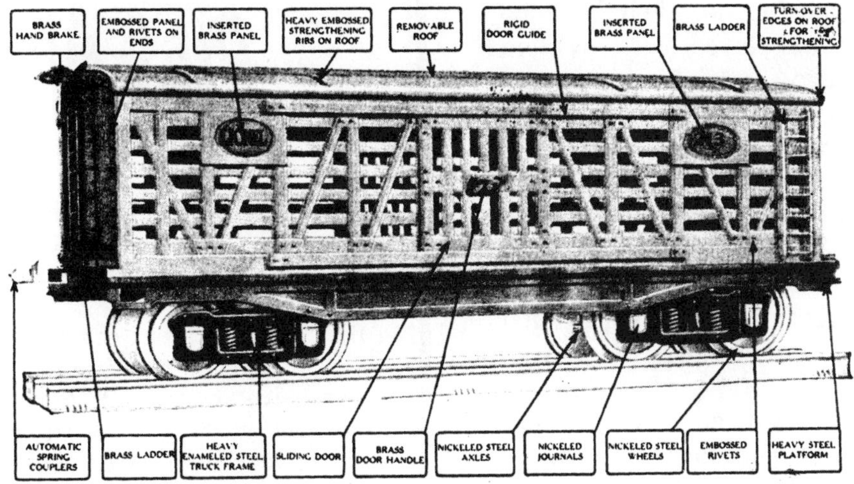

The cattle car was a foot long, but you had to provide your own livestock.

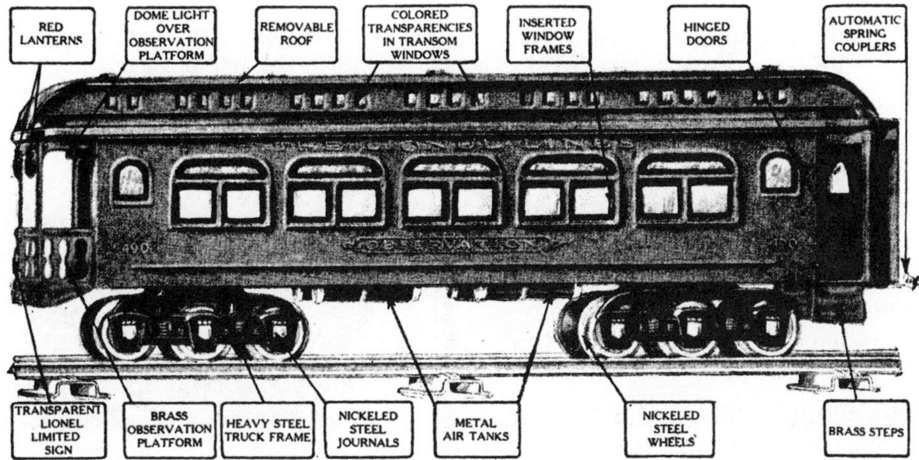

Open-porch observation car sometimes needed additional weight to keep it from whipping off sharp curves.

LIONEL WAS FIRST TO INTRODUCE—

Inserted panels in doors and windows of cars and locomotive bodies, which give great strength and add real detail to construction. Far superior to representing these details by lithographed process on tin. Patented July 16, 1918.

Inserted etched brass plates in locomotive bodies. Patented July 16, 1918.

A perfect die-cast wheel with nickeled steel rim over the tread—insuring accuracy and long use. Patented May 17, 1925.

Insulated fibre frogs on switches. Patented April 21, 1925.

"Lockon" Track Connections. Patented June 16, 1925.

Headlights with individual switches and green and red transparent side panels. Patented June 2, 1925.

Automatic Train Control—the only device that automatically controls the operation of the train. Patented August 21, 1917.

LIONEL WAS FIRST TO INTRODUCE—

All-steel car and locomotive bodies, hand enameled and rigidly assembled, instead of flimsy lithographed tin.

Trucks with nickeled journals.

Roller contact shoes on locomotives.

Three-bearing armature shafts on miniature motors.

Electrical sheets for motor and armature construction instead of cheap cold-rolled steel.

Drill rod shaft for armature, instead of commercial iron wire.

Reinforced phosphor-bronze bearings for armature shaft and wheel axles.

Automatic Crossing Gates.

Automatic Warning Signals.

Automatic Block Signals.

All-steel electric lighted miniature bungalows and villas.

Railroad—make him your assistant—he'll have just as much fun as you do. He'll be a boy again—chances are he played with a Lionel Train himself long ago."

Turning men into boys and boys into men: This was the special alchemy practiced by Cowen. But the baffling message behind the glowing catalog copy was that neither state was satisfactory. Why would men want to be powerless boys who in their turn were only yearning to be adult males directing swift freights? It is doubtful that Cowen recognized the illogic of his own rhetoric.

Man or boy: As far as Cowen was concerned, they both wanted to be railroaders. And Lionel would help. "Boys, Lionel will aid you to obtain a valuable technical knowledge of electricity and the principles of modern railroading," Cowen promised in 1926. The lesson was even more explicit by 1928: "There's knowledge to be gained from the study of Lionel Railroad operation—knowledge of electricity, of railroad control, and of transportation that will be valuable to you when you grow up to manhood. Hundreds of boys who were Lionel fans years ago are today occupying positions of trust on the great railroad systems of the country—helped forward by what they learned as boys through the operation of their Lionel Trains."

The other theme emphasized in the catalog was control and mastery. "Passenger trains, freight trains, work trains moving about at the will of yourself—the young engineer—operated by you from the switch tower, and absolutely under your control at any distance. You are thereby the master of your train," read the 1928 catalog. Boys—and failed men—could thus discover the power they lacked in their real lives. Lionel's world was under control even if the rest of the universe was not. Years later, in the fifties, the same idea was still in evidence: "Note to parents: Control of a Lionel train today—control of his life tomorrow."

Cowen was as modern in his advertising techniques as he was in his themes. He marketed Lionel trains nationally, eschewing the regional merchandising still practiced by some companies. Ads that were masterpieces of psychological manipulation, most of them playing unceasingly on Cowen's theme of "Lionel: The Father And Son Railroad" ("Real enough for a man to enjoy—simple enough for a boy to operate"). Cowen even went so far as to reprint Cadillac's famous ad, "The Penalty of Leadership," applying it to Lionel trains ("When a man's work becomes a standard for the whole world, it also becomes a target for the shafts of the envious few").

As early as 1921 he mounted a coast-to-coast ad campaign, explaining to dealers, "In addition to this space in the boys' own particular magazines, we help parents decide by using magazines of national circulation and of universal interest." In one year Lionel advertised in *American Boy, Boys' Life, Current Events, Youth's Companion, St. Nicholas, Boys' World, Boys' Magazine, Lone Scout, Popular Mechanics, Electrical Experimenter, Literary Digest, Collier's,* and *Sunset Magazine.* Combined circulation was over five million, with *Collier's* and *Literary Digest* selling more than one million copies each. Within two years, Lionel expanded the list to include more adult magazines, placing ads in the *Saturday*

DIES AND MOLDS

Both dies and molds have been used to make electric trains. Dies stamp out train parts from flat metal sheets, much like cookie cutters. They also press in surface detail. After the pieces are punched out, they are bent to form cars, locomotive boilers, and other inexpensive sheet-metal trains.

Heavier, more elaborate train parts, such as locomotive chassis, are cast in hand-carved molds. Liquid metal or plastic is forced into every nook and cranny of the mold to produce minute details.

Confusingly, the term *die-casting* generally refers to the use of molds in the manufacturing process.

BILD-A-LOCO

In 1928, Lionel reintroduced locomotives in kit form (they had appeared briefly in 1919), calling them Bild-a-Locos. One O-gauge and two standard gauge electric engines were available. Complete kits included all parts, locomotive cab and chassis, a small screwdriver, and enough track to make a circle. Prices ranged from $20 to $42.50 for the dark-green twelve-wheel 381U that eventually pulled the State Set.

The motor was removable, and when not being used in the engine, it could power construction toys. With Bild-a-Locos, Lionel was attempting to offer two toys in one and to compete with the A. C. Gilbert Company's Erector sets.

As with its trains, Lionel sold Bild-a-Loco on the basis of its educational value. "No boy can build a 'Bild-a-Loco' without getting a better understanding of electricity and mechanics," the catalog claimed.

But most boys wanted to play with trains, not be educated. Also, Lionel didn't offer any construction toys to use with the Bild-a-Loco motor. The standard gauge kits were on the market for only two years, although the O-gauge 4U was offered into the early thirties.

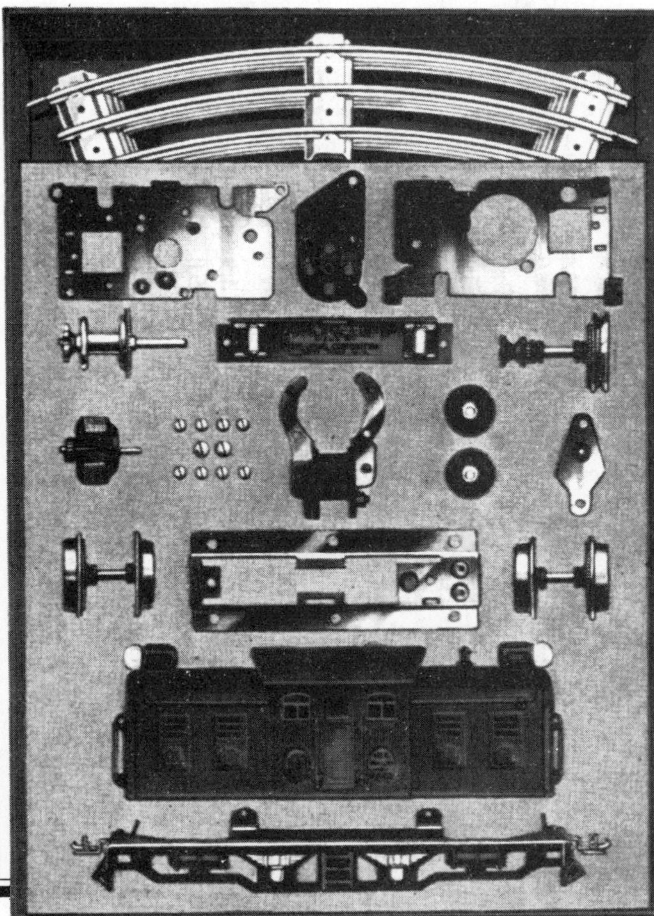

The Bild-a-Loco motor, assembled and with the wheels put in place. The motor was designed so that no wires had to be connected; all electrical contacts were made as the parts were assembled. A base and pulleys converted the motor for use in construction toys.

The motor and wheels are secured to the locomotive chassis. Rollers were attached to the bottom of the motor to pick up current from the center rail. The chassis had cowcatchers, ornamental springs, and ladders.

The locomotive body is fitted to the frame with screws provided. Preassembled contacts in the body carried current to the headlights at both ends of the engine. The small pantograph on the roof was not functional.

The orange 4U locomotive. In kit form, the engine cost twenty dollars, although if bought assembled it was only fifteen. (The extra pulleys and base for the motor made the kit more expensive.)

Even miniature billboards Lionel made for train layouts expressed Cowen's desire to turn boys into men and men back into boys.

Evening Post, Scribner's, Harper's, Century, World's Work, Review of Reviews, and *Popular Science Monthly.*

Cowen did not limit himself to magazines. Movies were becoming increasingly popular: At the start of the decade, thirty-five million people a *week* were paying ten cents or more to see Westerns and melodramatic love stories. By the time of the crash, weekly movie attendance was up to eighty million, and war and gangster films were the rage. Cowen was not able to worm Lionel trains into feature films (though he succeeded in the next decade), but he did produce his own movie, described as an "industrial film" in the 1925 catalog. Eight purported frames from the film (with their sprocket marks drawn in) were shown in the catalog. They portrayed manufacturing steps like "enameling, in which the famous everlasting Lionel finish is applied" and "transformer division, all parts are made and assembled under our own roof," with industrious Lionel workers shown going about their duties in the large-windowed factory in Irvington, New Jersey. In a probable exaggeration, the catalog mentioned that the film was five thousand feet long, which meant it would have run for hours.

Like movies, radio, too, matured in the twenties, especially as an advertising medium. The number of households with glowing tube sets in the parlor went from 60,000 to 13.7 million in eight years. Companies were quick to sponsor shows. Philco, Firestone, General Electric, Paramount, Stromberg-Carlson, Maxwell House, and Eveready (started supposedly with Cowen's flashlight) sponsored orchestras, while Kellogg's and Socony went for dramas and discussion programs. During the month preceding Christmas, 1929, Lionel bowed in with Uncle Don and his Lionel Engineers Club. Don Carney, a children's entertainer, was on the air in New York, Chicago, and Cincinnati every Friday night from six-thirty to seven with his nephews, Laddie and Alfred. Together, they played the piano, sang the brave song of the Lionel Engineers, and told railroad stories. As "Chief Engineer," Carney presided over the Engineers Club. All boys were eligible (despite the war work of their mothers, girls were still assumed to be uninterested in electric trains). To join, the boy or his parents had to buy some piece of Lionel equipment in the first week of December and send the receipt to Lionel. Members received a round badge *(Uncle Don's Lionel 1929 Engineer's Club),* a certificate with Carney's picture on it, and a subscription to a planned Lionel magazine.

A photo contest offering a total of $1,000 in gold "to the boys of America who own Lionel Electric Trains" coincided with Carney's original show. A first prize of $250 was offered for the picture of the most realistic Lionel layout. Cowen hosted a formal dinner at which entries were judged. He, Carney, and the presidents of the Erie and Lackawanna railroads (New Jersey concerns that later merged) gathered in tuxedos to go through the piles of pictures. Cowen supposedly ran a train around the large table at which the judges sat. This *Hors D'Oeuvres Special* carried cigars, nuts, and various *crudités* in its gondolas. Each judge could stop the train at his place, light up a Havana panatela, and then send the train on its way. Although the photograph of the deliberations that appeared in the new *Lionel Magazine* showed no such train, Cowen did in fact hook up "chuck wagons" for parties at his home. (Hamburger counters and soda fountains also picked up the idea of bring-

1928 lamppost, highway crossing, and hand-operated semaphore set cost $4.25 and included two extra bulbs in their own wooden containers.

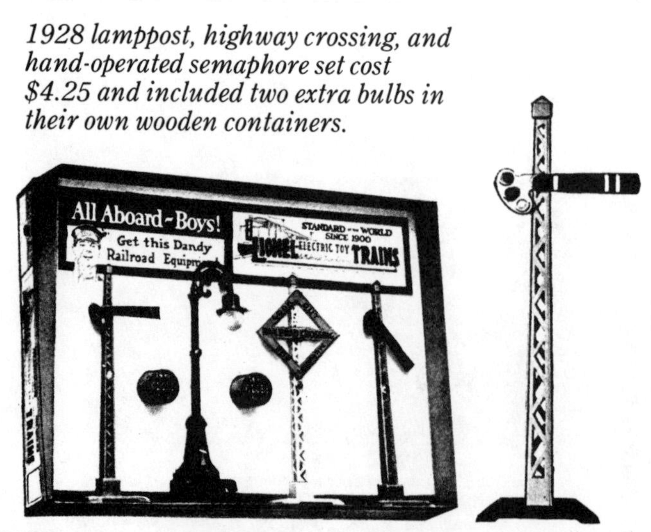

SONG OF THE LIONEL ENGINEERS

(TO THE TUNE OF *CASEY JONES*)

Come all you club members
if you want to hear,
A story about a young engineer.
Lionel is the little fellow's name
And he always runs
a Lionel electric train.

(CHORUS)

Lionel trains, nothing could be finer,
Lionel trains, powerful and strong.
Lionel trains, superpowered motors
That pull a train of twenty cars all
day long.

(SHOUT LAST LINE QUICKLY WITH GUSTO.)

Now, Lionel is going
to bring his train
Right up here to Uncle Don,
when he comes again.
We'll put the tracks together
all round the floor.
So be sure to listen in
and hear the engine roar.

(REPEAT CHORUS)

Judging Lionel's photo contest are (left to right): *J. M. Condon of the Erie Railroad, "Uncle" Don Carney, and Cowen.*

Surrounded by Lionel's magnificent 840 Power Station, a Lionel City depot and terrace, and freight and passenger specials, "Uncle" Don Carney sings out with gusto.

ing customers their orders on Lionel trains, especially in the 1950s, when comedian Jackie Gleason built a television skit around a train that ran on a bar carrying a shot of liquor.)

All was not sales promotions and photo contests, however. As the line became more grandiose, requiring more complicated tooling than had been called for by the simpler trains of the teens, Cowen sought ways of minimizing costs while preserving quality. He could save a small amount by buying raw materials astutely, but labor costs and other major expenses were rising. The highest-paid of Lionel's factory employees were the tool makers. Mostly Swedes and Germans, the tool makers designed and built the actual punches and dies that were fitted to Lionel's massive power presses, where the thousands of train parts were produced. Every car and engine, bridge and station required many tools and dies for both its basic body and for such details as bricks, stone ornamentation, and rivet heads.

At Caruso's urging, he and Cowen went to Italy from January to March 1922, to explore setting up tool making abroad. Even with the expense of shipping tools and dies back to New Jersey, and the complications of correspondence overseas, it might be cheaper to make Lionel's tooling in Italy, where labor was so much more economical. Caruso showed Cowen his native country. In Naples, they stayed at the elegant Hotel Vesuvio, where, during the preceding August, tenor Enrico Caruso (no relation to Mario) had died, gasping, "Doro, I can't get my breath." On the outskirts of the city the two executives dined in a restaurant housed in a distinguished stone mansion. Caruso, with the fine eye for real estate that had led him to move the Lionel factory to undeveloped Irvington, admired the mansion and the land surrounding it. A few years later, he bought both, eventually constructing a housing development around the old restaurant building that would become his office.

Cowen in Naples on the harbor-front promenade across from the Hotel Vesuvio.

The result of the trip was the establishment of the Societa Meccanica La Precisa "for experimenting, researching and manufacturing samples, models and tools." Caruso moved to Naples with his family to oversee the new company. For the next ten years, he traveled back and forth between New York and Italy, transporting tooling to the factory and taking plans for new products back to Naples. By the end of the decade, Lionel was putting almost $200,000 a year into La Precisa.

Making tooling in Europe caused some interesting problems. The Italian tool and model makers were naturally influenced by the trains they saw around them. European steam engines, traveling for shorter distances on more protected track than their American counterparts, had neither cowcatchers nor headlights on the front of their engines. La Precisa's designers did not go so far as to omit these important details from Lionel engines. But they did add metal bands to the locomotive boilers, which, while they looked colorful, were not representative of the latest in American design. It was one of the first things Joseph Bonanno noticed when he joined the company as a consultant in 1928. "I told Mr. Caruso, 'We don't have metal bands on locomotives in America,'" Lionel's future chief engineer remembers. "'But your designers and engineers and model makers over there see those locomotives in front of them all the time.' We began going to the railroads for their plans. Mr. Caruso very willingly went along with that trend and we started to design real American-type locomotives."

The Hellgate Bridge, the biggest, most de-

The house on the lower left was based on Louis Caruso's home, while his brother Mario's was duplicated on the right.

tailed toy train bridge manufactured by Lionel—a replica of the arched bridge spanning New York's East River—was designed in Naples from photographs. Still, Lionel's 1928 model was authentic in feeling. The Neapolitan tool makers cleverly modified the Lionel version so trains could pass through the bridge at ground level without having to approach it on elevated track, as was the case with the original. This made the Hellgate usable on even simple Lionel layouts.

Other accessory designs were based on scenes from Cowen's New York. The lovely lampposts that were produced during the twenties by Lionel were almost exact duplicates of the cast-iron street lights in Manhattan. Their one- and two-bulb posts were accurate even to the metal scrollwork in the crook of the shepherd's staff-shaped poles. Grand Central Terminal served as model for a Lionel City station introduced in 1931, the clock over its door perpetually reading "10:07." A pagoda-roofed switching tower with actual controls for the Lionel railroader to operate was based on similar towers along the Connecticut tracks of the New Haven Railroad. And the models were sometimes even closer to home. The undersized houses with dormers and sun porches that Lionel offered in 1923 were duplicates of the early brick homes of Caruso and his inventor brother, Louis, one block away from each other in Irvington.

It was during the twenties that Cowen assembled much of the managerial talent that would make Lionel the most successful toy train company in the world. Caruso was already firmly established as second in command to Cowen, serving as vice president and treasurer. Lionel's future sales manager and executive vice president, Arthur Raphael, was hired by Cowen in 1921 as a salesman. Raphael was to become Cowen's closest colleague, a brilliant merchandiser who brought the company its biggest department store accounts. Among his innova-

BRIDGES AND TUNNELS

Tunnels and especially bridges were among Lionel's most popular accessories in the twenties and thirties. For three or five dollars, you could make your track arrangement look special. But as trains became more realistic, short, foot-long tunnels began to look silly. Also, tunnels looked best when built as part of the plaster scenery and mountains on a layout. Bridges, on the other hand, were difficult to construct at home, and those offered by Lionel were very realistic. No tunnels were produced after World War II, although bridges continued to be best sellers for Lionel.

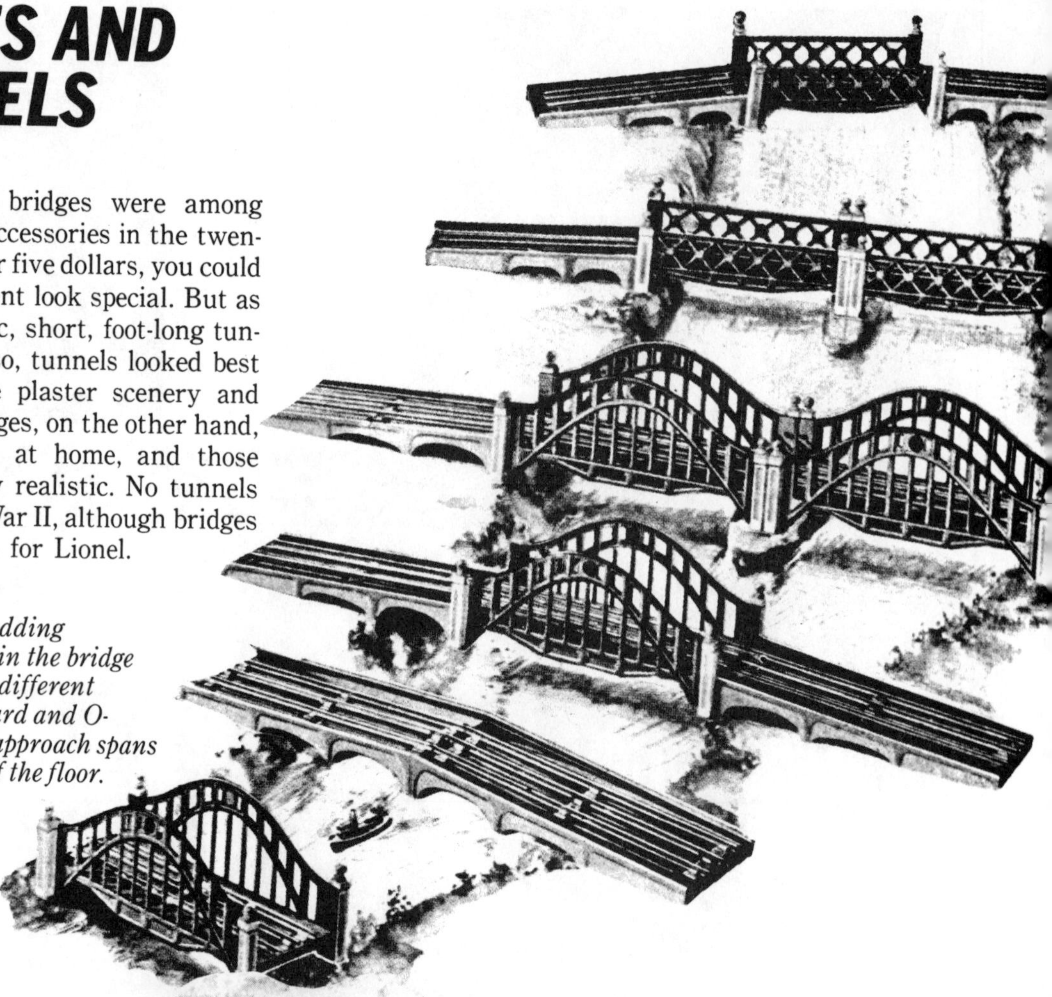

Bridges could be extended by adding additional center spans. Slots in the bridge floors held track in place, and different bridges were offered for standard and O-gauge track. The bridges had approach spans that raised track two inches off the floor.

Simple tunnels ranged from eight to seventeen inches long. All were made of steel. The smallest would admit only O-gauge trains (bottom) *while the largest could pass a Pullman Deluxe.*

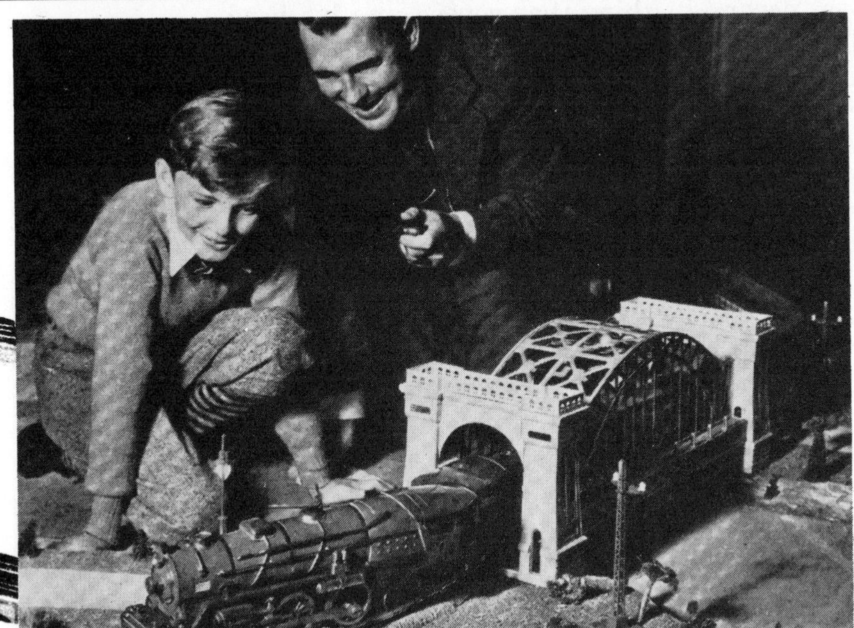

The Hellgate Bridge as interpreted by Lionel was almost two and a half feet long and a foot high, and was made out of enameled steel. Like many Lionel accessories, it came in two color combinations. The 1928 version was green and cream; a later model was painted silver, ivory, and red. It was designed for standard gauge trains (like the 400E steamer, left*), but O-gauge equipment actually looked more realistic passing through its portals.*

ROBERT MORGAN

Lionel's Hellgate (foreground) *duplicated the feel but not the actual proportions and detail of the 1917 bridge, which is 1,017 feet between stone towers. Properly known as the East River Arch Bridge, the Hellgate acquired its nickname because it passes over the dangerously swirling currents where the East and Harlem Rivers meet off the northeast point of Manhattan. The Hellgate completed the direct railroad route between New England and the rest of the country. While the real Hellgate was only the centerpiece of a several-mile-long viaduct linking the tracks of the New Haven and Pennsylvania Railroads, Lionel's bridge stood by itself and was never provided with approach piers.*

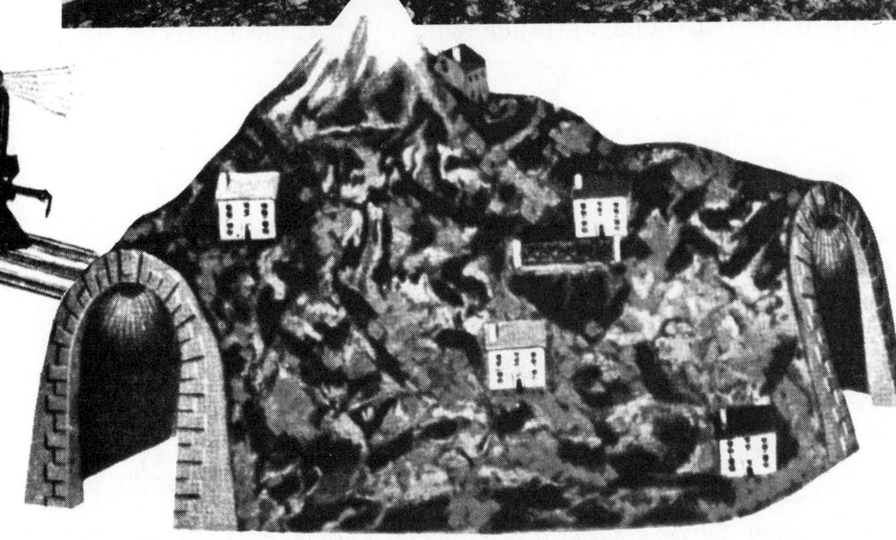

The largest tunnel Lionel made was curved (left) *and helped disguise those awkward corners on train layouts where it was obvious that the trains were turning because they had reached the end of the room. Both it and the straight tunnel* (above) *were lighted inside and had tiny metal houses and bridges scattered on their slopes.*

tions were what came to be known as "department store specials." These train sets, in different colors or with different combinations of cars than shown in the catalog, were made up especially for major customers like Macy's. The specials could be sold more cheaply without antagonizing Lionel's smaller dealers, who sold the regular line at list price. A witty raconteur who in his later years could get away with calling Cowen "bossy" and kissing him on his bald head, Raphael was also a playwright. During his years at Lionel he wrote material for Broadway musical revues, continuities for the *Superman* radio series, and a children's book, *The Great Jug,* which included a Christmas tree that grew its own electric trains.

Some of Lionel's best mechanical minds joined the company in the twenties, too. Bonanno, who eventually held two hundred patents mostly relating to electric trains, started consulting work on electrical circuits at the request of his uncle Mario. Charles Giaimo, who invented the whistle and was works manager after World War II, came to Lionel as a tool maker's apprentice. Thomas Pagano, who played in the factory as a young boy while his father made his watchman's rounds, spent his summers at Lionel, and felt triumphant when he could keep up with the regulars on piecework. He later became an assistant superintendent. Raphael hired Frank Pettit, who invented the operating cattle car and knuckle coupler, to work in the New York office stock room as a Christmas temporary. Raphael wanted college students working for him, so Pettit lied during the course of his interview.

"What are you studying?" Raphael queried.

"Dentistry," Pettit replied, saying the first thing that popped into his head.

"You're not tall enough to reach the patient," Raphael tactlessly said. Pettit was about Cowen's five-foot-five.

"Still, I'm studying dentistry," Pettit said.

He got the job, stayed on after the holidays, and eventually became head of the preliminary model shop at the factory, where most of the experimental work was done.

Caruso tightened his hold on the manufacturing end of the company through these appointments, for Bonanno, Giaimo, Pagano, and Pettit were all either related to him by blood or by marriage to his daughters or nieces. In addition, Caruso's brother, Louis, who invented Lionel's standard coupler, was a director of the company. In the thirties, Lionel's industrial relations director, Philip Marfuggi, also became related to Caruso when he married Louis Caruso's daughter. After the Second World War, when Giaimo succeeded Caruso, he too installed many of his relatives in the plant.

The irrepressible Raphael joked with Cowen about this. "Hey, Rafe," Cowen said one day, having just received the payroll figures from Irvington, "look at this. How many you think we have working at the factory?"

Raphael looked up at the ceiling. "Five hundred?" he guessed, giving an absurdly low figure.

"No," said Cowen, totally caught up in his enthusiasm about the size of the factory and taking Raphael's response seriously. "Three thousand."

"Oh, that's right," said Raphael, snapping his fingers. "I forgot Charlie Giaimo's relatives."

Cowen did not neglect his own family. Lionel's patent attorney was Joel Liberman, Cecelia's brother, who also became a director of

Completely landscaped layouts were available from Lionel. This standard gauge model, intended for store window display, cost eighty dollars, excluding trains and track.

ARTHUR RAPHAEL AND HIS NEUROSIS

Raphael's children's book featured a tree that grew electric trains,

Lionel's resident wit and sales manager, Arthur Raphael, was in the showroom one day when a popular musical entertainer came in and introduced herself. "I'm Evelyn and her magic violin," she said. "I'm Raphael and his neurosis," Raphael responded, without missing a beat.

Told by a Lionel secretary that she had dieted and lost thirteen pounds, Raphael quipped, "Seven of them were very attractive." Hearing that another secretary was marrying a man who had two degrees, Raphael said, "Then it will be twice as hard for him to make a living."

An amusing bon vivant who attended all the Broadway shows and wrote musical revues himself, Raphael occasionally dictated his clever letters to a secretary sitting on his lap. He was an office flirt who distributed gardenias and boxes of candy to the women workers. He was extremely generous, paying for the education of his secretary's deaf daughter at a special school. (When he died in 1952, Cowen continued to pay the tuition.) Another secretary, who spent her Thanksgiving typing a rush report for Raphael, found fifty dollars on her desk the next morning. Impulsively, he bought a set of paints for an office worker who expressed an interest in painting, which he loved. He used to say that an ideal vacation would be to fish all morning and to paint landscapes all afternoon.

Cowen relied heavily on Raphael's sales and marketing judgment, and the two men were close personally as well as professionally. After Cowen's wife died, he and Raphael frequently dined together. Raphael's cook served awful desserts and the two friends took turns sneaking them into the bathroom and flushing them down the toilet.

Raphael wrote Lionel's sales manuals in the form of dialogues between salesman and buyer. It was inevitable that when he wrote a children's book in 1936, *The Great Jug,* electric trains would figure in it. In the book, a brother and sister, Dicky and Betty, are transported first by kite and then by giant bird to a land where toys grow on trees. "One very big tree was outstanding," Raphael wrote. "It was absolutely covered with electric trains, all kinds and all colors. It took Dicky's breath away." The keeper of this magic forest, Claus Jr., explained to the children that toys were not so easily grown as years ago: "Toys are becoming harder to make all the time. Now you children want electric railroads . . . elaborate games and things like that. After all, an electric train cannot be made in a minute." A picture of the wonderful tree showed several streamlined, *Hiawatha*-type steam engines dangling from its limbs.

In the Lionel office, Raphael was the smiling, joking counterpoint to Cowen. "He was fun, fun, fun from the word go," a secretary recalled. "You respected Cowen, but you liked Raphael."

Lawrence in the fashionable evening clothes of the roaring twenties.

the company. Nephews worked in the showroom, especially at Christmas. Bertram Goodman, son of Cowen's sister Rose, sold on the floor while studying painting. He circulated among the display tables in the showroom (the switches were underneath, to hide them from children), covering for a salesman out to lunch, making the easy sales. Cowen would wander in: "How are things going, Bert?" he'd inquire. "Uncle Josh, this woman has a problem," Goodman might respond. "You mean this *lady* has a problem," Cowen would chide, politely but very firmly.

Another nephew, working as a permanent salesman on the road, told Cowen he had made a call when in fact he had skipped the customer. A while later, the customer appeared in the showroom. "Oh, I didn't know you'd added a new model," he told Cowen. "Didn't my salesman call on you?" Cowen asked, surprised. He checked his nephew's ledger, called him in, bawled him out, and fired him. (Being lied to probably infuriated Cowen more than his laxness.) Another nephew worked as manager of the New York office.

Cowen's problems at home were more complicated than those in the office. It was the roaring twenties, and the young people of America were wild and disillusioned. Wealthy parents tended to be overindulgent, and their children party-crashed and raced their gleaming sports cars over country roads, their laughter made more raucous by bootleg hooch. Lawrence, the smiling little boy who had adorned Lionel train boxes, graduated from Milford Academy in Connecticut and then attended Cornell. But the times were not conducive to serious study. If he was not the total sheikh, he did have the only Wills-St. Clair roadster at Cornell, and he spent more time with it than he did with his engineering books. A friend of Cowen's who was visiting at Cornell stopped to see Lawrence and was shocked to see Lawrence's fancy raccoon coat draped over the radiator of the car to keep the water warm.

Lawrence soon developed an interest in Wall Street, and the dazzling stock manipulations that created much of the wealth of the age. At eighteen he became a runner for a brokerage house at eighteen dollars a week, then a floor orders clerk in the Stock Exchange. He could not have been living solely on this meager salary, however, for at twenty he married Clarisse Bernard and they moved into the elegant Hotel Marguery on Park Avenue, where Cowen and Cecelia would eventually take an apartment. In early 1929, displaying much generosity but little financial acumen, Cowen bought Lawrence a seat on the New York Stock Exchange for $585,000. At twenty-one Lawrence was the youngest member of the Exchange. His seat was also said to have been the most expensive up to that time. Lawrence was happy, but Cowen never gave up trying to wean his only son of this "Wall Street foolishness" and bring him into Lionel. It took eleven years, but as in most things, Cowen finally had his way.

Lawrence's younger sister, Isabel, received an allowance of ten dollars a week from childhood until after she married, but she never had to spend it because her doting father delighted in buying her whatever she wanted. Only once did Cowen say no to her. Traveling in Europe with him, Isabel fell in love with an expensive, beautifully tooled leather jewel box. Cowen refused to buy it for her. But the first night out on the boat bound for home, the box was at her place at dinner.

Isabel married at age seventeen, which she later admitted was "much too young." Her husband, Jack Otis, was a handsome charmer, a natural salesman. Cowen took him into the

LIONEL'S SILVER JUBILEE

Lionel celebrated its twenty-fifth anniversary in 1925, even though its trains were probably not manufactured until about 1901. In fact, 1925 was the best year in the company's history up to that point. Net sales were $2,168,307, while the net profit of $248,553 was the highest yet recorded.

In addition to elaborate flyers to their dealers, Lionel marked its silver jubilee with ceremony at the New York office that included the presentation of a bronze plaque to Cowen and Caruso. Prepared by the prestigious Gorham jewelry firm, the plaque had an engraved medallion of Lionel's 402 electric engine (complete with reversing lever) in its center.

The inscription read: "To The Lionel Corporation; Commemorating Their Twenty-Fifth Anniversary, A Token Of Regard And Loyalty, And A Pledge To Perpetuate The High Ideals And Lofty Principles Inspired By Their President, J. Lionel Cowen, And Treasurer, Mario Caruso. Presented By The Staff Of The New York Office."

THOMAS PAGANO

On June 16, 1923, Lionel employees posed in front of the first Irvington, New Jersey, factory on Twenty-first Street. A huge, landscaped oval of track complete with bridges, tunnels, lampposts, and the Lionel City station was set up in the street. Cowen, in a dark suit, is in the third row from the bottom, to the right of the factory's keystone. Caruso is to his left (inset).

company. After two years, he became a director—on the same day in 1929 that Louis Caruso was elected to the board. When Otis and Isabel divorced a few years later, Otis resigned from the company, although Cowen would have allowed him to stay on. (Lawrence also divorced; both he and Isabel had long second marriages.) Cowen seemed to take the divorces stoically, though he later remarked that from then on, he was going to wait five years before giving newlyweds any wedding presents.

Early in the decade, Cowen had warned that the boom of the twenties would end in a depression. But as the stock market continued to climb, as sales of toy trains grew, he seemed to forget his own prediction. Things were going so well. During the decade, Lionel increased the value of its capital stock from $50,000 to $1.5 million, paying steady dividends. Cowen's personal wealth increased greatly. A nephew recalls Cowen turning to him at an outdoor cafe in Paris after reading the financial pages of *The Herald-Tribune.* "Well," Cowen said, "I've made $3 million since I've been away [the amount was surely a Cowen exaggeration]. But it can go down, too, just as it goes up."

Cowen also scored a major business triumph during the decade by gaining control of Ives. Lionel had pulled ahead of the Connecticut company during World War I. While Lionel concentrated on electric trains after the war, Ives was losing money with its line of boats and being undercut in the wind-up train market by companies producing cheaper models. Although Ives's electric trains were in some respects superior to Lionel's, the tradition-bound Yankee firm lacked the merchandising energy and cleverness of Cowen and Raphael. Ives sold almost $1 million in trains and boats in 1926 (less than half the amount Lionel was selling),

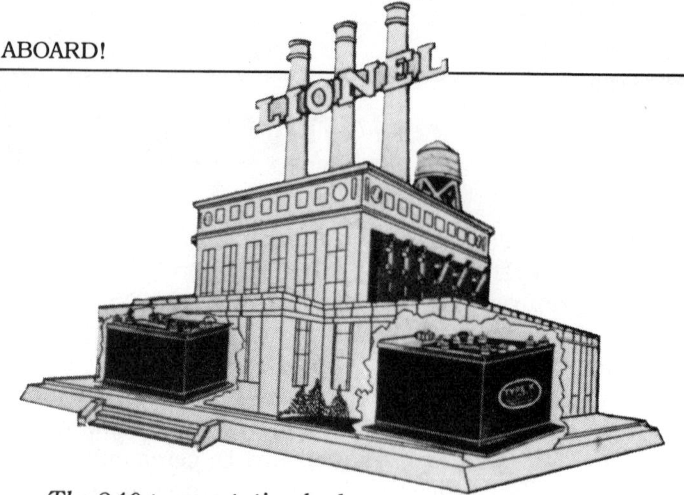

The 840 power station had room in it for two transformers.

but its cash flow was inadequate and before the end of the decade the company's creditors forced it into bankruptcy. Cowen and W. O. Coleman, of the Chicago American Flyer company, gained control of Ives and shortly afterwards Coleman sold his share to Cowen. Harry Ives, who had jousted with Cowen over his advertising methods, left the Bridgeport factory for the last time in September, 1929. He died seven years later.

As the crash of October 24, 1929, neared, Lionel gave no sign that the electric train business was anything but full throttle ahead. Lionel's most elaborate passenger train was introduced that year, a magnificent, nine-foot-long standard gauge set called the *Transcontinental Limited.* It was soon known as the State Set because its four passenger cars were lettered *California, Colorado, Illinois,* and *New York* (giving the train geographic ties to markets in all parts of the country). A three-page fold-out in the center of the catalog advertised the set, which sold for a whopping $110. Each of the cars was almost two feet long and had two bathrooms in which the toilet seats actually could be raised and lowered. The roofs opened to show off

The brown, 1930 State Set came with the twin-motored 408E electric engine, since the first green twelve-wheeler engine introduced with the set wasn't powerful enough to pull twenty-four pounds of massive state cars. The box label on the State Set carton displayed Lionel's top-of-the-line trains and accessories.

Lionel's switch towers and small power stations (above) *had controls on their backs or transformers inside them from which trains could be run* (below).

the interior detailing. At the head of the dark green train was a new twelve-wheel electric engine. All the great accessories were also in the catalog, including the Hellgate Bridge, the Lionel City rural station on its landscaped terrace (a Grand Central model was yet to come), and Lionel's power station, which was two feet square and could house two working transformers.

When the crash came, Cowen and Lionel were totally unprepared. Lionel was offering the most expensive, grandiose line in its history. By the end of October, virtually all of it had been manufactured and shipped. Like much of the country, Lionel would not feel the real impact of the Depression until 1930 and after. When it came, it would be devastating.

Cowen himself lost heavily in the crash. He had invested deeply in the stock market. Years later he said he had been ready to retire when the crash came, but that he lost so much he had had to keep working. Cowen's losses were surely real enough. But his retirement at age fifty-two from a business he gloried in was as plausible as a child's rejecting a Lionel train for Christmas.

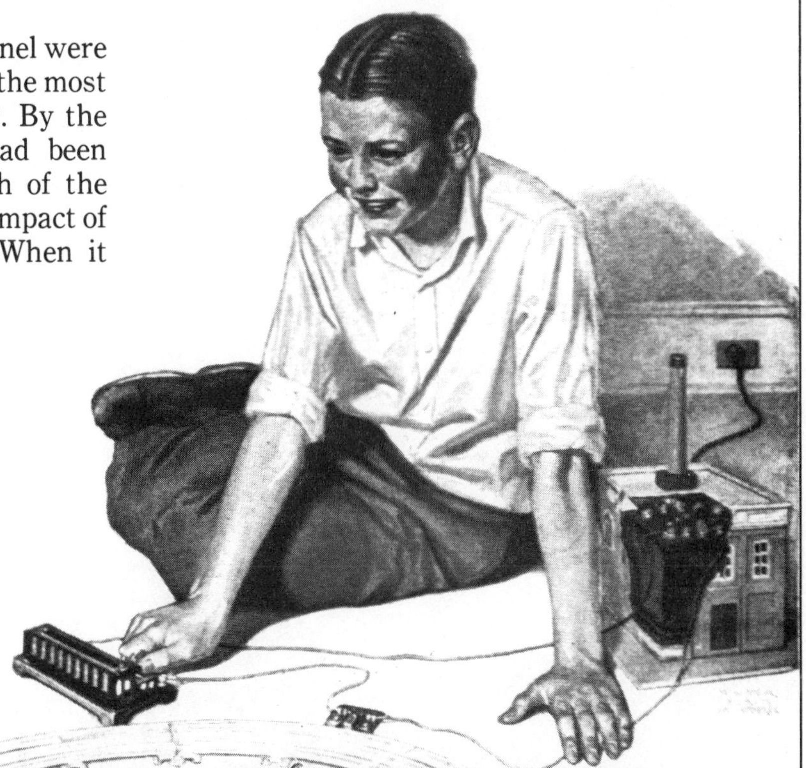

Despite the rigorous division between the worlds of men and boys in the early part of the century, Lionel trains could bring them together.

BOYS—PUT THIS AD SOME PLACE WHERE DAD WILL SEE IT

This Father Never Knew His Own Son

DOWN on the floor with his Lionel Train, *your* boy is tackling all of the problems of a man's world in miniature. *Today,* there is an opening for a partner in that railroad enterprise of his; no easy-chair "silent" partner, but an *operating executive* is required. *You* are wanted for that job.

Peel off your coat, Dad, and help him build Imagination Land. Show him how real trains are made up and started on their runs. Show him where the switches go and how the semaphore is used. He *wants* to know these things and he wants *you* to be the teacher.

In his mind's eye, his trains and his circles of track are but the raw beginning of a magic world. He sees them not as toys but as a little universe in which he is the master. And that boy of yours is ambitious. He pictures things that he can add, cities and scenery and splendor for his right-of-way. He knows what he wants to build—imitation lakes, sidings with tiny, h... factories, model cattle corrals, true-to-life scenic effects—but h... ...ucting them.

Avoid the disap... you as he grows up... with him and form...

LIONEL TR...

In 1934, Lionel Magazine *ran a series of ads directed at fathers with phrases including: "Keep young with your boy and he'll grow older with you" and "Don't have your boy grow away from you as he grows up."*

The number one father-son railroad team in the country, Cowen and Lawrence, enjoy a chuckle at pop's desk.

ROBERT PURDY

By the fifties, fathers and sons were ready to swap places, according to Lionel's ads.

BETWEEN STATIONS

FATHERS AND SONS

Even if he wasn't interested in toy trains, it was the rare father who could say he didn't want to be closer to his son. Lionel's advertising held out that promise.

"Here's a common meeting ground that will weld the bonds of a friendship that knows no age," a 1934 ad said. "There is a fascination about Lionel Engineering that you will find second only to the joy of close companionship with your boy. You will see his youthful affection transformed into a deep companionship that will keep him your friend for life."

LaRUE SHEMPP

Lionel distributed breakfast table cards on which son could inscribe his choices of trains for father.

Wearing the same caps, father and son enjoy the same hobby.

CARSTENS PUBLICATIONS

Gang car's workers went along for the ride but never got off.

Iceman worked up a sweat pushing ice into reefer car.

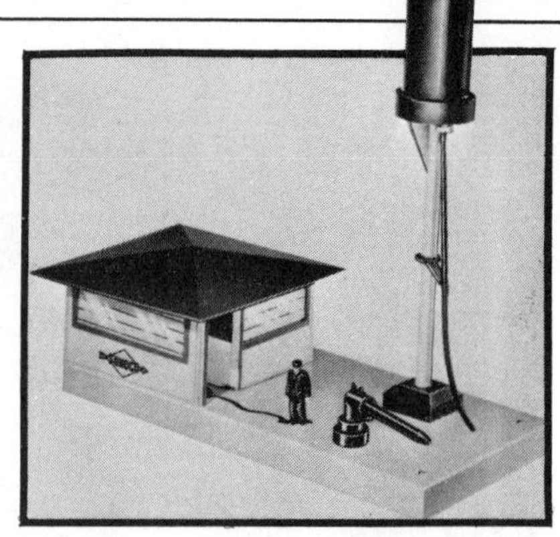

Diesel fueling station attendant manned filling hose.

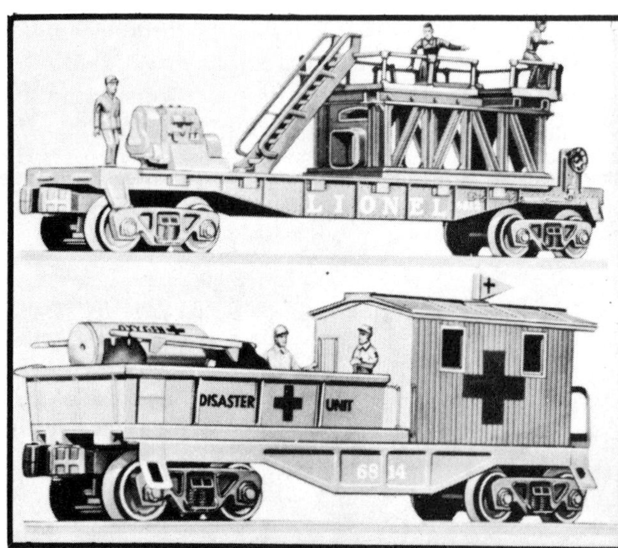

Maintenance and disaster aid were performed by steady workers who never left their posts.

Cop chased hobo around loaded gondola.

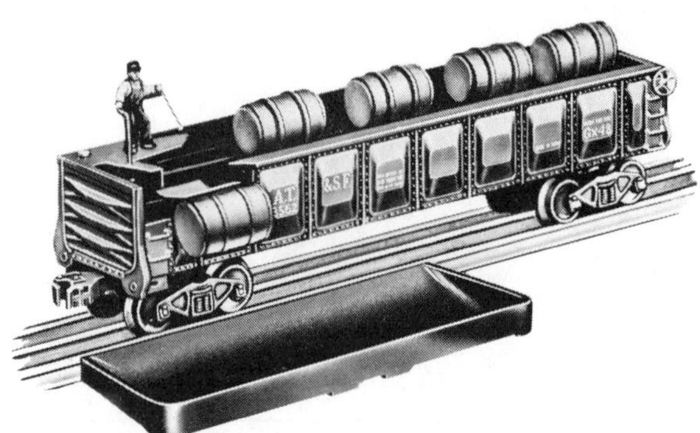

Barrel unloader dumped barrels into trackside bin or onto barrel ramp, where another worker pushed them along.

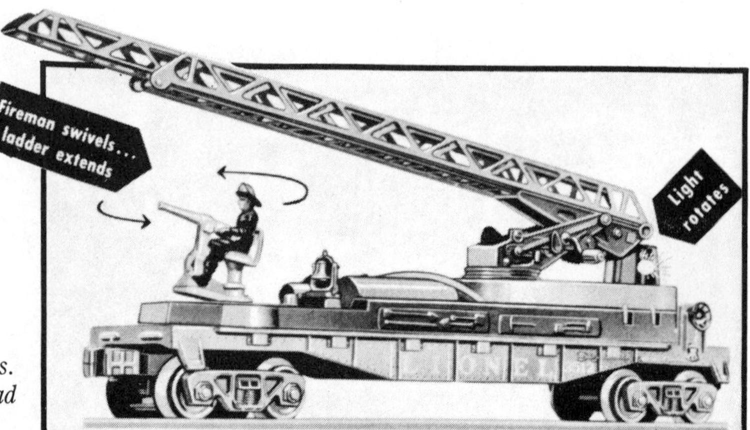

Fire fighting was important on Lionel Lines. Car at left was self-reversing, but flatcar had to be pulled by engine.

BETWEEN STATIONS

LIONEL'S WORKERS

The workers on Lionel Lines were not unlike their leader, Joshua Lionel Cowen. They were conscientious and took great pride in their work. Whether unloading milk cans or pumping handcars down the track, Lionel workers stayed at their posts until the job was done — and even afterwards.

These workers were usually made of rubber. Their faces and hands were painted pink, and their work clothes were often blue or gray.

Tower men in switch tower came downstairs as train passed.

CARSTENS PUBLICATIONS

Radar antenna rotates

It was breezy on open flatcar, but radar operator read his screen conscientiously.

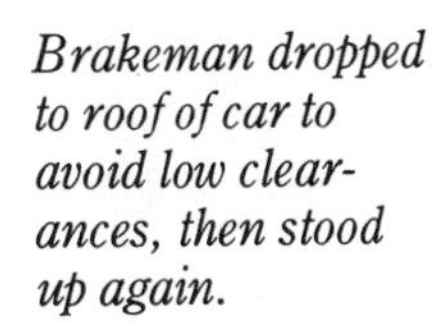

Brakeman dropped to roof of car to avoid low clearances, then stood up again.

Sweeper of poultry car (top) *fortunately only pretended to clean out floor of car. But mailman did throw a sack of mail held by a magnet to his stomach.*

Ballast tamper drove car that tapped down trackside gravel. Trackside trip activated tampers.

CARSTENS PUBLICATIONS

Whether the trains were cast-iron models of 1909 (top), *or Lionel's best of 1949, Christmas morning was the time to come thumping downstairs to find them magically set up on the living room floor under the tree.*

THE DAY AFTER CHRISTMAS

BY GEORGE C. ESKHOLME

Hello!-hello!-that you, Boss?
This is your senior clerk—
I've just called up to tell you
I can't get in to work!

Sickness?—no—no accident—
(Ain't even got a pain);
But Junior needs a helping hand
For his electric train.

He got the set for Christmas—
With engine, slick and neat,
With switches, lights, and tunnel,
And station, all complete.

You ought to see her veer and swerve
And speed around the hill
With certain grip on switch and curve—
I tell you, it's a thrill!

What?—give my job to Sandy?
You surely won't do that—
With Christmas only yesterday,
And gosh! it's left me flat!

Remember what you told us
When you gave your Christmas talk?
You said we need not worry—
That there'd be lots of work!

Don't you remember saying
That things go 'long the best
With close cooperation?
Well, surely—here's the test:

In setting up a railroad
There's lots of things to fix
That Junior can't manipulate—
You see, he's only six!

If I can just stand by him
Till things get on O.K.,
He'll operate the train alone
When once he's shown the way.

You know, when you were busy
With extra work to do,
You never had to ask me twice
To stay and see it through.

In all the years I've worked for you
I haven't failed you yet!
Now, when I ask a favor,
What answer do I get?

What! do you really mean it?
By gosh! can that be true?
Hey, Jane—get out your glad rags—quick—
I've got some news for you!

Put some water in the soup—
I'm out to get cigars—
The Boss is coming—right away,
TO HELP US RUN THE CARS!

—*Model Builder* Magazine
December, 1938

ANTHONY CAPRIO

MAX KNOECKLEIN

BETWEEN STATIONS

TOY TRAIN FOR CHRISTMAS

Trains — real as well as toy — have always been inextricably linked with Christmas. Real trains chuffing through snowy landscapes, brought people home for this major family holiday. Toy trains were a special and expensive gift, particularly appropriate at Christmas. The practice of setting up a crèche evolved into the building of a "Christmas garden," a miniature winter scene. This was but a short step to trains circling the Christmas tree.

AAR

Lionel's model railroading magazine of the thirties, its layout book of the fifties, and this Association of American Railroad's newspaper cartoon – all had the same message: Christmas and trains go together.

Today, foam pillows and urethane packing materials are being manufactured in the former Lionel plant in Irvington, New Jersey, where trains were made until about 1942.

Lionel's largest and last plant (foreground) *on Irvington-Hillside border.*

"Lionel Building" is still chiseled in keystone of old Irvington plant, whose windows are sealed against vandals.

BETWEEN STATIONS

THE PLANT

There was a succession of Lionel plants as the company grew, moving from New York to New Haven to New Jersey. The longest-lived and the biggest was on the Irvington-Hillside border.

"We'd poke through the junk outside looking for usable discards," recalls John Felber, who grew up near the plant. "One kid was lucky and found a bridge, but I only found a bunch of faulty flag stand bases."

In 1967, the machinery in the plant was sold at auction. Today, various firms occupy the fifteen-acre plant.

Lionel assembly line (top) *with train boxes piled up for photographer's benefit. Santa Fe boxcars have lettering but no doors or wheels.*

Reception area of Irvington-Hillside plant (right). *In engineering department, John Salles, Joseph Bonanno, and John Di Giralomo check diesel whistle.*

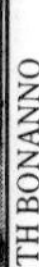

TOM PAGANO

President Eisenhower received Lionel's General *in Oval Office.*

Secretary of State John Foster Dulles with scale steamer.

Secretary of State George Marshall (second from left) *and Attorney General Thomas Clark (wearing the bow tie) at Lionel layout for war relief.*

King Ananda of Siam, ten, with Mickey Mouse handcar.

CARSTENS PUBLICATIONS

Sportscaster Bill Stern on Lionel showroom layout.

Paul Winchell and Jerry Mahoney at Lionel showroom entrance.

Eleanor Roosevelt with Cowen and Raphael at Herald Tribune *Fresh Air Fund benefit layout.*

BETWEEN STATIONS
FAMOUS FANS

Many famous people, from stripper Gypsy Rose Lee to Harvard president James Conant, relaxed with Lionel trains. Musicians Tommy Dorsey and Paul Whiteman were Lionel fans, as was actor Robert Montgomery. Playwright Ben Hecht staged railroad wrecks, then untangled them with his Lionel crane. Cowboys Roy Rogers and Gene Autry rode Lionel Lines. Arthur Godfrey had a huge layout, and Frank Sinatra still collects Lionels. Swimmer Johnny Weissmuller and Yankee third baseman Gil McDougald also had weak spots for Lionel.

Comedian Gary Moore runs Lionels blindfolded – and wrecks them!

Helen Hayes and son (kneeling) with Cowen at treatment center for infantile paralysis.

Yul Brynner takes break from The King and I *to enjoy American Flyers.*

Building a layout was a father and son proposition.

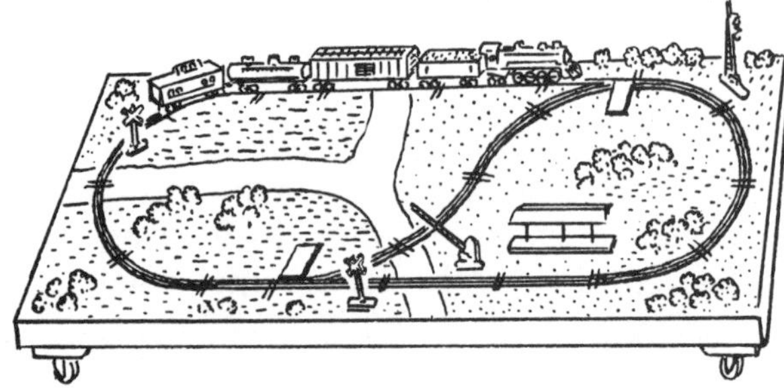

Lionel supplied plans and sketches for simple layouts that rolled away under beds.

Laurence Gieringer dusting off Roadside America. His brilliant Lionel layout is still open to the public in Shartlesville, Pennsylvania.

ALBERTA BERNECKER

AN EXCITING PANORAMA OF RAILROADING IN A SMALL SPACE!

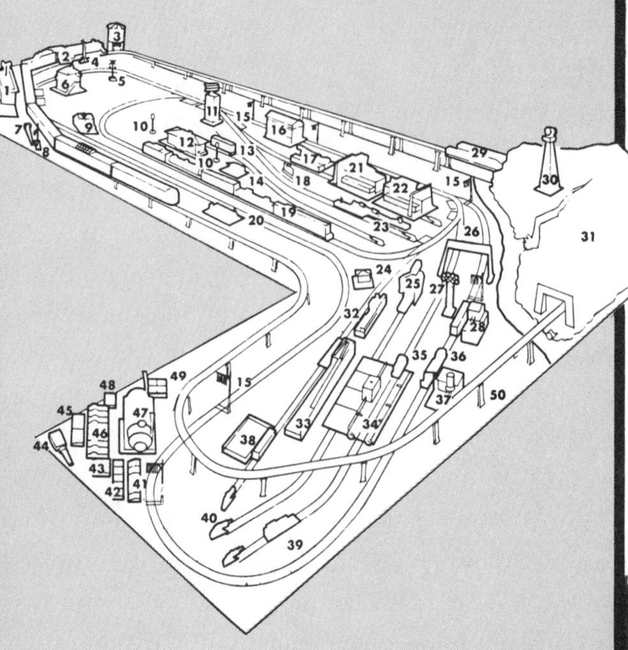

1. Sound Dispatching Station
2. Steam Passenger Train
3. Water Tank
4. Automatic Semaphore
5. Ringing Highway Signal
6. Automatic Switch Tower
7. Automatic Crossing Gate
8. Banjo Signal
9. Automatic Gateman
10. Lamp Post
11. Rotating Radar Antenna
12. Illuminated Station
13. Trolley
14. Animated Newsstand
15. Tell-Tale Poles
16. Operating Coaling Station
17. Operating Coal Loader
18. Billboard Blinker
19. Diesel Train
20. Milk Platform
21. Culvert Unloading Station
22. Culvert Loader
23. Operating Barrel Loader
24. Newsstand with Horn or Whistle
25. Operating Gantry Crane
26. Operating Signal Bridge
27. Floodlight Tower
28. Icing Station
29. Girder Bridge
30. Rotary Beacon
31. Mountain
32. Operating Lumber Mill
33. Operating Lumber Conveyor
34. Engine Transfer Table
35. Diesel Switcher
36. Diesel Switcher
37. Operating Diesel Fueling Station
38. Horse Corral
39. Track Cleaning Car
40. Illuminated Bumper
41. No. 90 Controllers
42. No. 364C Controllers
43. Transfer Table Controller
44. Microphone for Dispatching Station
45. Uncoupling Controllers
46. Switch Controls
47. ZW Transformer
48. Three-Lever Crane Control
49. Coaling Station Control
50. Graduated Trestle Set

BETWEEN STATIONS

BUILDING A LAYOUT

Building a layout — creating a miniature world that provided a proper setting for the trains — was the end toward which all Lionel activity was directed. Layouts might be a simple plywood board with sawdust dyed green to represent grass, or have weathered buildings, grimy factories, and rolling hills.

Lionel publicized especially good layouts like Roadside America and Delta Lines in its own magazine in hopes of inspiring less skilled modelers. It also provided plans for simpler railroad empires.

Frank Ellison's Delta Lines layout in New Orleans used outside-third-rail track and ran Lionel's scale Hudson.

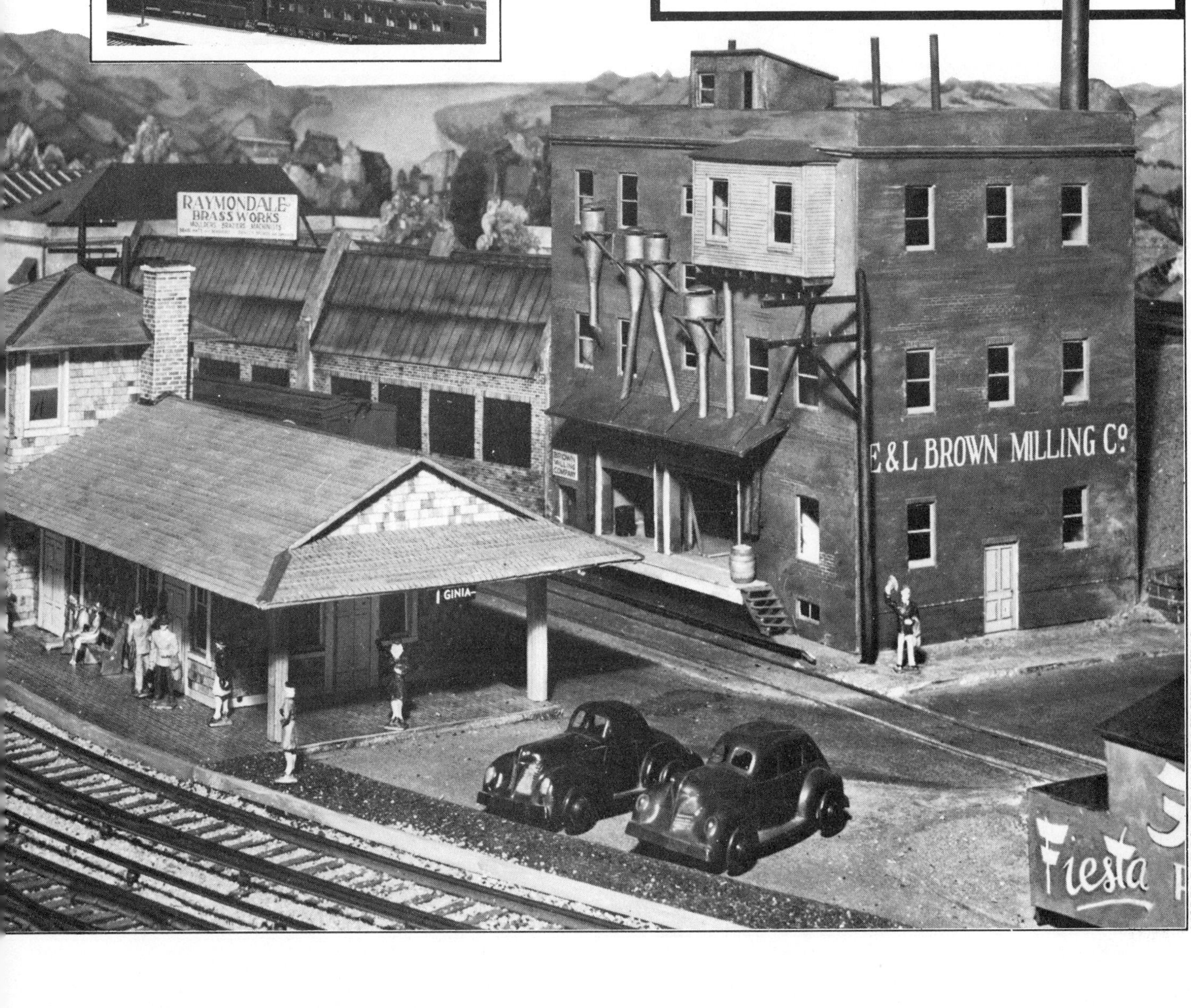

MODEL RAILROADER/KALMBACH PUBLISHING

The train store window—almost always with an operating layout—was as fascinating as the sales counter itself (left).

CLAY SENIOR

Altman's layout in New York at Christmas (left) *kept children (and Santa) occupied while their parents shopped. Lionel provided lighted displays to its dealers* (below) *to show off their trains.*

JOHN WEIS

Window of Model Railroad Equipment Corporation store in New York combined Lionels with American Flyers.

BETWEEN STATIONS

THE TRAIN STORE

Nothing could compare with a trip to see the trains! Whether they were in the toy train section of a large department store or in a small hobby shop, Lionels always attracted a huge crowd at Christmas time.

Usually there was an operating layout, often supplied already landscaped by Lionel (although larger stores like Altman's built their own). If the clerk was especially kind, he let you run the trains, but usually he was too rushed to consider such a request. Even if you didn't buy anything, the trip was worth it.

Macy's toy train counter in 1948 was a mob scene as shoppers vied for Lionel's turbine and accessories.

Northern Pacific engineer W. Brightfelt: "Lionel trains have made possible whole railroad systems."

New Jersey engineer W. Smith: "My grandsons enjoy the thrills of model railroading with Lionel."

AAR

Conductor and engineer ritually synchronize watches on the Missouri-Kansas-Texas (above).

Engineer Bob Butterfield with his grandsons and Lionel 400E (above), *and in the cab of his* Twentieth Century Limited *Hudson* (right).

ALVIN STAUFER

AAR

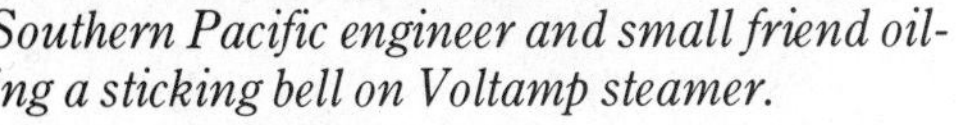

Southern Pacific engineer and small friend oiling a sticking bell on Voltamp steamer.

BETWEEN STATIONS

WHERE'S THE ENGINEER?

The Lionel catalog may have carried endorsements from railroad presidents and locomotive builders, but it was engineers like the *Twentieth Century's* Bob Butterfield who were the heroes of generations of boys.

"The Trains That Railroad Men Buy For Their Boys" was Lionel's slogan in the thirties, and Cowen backed it up by having Butterfield and others appear in the catalog testifying to the realism of Lionel trains.

Free, three-foot-high dealer display of thirties carried endorsement of unnamed engineer for five engines.

Santa Fe engineer W. P. McAfee: "It is natural for railroad men to buy Lionel trains for their boys."

ED WEIDNER/TTOS BULLETIN

Showroom was modernized after World War II, including Niagara Falls model on layout.

Balding Cowen and first sales manager Mark Harris selling trains in showroom in about 1914.

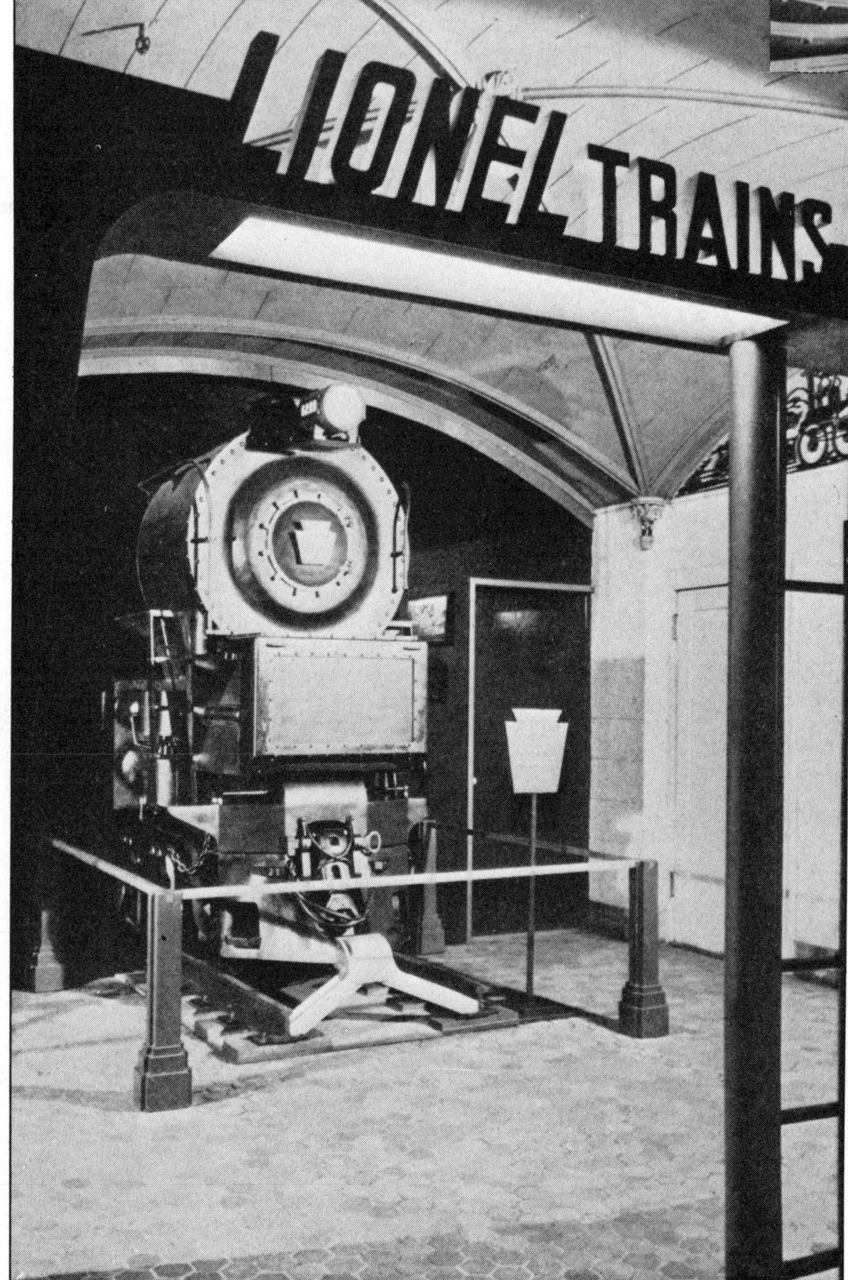

CARSTENS PUBLICATIONS

Showroom's most famous postwar layout had four transformers, track control board, roundhouse, and nonworking turntable. Entrance (left) had mock-up of Pennsylvania steam turbine.

Showroom layout of thirties and forties had more realistic T-rail track and was setting for photo contest.

BETWEEN STATIONS

THE SHOWROOM

Lionel's New York showroom at 15 East Twenty-sixth Street (after 1926) was a wonderland of elaborate operating layouts. Salesman William Gaston, who occasionally drew showroom floor duty after the war, recalls salesmen racing the trains to crossings and causing wrecks until Cowen had better block signals installed.

Cowen's office was just off the showroom floor. Once, seeing an unhappy-looking boy, Cowen repaired his balky engine on the spot. "Now go out and look at the trains," he then urged.

JOSEPH SADORF

Last New York showroom layout built in late fifties featured control booth and new Super-O track.

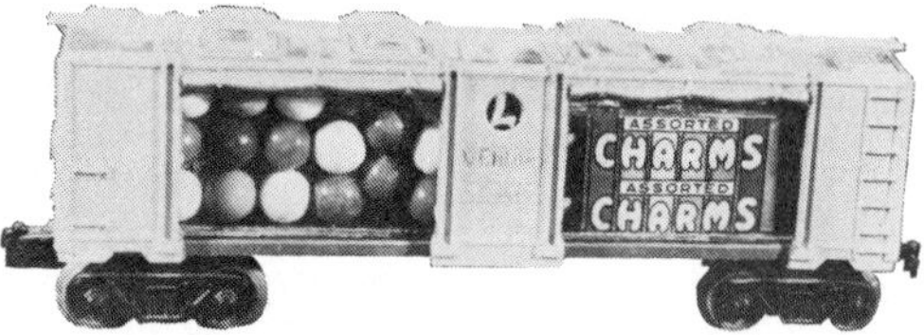

Car used for rolling bank and acquarium was also suggested as an actual candy carrier.

Proposed transformer would have had a lever for each of four trains plus speedometers.

Oversized conveyor belt was considered for loading and unloading crates.

Tank car body on trestles could have made inexpensive oil storage tank.

A bobbing giraffe car was actually made, but it had one giraffe, not two.

BETWEEN STATIONS

TRAINS NEVER MADE

Lionel manufactured a dazzling variety of trains and accessories. But still more were contemplated but never produced. A billboard whose message changed as a train passed, a device for turning hopper cars upside down to unload them, and an animated track repair gang were proposed but never released.

Prototypes for these and other hypothetical Lionels were constructed, sometimes of cardboard, sometimes by modifying actual cars. Many of the models still exist.

Spring-wound helicopter from Lionel flatcar was tried on a child's push-toy.

Flatcar with man apparently spraying track-side weeds or fires never left the factory.

Popular self-reversing gang car had an experimental load of a missile from Lionel's space trains.

5

SIDETRACKED

1930-1944

The thirties and early forties were as tumultuous for Cowen and Lionel as they were for the rest of the country. As the period began, Cowen found himself in the middle of a front-page bank scandal; as it ended, he was basking in the praises of a United States senator for his company's war effort. Lionel converted entirely to the production of military hardware during World War II, emulating locomotive manufacturers like Baldwin and Alco, who added gun mounts and howitzers to their own assembly lines. And like all its big brothers, including the Pennsylvania, New York Central, and Union Pacific, Lionel got through the war by relying more heavily than ever before on women workers. From the growth of the labor movement (Lionel unionized during the war) to Walt Disney (Mickey, Pluto, and Donald rode Lionel trains in the thirties), Lionel reflected America.

The crash of the stock market and the beginning of the Depression had an immediate and devastating effect on Lionel. From 1929 to 1930, sales declined from $2,278,000 to $1,932,000 and net profits dropped even more sharply, from $363,700 to $82,000. Though times were troubled, Lawrence went ahead with his Wall Street career, forming the brokerage firm of Cowen, Stark & Company. Lionel, too, heedless of the state of the economy, brought out elaborate products whose dies had been cast in Italy before most families' toy budgets were diverted to necessities like food.

The greatest steam locomotive the company ever produced came out as the Depression worsened: the standard gauge 400E, a two-and-a-half-foot-long monster steamer with red-spoked wheels and copper trim. To promote the 400E, Cowen hired Robert E. Butterfield, one of the actual engineers on *The Twentieth Century Limited*. Butterfield was already known to the public through the efforts of the New York Central's publicity department, but when Cowen put him on the cover of the 1931

Lionel conductor for store window displays stood almost four feet high. A battery-powered motor swung his arm and lantern back and forth.

JOHN WEIS

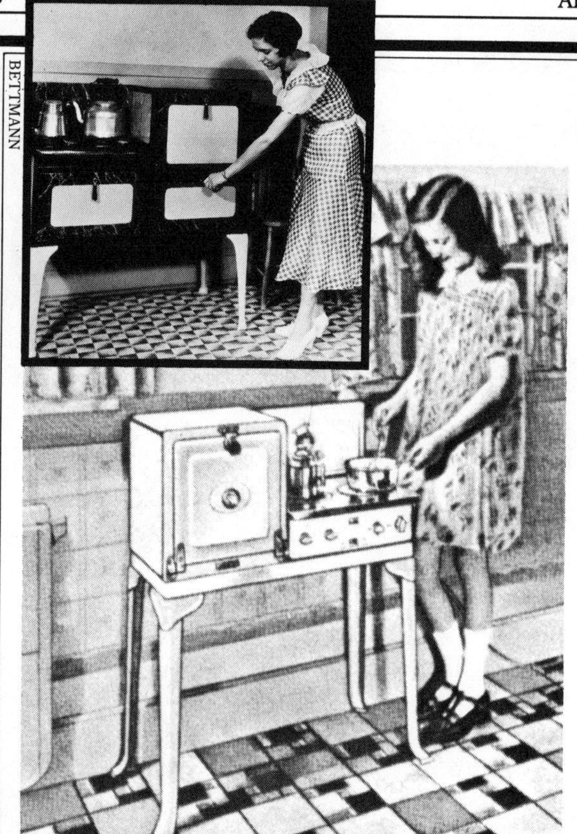

Lionel's stove was an accurate model of a real gas range of the period (inset).

ON THE BACK BURNER

In 1930, Lionel introduced its second product that wasn't a train (the first was its racing cars), which was also the first Lionel aimed at girls: a "real electric range." The stove had an oven with a built-in thermometer and two electric burners that actually worked. But at $29.50, the porcelain-finished range actually cost more than a real electric sewing machine or vacuum cleaner and about the same as a gas stove at Depression prices; in fact, the Lionel stove cost more than a teacher made in a week.

The stove occupied the entire back cover of the catalog, indicative of the importance Lionel placed on trying to reach the female market. On the other hand, coming after forty-seven pages of magnificent, powerful trains, it had something of the air of a booby prize.

Cowen brought one home for his granddaughter, Cynthia, but not many other girls got to bake biscuits in the oven. The stove was overdesigned and was far too expensive for the Depression market.

Lionel catalog, his immortality was assured. Butterfield was painted in front of the massive, six-foot driving wheels of his own Hudson locomotive, which pulled *The Twentieth Century.* His two grandsons, Richard and Robert III, stood beside him holding a 400E.

Despite this magnificent engine, plus a new station based on Grand Central Terminal, nonderailing switches, and other railroading accessories, Lionel suffered its first losing year in 1931, going into the red by $207,000. This was partly due to the quality of the line, priced high by Depression standards. At $42.50, the 400E cost as much as a three-piece bedroom set and, incredibly, only slightly less than a two-year-old Ford. Not many people were buying toy trains at those prices.

Cowen, may have been somewhat out of touch with these economic facts of life. Although he took a ten-thousand-dollar cut in salary, at fifty thousand dollars he was still making about six times as much as a United States Congressman and ten times the income of a doctor or lawyer. *He* could certainly afford a 400E, even if no one else could.

But the harsh realities of the Depression soon overtook Cowen himself. His salary dropped month by month until he and Mario Caruso were making the same amount—$12,750. And he also found himself embroiled in a financial scandal from which he barely escaped with his reputation.

The Bank of United States had been founded in Cowen's offices in 1913 by Cowen's brother-in-law, Joseph Marcus. Cowen himself was one of the directors. In December 1930, the bank failed. Cowen barely avoided being indicted along with several other directors and his nephew, Bernard Marcus, president of the bank. As it was, he was sued by the State Superintendent of Banks and forced to make restitution of almost $1 million.

Cowen testified that he had neither scrutinized the millions of dollars in unsecured personal loans the bank had made nor been aware of the manipulations of the bank's stock because he had relied on the judgment of Bernard Marcus. (Ironically, Marcus was the uncle of Roy Cohn, who thirty years later was to buy out Cowen and almost ruin Lionel.) Further testimony, reported verbatim in *The Evening Post,* indicated that Cowen had also invested $200,000 in a syndicate for trading the bank's stock and was never informed by Marcus that the syndi-

In 1930, Lionel came out with a new passenger train, *The Blue Comet,* based on the Central of New Jersey Railroad's train of the same name, which ran from New York to Atlantic City. The Lionel standard gauge *Blue Comet* cars were named after actual comets, just as the coaches were on the real train. Lionel's three were *Faye, Westphal,* and *Temple.* Lionel's *Blue Comet* was painted in two tones of royal blue with cream-colored window frames, although the real *Comet* was dark blue with black roofs.

After the *Transcontinental Limited* (State Set), *The Blue Comet* was the most elaborate passenger train Lionel made in its legendary standard gauge period. It was pulled by the massive 400E steamer in its own two-tone blue livery. The actual *Blue Comet* did not compare to such famous real trains as *The Twentieth Century* or *The Broadway Limited.* It made a short run down the Jersey coast to the then-fashionable resort of Atlantic City. Because the entire trip was only a few hours, *The Blue Comet* had only coach cars and no overnight Pullmans. However, Cowen was one of its frequent passengers, as he enjoyed the seaside resort city. It was surely because of his patronage that *The Blue Comet* was immortalized by Lionel.

SARASOTA LIONEL MUSEUM

The 400E (left) *paces* The Blue Comet *down the mainline. Trailing is Lionel's smaller standard gauge passenger train,* The Broadway Limited, *and its green Stephen Girard cars. Track on Sarasota Lionel Museum layout is handmade with third rail on one side for realism.*

cate had disbanded and his money was gone. Luckily for Lionel, Cowen was much too vital a man to contemplate the course chosen by twenty thousand other failed businessmen that year who committed suicide.

It must have been a great advantage to Cowen to have had a "friendly" bank, and perhaps he didn't look too closely at how it was being run. The toy business was very seasonal; manufacturers had to borrow money in the early part of the year to produce goods that would not bring in income until the last quarter. Toy makers were on a perpetual treadmill of borrowing and repaying, and Lionel suffered more than most because trains sold so heavily in December, in time for Christmas. When the bank failed, it emerged that Cowen had an outstanding loan of $500,000 unsecured by any collateral.

The case dragged on for three years. During this time Cowen repaid $850,000 in loans he had both made to himself and guaranteed for others. He put up an interest in Lionel and his $500,000 life insurance policy to make good on his share of the bank stock he held. All this was in addition to $700,000 he testified he lost through Marcus's manipulations. (The amount of restitution Cowen was able to make was an indication of how truly wealthy he had become as a result not only of Lionel's success but of his own investments in the stock market.) Finally, in 1934, Cowen paid a $5,000 penalty and was dropped from the $60-million suit brought by the State Superintendent of Banks against the directors.

Assortment of boxed O-gauge freight cars cost nine dollars.

Both Cowen's and the company's financial security were severely shaken by the Bank of United States scandal and settlement. But despite the deepening Depression and the continuing decline of train sales, Lionel kept producing top-of-the-line merchandise. In the real world, destitute veterans calling themselves the Bonus Expeditionary Force might march on Washington, but in Lionel Land it was clear that "what every boy needs [is] a roundhouse and weighing scale."

Cheaper trains were manufactured, although Cowen did not deign to put the Lionel name on them. The Ives Company, now controlled by Lionel, produced inexpensive wind-up trains. Lionel itself established a company named Winner to front a line of cheap O-gauge electric

Lionel's weighing scale (below) *actually weighed freight cars with tiny brass weights in an illuminated shed. It was based on a real railroad scale on the right that handled three and a half cars a minute.*

AAR

COWEN TESTIFIES IN BANK CLOSING

Joshua Lionel Cowen

Joshua L. Cowen, uncle of Bernard K. Marcus, took the witness stand and was questioned by Max D. Steuer (Assistant Attorney General) at the opening of the hearing.

Q. When did you become connected with the Bank of United States?

A. It was organized in my office....

Q. Did you ever borrow money from the bank?

A. Yes. In January, 1929, I borrowed $625,000, repaid $300,000 before May of that same year and later increased my indebtedness to $500,000.

Q. Did you give any security?

A. No. I offered it... but Mr. Marcus wouldn't take it.

Q. Are you related to Mr. Marcus?

A. Yes, he is my sister's son.

Q. Did you owe the bank in one name only?

A. Yes. Of course, I endorsed notes for my corporation.

Q. For what corporation and what loans?

A. I endorsed one note for $175,000 for the Lawrio Real Estate Corporation, a subsidiary of the Lionel Electric Train Company....

Q. Did you endorse notes for anyone else?

A. I endorsed a note for $100,000 for Mandel Frankel....

Q. ...Then came the formation of Bankus, which began to trade in bank units. Now when did you go into that syndicate?

A. Oh, that syndicate, I should say in 1927.

Q. But Mr. Cowen, there weren't any bank units then. Now I'm assuming that you are making an honest mistake. Will you try to remember just what the facts are?

A. Well, I was not a member of any syndicate formed to trade in City Financial stock.

Q. Were you a member of a syndicate which dealt in units, and if so what was your participation?

A. Yes, I was a member. I had an interest of $200,000 in cash, which was an eight percent participation.

Q.Have you paid your indebtedness on the syndicate debt?

A. No.

Q. But the syndicate disbanded in 1929.

A. I didn't know that. I was never informed.

Q. You mean to say that you hadn't heard that the syndicate stopped trading and the accountants had rendered their report?

A. No....

Q. Did you ever know that the bank examiner examined the bank in July, 1929?

A. No.

Q. Now, this is quite important. Were you never informed?

A. I don't think I ever was.

Q. Are you aware, Mr. Cowen, that when you became a director you took an oath to do your duty as a director?

A. I don't know.

Q. Well, I can tell you that you did.... Now in 1929, what did you do to inform yourself of the condition of the City Financial Corporation?

A. Not anything.

Q. In 1930?

A. Nothing....

Q. Well, what was the first you knew of this bank condition?

A. When I read it in the newspapers.

—*The Evening Post*
February 16, 1931

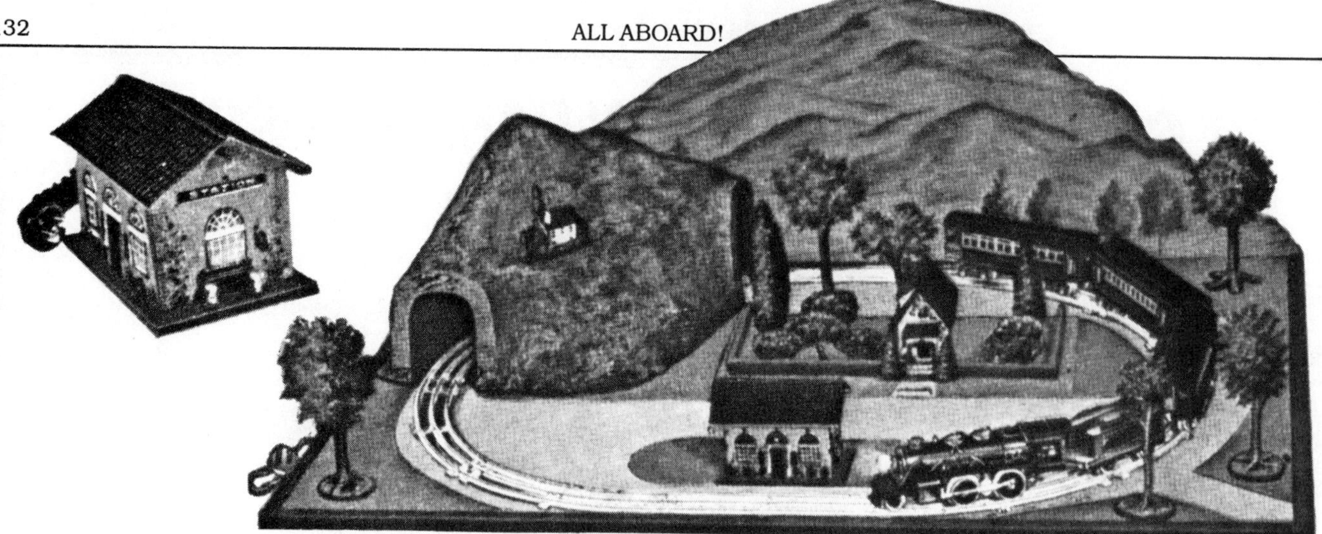

Lionel Jr. electric trains included transformer in a station. Landscaped layout slid under bed for storage.

trains using the Ives cars. "And Now! A Real Electric Train For Little Brother," announced the orange Winner flyer, which carried no hint of the prestigious (and higher-priced) Lionel name. For $3.25 the financially strapped family could have a three-car train, a circle of track, and a transformer cleverly housed inside a small, lithographed station that bore the name *Winner R. R. Co.* A completely landscaped railroad with curved tunnel, houses, and trees could be bought assembled for $11.75. But in 1932, Lionel's second consecutive losing year (the company lost $209,000), the line was dropped.

Cowen's enthusiasm was never behind Winner, and the trains were not included in the Lionel catalog. The line was too much of a compromise for a man who hated compromises in anything, least of all in the quality of his trains. (Sometimes Cowen had to be more flexible: The 400E steamer could not have negotiated Lionel curves if it had had a third set of driving wheels. But on other points he was adamant. He once yanked a line of freight cars off the assembly line because they had only one brake wheel instead of two.) Still, the Depression made compromise inevitable. The next year Winner trains were back as the Lionel Jr. line, and even wind-up trains were in the catalog.

Lionel Land had always been a refuge from the real world, where boys could be men and men could be boys. It was a fantasy universe; reality only intruded in the form of a copy of the newest locomotive or signal bridge. But as the thirties went their terrible way it became more difficult to keep the two separate. By 1933, unemployment was up 25 percent over 1929 and industrial production was half of what it had been before the crash. Between the economy and his own financial problems, Cowen had all he could do to keep Lionel going. In January 1933, Lionel's board of directors dissolved the faltering Ives toy company, all patents and trademarks becoming the property of Lionel. The upstart Cowen could take grim pleasure in his triumph. In his typical fashion, Cowen later claimed he took the Ives dies and hurled them into the Connecticut River. But, as the dies were valuable as scrap metal—weighing hundreds if not thousands of pounds—this was probably just typical huff and puff on Cowen's part.

Production of tools and dies in Mussolini's Italy became both too difficult and too expensive. Mussolini thought Lionel trains were fantastic and wanted to put them in every school in Italy, but he also demanded that La Precisa produce carnival glass and military goods. Labor was much cheaper in the United States during the Depression, anyway (wages were down 60 percent from 1929), and it was no longer necessary to maintain the Naples operation. Cowen and Caruso reached an agreement by which Caruso bought La Precisa from Lionel for $110,000. Caruso then moved back to New Jersey and continued to work for Lionel. Eventually his son became president of La Precisa, while Lawrence Cowen became president of Lionel.

The world of bread lines and apple peddlers intruded even more directly into Lionel's catalog. To save money, sixteen pages of the 1933 catalog were printed in black (actually dark green) and white. Sprinkled among the toy trains was the image of the blue eagle, symbol of Franklin Roosevelt's National Recovery Administration. The NRA regulated wages, working hours, and, by extension, prices.

COWEN AS REMEMBERED BY . . .
HIS COMPTROLLER

Edward Zier came to Lionel in 1931 as a temporary auditor from Price, Waterhouse. He found the company's books in disarray. "Their accounting was horrible and I put in some better systems," Zier remembers. "Cowen didn't like me too much to start with. I mean, here's a guy coming in and changing his world around. But he quickly saw the benefits. 'Christ, this was like having an automobile and not knowing how to use it,' he said. 'You want a job here?' "

Zier says Cowen was vain about his age and "covered it up." He also remembers Cowen wearing a hat in the office to hide his baldness, although in fact Cowen appears hatless in almost all photos of him. Zier does agree, however, with everyone who knew Cowen that he had impeccable taste: "It was impossible to buy a present for him. You couldn't match his taste in ties. I once got him a pair of gold cufflinks. They were expensive for me and he said he loved them, but a week later he brought them back to the store. Larry said Cowen once received twenty-nine Christmas presents and returned twenty-eight of them."

Cowen himself gave elaborate presents. Zier received several gold watches and even some gold golf tees and collar stays from him. Cowen personally chose Christmas presents for Lionel's major customers, giving them wallets from Cartier and silver cigarette lighters and crystal from Tiffany's. "Once I looked into the stockroom and there he was wrapping presents with the office girls," Zier recalls. " 'Christ, you must be the most expensive office boy in the country,' I told him. He didn't like that, and was angry at me for a while."

But Cowen rarely stayed angry for long, especially if the Yankees were in town. "Hey, what are we doing in here? It's a great day out. Let's go up to the Stadium," Cowen would say to Zier and the other executives. Zier remembers the occasions with mixed feelings. They were joyful outings, but Cowen's propensity for betting on every pitch made concentrating on the game difficult.

Above all, Zier remembers Cowen as a father figure. "I used to call him Pop, especially in the later years," Zier says. "Many employees felt he was like their father. If someone were ill, he sent his own doctors over and paid the bill. One of the girls had a nephew with a bad heart. Cowen paid for the entire treatment. If there were a family emergency, he'd grab the bill himself."

Lionel crew in the mid-fifties. Seated, left to right: *Edward Zier, Joseph Bonanno, Cowen, Charles Giaimo, John Giampolo (assistant superintendent for production).* Standing: *Tom Pagano, Philip Marfuggi (industrial relations director), Lawrence Cowen, Alan Ginsburg (vice president for sales), Sam Belser (sales manager), Frank Pettit.*

ELIZABETH BONANNO

Trying to reach a wider market, Lionel offered wind-up speedboats during the Depression. The boats were each $3.50 and—according to the catalog—ran for four minutes on one winding.

One page in the catalog epitomized the struggle Lionel had maintaining the illusions of Lionel Land in the face of the Depression. Across the top of the page was the headline, "The Fun Of Building A Lionel Model Railroad," with a picture of a spotless, perfect, poverty-free Lionel village. But in large type across the bottom of the page was the notice, "Prices in this catalog are subject to change if necessitated by operation of the National Industrial Recovery Acts." It must have galled Cowen, a staunch Republican, to have had to subject his trains to that alphabet of regulatory agencies set up by Roosevelt. But it must have upset him even more to have read Lionel's profit and loss statement. Despite the introduction of both a self-steering boat and something called a chugger to give a *choo-choo* sound to steam engines, Lionel lost over $200,000 for the third year in a row. In December, things were so bad the company had to borrow on the life insurance policies of Cowen and Caruso.

In the spring of 1934 Lionel was unable to secure the short-term bank loans it needed to produce its trains for the year. The company owed $296,000 and had only $62,000 in liquid assets to cover its debts. Sales had declined every year since 1927 and the company had made no money since 1930. The Lionel name was still magic to children, but it was not as palatable to bankers, especially with Cowen's involvement in the Bank of United States debacle. The company had tremendous assets in its plant and machinery and in its business name, but it was on the verge of going under for want of operating capital.

On May 7, with the only alternative being to sell off a piece of the company, which he didn't want to do, Cowen put Lionel in what was described as a "friendly" equity receivership. This meant the company would be overseen by receivers appointed by a federal judge in Newark, New Jersey. Cowen and Caruso would still run Lionel but the receivers, acting for the court, would approve all financial decisions. The receivership allowed Lionel to postpone paying its debts and to secure capital to manufacture the 1934 line.

Both receivers were acquaintances of Cowen's. Mandel Frankel, a director and secretary of Lionel, had received a hundred-thousand-dollar loan from the Bank of United States that

Cowen had signed for. In the 1930 catalog, which used code names to identify the sets so dealers could order them without confusion, one of the inexpensive O-gauge sets was code-named Frankel. The other receiver, Worcester Bouck, was associated first with a bank in Syracuse, New York, and then with Chase Manhattan, where Lionel later opened an account. Bouck eventually became vice president and comptroller of Lionel.

The receivership gave Lionel the capital with which to produce its trains, and, as happened so often, it was the railroads themselves that provided the inspiration (and the blueprints) for the models that took Lionel out of receivership and back into the profit column. Like Lionel, the real railroads were in trouble in the mid-thirties. Their glorious supremacy was being challenged by an expanding highway system. Passenger traffic was slipping away from them, diverted to cars and buses and the high speed excitement of the growing commercial aviation industry. The railroads needed something new to bring them back to the forefront of the country's consciousness. And that something was streamlining.

New trends in architecture and industrial design, lightweight metals, and diesel engines that did not need their machinery exposed for the complicated servicing required by steam locomotives made for a new, streamlined look in railroad trains. While Cowen was grappling with the financial problems besetting Lionel, chief engineer Joseph Bonanno was meeting with the Union Pacific to copy its new streamliner. The M-10,000, eventually known as the *City of Salina,* was unveiled by Pullman (who had built it) and the Union Pacific on February 12, 1934. It went on a sixty-eight-city publicity tour and was then displayed at the Chicago Century of Progress Exposition. Crowds lined the right-of-way to cheer it on, a shiny yellow and brown dart of hope in the gloom of the Depression.

Streamlining gripped the railroads. In April, the Chicago, Burlington and Quincy Railroad produced its gleaming Burlington *Zephyr* and sent it on a publicity tour. And in October the Union Pacific unleashed the M-10,001, the *City of Portland,* on a coast-to-coast speed run. The newspapers charted its progress from Los Angeles: "Streamline Train Eleven Hours Ahead of the Regular Time in Cheyenne;" "Expected To Do Even Better on the Plain of Nebraska;" "Hits Speed of 120 M.P.H." The Los Angeles-Chicago run was a record-smashing thirty-nine hours. Chicago to New York was more sedate, in deference to the New York Central's *Twentieth Century Limited,* shaming that train by only twenty minutes. (To put the Western pretender to the throne in its place, the New York Central pointed out that city ordinances forbade steam or diesel engines from entering New York under their own power, so the *City of Portland* had to suffer the ignominy of being towed into Grand Central Terminal. Put on display, it attracted 58,000 people.)

The Lionel factory was busy shrinking the steamliner down to one forty-fifth actual size. The Union Pacific train would have been too big and expensive in standard gauge, so it was produced in O-gauge. (O-gauge was the coming thing, a more democratic gauge for a middle class whose homes and incomes were not up to standard gauge.) The fact that the Union Pacific was on the cover of the 1934 catalog was indicative of the primacy O-gauge was assuming; standard was manufactured for another five years, but it never again appeared on the catalog cover. The Depression had put an end to the rich boy's gauge.

"The wonder-train that races to the Pacific Coast at the uncanny speed of 110 miles an

A LIONEL TRAIN

BY W. LARUE SCOTT

Through the tunnels and over the bridge,
Those sturdy cars and engines rush;
Over the valley and into the station,
Every car in correct formation.

The bells are ringing,
The gates go down;
And the train rushes off without a sound.

Around the curves it goes without screeches,
'Til soon the mountain top it reaches.
The brakes are loosened,
The train coasts down,
And soon it rolls into Lionel town.
Then on to another track it switches
And on to another engine it hitches.

Then away they go,
We all now see.
United they reach the Lionel factory.

—*Lionel Magazine*
March-April, 1932

LIONEL GOES STREAMLINED

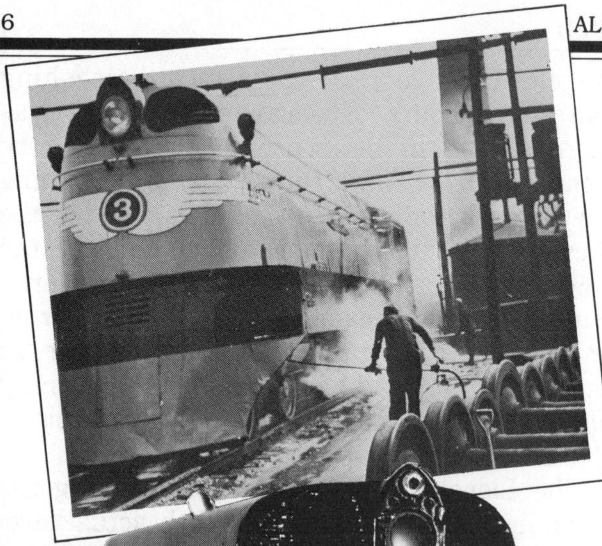

The real railroads had nothing on Lionel when it came to streamlining in the mid-thirties. Whether steam (like the *Hiawatha* or *Commodore Vanderbilt*) or diesel (like the *City of Portland*), Lionel seemed to have the railroads' newest blueprints as soon as their own engineering departments drafted them. Few streamlined engines ran on America's right-of-way that didn't also run in miniature on Lionel Lines.

CARSTENS PUBLICATIONS

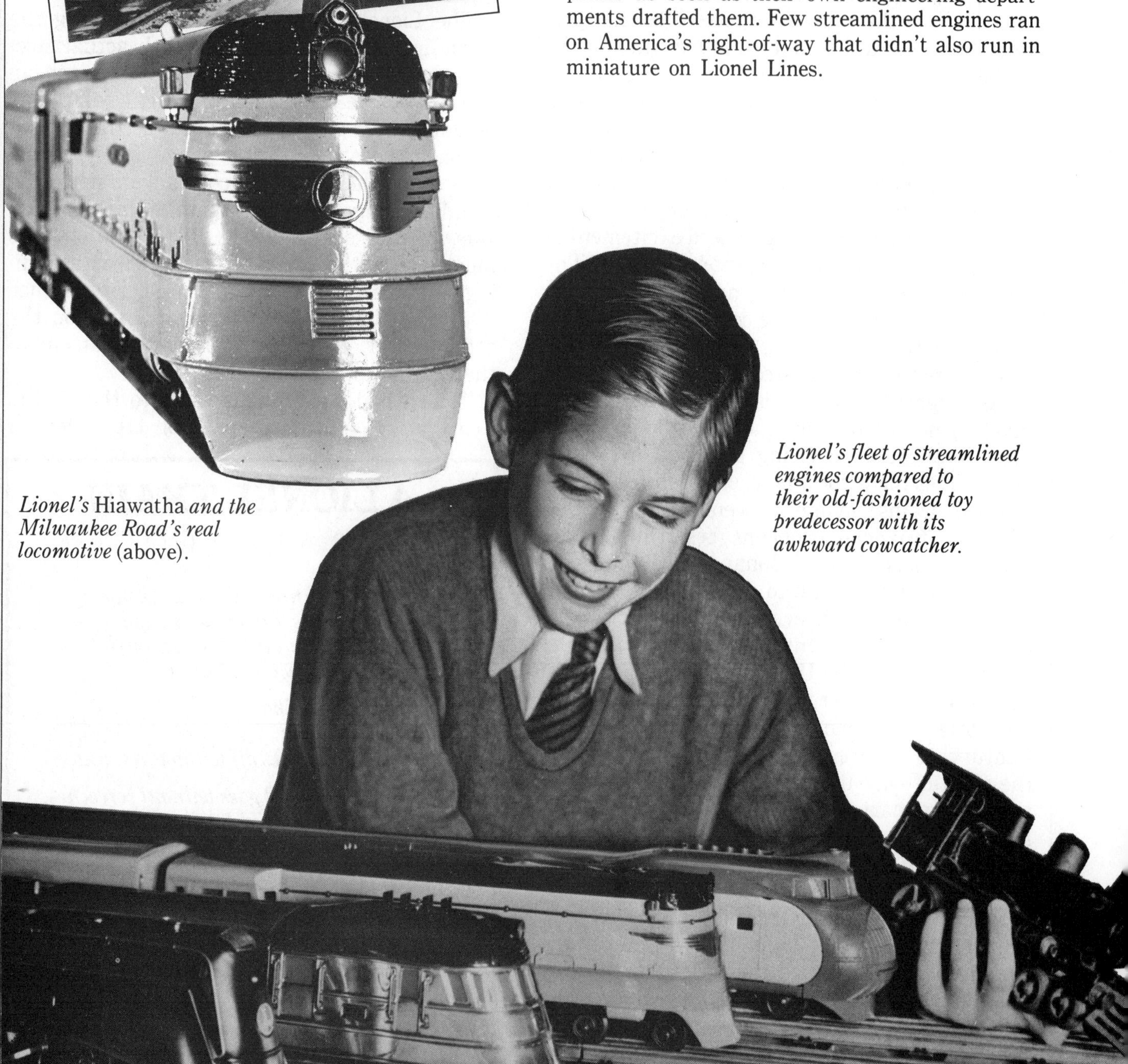

Lionel's Hiawatha *and the Milwaukee Road's real locomotive* (above).

Lionel's fleet of streamlined engines compared to their old-fashioned toy predecessor with its awkward cowcatcher.

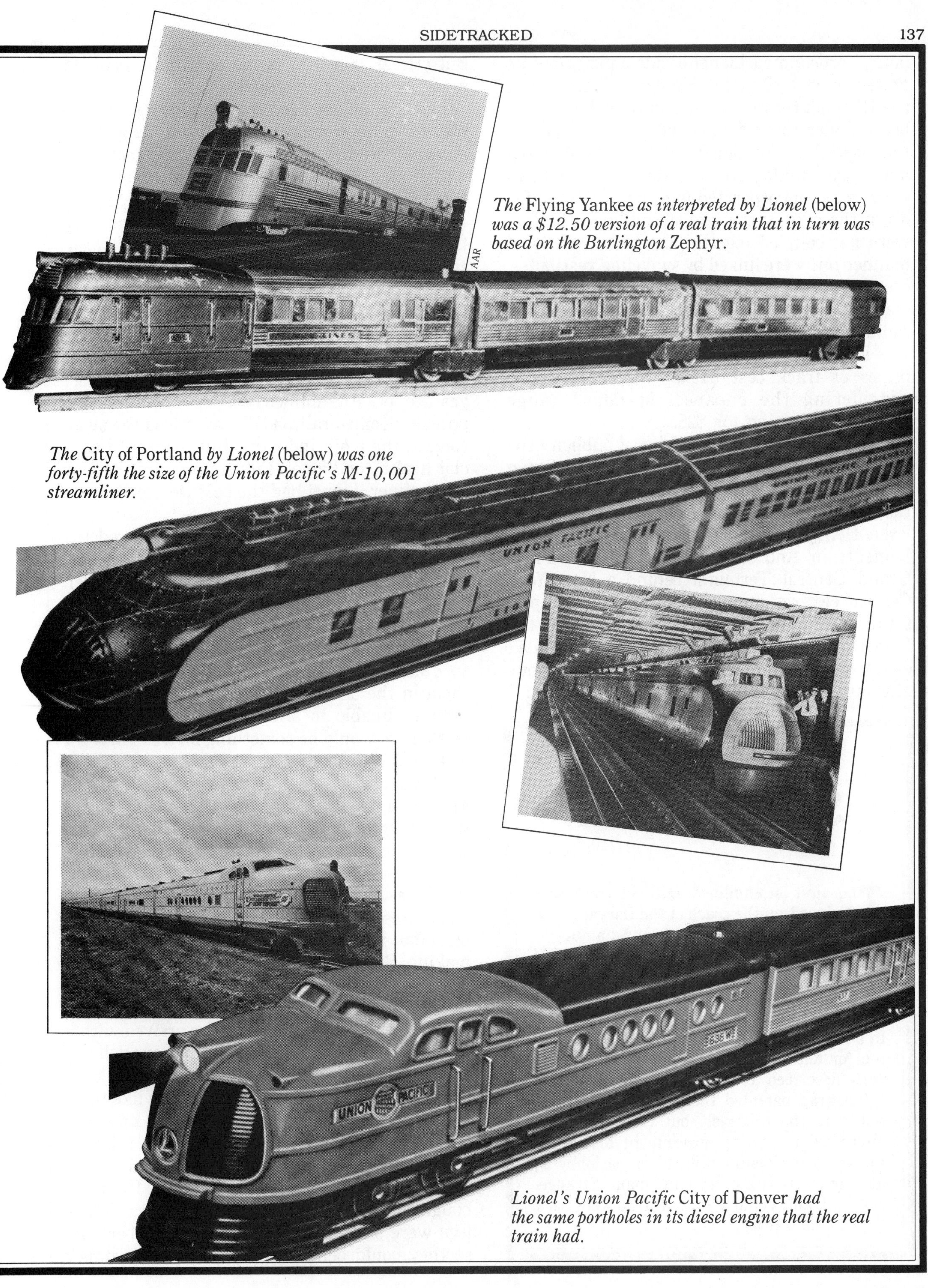

The Flying Yankee *as interpreted by Lionel* (below) *was a $12.50 version of a real train that in turn was based on the Burlington* Zephyr.

The City of Portland *by Lionel* (below) *was one forty-fifth the size of the Union Pacific's M-10,001 streamliner.*

Lionel's Union Pacific City of Denver *had the same portholes in its diesel engine that the real train had.*

hour," proclaimed Lionel beside a picture of its newest model. (The catalog was printed before the 120 mph record was set; for once, Lionel was being understated in its catalog copy). "This is the masterpiece of Lionel's engineers and craftsmen," the catalog crowed. Many new features were in fact incorporated into the Union Pacific. As in the case of the real streamliner, the cars were not coupled together in the conventional manner but were linked by swiveling vestibules, creating the impression of a sleek, one-piece train. The cars were too long for Lionel's sharp-radius curves, so new track with wider curves was introduced. The three-car train and twenty pieces of track cost $19.50, quite reasonable considering the cheapest standard gauge steamer was going for $25.

Lionel profited from every bit of publicity the Union Pacific Railroad received that fall. When the M-10,000 went on display in Chicago, Lionel's model was in a glass case beside it. Even Henry Ford praised the accuracy of the Lionel train. And when the M-10,001 glided into Grand Central Terminal behind a New York Central electric engine, Robert Butterfield presented the Union Pacific engineers with the Lionel model of their train. "From one railroad engineer to another, in commemoration of your glorious record-breaking cross-country run," Butterfield said over a national radio hook-up while newsreel cameras rolled.

Lionel supplemented this publicity with articles in its own magazine reaching "Lionel Engineers" around the country. The streamliner was touted as being the "train of tomorrow." But even Lionel knew what the real vehicle of tomorrow was. "Just think of it. A railroad train that travels as fast as an airship!" *Lionel Magazine* gushed, calling the Union Pacific's engineers "pilots." (Indeed, at the end-of-run ceremonies, the engineers wore ties and white mechanics' smocks that made them look more like doctors than fearless railroad men.) What *The New York Times* editorially called "one more gesture of streamlined defiance by the supposedly doomed railroads" was indeed the swan song of the train industry. But it meant financial health for Lionel. First to produce the new streamliner, Lionel had the best December in its history.

Lionel was also aided by two small rodents whose pluckiness set an example for Americans, helping them to forget their own troubles. When Lionel put Mickey and Minnie Mouse on a wind-up handcar and sold them with a circle of track for a dollar in the fall of 1934—producing them so quickly that there was no time to include them in the catalog—they were snapped up by families unable to afford an electric train. At least there would be something on track in front of the Christmas tree that year.

There are at least two stories of how the Mickey Mouse handcar came to be. According to what Worcester Bouck told the federal judge who eventually discharged Lionel's receivership, Bouck designed the car on the eve of the Christmas season. But a conflicting account came from Joseph Bonanno. Lionel's customers took a personal interest in what the company was making, Bonanno said, and often sent in suggestions and even models of new train ideas. Bonanno was at the factory one day in the summer of 1934 when a package arrived with a model of a handcar pumped by a Popeye doll. "It was huge," Bonanno said. "About a foot long. What are you going to do with a thing like that? You can't sell such a big thing. I picked up one of our wind-up trains and I said, 'This is the way we can use it.' That evening when I went home I stopped at a stationary store in Forest Hills and bought some Mickey and Minnie figures. Their legs were stiff, and we substituted rubber rods so they could bend up and down on a smaller

THE FIRST STREAMLINER

The first streamlined railroad train was designed by the coach of the Harvard rowing team in 1865. The Reverend Samuel R. Cathtrap was watching his team practice when it struck him that racing shells—like other boats—were long and tapered but that land vehicles were flat-nosed. He set to work. In a few months, he developed what he called the Air Resistor, which he somewhat irreverently described as a miracle train.

Cathtrap patented the design and tried to sell it to the railroads, but they were only interested in getting government money for the transcontinental railroad or on lobbying for contracts to carry the mail. Strange-looking trains could wait. Cathtrap went back to coaching crew.

DISNEY IN LIONEL LAND

The combination of Disney and Lionel was a natural. But Cowen, ever the inspired merchandiser, improved even on Mickey Mouse. Not content merely to have him and Minnie on a handcar, Cowen used Mickey on a wind-up train and created an entire circus set around him that sold for only two dollars. He put Mickey in Santa's bag, put Santa on his own handcar, and marketed that for one dollar. And to help stores sell the Lionel handcars, Cowen created three-foot-high animated cutouts of Mickey and Donald Duck powered by a single flashlight battery. They stood in the windows, pointing to Lionel's handcars at their feet.

Mickey and Minnie pumped Lionel into the head lines in 1934.

As Donald worked the handcar, quacking away, Pluto's head bobbed up and down.

EASTERN DIVISION, TCA

Cowen's proposed Mickey Mouse circus train outfit, as submitted to the Design Registration Bureau, was actually produced in 1935 as a paper tent with a wind-up train.

SELLING LIONEL

Gentlemen: You have been selected as Lionel demonstrators because in our opinion you correctly represent what we at Lionel believe to be our ideals. The Lionel Corporation, over a period of years, has assumed the proportions of a guild. We are not merely manufacturers of electric trains; we are, instead, specialists in bringing to a boy the realization of the enormous degree of fun and education to be found in Lionel Electric Trains....

"The successful store salesman has acquired the priceless knack of including with a nod or a smile the several other customers who may be awaiting his attention at the counter. Therefore, under no circumstances exclude from your attention people other than the one to whom you are talking. Let them know that you are well aware of the fact that they are waiting for you and that you are at the point of waiting on them....

"In all walks of life, a man is judged by his neat appearance, by the cleanliness of his collar, by the careful brushing of his clothes and polishing of his shoes. At an electric train counter, the salesman in charge is judged by the appearance of his counter. Nothing so mars an electric train layout as a frowsy display, with casual cars across the track, and accessories lying on their sides, with an appearance of carelessness and disinterest....

"There must be one, or several, trains in operation at all times. Bells must ring, gates must fall, whistles should be blown frequently, a railroad must be in evidence to attract the passerby.... Stretch the train out to its full length; the couplers must be connected, and the train must always be shown standing on track. Never stand electric trains on a step fixture unless they are on the track; otherwise, the cars are out of line, and the entire train set appears at its very worst....

"We are printing 1,000,000 four-color catalogs, an absolutely unprecedented quantity in this industry. There will be ample catalogs at your counter if you distribute them intelligently and selectively. You must learn, without giving offense to anybody, to distinguish between the person—whether a boy or a grownup—who wants a Lionel catalog either to cut out the pictures or because he happens to be a collector of catalogs, and the person who is really a prospective customer and desires to make a selection of Lionel trains. Make every catalog count....

"Every day while you are behind a Lionel counter, please remember that you represent the Lionel Corporation.... You are the man who can crystallize at the point of sale a feeling of friendship for the Lionel Corporation if you handle your task properly.... When customers talk to you, are they going to say to themselves, 'This top-notch organization is represented by an intelligent, helpful, courteous man'?"

—*An Address to Lionel Demonstrators,* 1939

JEAN BASECQ/ALAIN DEBORSU

Cardboard store display showed Lionel's major accessories—roundhouse, Hellgate bridge, and power station (missing its chimneys)—and left room for two train sets.

WILLIAM K. WALTHERS

Toy train trade show in New York in February 1938 had Lionel booth at left displaying Hiawatha, City of Portland, *and other engines.*

handcar. We made up a sample and the New York people came to the factory to see it. Worcester Bouck thought it was cute. Mr. Cowen said he could sell a hundred thousand to Macy's alone."

Conflicting claims of who was first with a new Lionel invention were not unusual, especially in the engineering department. Regardless of who did create the handcar, Lionel sold 253,000 of them that fall, turning down orders for another 100,000 because there wasn't time to get them out. Everyone wanted a Mickey Mouse car for Christmas, even ten-year-old King Ananda of Siam, who played with his on his knees on the palace floor. Lionel entered into a licensing agreement with Walt Disney that was extended in the next few years to include Donald Duck and Pluto on their own wind-up car. (Mickey graced some sixty toys in those years, including the two million Ingersoll watches that helped pull that company out of financial difficulty.)

The wild popularity of the Mickey Mouse handcar drew attention to Lionel's more profitable trains. (Included with every handcar was a brochure describing the rest of Lionel's line.) This enabled the company to finish in the black for the first time in four years. Lionel's 469 creditors were paid the $296,000 owed them. Bouck received a $20,000 fee for his services, while Frankel got $7,500. And Lionel was able to report a net profit for the year of $29,600. On January 21, 1935, the receivership was discharged and the company was turned over to Cowen and the board of directors.

A federal judge with the unfortunate name of Guy L. Fake congratulated Bouck and Frankel on the "successful operation of the company and placing it back on its feet. There is no case that I remember where more success was met with than in this case."

Bouck credited the Mickey Mouse handcar with saving Lionel, and the story was picked up with glee by newspapers and radio commentators hungry for happy financial news. "Little mouse saves big lion of a corporation" was the tone of most of them. Lowell Thomas commented on the fairy tale quality of Lionel's successful journey on the little wind-up railroad of Mickey and Minnie, bravely pumping around their circle of track. There was irony in the world's greatest electric train company being saved from extinction by a turn-of-the-century wind-up train. But the greatest irony was that

BLOWING THE WHISTLE

A separate controller worked the whistle.

Lionel's whistle hauntingly faded off at the end of its call, just like the real thing. When a short wave radio operator's son sounded his whistle while his father was talking on the radio, the person on the other end swore they lived by railroad tracks. While the whistle chamber was originally made of metal, plastic was later substituted, but the authenticity of the sound remained.

OFFICIAL WHISTLE SIGNALS

● means a short blast, – a long blast.

●	Apply brakes. Stop.
– –	Release brakes. Proceed.
– ● ● ●	Flagman go back and protect rear of train.
– – – –	Flagman return from west or south.
– – – – –	Flagman return from east or north.
– – –	Train in motion has parted.
● ●	Answer to any signal not otherwise provided for.
● ● ●	When train is standing, back.
● ● ● ●	Call for signals.
– – ● ●	Approaching highway crossing at grade.
———	Approaching stations, junctions and railroad crossings at grade.
– – ●	Approaching meeting point of trains, on a single-track road.

A succession of short blasts is an alarm for persons or live stock on the track.

LOU REDMAN

the story wasn't true. There was simply not enough profit margin in a one-dollar toy to have brought Lionel the income needed to save the company. (One dollar was the retail price. Lionel sold the handcars for closer to sixty cents apiece, and the cost of labor and materials plus Disney's percentage had to be deducted before computing profit.) No doubt Mickey's publicity helped greatly, but it was the Union Pacific followed by the rest of the electric train line that put Cowen behind the throttle once more.

With a new head of steam, rid of the demoralizing effects of the receivership and the bank scandal (settled the same year), Cowen and Lionel roared into the second half of the decade. New trains and inventions poured from the Irvington factory. If 1934 had been the year of the streamliner, then 1935 was the year of the whistle. With Lionel engineers vying to create the most realistic and exciting devices, the appearance of an authentic-sounding steam whistle was a signal event. To be able to reverse a locomotive automatically without having to touch it was good. To throw switches electrically rather than by hand was fine. But to sound a deep, throbbing steam whistle with the push of a button, to warn pedestrians off the tracks, to interrupt parents in their adult conversations by filling the house with the pulsing call of imminent journeys—that was sheer joy. In childhood bickerings over whose turn it was to be engineer, blowing the whistle ranked second only to running the trains, and far outclassed pressing the red button of the automatic uncoupling track.

There had been many attempts prior to 1935 to create a satisfying toy train whistle. Some worked off the motor, like the bell that tinkled on wind-up trains, but these were dependent on the movement and pace of the engine. Others tried to utilize air rushing over the speeding train. Bellows produced a wheezing, cowlike sound totally unlike the long, drawn-out notes of the steam engine. Arthur Raphael even commissioned an inventor to create a whistle. The inventor came up with a compressed air storage tank: When the train went over a device on the track the air was released through thin pipes, making a faint, brief *tweet* before being exhausted. But this was not Raphael's idea of a steam locomotive whistle, and it was never produced.

There were two problems in creating a satisfactory whistle. It had to sound authentic, and you had to be able to blow it whether or not the train were moving so that real railroad whistle signals could be given. Charles Giaimo's invention solved both problems. Giaimo placed a tiny motorized fan in the tender. The spinning fan blades sent air through resonating chambers and out a hole in the top of the coal pile of the tender. The resonating pipes were "tuned" like an organ (Lionel engineers studied organs to figure out the proper dimensions of their whistle's pipes). One pipe was longer than the other in the ratio of five to four to give the note of F, the same pitch struck by real railroad whistles.

The true brilliance of Giaimo's whistle, however, lay in the fact that it was activated by direct current while the train motor ran on alternating current. When the whistle controller at the transformer was pushed, a small charge of DC current sounded the whistle without interfering with or being dependent on the train's motor. Raphael was ecstatic. "Looks like an instrument, Joe, looks like an instrument," he told Joseph Bonanno, Lionel's chief engineer. Bonanno spent part of his summer vacation developing a relay that would respond to direct but not alternating current.

The whistle was installed immediately on the *City of Portland* and on the other new engines. To give voice to older, mute locomotives, separate whistle tenders with controllers were made available. A copy of "Official Whistle Signals" was printed in the catalog so little engineers could produce authentic sounds.

In the meantime, the railroad companies followed the successful lead of the Union Pacific and Burlington and began streamlining their trains. The Boston & Maine copied the Burlington's *Zephyr,* producing its own streamlined *Flying Yankee.* The New York Central, still relying on steam power, placed a streamlined outer skin on a traditional Hudson locomotive and named it the *Commodore Vanderbilt,* after the line's founder. The *Commodore* immediately went to work pulling *The Twentieth Century Limited.* In the Midwest, the Milwaukee Road

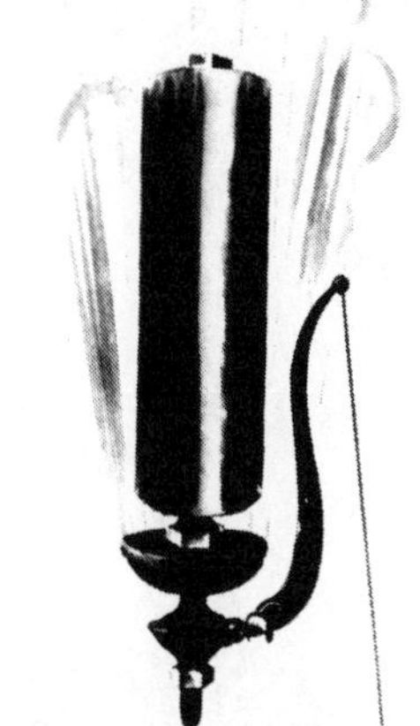

COWEN AND THE WHISTLE

Although Charles Giaimo actually invented Lionel's whistle—with an assist from Joseph Bonanno—as far as the press was concerned, the whistle was Cowen's baby. "The publicity people came to me," Bonanno recalls, "and said was it all right if they said that Mr. Cowen created the whistle. I said fine, whatever they wanted."

Thus was born a rollicking tale. Cowen, according to his publicists, was strolling beside the Hudson one afternoon when a passenger train sounded its whistle. Entranced, he rushed back to Lionel's engineering department. "Men, the New York Central's got a new whistle!" he announced. "We've got to have it. Drop everything else for the time being."

Cowen then supposedly led his best engineers, armed with recording machines and other devices, back to the tracks. They stayed there for days, trying to capture the sound of a wailing whistle. "Did you get it, Jake?" Cowen supposedly asked an assistant. "Take your time! Don't rush it. There's another along at four-eighteen."

Recorders, oscilloscopes, and other sophisticated instruments *were* used to study the sound of a real railroad whistle, Bonanno says. But the railroad was the Lehigh Valley, not the more glamorous New York Central. The location was not the romantically verdant banks of the Hudson, but the industrial area beside Lionel's Irvington plant where the tracks of the Lehigh Valley ran. Finally, as far as Bonanno knows, Cowen was not involved in the sessions.

First design of the Santa Claus handcar showed a battery-lit Christmas tree on front of the car, but final version was unlit.

had an all-new streamlined steam locomotive and passenger train built for its high-speed Chicago-St. Paul/Minneapolis run. The train was the *Hiawatha,* designed by industrial stylist Otto Kuhler.

For each of these new streamliners there was a Lionel counterpart, complete with whistle. The orange and gray *Hiawatha* used the same close-coupled cars as did the Union Pacific. The *Flying Yankee* also had the same sinuous look, but it was chrome-plated, smaller, and less expensive. The *Commodore* was a medium-priced engine that pulled both freight and passenger trains for Lionel Lines. Lionel never made the much-publicized Burlington *Zephyr* (although the *Flying Yankee* looked just like it), inasmuch as the Burlington was a Chicago-based railroad and American Flyer, located there, came out with is own *Zephyr.* Also, the Western routes covered by the Burlington went through some of the same toy markets as the Union Pacific's M-10,000. And anyway, the Lionel model of the Milwaukee Road's *Hiawatha* represented the Midwest railroads.

The success of the Mickey Mouse handcar led to further use of cartoon characters at Lionel. Cowen dreamed up a mechanical handcar for the Easter season, a Peter Rabbit Chick-Mobile pumped by a white rabbit with a basket of jelly beans or an Easter egg on the other end. "For years there have been candy rabbits, chocolate rabbits, fluffy rabbits for Easter, but never a real rabbit toy," Cowen said. "So we conceived the Peter Rabbit Chick-Mobile. This enables the toy department to participate for the first time in the profits from heavy Easter spending." Two versions were made, one with flanged wheels to fit on Lionel track and one with plain wheels for floor use. But people bought new clothing at Easter, not toy trains. Peter Rabbit (who was a cartoon character in *The New York Herald Tribune* as well as the subject of a children's book) never appeared in the Lionel catalog, which was geared to fall and winter sale, and Chick-Mobile sales were low.

Mickey Mouse suffered from no such seasonal identification. His handcar was followed by a small wind-up *Commodore Vanderbilt* with Mickey shoveling coal from the tender. Three lithographed circus cars, a cardboard circus tent, a gas station, fake circus tickets, and a Mickey Mouse ringmaster were included in the circus set. The red *Commodore Vanderbilt* had a battery-operated headlight and a bell. Complete with track, the set cost only two dollars. It probably functioned as a loss leader for Lionel, something on which the company made little or no money but that drew attention to its more profitable items. Mickey also appeared in the toy sack of a Santa Claus figure who pumped his own handcar, though Santa must have had trouble seeing where he was going—he had a Christmas tree on the front of his car.

Lionel was climbing out of the Depression faster than Shirley Temple could tap dance. An automatic gateman who came rushing out of his shack waving a lighted lantern when a train passed appeared in 1935. This became one of Lionel's most popular accessories and was never again absent from the catalog. Two powerful wind-up speedboats that steered themselves were produced so Lionel railroaders would have something to do in the summer, when it was too nice to stay inside and play trains. At the end of the year, Lionel's profit was $154,000, more

Preproduction mock-up of Chick-Mobile had removable paper basket and crouching rabbit. Manufactured model had molded basket and standing bunny.

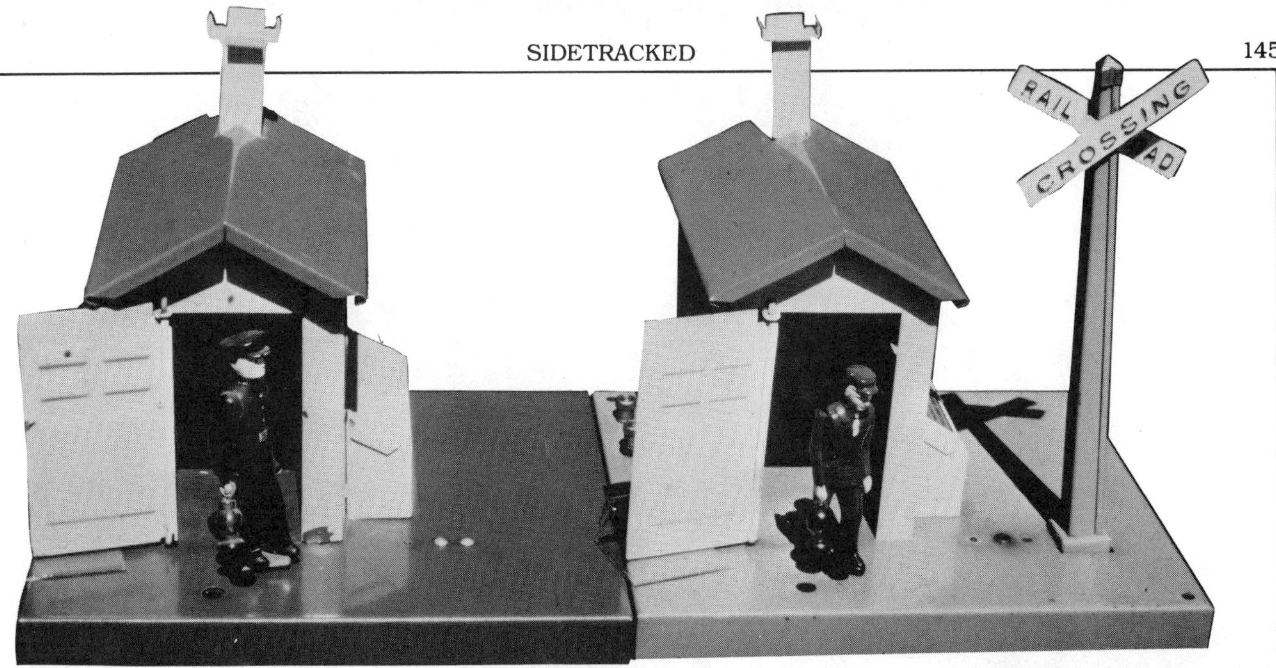

RICHARD CLEMENT/TOY TRAIN MUSEUM

The crossing gateman was so popular that after World War II, the Soviet Union plagiarized the design, though changing the uniform to a Russian-style overcoat (left).

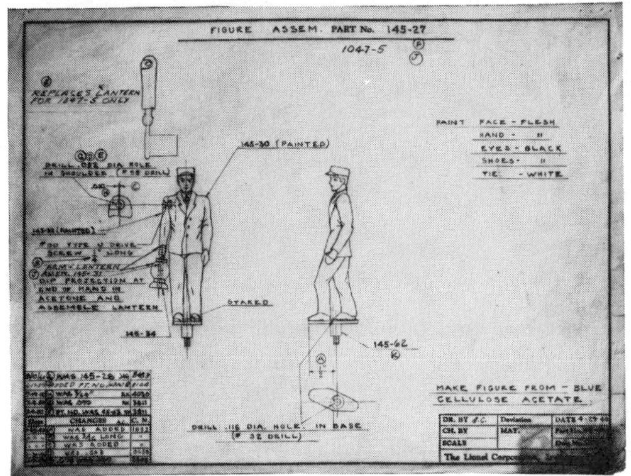

Assembly and painting sheet for Lionelville's most famous citizen, the crossing gateman.

Testing gatemen at the factory.

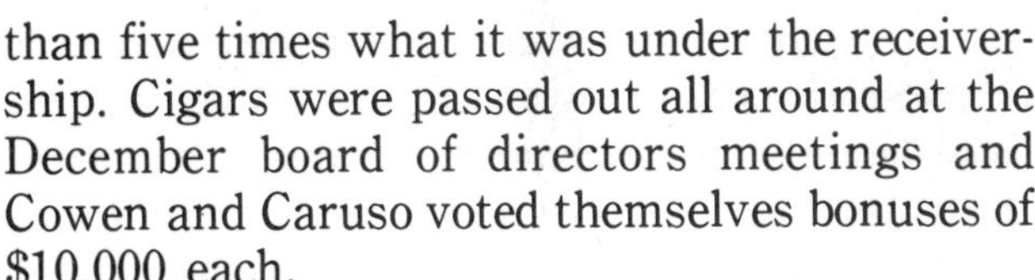

than five times what it was under the receivership. Cigars were passed out all around at the December board of directors meetings and Cowen and Caruso voted themselves bonuses of $10,000 each.

It seems appropriate that during the Depression, a time when the nation was confronted unavoidably with the realities of life, electric trains began to look less like toys and more like the real thing. As the thirties wore on, Lionel continued to base its trains on specific models of the real railroads, working from actual blueprints provided by various engineering departments. Streamlining became more and more popular. When the Union Pacific produced the *Overland Express,* Lionel was right there with its model. The Pennsylvania turned out a sinister-looking steam engine nicknamed the *Torpedo;* Lionel's model appeared on the cover of the catalog, superimposed on a blueprint of an actual steam locomotive. Even Lionel Jr. trains, the cheaper "starter" sets, had smaller *Torpedo, Commodore Vanderbilt,* and *Flying Yankee* models. Electric toy trains were maturing with the country and there was less room for the fanciful standard and O-gauge locomotives, with their copper-colored piping and red cowcatchers.

Streamlining notwithstanding, the most modern means of transportation, as Lionel well knew, was the airplane. In 1936, Lionel added a plane to its line, enabling it to claim in a flyer to dealers: "By air, land, sea, we're headed your way with profits." The plane was the type seen

Children jammed Brooklyn's Fox Theatre (inset) *when Lionel's pylon-controlled electric airplane debuted with a new adventure serial.*

in penny arcade games attached to a pylon and controlled by a cable. And since the company's largest station was Lionel City, it was only natural for Cowen to offer a Lionel Airport for the plane to land at. The advertising copy accompanying the airplane was sadly reminiscent of the ballyhoo that had once surrounded Lionel railroads. "With every boy and girl—every adult in America—vitally interested in Aviation—with every headline stressing the importance of Aviation—here is an ace showmanship hook-up sure to bring r-e-t-u-r-n-s," a dealer brochure promised.

Lionel was unable to meet the demand for the plane. When Columbia Pictures came out with a thirteen-week serial, *The Mysterious Pilot,* with Frank Hawks, Lionel mounted a promotional campaign in which the plane was demonstrated in the lobby of theaters showing the Saturday afternoon cliffhanger. It was then given away as a door prize.

The Fox Theatre in Brooklyn, first to employ the stunt, was delighted with the results. The theater used the plane to announce the upcoming serial in a two-week lobby display. "An usher was at the controls at all time," a theater official wrote Lionel. "Repeatedly, large crowds, sometimes numbering a hundred or more, came into the lobby off the streets and stood gaping at the zooms, back spins and whirl-about they saw before them. As pure entertainment, it was first class, for crowds, made up in a large part of overgrown men as these were, are bigger kids at heart than most kids."

As the Depression abated, Lionel's profits increased. By 1937, Cowen's and Caruso's salaries were back up to $35,000 plus $1,200 expense accounts. The company was producing 350,000 train sets a year. Its premier position was helped by protective tariffs, which had the effect of restricting the foreign competition that had plagued America's toy industry in the years before World War I. Electric trains were now classified with watches and jewelry, and a high

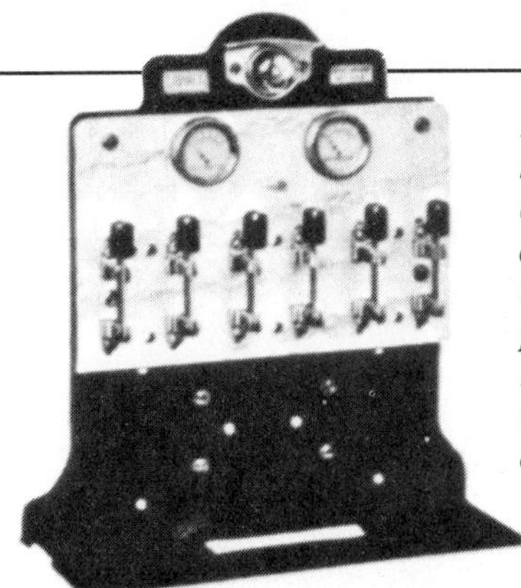

Lionel's panel board's knife switches could operate lamps and accessories, but the two meters were just painted on. Joseph Bonanno's design for real meters was rejected as too costly.

import duty was placed on them. The result was that European toy trains were no longer competitive with American.

Lionel Lines continued to emphasize realism. Model railroading was becoming a hobby for adult men, who weren't interested in a circle of track with an ill-proportioned locomotive under a Christmas tree, however charming. They wanted a fully landscaped permanent layout with a locomotive so accurately detailed that if it were magnified forty-eight times it could match the *Twentieth Century Limited* gear for gear. These men did not find it amusing that Lionel's 400E steamer was short a set of driving wheels; they found it heretical.

A number of small companies sprang up to cater to this adult hobby, which was growing rapidly, due partly to the shorter work week that unionization had produced and the resulting emphasis on leisure time activities. These *scale modelers* (every engine, car, piece of rail, and tree on their layouts was "in scale" by a set ratio) did not hide behind their children, pretending the small trains were for them. Nor did they say they were "playing" with "toys." Instead, they explained they were building model railroads. In 1937, Lionel appealed to these modelers directly with an exquisitely accurate rendering of the New York Central's Hudson-type steam locomotive, which did in fact pull *The Twentieth Century Limited* and other crack trains. (The engine was named the Hudson after the river along which the Central's tracks ran.)

The detail on the Hudson was accurate enough for engineer Bob Butterfield. If he had been shrunk to one forty-eighth his size, Butterfield would have felt at home with the Lionel Hudson, so thorough was Lionel's attention to the esoterica of locomotive external anatomy. The eccentric crank, valve actuator, booster wheels, Baker reversing gear, and injector delivery pipe were all reproduced. (Though if, in fact, Butterfield had found himself inside the cab of Lionel's Hudson, he would have been without a throttle—one piece of detailing Lionel felt the model could do without). The Hudson was a wonderful engine, and a great departure from Lionel's usual toy trains, which, even when they were described as being blueprint-accurate, had been more approximations than one-to-one representations. It cost seventy-five dollars—as much as the complete top-of-the-line standard gauge *Blue Comet* with three passenger cars and the 400E locomotive. For the same price, you could travel by real train from Chicago to San Francisco, spend sixteen days, and return.

Cowen was inordinately proud of his model of the engine that often had taken him between New York and Chicago. "It was the most beautiful thing I ever saw," he said. The brass handmade model from which the molds were cast by a Brooklyn-based Swedish firm was put in a glass case behind his desk. Even the tender that carried the Hudson's coal and water was a source of joy for Cowen, who claimed the simulated coal pile had first been laid out with real coal and then sculpted to give the proper artistic effect of heaped up coal to the model.

No detail was omitted, Lionel claimed, even to the number of rivets on the side of the tender.

At Twenty-Third Street and Broadway in Manhattan, Lionel street lamp (right) *and real city lamppost frame the Empire State Building.*

SCALE HUDSON

Just like its big brother on the New York Central, no expense was spared in creating Lionel's Hudson steam locomotive. The cost of tooling for the one-forty-eighth-scale model was put at $75,000 by Joseph Bonanno, who visited the American Locomotive Company's shops in Schenectady, New York, to get its blueprints of the real passenger engine. It then took more than a year to make the first scaled-down model in brass, and another six months to prepare the tooling.

The lettering on the tender was in approved New York Central style. Central president Frank Williamson was so pleased with Lionel's Hudson that he put a model of it on his desk (mounted on Lionel's presentation board for the Hudson), and appeared in the catalog and in ads vouching for the accuracy of Lionel's trains.

Catalog highlighted the Hudson's detailed reversing gear.

The Hudson lacked only smoke (when you looked down its smokestack, you saw the head of a screw that held the headlight in place) and the sound of escaping steam (finally added to Lionels in the 1970s). When Lionel issued its first public stock certificates in 1937 (left), *it bore an engraving of the Hudson being admired by a boy in tie and white shirt.*

"Sixteen hundred model rivet heads dot the sides of the tender," a special Lionel brochure boasted, "rivet by rivet exactly as in prototype." But soon after the Hudson's release, a customer with the typical high standards of adult model railroaders wrote a letter of complaint to Cowen. The man had been spending some time in the New York Central yards at Harmon, north of New York, comparing Lionel's tender with the original. Not only did Lionel's tender not have 1,600 rivets, as advertised, but the Central tender on which it was supposedly faithfully modeled did not have 1,600, either. Several recounts by the customer, who had to wipe coal dust off the 14,000-gallon Central tender to count them, showed Lionel's model to be three rivets shy of its larger counterpart. Flabbergasted, Cowen rallied his forces for a countdown. The final score was New York Central 1,402, Lionel 1,399. "It was true," a mortified Cowen admitted later. "We don't yet know how it happened." But to prevent any future slurs to the Lionel reputation, he created the position of rivet counter at the factory.

If it were thought of as a toy train, the O-gauge Hudson engine was very expensive. As a die-cast, elaborately detailed metal *model,* it was cheap. Comparable models made by small, low-volume companies cost several hundred dollars. With its large production facilities and expectations of greater sales, Lionel was able to undersell these small hobby companies. Producing the Hudson took two years; its tooling was estimated to have cost from forty-five to seventy-five thousand dollars. The company needed to sell approximately fifteen hundred engines to break even. It apparently exceeded that number in the first year, even though there were problems with a cowcatcher that sometimes shorted when it touched the center rail and warped boiler castings caused by an impure zinc alloy.

The Hudson was created in recognition of the desire of male adults to run model trains, a desire that was enthusiastically shared by Cowen. It was featured on the cover of the 1937 catalog, which went to boys, but it was really aimed at their fathers. Besides its price, the locomotive was set apart from the rest of the line by the inclusion of a walnut display stand for use on a "mantle-piece or as a decoration in the hobby room," acknowledging that some of the customers bought the engine not to run it but just to look at it. Those who did operate it had to use new track that had wider, more realistic curves than other toy track and whose rails had the solid *T* shape of regular railroad track. Another distinguishing feature of the Hudson was that it could be adapted to run on two-rail track with an outside power rail, a more realistic-looking track favored by adult modelers. Lionel itself did not make such a track, but recognized the Hudson was too fine to be limited to its own three rails.

The Lionel Corporation went public in 1937, issuing 77,500 shares of stock at $12 a share for a total value of $930,000. The money went to repay bank loans and to provide working capital as new machinery was added to the factory. And, for the first time since nine-year-old Lawrence's picture had appeared in the catalog and on train box covers, the younger Cowen became involved with the company.

Lawrence became a director in what he described as an "advisory capacity," remaining with his brokerage firm and only attending Lionel board meetings. He still preferred the financial challenges of Wall Street to those of running a manufacturing company. But Joshua Cowen was not a man to be denied, especially where his only son was concerned. Bit by bit, Lawrence was drawn into the company, becoming assistant treasurer and then a vice president and comptroller. In 1940 he relinquished his ties with his brokerage house and went to work full time for his father.

There had always been an air of paternalism about Lionel, stemming from Cowen's and especially Caruso's dream of creating a self-sufficient factory-based community that would raise its own food in the style of a European commune. In fact, Caruso relished the role of grand seigneur and actually brought baskets of food to his workers' homes at holidays. (On one such visit, he discovered an elaborate collection of Lionel's best trains. A worker had smuggled them out of the factory by hiding the unformed cars under his shirt. Once home, he assembled the trains.) Cowen and Caruso would provide. The workers had only to trust them and accept their benevolence.

This may have been fine in the twenties, but the thirties were a time of unionization and worker assertiveness. In 1937 Lionel experienced its first strike. More than two hundred workers walked off the job, seeking union recognition, a forty-cent-an-hour minimum wage, and "proper ventilation, sanitation and safeguards

COWEN AS REMEMBERED BY . . .

His Granddaughter

"When I was a child, I believed as long as my grandfather was there nothing was ever going to go wrong," Cynthia Otis Saypol says. "He could fix it or he could protect us, take care of us. When I think of him I see a very tall, very strong . . . a very cute man, though in fact he was of course short. What I felt was, 'This person truly loved me.' He was not a friend, but pure love to me. He represented the male image in my life, as my father wasn't there very much."

Cynthia Saypol is the daughter of Cowen's daughter, Isabel. She grew up in Manhattan where "Bankan," her childhood name for Cowen, was a kind of fairy godfather to her. It was Cowen who stayed up Christmas Eve wiring Cynthia's dollhouse so that each of the twelve rooms had its own light and a separate switch. When she was six, Cynthia told her grandfather that she wished she had a "dickey bird" (canary). The next morning at nine a canary in a beautiful carved mahogany cage was on Cynthia's doorstep. A few nights later, Cynthia was staring out the window. "Look at the moon and stars," she said. "For goodness sake, don't let your grandfather hear you," someone said, "or he'll come up with those, too."

Cowen gave Cynthia an allowance and taught her bookkeeping. He showed her how to fix plugs and to make other household repairs, "things girls didn't usually do," she notes. "In fact, he was closer to the girls in the family than to the boys. In the house, men and women were always together. It wasn't at all like the women had to go into the other room. He went to the fights at the old Madison Square Garden with Isabel because no one else would go with him. He was a patient teacher. He never talked baby talk. I can never remember the man talking down to me. The only thing you couldn't be in front of him was stupid. He was not a man to suffer fools."

Cowen required that young people behave with decorum. "No one ever scrambled around in front of him," Cynthia recalls. "You didn't come into the house with filthy shoes, for instance. Children sat at the table with the grownups. We drank out of china cups. He adored young people—as long as they were neat." Cowen himself was the model of propriety. He never came to dinner without a jacket, never wore baggy pants or an old sweater. His small home workshop, in a large hall closet, was immaculate, each tool hung by size in its precise place. "You'd think nobody ever went in there, but he always had something he was working on," Cynthia says. Even when he was down on the living room floor making repairs on a balky engine, Cowen appeared unrumpled. "He laid his tools out neatly in a row in front of him. He had beautiful, expressive hands, very adept. He could take the whole locomotive apart—he couldn't stand anything not working—and never got dirty or even removed his jacket," Cynthia says reverently.

Cynthia's family had trains, but, like so many girls, she recalls, "My brother wouldn't let me play with them." Cowen brought her a Lionel electric range and a tiny gold locomotive to hang on her charm bracelet. "There was never a present given that wasn't 100 percent the best of whatever it was," she says. "If it was gold, it was fourteen or eighteen karat, not plated. When I was five I got a tiny gold rabbit with diamond chips. He shopped at Van Cleef's or Steuben or Tiffany. There was nothing he gave that wasn't perfect."

As a child, Cynthia walked through the Lionel factory holding her grandfather's hand. Sometimes he'd halt an assembly line to show her something new. He addressed the workers by name and they'd wave to him. "I never had the feeling it was anything but incredible fun to run the business," she says. "I think it meant more to him to have a good time in what he did than to make money. Sometimes we'd think of how much money he could have made if he'd kept the flashlight invention, but he was never upset about it at all."

Even better than the factory was the Twenty-sixth Street showroom. "The most fun was to be allowed under the railing around the layout, to get up close to the trains, because I was my grandfather's darling," Cynthia remembers. Later, her daughter, Cathy, led her first grade class in a privileged romp around the showroom, which Cowen closed to the public for the day.

The temper that Cowen displayed so frequently at the office was not in evidence at home. "He was interruptive, he never waited for people to finish a sentence, but he never got angry or raised his voice. I never remember hearing him lose his temper," Cynthia says. "His voice sounded strong, secure, which was probably why I thought he was tall. At home, he was never without an opening for humor. He laughed easily. If he did something naughty, as he often did, he acted almost like a bad boy."

on machinery." The factory continued to function, but only two-thirds of the employees remained at work.

Unions were anathema to an autocrat like Caruso. Predictably, he refused even to consider the demand for union recognition. (Cowen stayed out of the fray; at the New York office, loyal secretaries, clerks, and bookkeepers were far less organized than the blue-collar factory workers.) After two weeks, the strike was abandoned and the workers accepted Caruso's original offer of a 15 percent increase in pay, keeping wages under the forty-cent-an-hour minimum sought by the strikers. Unionization was inevitable, however. Caruso was able to fight a delaying action for another five years, but in 1942, with the labor force almost half women because of the war, the United Paper, Novelty and Toyworkers' Union won an election under the supervision of the War Labor Board. Paternalism was on its way out at Lionel.

The postwar Lionel trains that would captivate America in the early fifties had their foundation in the years preceding World War II. The sheet metal locomotives that had characterized standard gauge gave way to entirely die-cast engines like the Hudson. Following the Hudson's success, Lionel introduced cheaper die-cast engines. The die-casting process, in which molten metal was forced under high pressure into the cracks and crannies of hardened steel dies, produced highly detailed locomotives. Pipes, rivets, compressors, air tanks, and even a miniature locomotive builder's plate (BUILT BY LIONEL) were all cast into the engine in one piece. The locomotives were a somber black, like most of their big brothers on the real railroads. They were serious and meant business, unlike the gaily-colored locomotives of Lionel's pre-Depression days. The detailed look of the Hudson was also duplicated in a miniature size called 00-gauge. 00 trains were one seventy-sixth actual size, versus the one forty-eighth of the Hudson. A circle of 00 track covered only twenty-seven inches, while the broad-radius track of the Hudson took up seventy-two inches. "What a gift to father and son who live in a city apartment where room is at a premium!" the catalog said, recognizing the change in living quarters that was occurring in America as small towns and the countryside were abandoned for the big city.

With the trend toward realism came the invention of new devices to make toy trains more lifelike. Couplers that opened at the touch of a button were introduced in 1938. When the car was on a special track, it could be uncoupled from the rest of the train without the operator's actually having to touch the car. The uncoupling track had two extra rails that conducted

Heavyweight boxing champ Gene Tunney (left) *learns about 00 gauge from Lionel's Chicago sales manager, Jack Caffrey, in the Chicago showroom.*

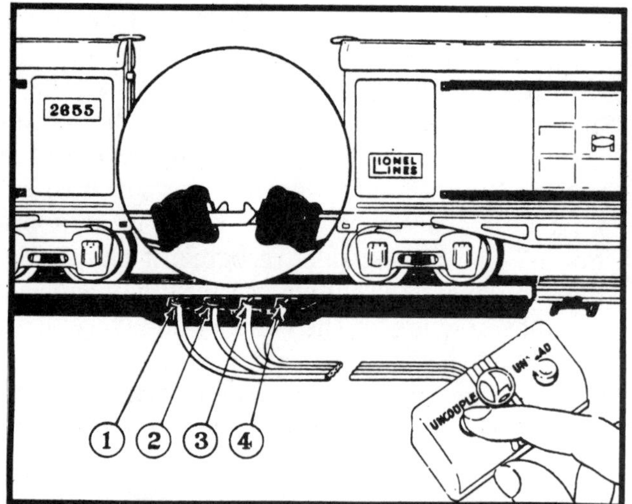

Pressing the uncouple button on the left side of the controller caused the 1938 box couplers to disengage. Box couplers, however, were as outdated in appearance as the real railroads' link-and-pin couplers (right), *which were replaced by knuckle-type couplers in about 1882. Lionel knuckle couplers would be introduced after the war.*

Remote control uncoupling relied on a special straight track that had five rails and a controller connected to it. The track replaced an ordinary piece of track in the train layout. It got its power from the regular current running through the rails.

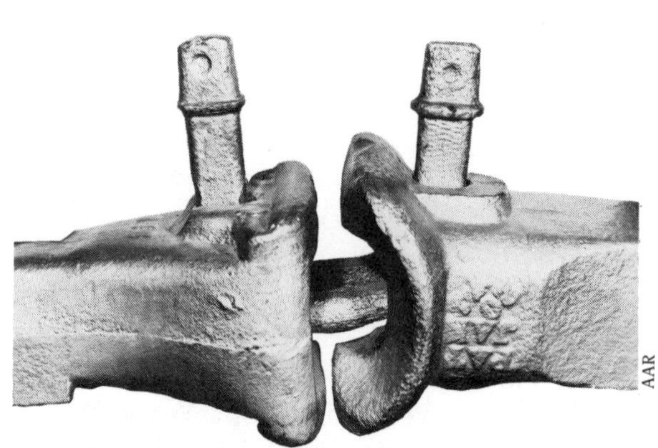

AAR

power to the car's couplers when the red *uncouple* button was pushed. (The couplers didn't look anything like real railroad knuckle couplers, but they worked well.) Another button connected to the same track made the car unload. The new cars dumped coal, expelled barrels, tossed out packing crates, and rolled logs into receiving bins.

Action was also added to what Lionel called its accessories, that delightful rear half of the catalog full of crossing gates, semaphores, bridges, tunnels, stations, powerhouses, signal towers, street lamps, and track and switches, which accounted for 40 percent of the company's sales. The early accessories had been basically static. Lamps might go on and off, but most accessories didn't really do anything except sit beside the tracks and look pretty. All of that changed in the late thirties and early forties. Coal loaders with clanking bucket scoops, log conveyors with endless chain lifts, electromagnetic cranes that delivered scrap iron to waiting gondola cars, and bascule bridges that raised automatically to provide clearance for passing ships were added to the line. They all operated at the push of a button. The Lionel engineer could command these ingenious wonders without ever going near them. He didn't even have to be in the same room. This was the dawn of Lionel's highly-touted *remote control,* a phrase the company would drum into the heads of America's youth.

Remote control meant just what it said. Lionel engineers could control everything from a distance by pushing buttons, levers, and switches. Not only inanimate objects like bridges and barrel loaders but eventually cattle, horses, and even people could all be made to move and to labor by remote control. It gave a child power over a Lilliputian universe, compensating for his helplessness in the real world.

Remote control was a great selling point. But it also took the trains still further away from those simple "hands on" days when the legs of an armchair were a tunnel portal, cars were uncoupled by hand, freight was empty thread spools or building blocks or filched clothespins, and passengers were toy soldiers laying on their sides in open cars. Remote control was progress. It made the trains more realistic. But it also gave children less of a chance to exercise their imaginations, less of a reason to crawl on the

RAILROADING BY REMOTE CONTROL

Whether it was coal, scrap metal, logs, or draw bridges, Lionel found a way of moving raw materials by remote control in the late thirties. Each accessory came with its own controller. Some, like the bascule bridge, had only one button. Others, like the electromagnetic crane, had five. Ranged beside the transformer, whistle box, levers for track switches, and lights, the controllers made an imposing operating panel that was as fascinating as the trains themselves.

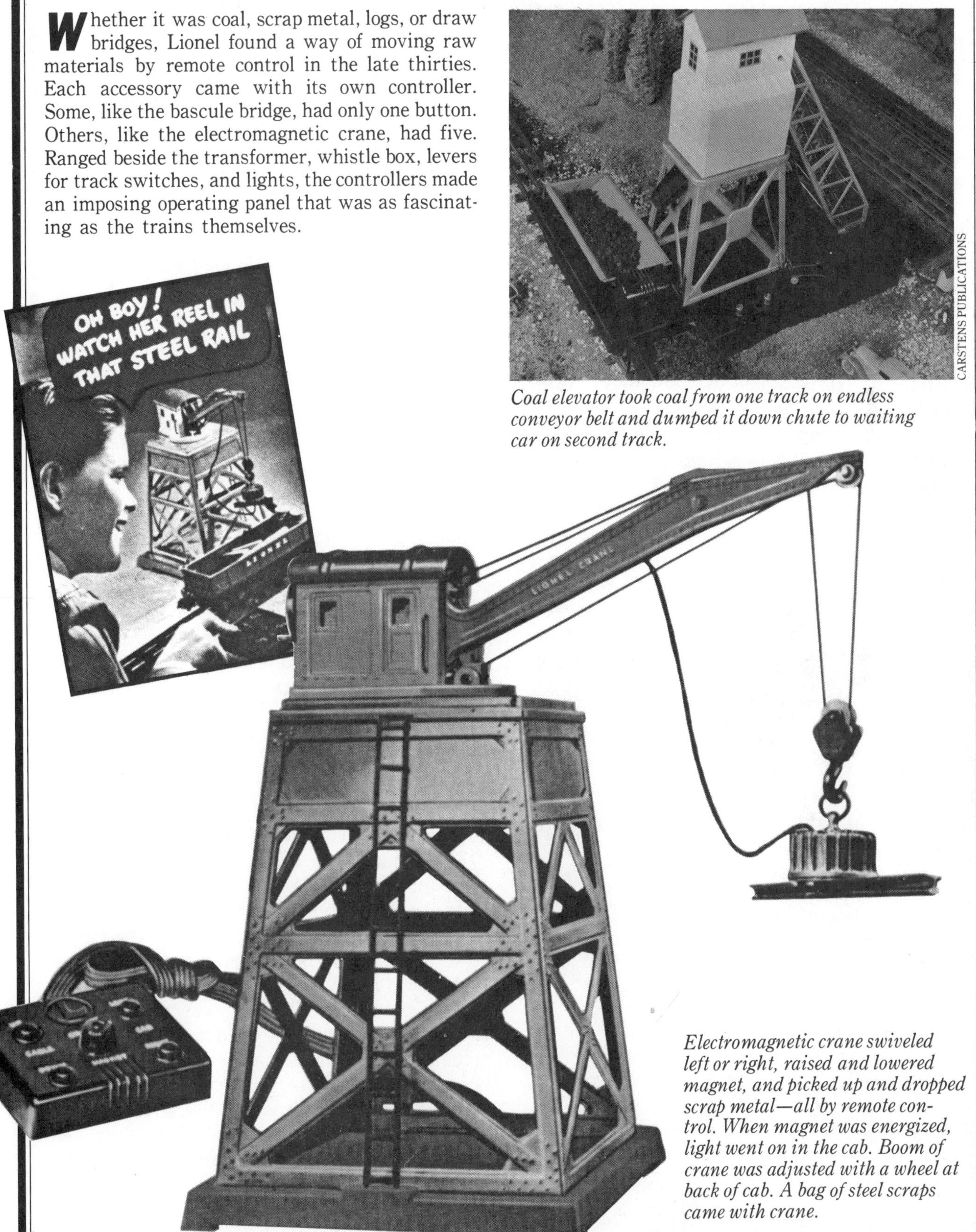

Coal elevator took coal from one track on endless conveyor belt and dumped it down chute to waiting car on second track.

Electromagnetic crane swiveled left or right, raised and lowered magnet, and picked up and dropped scrap metal—all by remote control. When magnet was energized, light went on in the cab. Boom of crane was adjusted with a wheel at back of cab. A bag of steel scraps came with crane.

floor. Choosing the correct button was a big responsibility. Physical contact with the train was discouraged. There was suddenly less frivolity and fun in Lionel Land. Remote control became symbolic of the button-pushing and emotional distancing that would be required of men in the modern world.

The train business was changing. In Chicago, the American Flyer company was sold to A. C. Gilbert, creator of Erector construction sets and Mysto magic tricks. Gilbert would move Flyer to New Haven, Connecticut, where the line would be modernized and made more realistic. American Flyer would become Lionel's biggest competitor after the war (though Flyer ran a poor second, selling one train for about every three sold by Lionel). Flyer's biggest attraction would be that its trains were more realistic than Lionel's.

The toy like standard gauge was discontinued by Lionel in 1939. It was perhaps fitting that the end of an era of toy trains that had been characterized by their colorful and fanciful brass and nickel nameplates occurred the same year Hitler invaded Poland. The world was too somber a place for the standard gauge two-tone Blue Comet locomotive with its flirtatious red-spoked driving wheels. Lionel exhibited in the "Children's World" building at the World's Fair, joining the country's railroads in making a brave show of normalcy. But the company's efforts were already increasingly directed toward securing war contracts rather than toward producing new trains.

A. C. Gilbert on American Flyer's postwar showroom layout, which boasted two-rail track

LIONEL AND THE AMERICAN WAY OF LIFE

"Your management is united with all other patriotic Americans in determination to do whatever must be done—to fight and win this battle of production—in order to bring about an early and successful conclusion to this war—*and a return to the days of Electric Trains and the American mode of living they symbolize.*"

—Joshua Lionel Cowen
May 29, 1942
The Lionel Corporation Annual Report

By the time Pearl Harbor was bombed, Lionel had $5.5 million in government contracts. That was almost double what it had made during its best year of train sales in the period preceding the war. At the board of directors meeting four days after the Japanese attack, Caruso suggested the company buy $50,000 worth of savings bonds as a patriotic gesture. The sales staff was kept on a week to week basis because it was unclear how long Lionel would continue to manufacture trains. By June 1942, train production was suspended for the war.

There was still a catalog, though, with an announcement about Lionel's war work. "Lionel Goes To Sea; Lionel Machinery and Manpower Now Work to Help Win the War," the catalog read. "Illustrated below are a few of the products Lionel is now building to help beat the Axis. If you have difficulty in locating the Lionel equipment you want for your model railroad, remember that the material and manpower normally devoted to its production is now assigned to help win the war." "Illustrated below" were binnacles to hold ships' compasses, peloruses and alidades for navigation, lifeboat binnacles, and percussion primers for antiaircraft shells.

Lionel also made alcohol-filled compasses, and

that led in a roundabout way to Caruso's finally acquiring the company farm he yearned for. A special alcohol-resistant paint was needed to coat the bowls of the compasses, and egg albumin was used as the base of this paint. The eggs had to be very fresh, chief engineer Bonanno discovered, so every morning Lionel sent a truck to the local farms in rural New Jersey to pick them up. However, Lionel still had trouble getting uniform results. "We found that the paint had to be mixed and used within a few hours from the time the egg was laid," Bonanno said. Enter Caruso, who gleefully ordered two dozen white leghorn hens and housed them in a temporary hen house on the corner of an employee tennis court. Two dozen eggs a day provided enough paint for sixty compasses. Caruso had the engineering department design a trap nest with a red light that went on when an egg was laid.

Since only the egg whites were needed for the paint (whose formula had been devised by Caruso during World War I), Lionel was left with sixty or more yolks a day. "At first the people who did the spraying and mixing drank them," Bonanno said, "but they soon tired of that. They were finally consigned to the chef, who prepared omelets for the employees' lunch." Caruso didn't stop with chickens, however. He bought two pigs to go with them. "We like to produce everything we need here," he pompously told a local reporter, "and there is lots of garbage from the cafeteria going to waste. We shall feed the pigs the garbage and they will raise a family. Then we will have our own hams and bacon." And, continued Caruso, what he

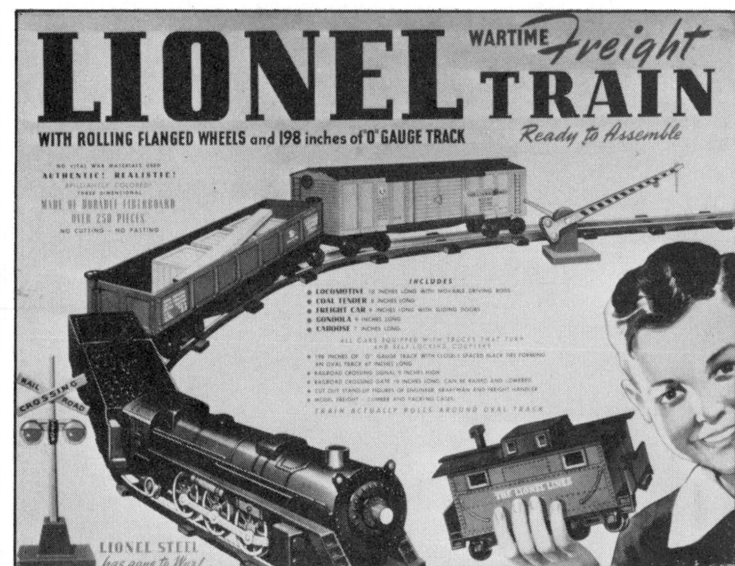

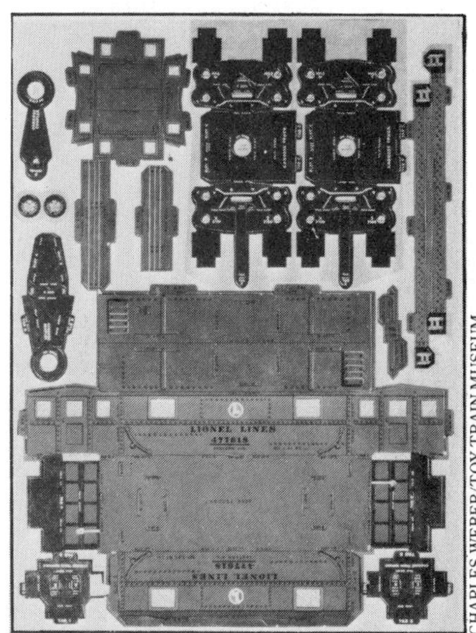

The paper train required dedication to assemble. Flat sheet of parts (above) *produced caboose* (below).

really wanted was a cow. "We haven't enough land now," he said, "but we are trying to lease some from the Lehigh Valley Railroad [which ran past the factory]. When we get that we shall have a cow."

Due to the shortage of materials and the urgency of war work, Lionel produced no electric trains in 1943 and 1944. Nor were there train catalogs to fantasize over. So as not to leave the boys of America entirely bereft, the company did produce a cardboard train that could "run" on cardboard track. "Lionel Steel Has Gone To War," was the legend on the box containing 250 intricate pieces of a freight set based on Lionel's regular O-gauge line. The set was actually produced by the "premium king" Samuel Gold, who made prizes for candy manufacturers. Gold had gone to Cowen with an idea. "Look, if Lionel goes to war," he argued, "what happens to the generation of boys you lose, who don't grow up with train sets?" Gold proposed what came to be known as the "paper train." While the flat box in which the train came said, "Ready to Assemble," in fact the paper train, with its tabs and slots and pieces to be folded, was monstrously difficult to put together. Many a father gave up in despair on Christmas Eve.

Deprived of steel, Lionel also turned to wood for several abortive toy lines during the war. A series of railroad buildings, including a finely-detailed freight station and a bay-windowed passenger depot, was advertised to dealers. Pull toys called Lion-Eds, "with flirting eyes and impish smiles," were offered. The horse, lamb, and dog Lion-Eds had "roguish eyes not just painted on," according to a Lionel flyer. Preschool toys of simple building blocks were also merchandised by Lionel. But none of these made much of a contribution to sales, and it is not even clear they were produced in any quantity.

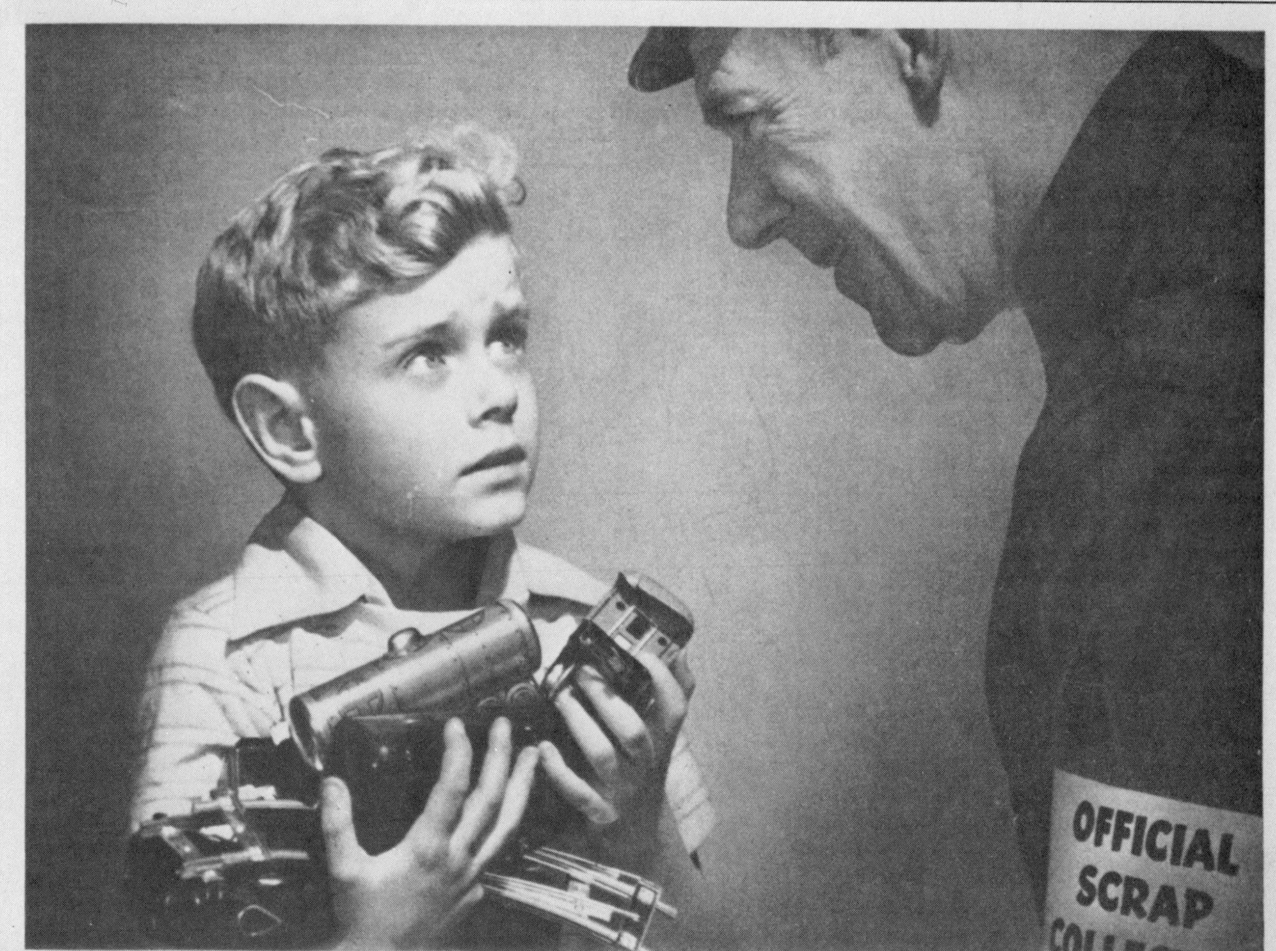

MAURICE DEMERS/TTOS BULLETIN

Sparton radios sponsored ad in 1943: Even toy trains had to be sacrificed in wartime scrap metal drives.

Cowen accepting the Victory Fleet Flag for outstanding production. Inset (left to right)*: Senator Albert Hawkes, Cowen, Mayor Murphy of Newark, Caruso.*

The war was extremely profitable for Lionel. Sales rose from $3.5 million to $5.4 million to a high of $7.2 million in 1943. Dividends of $1.30 per share were declared while net profits duplicated the twenties high of over $400,000. However, there were problems associated with Lionel's success. Its agent for securing government contracts, who received a healthy 5 percent commission from Lionel, was indicted for making commissions while still an employee of the Federal Housing Administration. Lionel terminated his contract and deducted the 5 percent from what it was charging the Navy. Lionel was also twice reprimanded by the Price Adjustment Board for making excessive profits on its war contracts. In 1942, the company was required to refund $300,000 and deduct 20 percent from future Navy bills. At the end of 1943, Lionel had to return $325,000 to the Navy for exceeding what the government determined were its guidelines for legitimate profits. Such renegotiation was not uncommon during the war, however, and Lionel was by no means alone in having to return money to the government.

The Lionel catalog had always promised to unite fathers and son; it was now doing just that for the Cowen family. As vice president and comptroller, Lawrence was third in command under Cowen and Caruso. His influence was growing, especially during the war, when there was less emphasis on Raphael's selling skills or Bonanno's or Giaimo's engineering and manufacturing expertise. Lawrence dealt with many of the government contracts once Lionel's procurement agent was indicted. In the summer of 1943 it was Lawrence who applied to the United States Maritime Commission asking that Lionel be granted the Commission's *M* Award for Merit for outstanding wartime production. On September 9, the *M* Pennant and the Victory Fleet Flag were awarded to Lionel in elaborate ceremonies at the factory. New Jersey Senator Albert Hawkes praised Lionel's war effort as "symbolic of what America can really do when it rolls up its sleeves, goes to work, and sees victory in sight." While Cowen and Caruso sat beside each other on folding chairs on the bunting-draped platform, Hawkes paid elaborate homage to the women working at Lionel. "I know there is a type of job suited to every patriotic woman who wants to do her part," Hawkes said. "I am sure

Issued in 1944, the forty-page Planning Book *helped you to prepare your railroad for the trains that would be available after the war.*

that, in our own area, women will fill the depleted ranks of manpower and contribute, as you are doing, their full measure of time and effort and devotion to the cause of victory." Before the war was over, Lionel earned three gold stars to add to its *M* in recognition of meeting production goals.

Although there were no trains during the war, Lionel had no intention of losing the momentum that had built up before 1941, when an estimated 250,000 toy and model railroaders in the country spent $11 million annually. During the war years, Lionel's publicity department pumped out Lionel's own railroading magazine, *Model Builder,* to fifty thousand subscribers every other month. *The Lionel Railroad Planning Book* told the young engineer what to do while waiting for the war to end. "Start now to plan a postwar railroad," a booklet urged. "Don't wait until the last shot is fired and until Lionel is again manufacturing trains before starting plans and preparations for a miniature railroad system of your own." Track plans could be sketched; benchwork to support the trains could be built; scenery could be constructed.

But while the company was doing well financially and looking with confidence toward the resumption of peacetime production, internal strains were breaking up the management team of Cowen and Caruso that had guided Lionel for forty years. It was obvious that Lawrence would succeed his father as president of the company, and this made Caruso's position untenable. Caruso was also disturbed that Cowen's son would benefit from his father's position while his own son, Anthony, would not.

The union that had been voted in at the plant in 1942 also cramped Caruso's style. A man who had fired workers at the snap of a finger now had to arbitrate and negotiate with his employees. It was an affront to Caruso's dignity. On October 5, 1944, Caruso told the board of directors that he and his family were putting up for sale the fifty thousand shares of Lionel stock they held. "In view of this proposed sale, I feel that it is appropriate that I sever my connection with the Corporation with which I have been associated as Works Manager for the past forty years," Caruso wrote. "It is with the greatest regret that I feel compelled to take this action, and in the sincere belief that it will not adversely affect the war effort."

Cowen read the letter to the board, as well as a second one in which Caruso agreed not to become involved in any corporation whose products competed with Lionel's. The board then expressed its "deep appreciation of the many years of loyal and efficient service which Mr. Caruso has given to the corporation, and the high regard and personal affection the other members of the Board have formed for Mr. Caruso." Caruso was voted his year's salary of $37,500 as severance pay and was given the traditional wrist watch as a departure gift. By November 1 he was gone, succeeded as works manager by Charles Giaimo.

After his departure, Caruso founded C-Eight Laboratories in Newark, New Jersey, (named for the eight Carusos in his family), a company that developed coin-operated vending machines. But he was unable to compete in an industry infiltrated by organized crime. He then returned to Naples, Italy, with his family. Using the Lionel-founded La Precisa as a base, he expanded into construction, real estate, and farming.

Caruso had been with Cowen almost from the beginning, and together they had made the company the largest manufacturer of electric trains in the world. But neither Cowen nor Caruso could have imagined the glories that lay ahead for Lionel in post-war America.

Lionel apologized for the absence of trains during the war by explaining the war work it was doing.

LIONEL TRAINS
NEW YORK, N.Y.

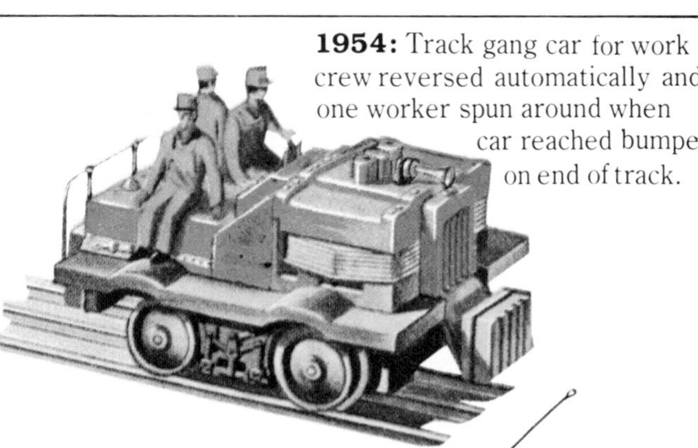

1954: Track gang car for work crew reversed automatically and one worker spun around when car reached bumper on end of track.

1955: The first Lionel trolley made since the teens had a roof pole that swiveled and changed direction when the trolley did.

1949: The perfect family ogles the perfect trains on a typically crowded layout combining pre- and post-war operating accessories.

CATALOG YEARS

1949–1955

The Lionel catalog was the wish book supreme for boys in postwar America. It was required reading, its forty-four pages demanding Solomon-like choices among engines and accessories. Hidden in a notebook, it was an antidote to the dullest of teachers. More than one million were distributed annually, many free or for as little as ten cents. Only the Sears and Montgomery Ward catalogs were better known.

Lionel '027' Diesels with Magne-Traction

No. 2032 ERIE TWIN-UNIT DIESEL — This is the black-and-gold Erie Railroad model of the ALCO-type double "A" unit Diesel. Has sturdy worm-drive motor with *MAGNE-TRACTION*. Contains built-in horn. This Diesel has operating knuckle couplers and headlights on both pilot ends. Length 22". **$39.95**

No. 2031 ROCK ISLAND TWIN-UNIT DIESEL — A wonderfully accurate reproduction of the Rock Island ALCO-type double "A" unit Diesel. It has a worm-drive motor, built-in horn and *MAGNE-TRACTION*. Knuckle couplers and headlights on both pilot ends. Length of twin-unit 22". **$39.95**

No. 2033 UNION PACIFIC TWIN DIESEL — Another double "A" unit Diesel of the ALCO-type, in gleaming aluminum finish with the herald of the Union Pacific. Equipped with worm-drive motor, *MAGNE-TRACTION* and built-in horn. Operating couplers and headlights. Length 22". **$39.95**

No. 2245 "TEXAS SPECIAL" TWO-UNIT DIESEL — Brilliant new Diesel patterned after the loco that speeds through the Southwest. It's an "A" and "B" combination with *MAGNE-TRACTION* and built-in horn. Operating knuckle couplers and headlight. Two units measure over 2 ft. **$39.95**

No. 623 SANTA FE DIESEL SWITCHER — Fast and able — b sure to see it in action! Markings are of the A.T. & S.F. This GM-typ switcher has a worm-drive motor and *MAGNE-TRACTION*. Operatin knuckle couplers on both ends. Powerful headlight. Length of switche 11⅝". **$25.0**

No. 624 CHESAPEAKE & OHIO SWITCHER — The yellow an blue C&O switcher is another top performer! It's a GM-type like th Santa Fe, with worm-drive motor and *MAGNE-TRACTION*. Headligh and knuckle couplers on both ends, making it ideal for switchyard us Length is 11⅝". **$25.0**

30

1954: Agonizing decisions faced the reader of the catalog as he tried to choose between the diesel might of nine railroads in one year (still other lines were represented in steam).

No. 115 Illuminated City Station. Just like magic your train automatically comes to a stop in front of this station, is detained for an instant and is then released! Heavy enameled steel embossed to represent stone construction. Skylight removable. 13⅞" long, 9¼" wide and 8½" high. $16.50

Station automatically halts train!

No. 93 Water Tower. Ease your steam type locomotive onto the siding and pretend to take on "water" from this realistic tower. Stands 8¾". $1.75

No. 156 Illuminated Station Platform. Richly-enameled and deeply-ribbed roof. Massive, die-cast structural columns. Real picket fence contains colorful billboards. Detailed platform cross-reinforced. Twin bulb roof illumination. Use in multiple! Is 12" long, 5⅛" high, 3¼" wide. $4.50

No. 152 Automatic Crossing Gate. It's a real thrill to watch the red warning light glow and the gates automatically lower as your fast limited speeds along the rails, approaching the crossing. When train passes, light is extinguished and gates rise. Accessory measures 10½" long. $4.50

SUNOCO DYNAFUEL
For Better School Marks Remington PORTABLE TYPEWRITERS
DOGS PREFER RIVAL DOG FOOD
Enjoy Baby Ruth Every Day

No. 314 Plate Girder Bridge. Every model pike should have several of these! Bridge is die-cast, rivets projected in sharp relief. Die-cast structural steel sides and heavy steel platform. Precisely scaled for "O" Gauge and "027". Single span is 10" long. $2.50

No. 316 Trestle Bridge. Scaled-down model of the big steel railroad bridges that span real rivers and chasms. Made of heavy rolled steel. Deeply embossed structural details. Welded assembly! Brilliantly enameled in rich aluminum. Measures 24" by 6⅛". $2.75

SP Smoke Pellets. For use in all steam-type smoke locos illustrated in this catalog. Pellets load into stack. Harmless, odorless. Creates clean white smoke. About 50 in bottle. $1.00

No. 167 Whistle Controller. For use with Lionel Transformers which do not have built-in Whistle Controller. One button blows Whistle, other stops and reverses locomotive. $3.25

No. 919 Bag of Grass. Make scenic and texturing effects of real beauty with this strikingly realistic artificial grass. 50¢

No. 206 Artificial Coal. Dustless, non-smudging, clean. Made expressly for Lionel coal accessories and coal cars. 35¢

No. 88 Reversing Controller. Press button and locos with remote control unit stop, reverse. $1.25

No. 0209 Set of Barrels. Replicas of fuel oil drums, etc., used in rail shipments. Set of four. 50¢

No. 925 Tube of Lubricant Specialty compounded for working parts of locomotives. Two ounces. 35¢ 37

1949: The accessory pages at the back of the catalog offered enticements ranging from automatic stop stations to extra barrels for gondolas.

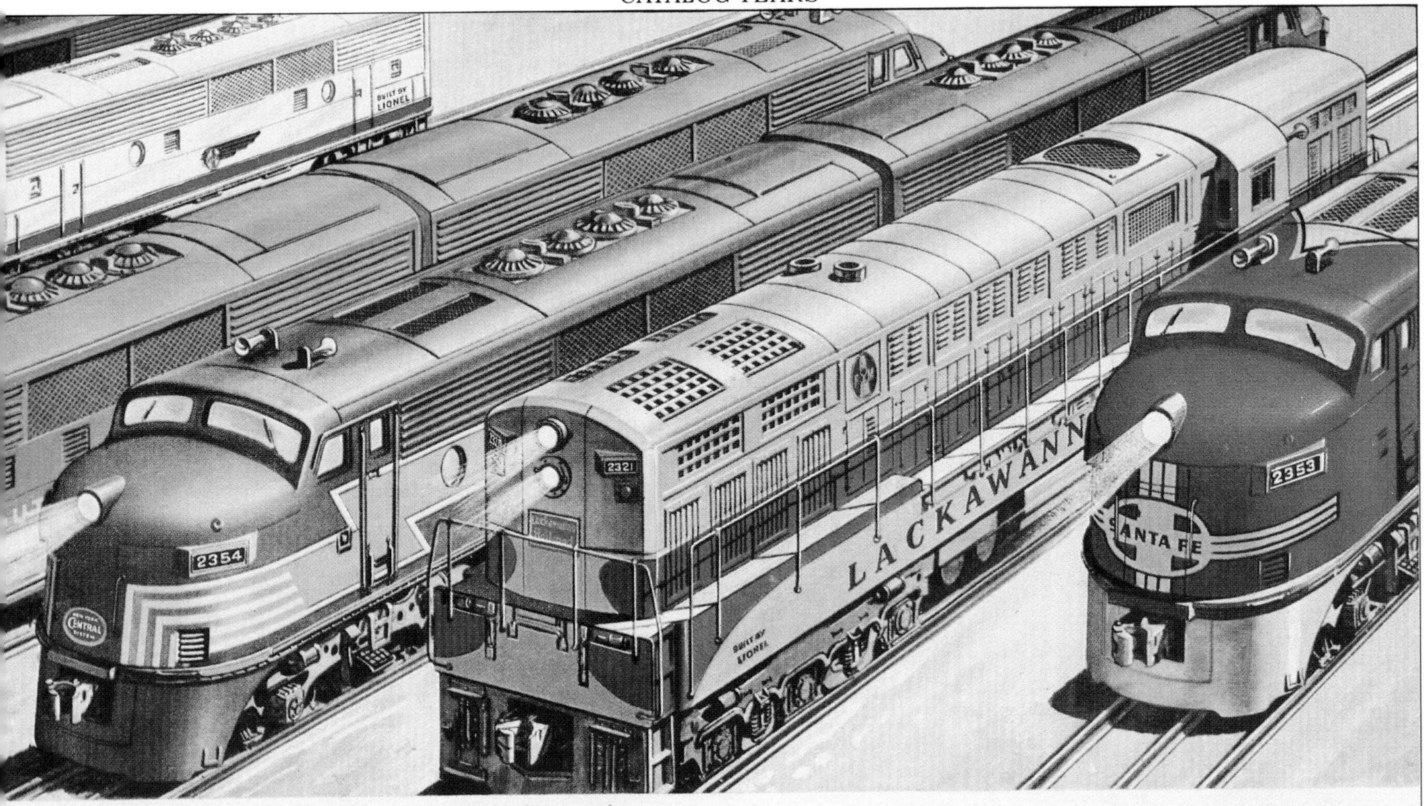

ionel 'O' Diesels with Magne-Traction

lo. 2356 SOUTHERN RAILWAYS TWIN-UNIT DIESEL—Take look at Southern's great green twin-unit Diesel — equipped with two orm-drive motors, built-in horn and *MAGNE-TRACTION*. It consists of wo GM-type "A" units — has headlights and remote control operating nuckle couplers on both ends. Overall length 26½". **$47.50**

lo. 2354 NEW YORK CENTRAL TWIN DIESEL — Pride of the lew York Central — these big twin GM "A" units. Lionel model coun-erparts have two worm-drive motors in the forward unit. They're quipped with built-in horn and *MAGNE-TRACTION*. Overall length f both units is 26½". **$47.50**

No. 2321 FAIRBANKS-MORSE DIESEL — Brand new Diesel type. Modelled after the Fairbanks-Morse loco built for the Lackawanna R.R. Has two worm-drive motors, *MAGNE-TRACTION* and built-in horn. Head end is completely illuminated, including headlight, Mars light, classification lights and markers. This Diesel is 17" long. **$43.50**

No. 2353 SANTA FE TWIN-UNIT DIESEL—Everybody is familiar with this Santa Fe powerhouse — it pulls the Emperor Chief. Like all these big Lionel GM double "A" units it is equipped with two worm-drive motors, built-in horn and *MAGNE-TRACTION*. Length 26½". Has headlights and operating knuckle couplers on both pilot ends. **$47.50**

"B" UNITS FOR GM-TYPE DIESELS—This year Lionel makes available three Diesel "B" units to match the double "A's" shown above. They are blueprint-accurate in design — measure more than 13 inches long. Used between your big "A" units they'll make an engine nearly 40" long.

No. 2343C SANTA FE
No. 2344C NEW YORK CENTRAL
No. 2356C SOUTHERN RAILWAYS

Each **$9.95**

31

WOW! IT'S A "LIONEL"

1949: A rubber brakeman opened the door and looked out when the remote control button that activated the operating boxcar was pressed. The door closed by hand.

Lionel's miniature billboards advertised real products like Nash, Frigidaire, and Halicrafters TV sets. Some came free with the catalog. Eight million cardboard signs were printed in one year.

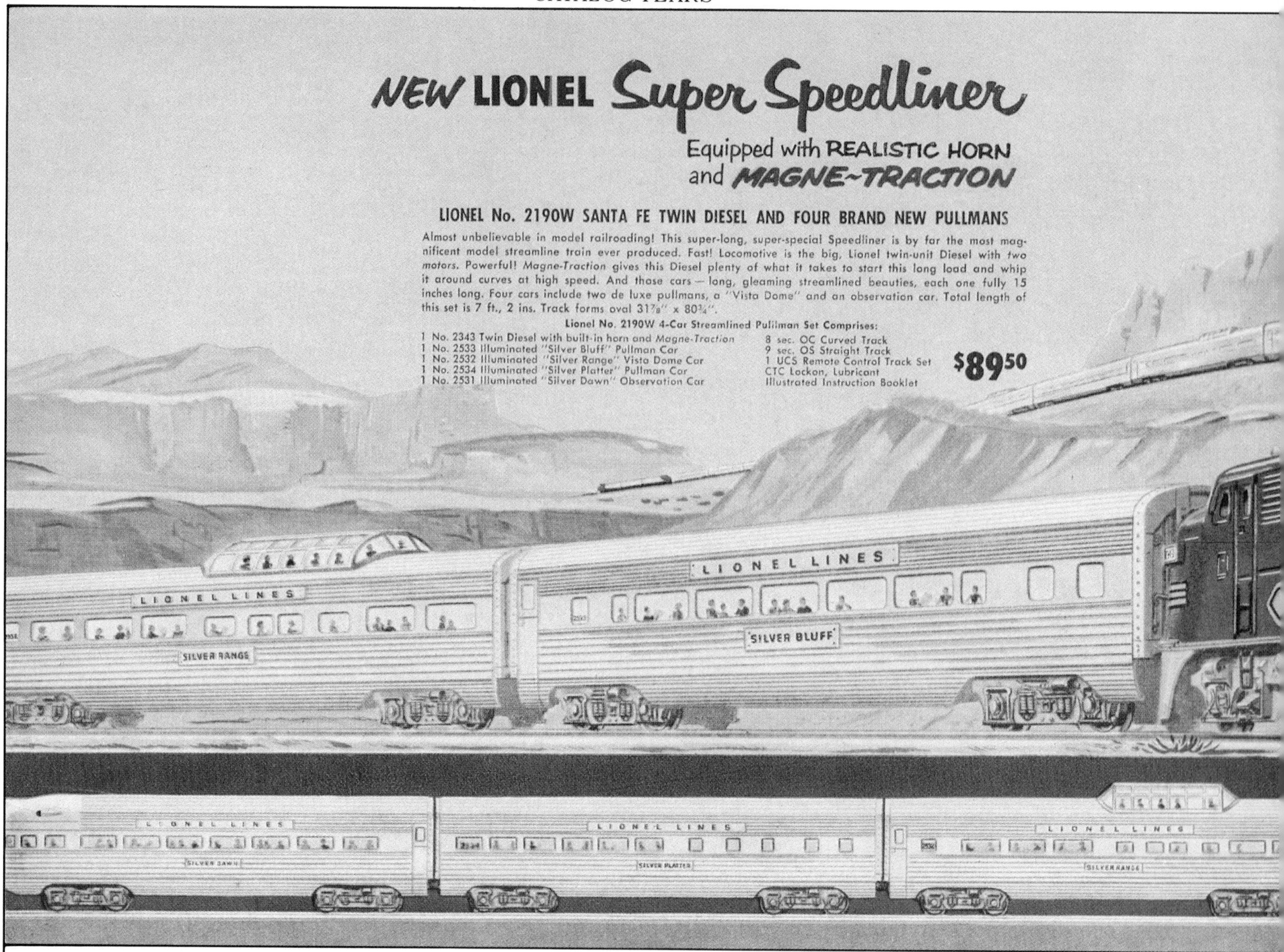

NEW LIONEL Super Speedliner

Equipped with REALISTIC HORN and *MAGNE~TRACTION*

LIONEL No. 2190W SANTA FE TWIN DIESEL AND FOUR BRAND NEW PULLMANS

Almost unbelievable in model railroading! This super-long, super-special Speedliner is by far the most magnificent model streamline train ever produced. Fast! Locomotive is the big, Lionel twin-unit Diesel with *two motors.* Powerful! *Magne-Traction* gives this Diesel plenty of what it takes to start this long load and whip it around curves at high speed. And those cars — long, gleaming streamlined beauties, each one fully 15 inches long. Four cars include two de luxe pullmans, a "Vista Dome" and an observation car. Total length of this set is 7 ft., 2 ins. Track forms oval 31⅞" x 80¾".

Lionel No. 2190W 4-Car Streamlined Pulilman Set Comprises:

1 No. 2343 Twin Diesel with built-in horn and *Magne-Traction*
1 No. 2533 Illuminated "Silver Bluff" Pullman Car
1 No. 2532 Illuminated "Silver Range" Vista Dome Car
1 No. 2534 Illuminated "Silver Platter" Pullman Car
1 No. 2531 Illuminated "Silver Dawn" Observation Car

8 sec. OC Curved Track
9 sec. OS Straight Track
1 UCS Remote Control Track Set
CTC Lockon, Lubricant
Illustrated Instruction Booklet

$89.50

LIONEL LINES

SILVER RANGE

SILVER BLUFF

1952: The Santa Fe, with its aluminum passenger cars, covered two pages of the catalog and half the living room.

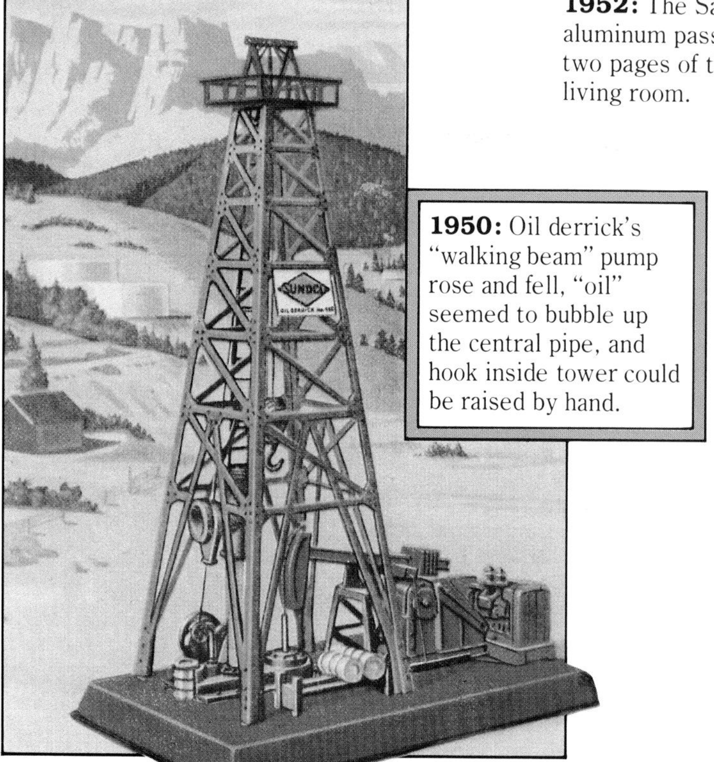

1950: Oil derrick's "walking beam" pump rose and fell, "oil" seemed to bubble up the central pipe, and hook inside tower could be raised by hand.

1954: Electromagnetic gantry crane picked up scrap iron. It could be rolled by hand on its small wheels.

1955: The *Berkshire* was Lionel Lines' biggest steam freight locomotive. Unfortunately, the detailed turntable existed only in the catalog.

1955: The ice depot had a worker who pushed blocks of plastic "ice" (complete with bubbles inside) into the open roof hatch of a refrigerated produce car.

1952: Dreams of realistic railroad empires were launched with accessory pages like these.

NEW, REALISTIC LIONEL ACCESSORIES

Lionel layouts are tops in model railroading because they "do more things" than any others. Lionel railroad accessories, as well as rolling stock, provide real railroad action. These brand new accessories are good examples of Lionel engineering realism — they move, they light up — they give your pike "real life".

LIONEL No. 450 NEW OPERATING SIGNAL BRIDGE

Here's the accessory you've been waiting for — the Operating Signal Bridge! Targets, switch boxes, steel girder construction are all direct copies of the real thing. Spans two parallel tracks easily. There are two red-green lights on the bridge, one for each track. The signal lights are operated by passing train (on the block signal principle). Has provisions for mounting additional targets, facing either way. For wiring additional lights or manual operation see instruction sheet included with the bridge. Dimensions: Inside width 7½". Inside height 6". **$5.95**

No. 450L Extra Light and Target, each $2.00

LIONEL No. 445 NEW OPERATING SWITCH TOWER

Now — a true touch of railroading for your yards or outland junctions — the Switch Tower! Watch the action as passing train automatically puts the tower into operation. Towerman on the platform goes back into the tower, while the other one runs down the stairs with a lantern. After train has passed, one towerman goes back upstairs and the other comes back out on the deck. Tower building has clapboard sides, shingle roof, inset doors and windows. Be sure to see this accessory in action! Base 6¼" x 5½". Tower is 7" high. **$7.95**

No. 157 STATION PLATFORM

Here's just the ticket for commuter use or for local stops. Station platform has deeply-ribbed roof and detailed, upright columns. Realistic picket fence contains reproductions of advertising posters. Simulated tile platform. Twin bulb illumination. Extra picket fence section provided so that you can join two platforms for a real long station. Base measures 12" by 3¼". Height 5⅛". **$3.75**

LIONEL No. 362 NEW OPERATING BARREL LOADER

Fun every minute with this amazing barrel loader! Just press your remote control button and see it work. Vibrating action of lower platform moves upright barrels over to chute where they are tipped over to ride up to the upper deck. Here they roll over tilting stakes into awaiting car. Active little workman superintends the whole operation. Base of platform is 19" by 4⅛". Height 4". Barrels are included with unit. Car and track shown are *not* included. **$7.75**

LIONEL No. 356 NEW OPERATING FREIGHT STATION

Another new Lionel creation — remote control operated. Touch a button and miniature scale baggagemen run their electric, baggage-loaded trucks out on the platform and back into the station again, adding dramatic action to freight-yard or passenger installations. Station itself is an excellent piece of scale designing. Clapboard sides have inset windows and bulletin boards. Set includes interesting set of adhesive posters for use on bulletin boards, if desired. Building is illuminated. Base is 5" by 15". Roof 5½" high. **$7.95**

22

1954: Complete train sets always came first in the catalogs, followed by individual engines, cars, and accessories. These three passenger cars were named for towns near Lionel's New Jersey factory.

LIONEL 027 TRAINS with TRANSFORMER MAGNE TRACTION

LIONEL LINES NEWARK 2436 · LIONEL LINES CLIFTON 2435 · LIONEL LINES SUMMIT 2435

HEAR THE TRAIN BLOW!

LIONEL BUILT-IN WHISTLES AND HORNS. Lionel steam whistles and Diesel horns have been developed through years of research. That's why they sound just like the real ones.

eight or Passenger — LIONEL Trains are tops

No. 1516WS "027" 3-CAR PASSENGER

New Loco with Smoke, Built-in Whistle and MAGNE-TRACTION

KYLARK — Watch her race around curves, billowing smoke, whistling for the ... A fast, high-balling streamline pullman, drawn by the big No. 2065 steam ... Sleek, gleaming cars include the pullman, the boat-tail observation car and ... Vista-Dome car from which your passengers view the starlit sky as well as the ... All cars are illuminated and show tiny passengers looking out the windows. ... measures 4 ft., 7½ ins. long. Track oval is 53¾" x 27¾".

Lionel No. 1516WS 3-Car Passenger Set Comprises:

...65 Locomotive and ...W Whistle Tender; ...34 Pullman Car "Newark"; ...32 Vista-Dome Car "Clifton"; ...35 Observation Car "Summit"; ...o. 1013 Curved Track; 5 sec. No. 1018 Straight Track; 1 No. 6019 Track Set; 1 No. 1033 90-Watt Transformer; Lockon, Lubricant, Smoke Pellets and Instruction Booklet

$59.95

No. 1517W "027" 4-CAR FREIGHT

New Double-unit Diesel with Built-in Horn and MAGNE-TRACTION

THE TEXAS FAST FREIGHT — A big, long freight hauler with the colorful "Texas Special" double-unit Diesel at the head end. This loco is unusual in model railroading — made up of GM "A" and "B" units. Your train includes the handsome black Southern Pacific box car, green NYC gondola and the cable car from which you can remove the reels and use for other loads. The caboose is of the very latest design. Train measures 5 ft., 5 ins. long. Track oval is 53¾" x 27¾".

Lionel No. 1517W 4-Car Freight Set Comprises:

1 No. 2245P Power Car; 1 No. 2245C "B" Unit; 1 No. 6464-225 Scale-Modelled Box Car; 1 No. 6561 Scale-Modelled Cable Car; 1 No. 6462 Gondola Car; 1 No. 6427 Illuminated Caboose; 8 sec. No. 1013 Curved Track; 5 sec. No. 1018 Straight Track; 1 No. 6019 Track Set; 1 No. 1033 90-Watt Transformer; Lockon, Lubricant and Instruction Booklet

$59.95

Are you a fisherman family? See back cover for those wonderful AIREX Spinning Reels. AIREX is a division of LIONEL.

11

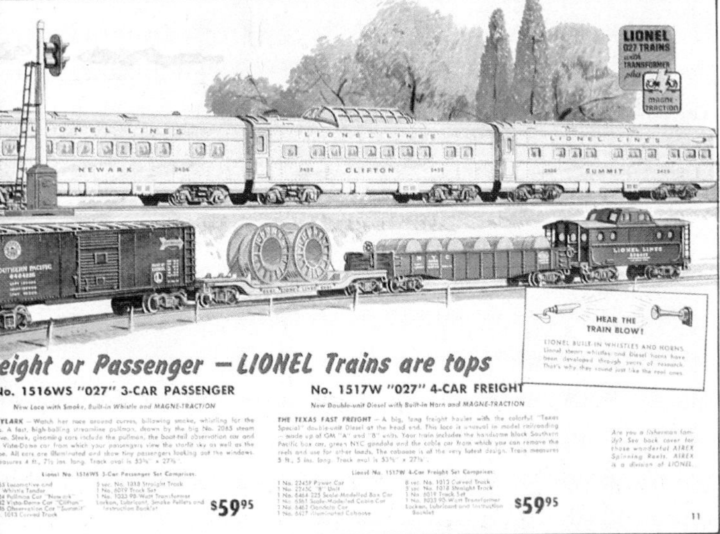

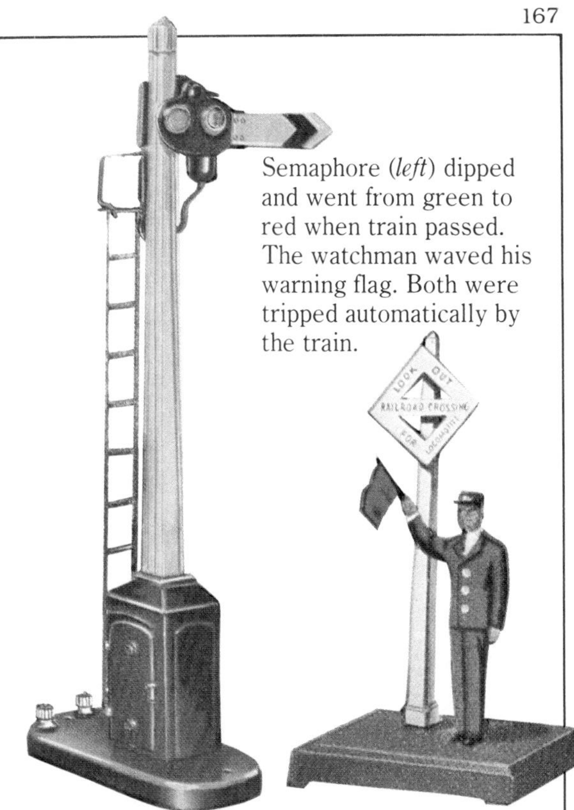

Semaphore (*left*) dipped and went from green to red when train passed. The watchman waved his warning flag. Both were tripped automatically by the train.

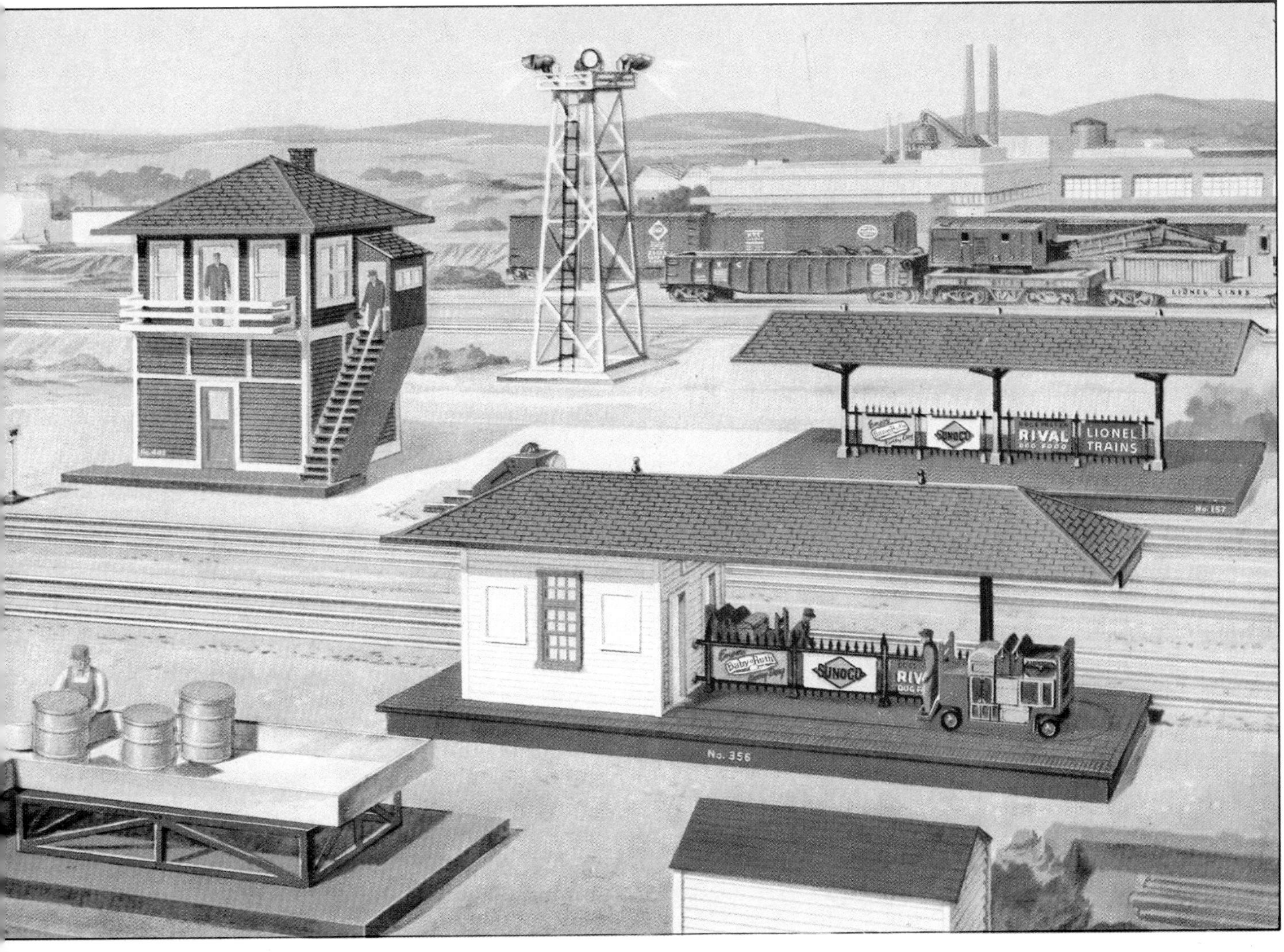

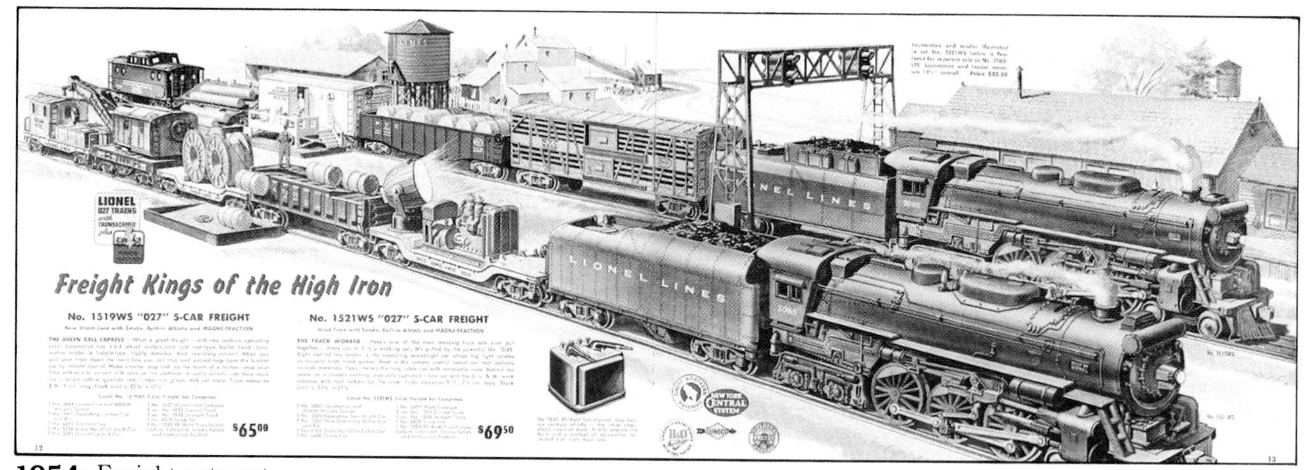

1954: Freight sets outsold passenger by twenty to one because, as Cowen was fond of saying, you could "do more" with them.

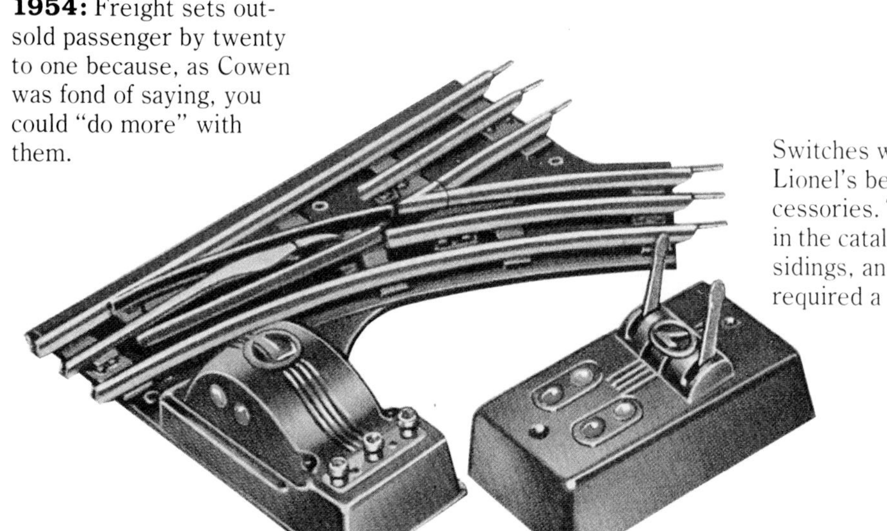

Switches were one of Lionel's best-selling accessories. Track diagrams in the catalogs were full of sidings, and every siding required a switch.

1952: The catalog showed you how to make realistic railroad scenes. Coal from the hopper on the ramp flows into the coal conveyor, which will load it into a car on the second track, all by remote control.

1951: Diesel sound effects record (steam sounds were on other side), Lionel catalog, and ten miniature billboards cost twenty-five cents.

PEAK YEARS
1946–1957

Toy trains became part of American culture after the war. Fathers and sons were supposed to develop special bonds through them, and they were on magazine covers and in TV skits. The most clever trains and accessories were developed during this period. But when the country changed, not even rocket-firing engines could preserve their position as *the* toy of boyhood.

1946: Lionel trains doing what Cowen claimed they were best at: "creating a life-long comradeship between a boy and his dad."

"Which—LIONEL do you want, Son?"

RICHARD NAPPI

The engineer's lantern moved back and forth in this store display.

TCA MUSEUM

The operating cattle and milk cars were the most popular postwar cars that "did" something. These are both pre-production models from the Lionel showroom. When manufactured, the cattle corral had a shorter base than the one shown, and the milk car platform was painted a brighter green.

JOHN WEIS

1957: Super-O track layout in Lionel showroom with the J.L.C. Manufacturing Co. at left of center.

DAVID EISENDRATH

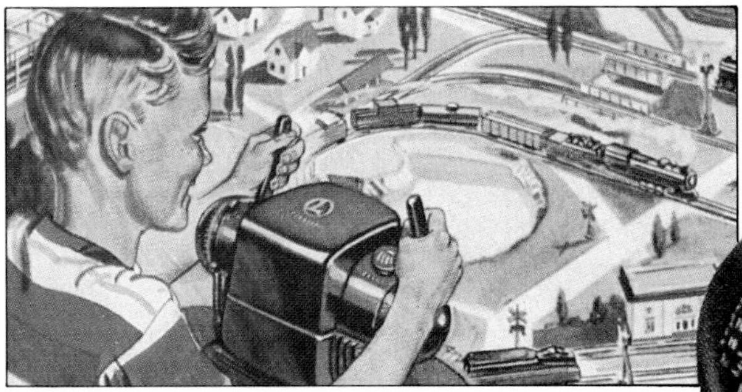

1948: The ZW transformer, Lionel's largest, was later increased to 275 watts and could run four trains plus accessories.

No Lionel engineer could handle his fast freight without a lubrication kit and a good supply of smoke pellets.

1947: Steam locomotives *were* big, but the catalog specialized in making them seem immense.

MARTIN VEHSTEDT

No. 2350 LIONEL'S replica of NEW HAVEN'S ELECTRIC LOCOMOTIVE

JAMES BURKE

Lionel-O-Rama paper cut-outs were offered as premiums in boxes of Nabisco Shredded Wheat in the mid-fifties.

1953: *Saturday Evening Post* ad says, "Mom knows everything is running smoothly" because Lionel brings her family together.

1949: A. C. Gilbert advertised American Flyer trains in the *Post* as having the same dependability and realism as his Erector sets.

YOURS HAS SMOKE AND MAGNE-TRACTION, TOO!

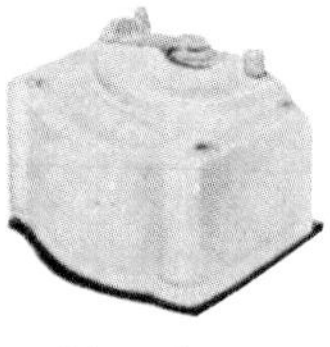

Lady Lionel came complete with an ivory and gold transformer.

1957: Lionel's ill-conceived "pastel train set for girls in fashion-right colors" produced a lot of publicity but few sales.

LIONEL LINES
RAIL ROAD CROSSING
A.T.&S.F.

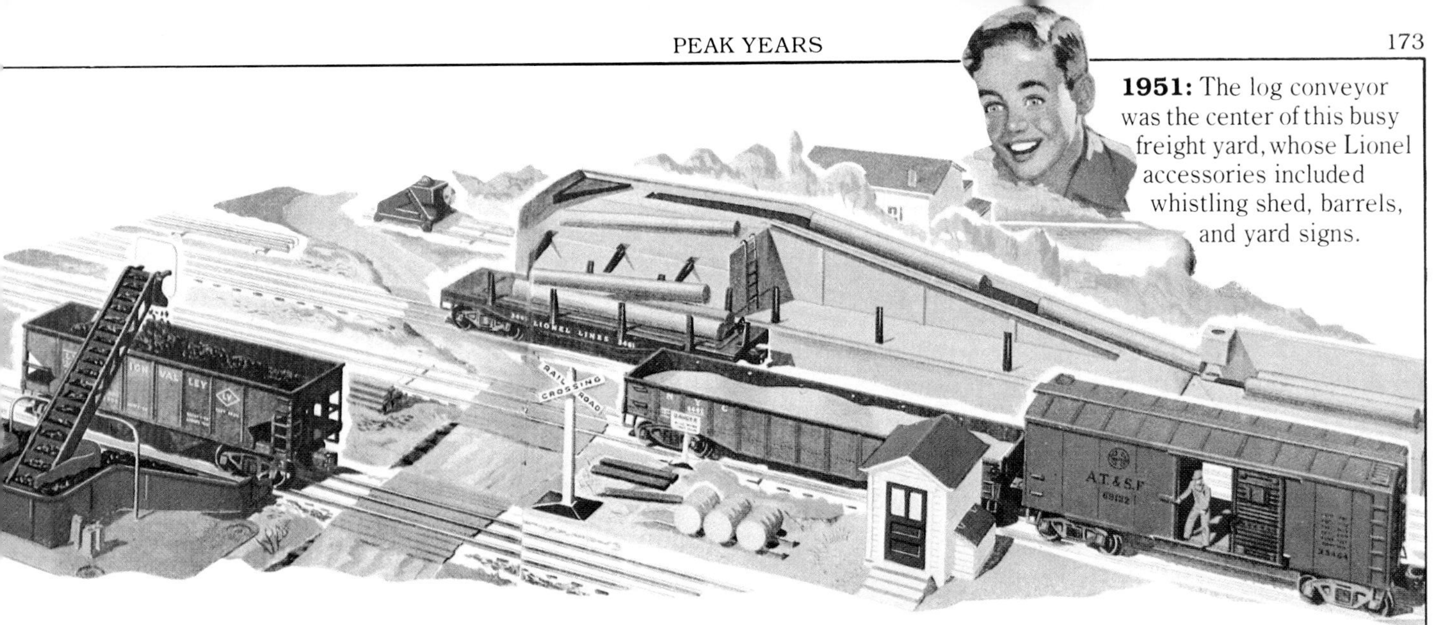

1951: The log conveyor was the center of this busy freight yard, whose Lionel accessories included whistling shed, barrels, and yard signs.

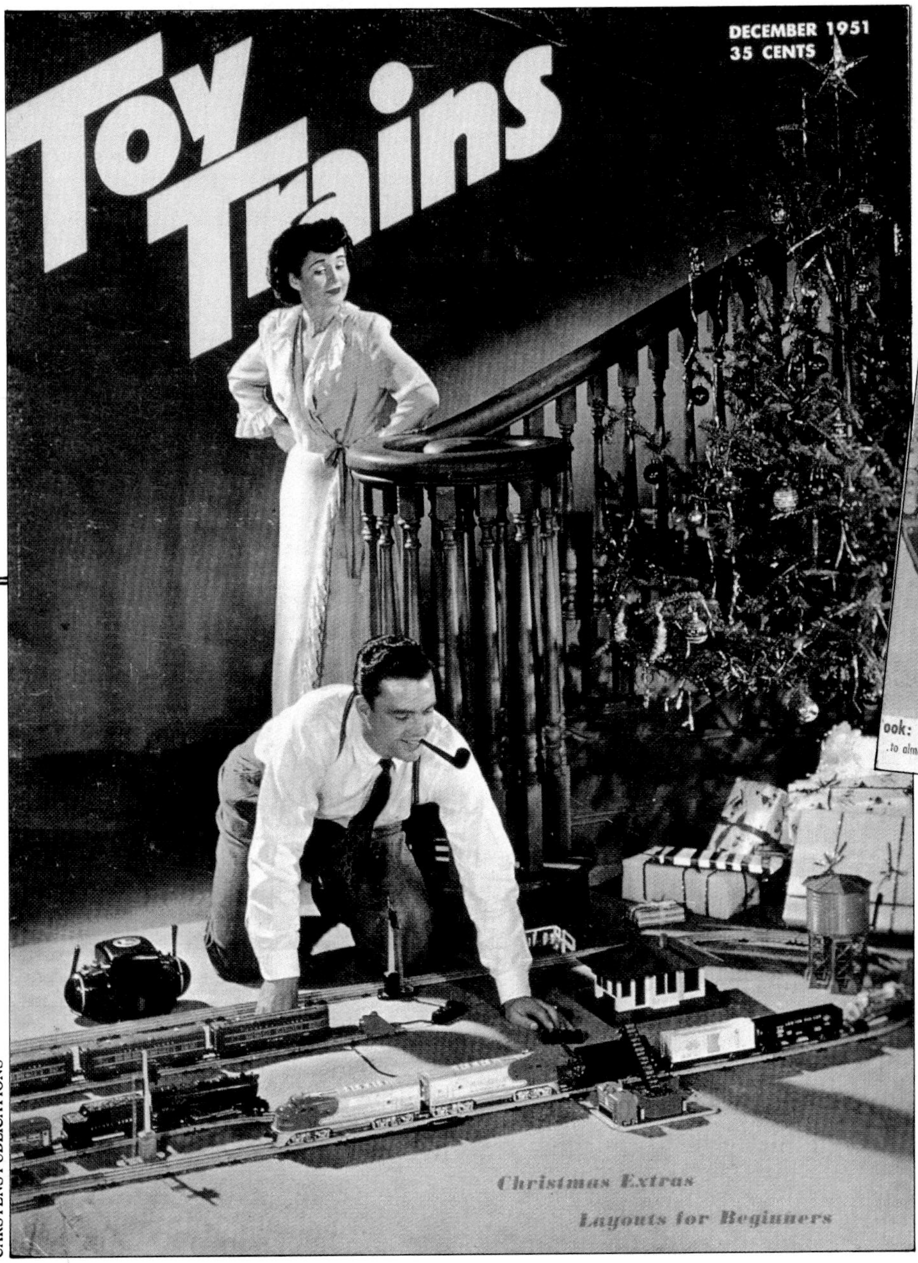
DECEMBER 1951
35 CENTS
Toy Trains
Christmas Extras
Layouts for Beginners

CARSTENS PUBLICATIONS

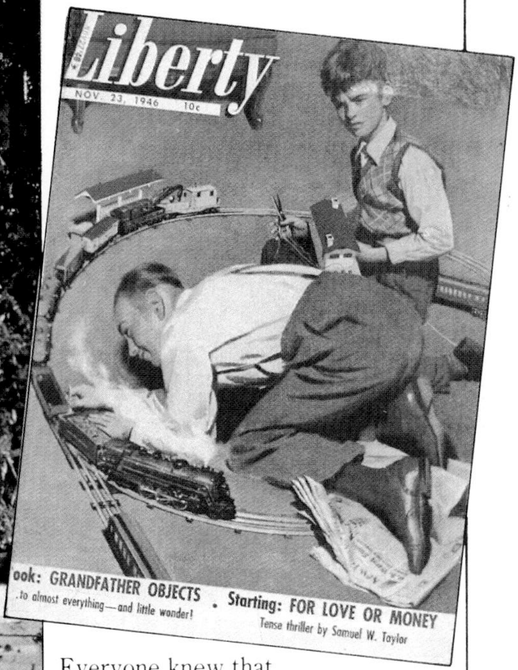
Liberty
NOV. 23, 1946 10¢
ook: GRANDFATHER OBJECTS
to almost everything—and little wonder!
Starting: FOR LOVE OR MONEY
Tense thriller by Samuel W. Taylor

Everyone knew that fathers were closet Lionelers at heart. Either they took over your trains on Christmas Eve (to their wives' slightly condescending bemusement), or they pushed you aside the next day, leaving you holding the station. Lionel's 1946 catalog was printed in *Liberty* magazine because of the postwar paper shortage.

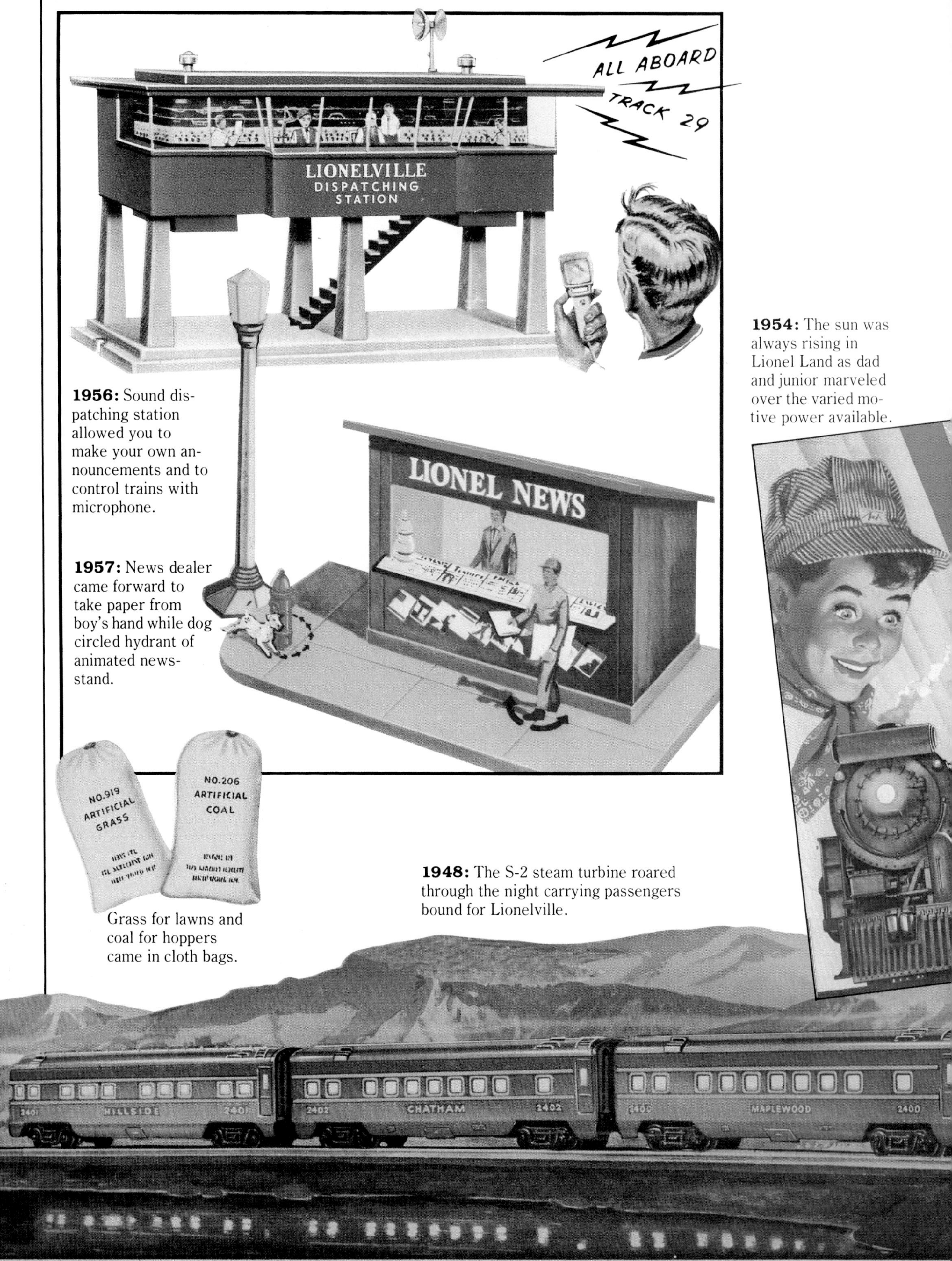

1956: Sound dispatching station allowed you to make your own announcements and to control trains with microphone.

1957: News dealer came forward to take paper from boy's hand while dog circled hydrant of animated newsstand.

1954: The sun was always rising in Lionel Land as dad and junior marveled over the varied motive power available.

Grass for lawns and coal for hoppers came in cloth bags.

1948: The S-2 steam turbine roared through the night carrying passengers bound for Lionelville.

Cowen (*left*) and son Lawrence in Cowen's office in 1950 examine the Union Pacific diesel issued for Lionel's fiftieth anniversary. On second shelf on wall behind them is brass model of 1937 scale Hudson.

The rotary beacon to warn aircraft had a red and green danger light. The heat of the lamp inside caused it to turn. Later a vibrator mechanism was substituted.

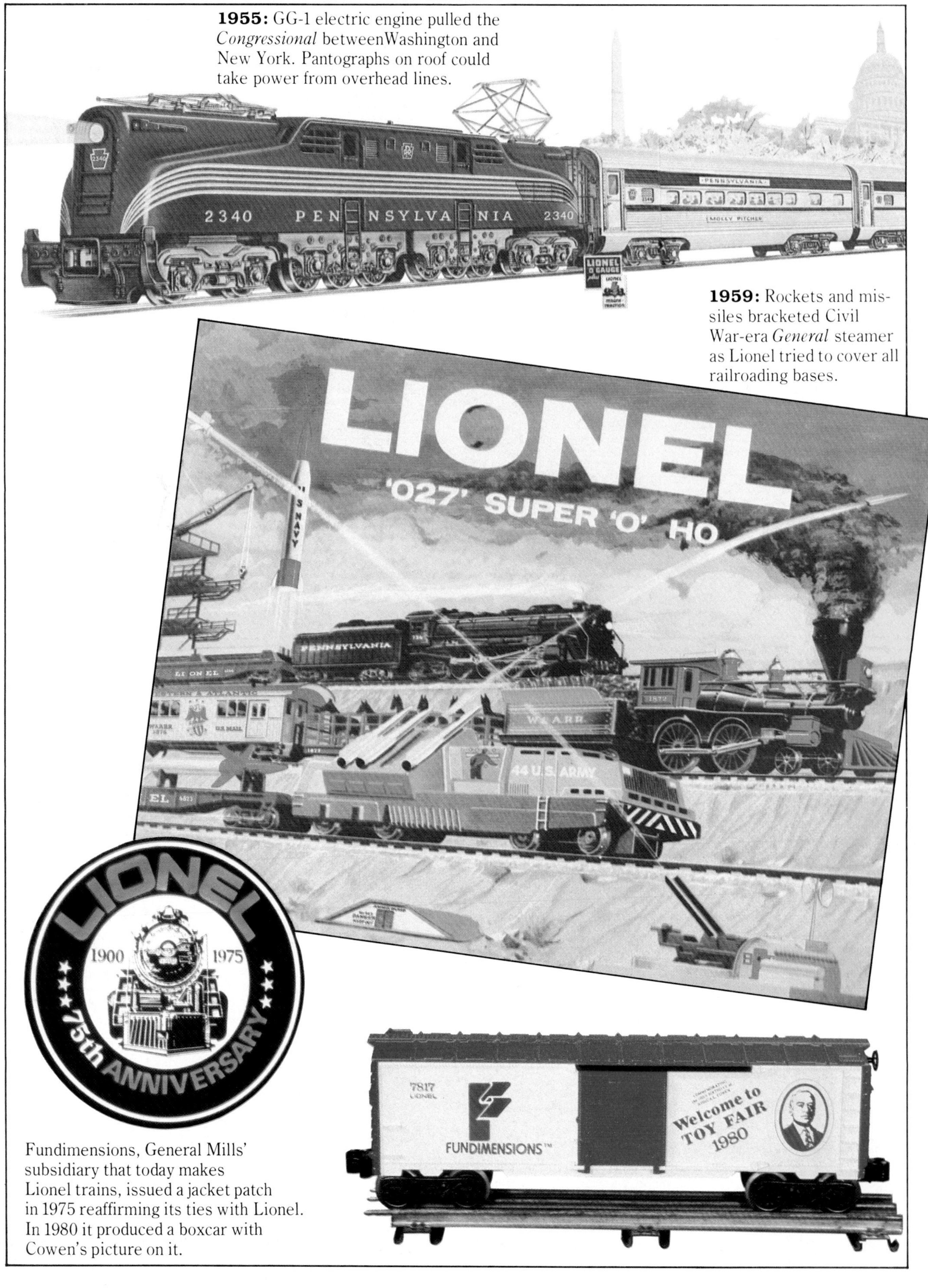

1955: GG-1 electric engine pulled the *Congressional* between Washington and New York. Pantographs on roof could take power from overhead lines.

1959: Rockets and missiles bracketed Civil War-era *General* steamer as Lionel tried to cover all railroading bases.

Fundimensions, General Mills' subsidiary that today makes Lionel trains, issued a jacket patch in 1975 reaffirming its ties with Lionel. In 1980 it produced a boxcar with Cowen's picture on it.

LIONEL TRAINS
NEW YORK, N.Y.

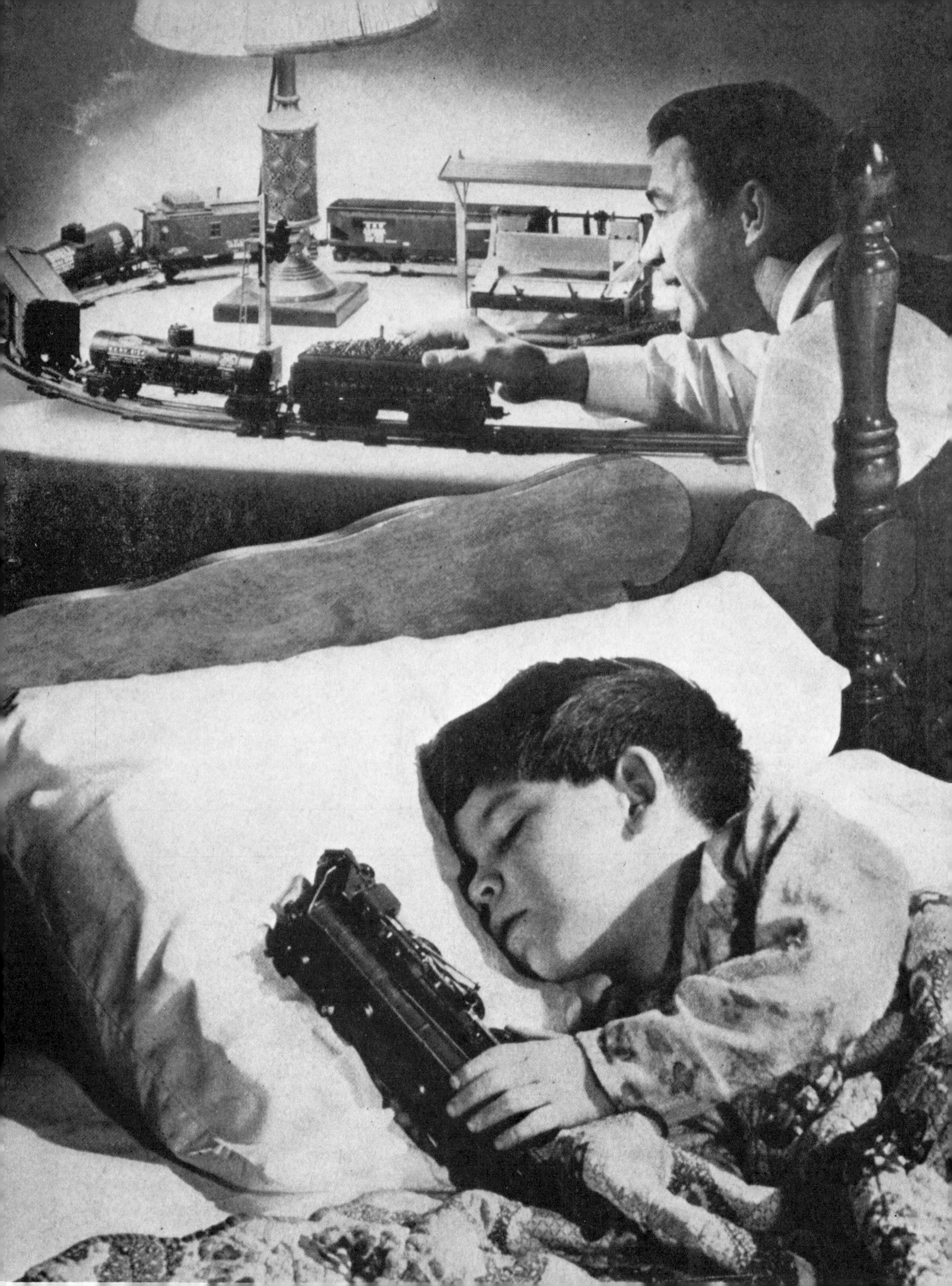

6

RIGHT ON SCHEDULE

1945-1953

With the departure of Mario Caruso, Lionel entered a decade of what would become undreamed of success. While continuing to produce war goods in early 1945, Lionel's Engineering Department was busy doodling up inventions that were as secret as anything produced for the Allies. Joseph Bonanno's draftsmen and inventors put the finishing touches on a number of soon-to-be-announced toy train miracles—real smoke, realistic knuckle couplers, radio-wave transmitters that controlled individual cars, and a detailed model of the Pennsylvania Railroad's twenty-wheel steam turbine locomotive. Until the Axis was defeated, no production facilities could be spared for such frivolities as electric trains (nor were raw materials available). But it was understood that when defense contracts were terminated at the end of the war, the race would be on to feed the luxury-deprived American appetite and to appeal to incomes augmented by defense overtime, working wives, and a four-year absence of major consumer goods.

Remembering the sales peak Lionel had reached in the post-Depression thirties and early forties before the war brought train production to a halt, Cowen and Arthur Raphael were prepared not merely to take up where they had left off but to develop the line even further. The charming standard gauge, with its excessively large track, could never be revived. For one thing, train sets would have to be cheaper so that everyone could afford them. And a new emphasis on realism, epitomized by the scale-model Hudson steam locomotive, eliminated anything as fanciful as standard gauge. Boys wanted trains that looked like the real thing, and so did their fathers, who were taking to model railroading in increasing numbers. The whistle was a move in the right direction. Now they had to follow it with puffing smoke and

JOHN FELBER

Lionel store poster showed range of postwar production.

proper-looking couplers so that Lionel Lines would be even more realistic.

Even aside from Cowen's unquenchable optimism and ambitious plans, factors were coming together that would make postwar America an ideal market for electric trains. The country was more railroad-conscious than it had been in years. The war had had a strange effect on domestic transportation. While great advances had been made in military aviation, railroads had become essential in moving vast amounts of goods and personnel within the country. Every bit of rolling stock and track was utilized as seemingly endless trains carried raw materials to belching factories and then transported cannons, tanks, trucks, jeeps—even amphibious landing craft—on strings of flatcars to ports for shipment overseas.

Troop trains took soldiers from enlistment centers to training camps, brought them home on leave, and then carried them away to embarkation points. At war's end trains met the packed troop transports and brought them back to railroad stations across the country. And in case anyone hadn't noticed that the railroads were doing a great job, the Association of American Railroads sponsored a series of dramatic ads throughout the war to keep the impressive statistics before the public. Because wartime production had gone to defense goods, leaving the railroads to make do with what equipment they had on hand, the war even gave a brief reprieve to the beloved but inefficient steam locomotive, allowing it one last chance to whistle hauntingly to the restless and horizon-bound. This final, glorious fling also kept the steam locomotive in the fantasies of worshipping children, augmenting the siren call of the Lionel catalog.

The fact that no toy trains had been produced during the war made them all the more desirable as the war neared its end. Far from being forgotten, four years of being without made children and adults yearn for their return to Lionel Land. Cowen himself was surprised at the requests that came in for *The Lionel Railroad Planning Book.*

It was clear to astute men like Cowen and Raphael that there would be more than enough customers for Lionel trains. Raphael had long studied birth statistics to enable him to predict the future train market, and predictions now were enough to make any vice president for sales giddy. There were sixteen million babies born during the war and a postwar baby boom of unprecedented proportions was forecast. Since electric trains were generally first bought for children six to nine years of age (excluding those elaborate layouts bought for month-old sons) and were then added to for the next five years, it was apparent that the early 1950s would be wonderful for Lionel if it could keep its dominant position in the industry.

The war had spurred the development of both materials and manufacturing methods that would vastly improve postwar toys. Technology developed during the war by more than 150 toy manufacturers who had fulfilled war contracts of $100 million annually would now be applied to toy production. One area of major innovation was in plastics. Five hundred new ones were on the market. Lionel would turn increasingly to plastic for freight and passenger cars; diesel locomotive bodies could be molded with more surface detail and at a lower cost in plastic than in metal. Also, lightweight plastic cars allowed an engine to pull a longer train. (The real railroads had turned to stainless steel and other modern materials to solve the same weight problem.)

The shortage of toy trains during the war, the

The future of America and of her railroads were one, according to Association of American Railroads ads.

COWEN IN PROFILE

BY ROBERT LEWIS TAYLOR

Joshua Lionel Cowen, a small, bustling, choleric man of sixty-seven, is perhaps the country's most progressive and farsighted railroader. A magnate of exceptional and refreshing immodesty, he considers his contributions to the industry at least as impressive as those of run-of-the-mill pioneers like James J. Hill and E. H. Harriman, and he feels that Robert R. Young [president of the New York Central], although shooting in the right direction, is still pretty much an upstart. Cowen is chairman of the board of the Lionel Lines, some of whose terminals are separated by as much as thirty feet.... At times he has served — together with important officials of other railroads, like the Pennsylvania and the Baltimore & Ohio — on the boards of large corporations, and he gives up-to-date methods a clamorous endorsement.

"Look alive!" he once shouted at the meeting of the board of an insurance company. "Keep moving. Never stand still. You stand still and you're moving backward. It's the same in everything. If you're a railroader," he added, directing a somewhat bilious glance toward a couple of railroader members of the board, "you need to keep your tracks in shape, put out new engine and car models, work up other modern equipment—in short, step out of the eighteen-nineties...."

The chairmen of many corporation boards try to maintain a certain detachment from routine operations; Cowen, who is crazy about toy electric trains, even after forty-seven years, cannot take them or leave them alone. Separated from his plant for very long, he gets jumpy and tense....

Cowen is short, standing just over five feet five, and has a ruddy complexion and gray hair. For his years, he appears uncommonly youthful. Some of his friends think he looks like ex-Governor Lehman, but other authorities have described him as resembling an anxious cherub. Cowen's harassed expression can be traced to his long-standing suspicion that the A. C. Gilbert Company, his only major business competitor, is trying to make good trains, too. Although the Lionel company is by far the largest of the toy-train manufacturers and has symbolized the industry for two generations, Cowen regards anybody else's appearance in the field as rash and highly presumptuous....

He has always felt that the children of America were looking over his shoulder as he worked. Furthermore, he has, he thinks, the viewpoint of a child himself, and he thus keeps a detached but automatic check on his progress. This picture of Cowen looking over his own shoulder while seated at his desk provides the best explanation of Lionel's somewhat exalted niche in the toy-train world. Any sacrifice of excellence for expediency would tax his conscience severely, and might even age him out of his juvenile viewpoint....

– *The New Yorker*
December 13, 1947

public's increased spending power, the baby boom, and improved technology all contributed to the astounding success Lionel would enjoy after the war. But this didn't account for what would become almost a mania for electric trains. Why did a mere toy come to play such an important part in the social history of postwar America?

Perhaps the answer lies in the war itself. The upheaval and tragedy of the early forties produced a hunger for normality in the country. Men wanted to return to jobs and careers. Rosie the Riveter—who had probably gone out into the world for the first time during the war—was told it was up to her to return home and raise a family. "The war was over. Nobody had causes anymore," said Roz Relin, Lionel's first public relations account executive. "You just wanted to get on with living, have dates, get married, have children—all of it." And you wanted to do it all at once, to make up for those lost war years. Home, hearth, and children became practically patriotic, testament to the feeling that everything was going to be all right.

Into this setting came improved, aggressively merchandised Lionel trains. For forty years Cowen had been advertising the train as the toy that would bring the family together. Those masterful ads from the thirties extolling Lionels as "the perfect instrument of father-son fellowship" would have an even more receptive audience in the postwar forties. Not only would Lionels "introduce you to your boy"; they would serve as proof positive that all was as it should be in your family. A Lionel in the living room at Christmas was as American as apple pie. The

Lionel's Board of Directors in Cowen's office in about 1949. Left to right: *Joel Liberman, patent counsel and Cowen's brother-in-law; Lawrence; Herbert Marache, of Granberry, Marache, a Wall Street firm; Cowen; Charles Giaimo; Philip Marfuggi; Joseph Bonanno; Arthur Raphael; Roy Duke, of Fidelity Union in Newark.*

war had been fought so that fathers could "play trains" on the floor with their sons (or, less frequently, daughters). The innocence of the "little-train-that-could" would grow more and more attractive as the postwar years became increasingly complex, as inflation grew at home and Iron Curtain threats proliferated abroad, as the specter of the atomic bomb and fallout shelter drills, the Red Menace and then the Yellow Peril, clouded the dream of a simple, peaceful suburban idyll.

This was all in the future, however. With V-E day in April, the Lionel factory workers—almost half of the approximately two thousand employees were women—could sense that a return to train production was near at hand. At the June meeting of the Board of Directors, Lawrence Cowen was elected president while his father was elevated to chairman. Raphael became executive vice president and sales manager and both his and Lawrence's salaries were increased to $25,000 a year, plus 3.5 percent of the net profits. As if to further signify the transition to a new era, the old Irvington plant was sold for $80,000. It had become superfluous with the development of the main Irvington-Hillside factory.

The atom bomb was dropped on Hiroshima on August 6, 1945. The next day Lionel's war contracts were terminated. A frantic period of retooling and retraining began at Lionel and other toy makers as they rushed to have consumer goods in the stores for the coming Christmas. While train production would not actually begin until late October, the Cowens felt it would be better to have excess demand even if all orders couldn't be filled, and they launched a massive, expensive advertising campaign to announce the return of Lionel trains. Despite the fact that the advertising budget contributed to an operating loss of $90,000 for the year, it was money well spent, helping to give Lionel a lead over its competitor, American Flyer, that was never to be challenged.

Lionel managed to get a line out before Christmas 1945. The East Twenty-sixth Street Lionel showroom was redecorated for the November 15 unveiling. Curved glass cases were built into the walls to show off train sets. Small tables were scattered about where salesmen could close deals with major buyers. The latest in recessed, indirect lighting illuminated models of the Grand Canyon and Niagara Falls on the obsolete prewar layout with its four loops of track. Light wood, curved surfaces, and art deco styling created a swank aura. Newspapers covered the event ("Lionel Trains, First Since '41, Put on Display"), recognizing the significance of what was happening: If electric trains were back, the war was really over and good times were ahead. It was news people wanted to read, news that would make them smile.

The trains themselves were disappointing. There was only one set, a middle-of-the-line freight from before the war with the unexciting manifest of gondola, boxcar, tanker, and caboose. The engine was a solid, die-cast steamer and the tender had a whistle. At $33.50 including track (but with no transformer), it was slightly more expensive than it had been when last offered in 1941. Cars were prewar models with the exception of the gondola, which was both the only new car and the only plastic one in the set. The train had been put together too quickly to allow time to include Lionel's biggest postwar feature,

Cowen and his daughter's son, Anthony Otis, take delivery of Lionel's first postwar train set for publicity photo.

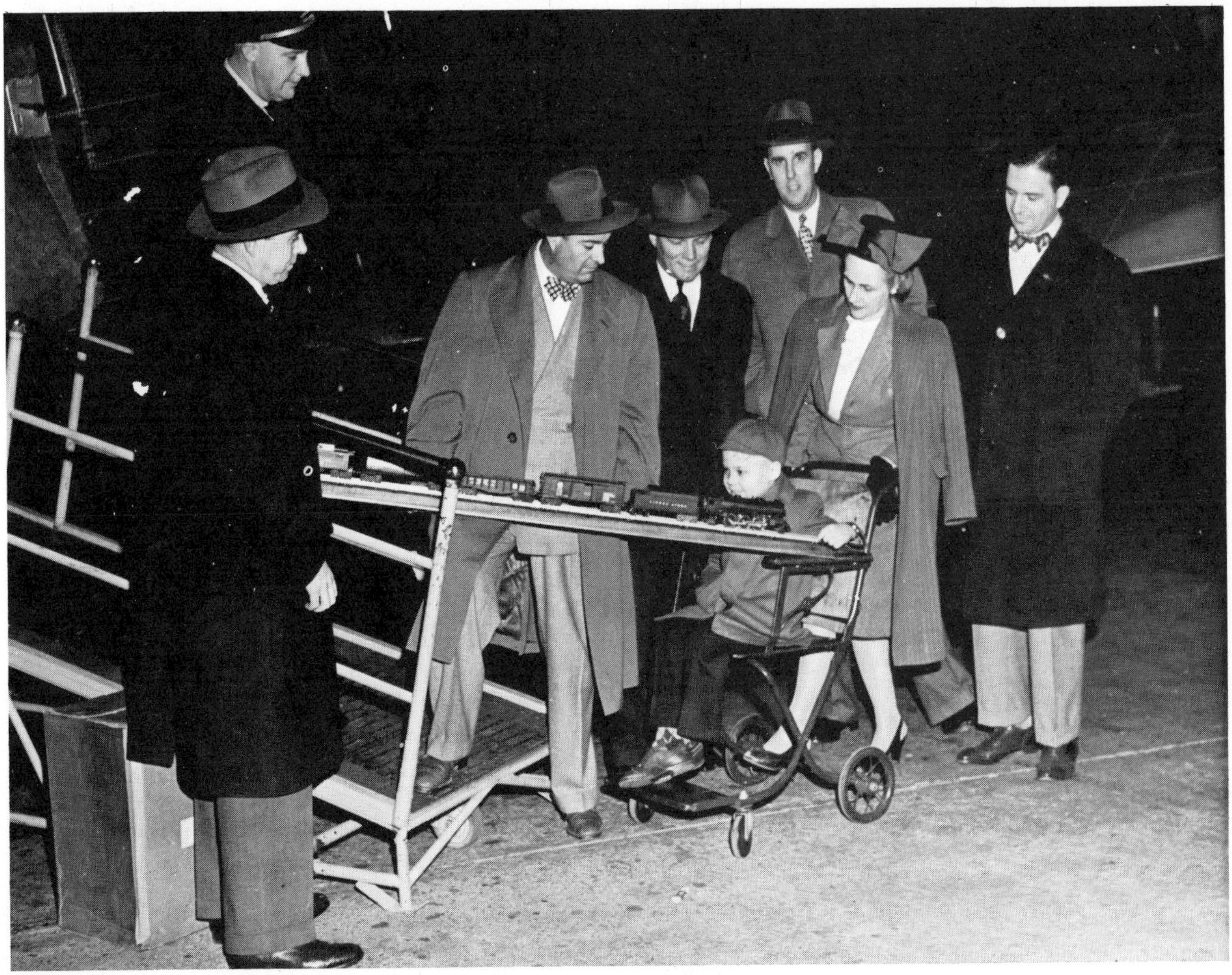

Lionel publicized its use of air freight to rush out trains for Christmas 1945 by having handicapped children receive the first sets in such locations as the St. Louis airport.

COUPLING TOGETHER

Toy trains have been coupling and uncoupling in endless variation ever since some imaginative boy tied empty cigar boxes together with string and pulled them across the floor.

Linking toy trains together was easy enough. The trick was to devise a linkage that would also uncouple reliably. Lionel tried many devices. Mario Caruso's brother, Louis, invented the latch coupler, which served from 1924 to 1938. Cars could couple together by backing into one another (it took a few tries). But the coupler had to be opened by hand to separate the cars.

Lionel achieved remote control coupler operation before the war, but it had not created a coupler that both worked and looked realistic. The prewar "box" coupler—even with remote control—was not acceptable in the competitive postwar market. The real railroads had couplers that resembled the bent knuckles on a tightly closed fist, and that's what Lionel wanted.

smoke, or the even more sophisticated radio-wave control (which Lionel would call electronic control). But the relatively few sets that did reach lucky homes that Christmas were the first to include one of Lionel's major postwar improvements, the knuckle coupler.

The new line featured at the annual Toy Fair in New York in March, 1946, was a great triumph. Smoke, electronic control, the new Pennsylvania Railroad's twenty-wheel steam turbine, a water tower that actually seemed to fill the locomotive tender's tank, and a host of new freight cars with fine detailing made their debuts. Salesmen wrote $9.5 million in orders, the greatest amount in company history, even though the country was still settling down and many of Lionel's greatest trains were yet to be revealed. Toy buyers were banking on the American public's expanded, half-a-billion-dollar buying power, more than twice the prewar figure.

Displayed on shiny tables around the showroom were the new trains. The steam turbine locomotive, modeled from blueprints supplied by the Pennsylvania Railroad, so pleased the railroad that it constructed a twelve-foot mock-up of the front of the engine that Lionel placed at the entrance to the showroom. While the turbine would go on to be a huge seller for Lionel, the real engine upon which it was modeled was a flop. Coal-burning steam locomotives were already obsolete, and even the turbine's new design could not save it. Although Lionel probably made hundreds of thousands of these S-2 turbines, the prototype proved so inefficient that Pennsy made only one. (The S-2 may have been an attempt to reassure coal producers that there was a future in coal-fired steam locomotives, for the Pennsy hauled approximately half of all coal mined in the United States.)

While Lionel's turbine was minutely detailed, it was actually out of scale in comparison to the other engines on the Lionel roster—too small for the locomotive it was supposed to represent. However, such fine points were lost under piles of wrapping paper on Christmas morning as steam turbines ("a magnificent giant of the rails") lined up under the nation's Christmas trees.

It was with the turbine that Lionel introduced the biggest innovation in its history: white smoke, which came out of the stack in time to

"BUT WHERE'S THE WATER?"

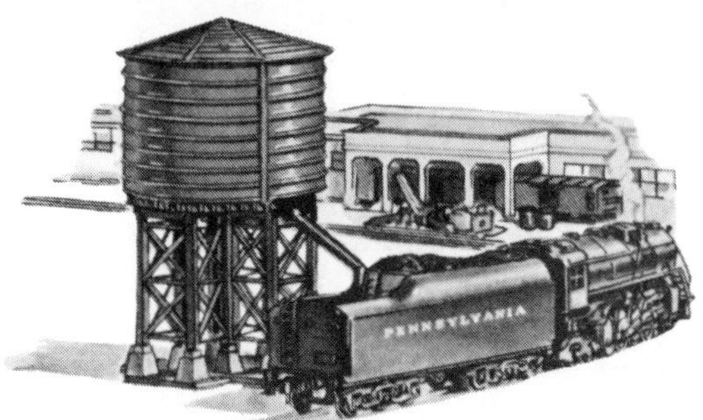

Taking on "water" from water tower's lowered spout.

Steam locomotives need water as well as coal to operate. Lionel had produced an operating coal loader even before the war, but its water tanks just stood there and looked pretty. In 1946, however, Lionel engineers came up with a realistic-looking water tower whose spout actually lowered at the touch of a button to simulate putting water in an engine's tender.

Cowen took one look at the preliminary model of the new accessory and reportedly said, "But where's the water?"

He went home and started tinkering. Soon he was back at the office with his own version of the tank: When the spout lowered, a thin column of glass appeared from the mouth of the spout, simulating water flowing into the tender. Cowen's design never went into production, but it apparently did inspire the clever model that Lionel ultimately manufactured.

In the final version of the water tank, real water was placed in the translucent yellow tank through an opening in the roof. Tablets of vegetable dye were provided to make the water visible through the walls of the tank. When the spout lowered, the water level in the tank dropped, giving the appearance that water was draining out of the tank. Actually, the tank had double walls and a hidden internal reservoir. The water was pumped into the reservoir to create the illusion that it was emptying out of the tank.

But the tank was overdesigned and too expensive, and there was still the danger of leakage. It was manufactured for two years and was then replaced by the original design—without water.

CARSTENS PUBLICATIONS

Lionel's water tower had realistically massive underpinnings and an operating spout, but what was that compared to filling your tender with seltzer?

the rhythmic turning of the locomotive drive wheels in typical "choo-choo" fashion. The only problem was the real, full-size turbine, having no pistons, did not belch smoke puff by puff but simply expelled it in a steady stream. But the inconsistency was obscured in the clouds of smoke that billowed from the engine, delighting adult and child alike.

Of all the clever devices associated with toy trains, none made more of an impact than the smoke that came wafting up from furiously churning locomotives circling living room floors in 1946. Other inventions were exclaimed over: the milkman who delivered tiny milk cans, the cattle that trooped in and out of a stock car, the railroad crossing man who came out of his shack and waved his lantern at passing trains, the crossing gates that went up and down. Many became big sellers and are remembered fondly. But today, when people recall trains from the postwar years, the first thing they invariably talk about are "the little white pills you put in the locomotive that made smoke come out." Cowen would later reveal that "the little white pills" cost about $17,000 and took five years to develop.

Every sort of device had been considered in the attempt to make smoke, many of them strange or elaborate. Toy locomotives with places for cigars or cigarettes inside them had been tried, as had others that burned cones of incense. Smoke screen machines used by the military were studied. Advertising devices, including a huge "cigar" that gave off smoke and billboards that sported figures puffing smoke as

JOEMINE MARFUGGI

Raphael, Cowen, and Lawrence by the showroom's museum with Lionel's earliest 2 7/8-gauge trains behind them at left.

they promoted particular pipes or cigarettes, were evaluated. Chemical compounds were tried. The first gave off poisonous fumes. Another exploded when compressed into the aspirin-size pill Cowen was seeking. A third was nontoxic when gaseous, but the pill itself was poisonous. Lionel finally settled on ammonium nitrate, although as late as January 1946, its potential toxicity was still worrisome, and the company planned to package each pill in Cellophane to keep them from small children. (This was actually never done, and the pellets were made available in small plastic containers with wire bale fasteners.)

Competition was fierce between Lionel and American Flyer as to who would first come out with smoke. Both introduced it in the 1946 line. Sales offices of the two companies, across from each other at Madison Square Park, considered the matter hush-hush. At the Gilbert factory in New Haven, where the Flyer smoke was developed, employees were forbidden to mention smoke at all. To keep the news from being leaked, Flyer laid out the preliminary drafts of its oversize 1946 catalog without the word appearing. Instead, there was an *X* where *smoke* would be in the final version. But a proofreader was careless, and the printed edition of the Flyer catalog, distributed to hundreds of thousands of children across the country, described a particular switcher engine as having both "Choo-Choo and X."

Flyer and Lionel played a waiting game before the Toy Fair that March, each wanting to withhold release of the new smoking locomotives until the last minute to make the biggest impact at the toy buyers' fair. But a radio news program broke the information a few days early. Caught flat-footed, Gilbert rushed several technicians to the New York showroom. Working all night, they set up the new smoking locomotives on the big Flyer layout. At dawn, passers-by peering through the circular porthole windows of Flyer's street-level showroom could see fleets of steam locomotives sending smoke up to the ceiling.

Flyer's smoke came from a liquid that smelled faintly of pine. Contained in a small capsule, it was inserted in a hole in the top of the locomotive tender. A tiny motor pumped the smoke through a tube and out the engine's smokestack. Lionel's smoke was simpler. The pill was placed in the engine's stack, where it rested on a heating bulb (which doubled as the headlight).

Lionel's 1948 catalog cover featured a turbine that produced copious quantities of smoke.

American Flyer's 1946 ad touted Erector and chemistry sets as well as smoking locomotives.

Lionel's smoke pellets came fifty to the bottle. The instruction manual cautioned against putting more than one pellet at a time into the engine's smokestack.

STEAMING WITH THE TURBINE

AAR

The Pennsylvania Railroad's innovative turbine locomotive.

The twenty-wheel turbine engine, modeled after the Pennsylvania Railroad's turbine, became the mainstay of Lionel Lines' steam motive power after the war. Selling for about thirty-five dollars, the turbine was in the upper middle price range for Lionel steam locomotives. It pulled both freight and passenger trains. Although its twenty wheels didn't make it more powerful than other engines (the two middle drive wheels on each side were for show and weren't even always in contact with the track), they did give it an imposing appearance.

Lionel's turbine went through several changes from 1946 to 1955, when it was dropped. The turbine's first tenders were square-shaped, but later tenders were streamlined with simulated water scoops under them. (A few tenders even had back-up lights.) The last model of the turbine had a fancy white line painted on the edge of its running boards and extra valve gear on the wheels.

An ecstatic owner of a new turbine.

Lionel's turbine – smoke streaming – had rounded, twelve-wheel tender with simulated water scoop for picking up "water" on the fly.

CARSTENS PUBLICATIONS

Joseph Bonanno (right) *and draftsman Al Cammarata confer over plans for a more streamlined tender for the turbine based on Pennsylvania Railroad blueprints.*

Cowen and Lawrence with a cutaway display model of the turbine that showed its internal worm gear drive train.

When the pellet was heated, it produced smoke. A flap connected to the engine's drive wheels moved up and down with each turn of the wheels, pushing the smoke out the stack in an amount proportional to the locomotive's speed. (The heating bulbs were changed the next year to high resistance wire similar to those in toasters, to go with a new, improved smoke pellet.)

The company now needed a suitable way to announce the two great new products—the S-2 turbine engine and the wonder of smoke—available to Lionel railroaders. Normally such good news would be disseminated through the catalog. But a postwar paper shortage severely limited the number of catalogs that could be printed. Lionel's advertising manager, Joseph Hanson, came up with the idea of inserting the catalog in a regular issue of *Liberty* magazine. Lionel bought sixteen color pages in the November 23, 1946 *Liberty,* the largest purchase of advertising space in a magazine up to that time. With a circulation of two million and a readership of six million, *Liberty* was the perfect vehicle to carry the message of the new Lionels.

A special advance brochure was prepared by *Liberty* promoting what the magazine called "the biggest thing in toy history... a complete, colorful line-up of the new Lionel trains for a nation of kids (and dads) panting for news of the wonderful new Lionels." *Liberty* had artist Percy Leason paint a cover illustration called "Father Takes Over," which depicted an enthusiastic father playing with the trains while his unhappy son looked on. Clearly recognizable was Lionel's new crane car and work caboose with searchlight, as well as the distinctive three-rail track. The steam locomotive, though not a turbine, was puffing smoke for all it was worth.

The catalog in *Liberty* was a great success. Lionel sold out its entire production run, and its dealers cleared their shelves. More trains were produced than in any year in Lionel's history, and sales were $10 million, also a company record.

Despite these accomplishments, Lionel still had to contend with its own problems of postwar adjustment. The corporation was experiencing in microcosm many of the phenomena facing America. Was there a housing shortage and were many Americans enduring temporary quarters? Likewise, Lionel had to buy two Quonset huts at $12,500 each for temporary storage space at the factory, and had to purchase a home for its new Chicago sales manager, Jack Caffrey, because he couldn't find housing for his family. Was the country in the throes of a marriage and baby boom? Lionel's in-house magazine started in 1946, *All Aboard at Lionel,* had photographs of 108 new "Lionel" babies in its first issue, and enough pictures of newlyweds to make it look like a wedding photographer's brochure. Was there at the same time concern that women, having worked during the war, might not be willing to give up their jobs to the returning men without a fight? At Lionel, the hottest debate in *All Aboard* was whether "girls" should wear slacks to work. Some of the comments: "Disgusting! Pants were made for men to wear, not women!" "Everyone asks if I get up before my brother so I can wear the pants in the family!" "Swell for work... but not any other time."

Lionel's postwar difficulties would be surmounted, but Cowen was soon to suffer a loss that would considerably mute his joy in the company's accomplishments. Cecelia Cowen had long had a heart condition. On June 12, 1946, she complained that she wasn't feeling well. A doctor was called; when he went into her bedroom, he found her dead. She and Cowen had been married forty-two years.

Despite his loss, Cowen insisted on chairing the monthly Board of Directors meeting as usual on June 20. When the regular financial business of the meeting was concluded, Raphael requested the chair. With his usual sensitivity and tact, Raphael moved an expression of "deep sympathy" by the board for his boss and friend of so many years, Cowen; for Lawrence, whom he had watched mature to the presidency of the company; and for Joel Liberman, Cowen's brother-in-law, fellow director, and Lionel's patent attorney.

Cowen moped around the office following Cecelia's death. He looked so dispirited that Fanny Mann, one of the women in the credit department, brought him a flower for his buttonhole to cheer him up. Like many of those in the New York office, Mann thought of Cowen as a father figure, wise and benign, to whom she could turn for advice or even a loan. Cowen appeared to enjoy the flower so much that every day after that, Fanny bought a flower and put it on his desk. When she left him a rose, people in the office talked, but she didn't care. The loyalty Cowen inspired transcended mere gossip.

FATHER'S DAY

A happy father stretches out on one of the showroom display tables to play with a steam switcher, while another examines the bascule lift bridge and simpler girder bridges. Children wait outside.

Cowen had no patience with the notion that electric toy trains were for children and that grown men had reason to be apologetic if they were caught playing with them. "It makes me mad," he fumed. "Why shouldn't a man run a train? Why, operating a good train layout is one of the greatest challenges I know!"

With great relish he pointed to one of the many customer letters he received. "To hell with Junior!" the letter began. "I've had electric trains all my life and never really started to enjoy them until I was old enough to vote. Kept my trains with me all through college and found them better bait for the female of the species than my car. My trains were the pride of the frat house and afforded more than one occasion for impromptu parties. Took them with me to Alaska during the war and finally gave them to a bunch of Eskimo kids. . . ."

So naturally Cowen loved the idea proposed by publicist Roz Relin that the Lionel showroom be put off-limits to children for Father's Day, June 1946. Only fathers would be allowed. And they had to bring three proofs of paternity: a photo of their offspring, a proud-parent anecdote, and a receipt from a maternity ward.

When the doors opened at 8:30 A.M., the fathers and father-poseurs were already lined up, some with their own improvised credentials. One carried his son's crayon drawing of an engine (steam, naturally). A pink baby sock, children's birth certificates, and even a copy of a job application describing one man as "father of three-year-old girl" were proffered. Raphael's favorite was the father who arrived with his infant son's diaper folded like a handkerchief in his breast pocket.

Several ex-railroad employees showed up on wistful busman's holidays. A former engine watchman with the New York Central brought a brown saddle shoe belonging to his fourteen-month-old daughter, although he admitted the passenger and freight trains at home belonged to him. A former New York Central brakeman arrived early and asked Cowen, "Do you need an expert brakeman to operate the toy train?" Cowen put him to work.

All told, more than 550 fathers came to the open house. In addition to being a lot of fun and a good publicity stunt ("Dads Ga-Ga Over Toy Trains; Fake Fathers, Bachelors Crash Exhibit"), the special promotion sold trains. Helped by the attention given the Father's Day Special, Saks department store sold $14,000 worth in the usually slow month of June.

For a while Cowen rattled around in the large apartment he and Cecelia had shared in The Marguery, at 270 Park Avenue. (He later moved to a smaller apartment in the same building.) He saw a lot of Saul Goodman, husband of his older sister Rose. They played gin rummy and talked selling (Goodman was a salesman in a clothing store). When Raphael and his wife and daughter went to the New Jersey shore for the summer, Cowen stayed at their apartment on East Seventy-Fifth Street so he wouldn't feel quite so lonely. There was an apocryphal tale that Cowen, the tireless tinkerer, spent his solitary summer evenings rerouting the wiring in Raphael's apartment so the phonograph went on when the bathroom light switch was pressed and the toaster popped up when the radio was turned on. Supposedly the family returned just in time to catch Cowen installing a jump-out boxing glove in the wall.

Cowen's attention was brought back to business by the unstable economy. After the first burst of postwar spending, people were growing more cautious. Electric trains were expensive, especially Lionels, with their large engines and heavy, three-rail track. American Flyer took advantage of the situation by introducing more realistic (and economical) two-rail track, with scaled-down trains to match. While Lionels were built on the approximate scale of one foot to a quarter of an inch, Flyers were built to a scale of one foot to three-sixteenths of an inch. By making American Flyers smaller, the A. C. Gilbert Company could make them for less money.

Two-rail Flyer track versus three-rail Lionel became the focal point of a debate among postwar children that was as heated as were their parents arguments over Truman and Dewey. Flyers were said to be more realistic because all their equipment was in proportion. But Lionel had far more "operating" cars and accessories, and its trains could "do" more. Flyer two-rail track was closer to the real thing than Lionel's three. But because of electrical complications due to the two-rail track, Flyer layouts could not be as complex. Feelings ran high, especially among Flyer children, who were hopelessly outnumbered by the Lionel three-railers. Having been given Flyer trains one shining Christmas morning only to come out on the block and find you had to defend them was early and painful preparation for the differences that divided the adult world.

O AND O-27

Two sizes of Lionel track and switches, O and O-27, were very similar. While both were the same gauge (the distance between the outside rails), the space needed for a complete circle of each track differed.

O-gauge track made a minimum circle of thirty-one inches in diameter. The height of the track was eleven sixteenths of an inch.

O-27 track made a circle only twenty-seven inches in diameter. The height to the top of the rail was seven sixteenths of an inch.

O-27 trains were slightly cheaper and smaller line than O. All O-27 engines could negotiate O curves, but some larger engines made specifically for O track would derail on the tighter O-27 curves.

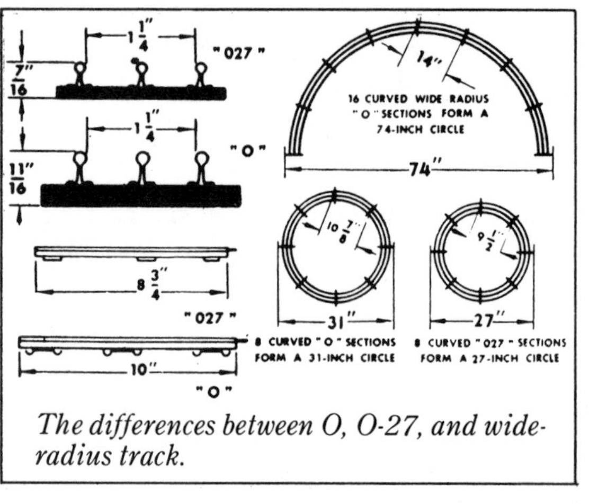

The differences between O, O-27, and wide-radius track.

The competition from Flyer and the slowing economy caused Lionel to lower its prices in 1947. Top items were reduced and train production was reorganized so that more of the lower-priced sets could be manufactured. Employees were urged to perform more efficiently so Lionel could lower prices without sacrificing quality and still make a profit.

One of the improvements that had driven up the cost of the trains was the smoke device. The bulb used to melt the smoke pill, manufactured by General Electric, was extremely expensive. It also burned out quickly, and was contained in a die-cast housing that was costly to produce. It was unthinkable to abandon the smoke feature on the locomotives, so a cheaper way of making smoke was needed. The solution came from within the company. It illustrated not only the creativity of Lionel's own staff, but the constant maneuvering for power and recognition at the factory.

Tom Pagano had risen to the position of assistant superintendent for parts production. He was in his office when Mario Mazzone, a chemist who was in charge of Lionel's plating operation and worked under Pagano, came in to tell him he had developed a new, cheaper smoke pill that would vaporize without a bulb. Mazzone was working on the chemical part of the process and Frank Pettit was building the mechanical device to heat Mazzone's pill. "How do you think I should present this?" Mazzone asked Pagano. "I don't want somebody else getting the credit."

"Here's what I would do if I were you," Pagano said, leaning against the shelves in his office that displayed Lionel's current products. "I'd put it all together and put it in a small locomotive to show it was economical to produce and didn't take up as much room as the bulb arrangement. Then when the old man and Larry and Raphael come here, I'd demonstrate it for them directly."

Mazzone liked the suggestion. He didn't want to have to go through Giaimo or Chief Engineer Joseph Bonanno, whom Pettit worked for. He went ahead with the new smoke device, while Pagano told Giaimo what was happening. "He wants to get credit for it, and also some extra financial reward," Pagano explained to Giaimo.

At last the big day arrived. The New York triumvirate was at the factory on its weekly visit, checking on any new items coming off the line and considering mock-ups of proposed products. (The engineering department under Bonanno rarely discussed anything in the abstract with Cowen. It prepared a model first so there would be something on which to try different colors, a chimney or a light, a railing or a pair of driving wheels.) The customary big lunch, complete with wine, had been eaten in the executive dining room, and the group moved to Pagano's office. A long table with two ovals of track for testing new trains was at the center of the room; under the table were drawers where experimental models were stored.

"Frank has something he wants to show you," Giaimo told the three men. (Pettit frequently demonstrated new products.) Like children eager to see a new toy, the group crowded around the table. Cowen was in the middle, with Raphael at his accustomed place just behind his shoulder. Pettit placed an ordinary small diecast steam locomotive and tender (one of Lionel's

HIGHWAY SAFETY

Cowen ran a safety first railroad, and Lionel Lines went out of its way to protect the motorist at highway grade crossings. Flag-waving watchmen, gates, and blinking red lights all helped to keep fatalities down. Such accessories usually cost less than six dollars and offered a lot of action for the money.

Passing train made watchman wave flag and crossing gate descend.

Crossing gateman's shack was white plastic and resembled clapboard siding in the fifties.

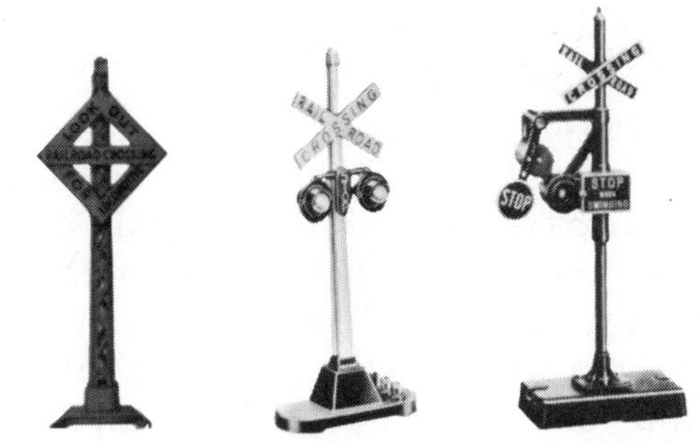

Grade crossings were protected by warning signs, blinking red lights, and banjo signal that swung back and forth.

cheaper models) on the track. Then he added a common black gondola and a caboose. He dropped a white smoke pellet down the stack of the engine and turned on the transformer. Beautiful white smoke started rising from the stack almost immediately (the bulb device had required a long time to warm up). Pettit advanced the transformer lever and the little locomotive chugged around the track leaving a cloud of smoke hanging in its wake.

There were big grins on the faces of Cowen, Lawrence, and Raphael. As soon as Pettit stopped the train, Cowen picked up the locomotive and turned it over in his hands to see if any liquid would spill out, as it used to with the first smoke generator. Only the partially consumed pill landed in his palm. "Great!" he exclaimed. "Great, great. That's terrific! Rafe, Rafe, what do you think of that? Great, eh, great, isn't it?" Raphael nodded enthusiastically at Cowen's shoulder. "What do you think, Larry?" Cowen said to his son, holding out the still-warm locomotive. Then he turned to Giaimo: "Charlie, let's figure on making it that way. How soon can we get it out? Joe, see what the guys have in it, get it designed. Go ahead right away!"

Pettit explained to Cowen that he hadn't been alone in creating the smoke mechanism, that it was Mazzone who had discovered the all-important new chemical formula for the pill. Pettit knew Cowen would take care of him; while not part of top management, Pettit was highly regarded by Cowen, who was also personally fond of him. Mazzone, however, had no such assurances. As soon as the demonstration was ended, therefore, he showed up in Pagano's office. What am I going to get out of this? he asked Pagano. I don't want just some Christmas bonus or some little extra added on. It's my formula and I want to make the pellets and sell them to Lionel.

Pagano was astonished. "Mario, you're not going to get away with that, not now," he said. "Set up here, make the pellets, and maybe in a few years you'll be able to show the company you can make them for less outside on your own." Mazzone was reluctant. "I'll go to bat for you," Pagano promised. "I'll get you a good bonus and a raise, besides." Pagano then went to Giaimo and told him Mazzone simply didn't want to give up the formula, that Lionel would have to pay him well for it, and even then Pagano wasn't sure Mazzone would part with it.

Mazzone was left in charge of production

Tom Pagano in his office, with new trains on the shelves.

(using a pill-making machine similar to those employed by drug companies). And although he had to reveal most of the formula to his staff, he managed to withhold the identity of one ingredient, the catalyst used to produce the chemical reaction. Production went forward with Mazzone adding the crucial chemical on his own. Pagano was never sure whether Giaimo and the others knew what was happening, but he suspected they did. As long as the smoke pellets were being produced, however, he felt it better not to press the issue. Within a year, fifty million pills were being manufactured.

Several years passed, and Mazzone finally did show Lionel he could produce the pills independently for less than it cost the company. He set up a small shop in Brooklyn with the help of his brother, and Lionel received weekly shipments of the precious white pellets. Eventually a liquid smoke was developed that required a simpler heating system, and the pills became obsolete.

In addition to smoke, Lionel introduced a whole fleet of new railroad cars that year, many of which provided what Cowen delighted in calling "real railroading action." Of all Lionel's so-called operating cars, those push-button delights that unloaded logs, coal, crates, barrels, cattle, and horses, the most popular was the automatic milk car. The tiny man who popped out of the white car and delivered silver milk cans to a trackside platform charmed even mothers, who were generally unmoved by the lure of clanking coal loaders and magnetic cranes. At each press of the button, out jumped the man in his spanking white uniform with another can. When all seven were unloaded, they could be returned to the car through a hinged roof hatch. It was not uncommon for peas, small marbles, B-Bs and other objects to be placed in the roof hatch by curious boys, but these only jammed the mechanism. The steadfast milkman would deliver only Elsie's finest.

The milk car was a sensation when it was introduced in 1947. Production schedules at the factory were rearranged to produce more of the plastic cars, but many orders went unfilled. Cowen was entranced with the milk car and often came out in the showroom to watch it work. He pushed the little red button on the controller for the car's special track and chuckled with delight each time a can plunked out on the green and white loading platform. "Marvelous, isn't it?" Cowen would say to whoever was standing beside him. Often he pretended he was just an ordinary member of the public who had happened into the showroom. "Now look at the smoke coming out of the locomotive," he would exclaim to some unsuspecting bystander. "Isn't that something? They say it's little pellets you drop down the stack. Wonderful! What will they come up with next?"

The milk car was a success primarily because it was the first car that actually contained a tiny figure who delivered freight by hand. Bulk commodities like coal and logs were simply dumped into bins in earlier operating freight cars; a prewar boxcar threw out packing cases at the touch of a button, but the cases tumbled out every which way. The milk car had an actual "attendant" who rode in the refrigerated car (he must have gotten pretty cold!), always ready to jump out and go to work. With his cap and overalls, stooped conscientiously over his heavy milk cans, going back and forth between car and loading platform with never a pause, the milkman looked almost animate. Best of all, it was the young railroader himself who determined with the push of a button whether the milkman worked or rested, controlling not only mighty steam engines but even adults (albeit miniature ones).

The milkman was not the only reason for the milk car's appeal. While most toy train freight cars carried loads that few people ever came in contact with, such as coal or oil or logs, the milk car carried something that was on practically every breakfast table in America. Every grade schooler had studied milk, learning how it "builds strong teeth and bones," following its romantic journey from the country to the city in refrigerated railroad cars that sped through the whistle-haunted night with their perishable cargoes. People had a positive feeling about milk (and about the milk car) that they could never have had about, say, barrels, no matter how cleverly a car might dump them out.

After the milk car was a huge success, Cowen gave the impression to the press that the invention had been sent in by a young Lionel railroader, some teen-ager who had been doodling and came up with the most successful car in toy railroad history. It was a good story, but it never

Cranes were favorites on Lionel Lines. The burro crane (left) *was self-propelled and had a motor-driven hook. The railroad crane was hand operated and was based on Bucyrus-Erie's 250-ton model.*

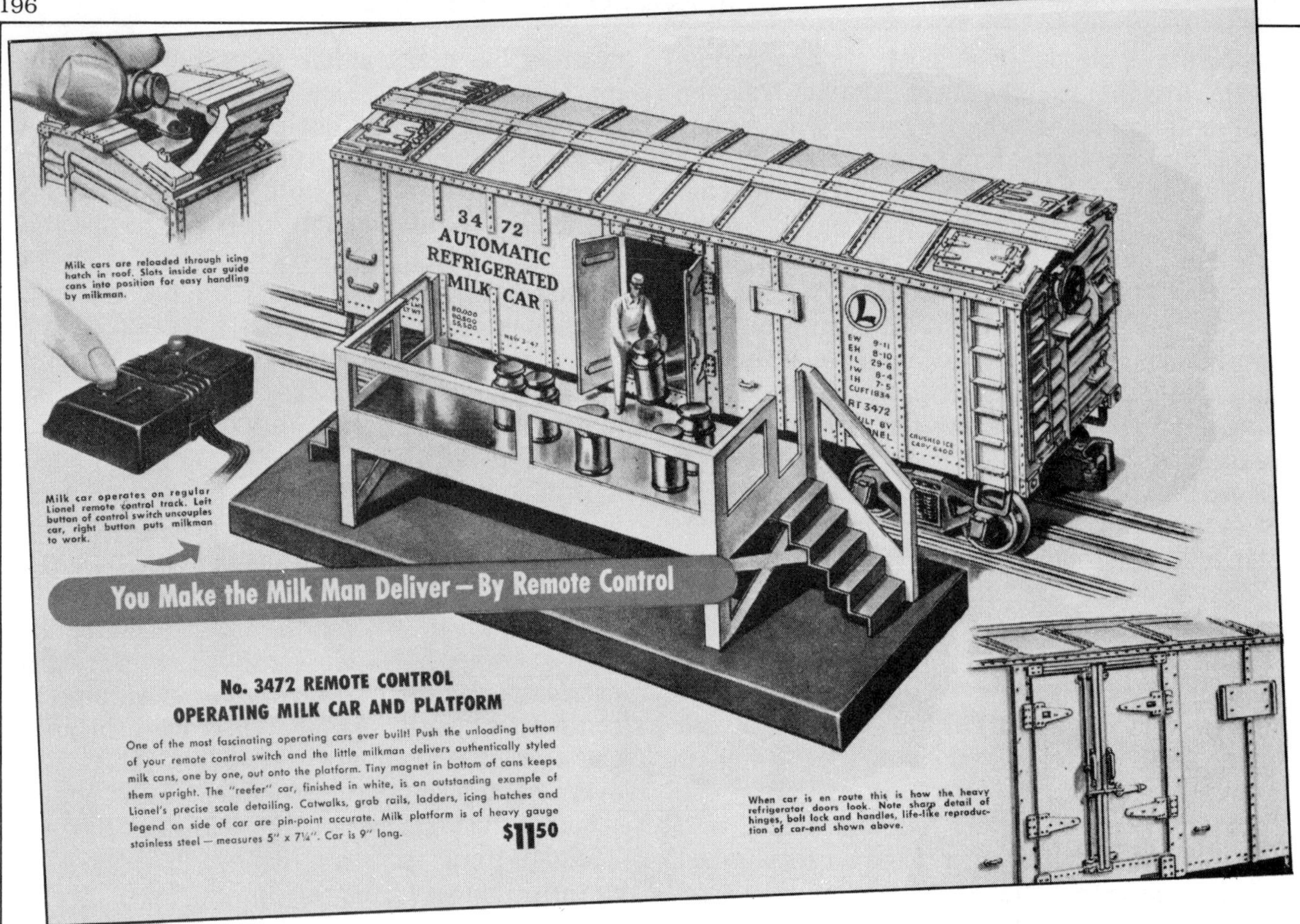

The milk car's magnetized cans were evocative of the small dairy farm, even then a vanishing part of America. The white car stood out in a time of dull reddish brown or black freight cars.

happened. The marvelous milk car came not from Lionel's engineering department but from an unsophisticated upstate New York carpenter who liked dabbling with toy trains. Richard G. Smith worked alone in his home workshop between carpentry jobs, building models of operating cars and accessories out of whatever materials he had at hand: sheet metal, stovepipe, scrap iron. Smith was not an engineer, and his inventions relied on mechanical cleverness rather than on new principles of electricity or chemistry. Lionel had been buying inventions from him since at least 1938. When Cowen received Smith's letter about the possibility of an operating milk car, Smith had already built a working model and was in the process of having it patented.

Always working independently, Smith created at least eighteen cars and accessories for both Lionel and American Flyer. Among them were a number of best sellers. For Lionel, Smith invented the milk car, a barrel unloading car, a log dumping car, a log loader, an icing station, a culvert loader and unloader, and an operating fork lift truck that actually loaded lumber on a flatcar. Smith also designed two of American Flyer's best-known cars: the Railroad Post Office car, which picked up and simultaneously threw out a sack of mail on the fly, and the unloading flatcar, which sent an armored car (in later versions, a stylish coupé) down a ramp from the railroad car. Smith also invented Flyer's oil drum loader, which came with a fork lift truck that dumped oil drums into a gondola car.

Although Smith invented the milk car in 1944, it was not manufactured until 1947. Its main feature, as described in his patent, was that the cans would be unloaded upright onto a trackside platform by "a can pusher, which can be made up to simulate an attendant." Despite his previous dealings with Lionel, Smith was nervous when he came into New York to demonstrate the car for Cowen. Cowen was immediately impressed, however, although the car was a crude model in which the cans were loaded through the side rather than through a roof hatch. Such refinements as the milkman and the charming platform design, with its railing and two flights of steps, were also missing. But Cowen knew a winner when he saw one. On April 18, 1944, he entered into an agreement with Smith whereby Lionel would pay him 2 percent of the wholesale price of any milk cars with platforms sold. Lionel made a down payment to Smith of $250, to be deducted from his royalties.

Smith was uneasy with the royalty arrangement, having previously sold his patents outright to Lionel. (In 1940 Lionel had paid him $2,250 for his patents for log and barrel loaders.) Returning the signed milk car contract to Cowen, Smith wrote, "I fully realize that it is possible for you to go around these contracts if you wished to attempt it, however I am taking it for granted that you will not. It is very unlikely that these are the last ideas along this line I will have and as long as you are on the level with me you can have first chance to get them. The royalty is not so large but that it may be worth paying just to have a chance at furture [sic] ideas along the same line."

Cowen wrote back instantly: "Frankly, we do not believe you were serious when you wrote the second paragraph. Our Corporation has earned an enviable reputation during the last forty years for its integrity, and surely after that long period it is far from our intention to break that record. Your patent attorney writes that in his 'opinion these contracts are proper and fit the situation.' All we ask you, Mr. Smith, is to share his opinion."

The milk car was introduced at a retail price of $8.95, which was raised to $11.50 during the Korean War. Based on wholesale discounts, Smith made approximately eleven cents on each car. Lionel had expected to pay him approximately $1,200 a year in royalties, corresponding to 11,000 cars. But in 1952 alone, Lionel manufactured the astounding total of some 180,000 milk cars, and Smith made about $20,000 in royalties.

Smith's carpentry soon passed by the board. Asked by a smiling American Flyer official how it was coming, Smith replied in his homey, country way, "Oh I don't carpenter any more. When it's spring, there's good fishing. In the summer, well, it's too hot. In the fall, then there's hunting. No, I don't do too much carpentering nowadays. It's pretty much mostly railroading with me now."

With its operating cars in action, steam engines smoking along, and whistles wailing,

MORE THAN TRAINS

Lionel offered more than just trains. The Lionel Chem-Lab, introduced in 1941 and available after the war, had a broad marketing approach ("Exciting Chemistry Experiments for Boys and Girls"). It is puzzling that while Lionel thought girls might like chemistry sets (there was, after all, the precedent of Mme. Curie), it continued to exclude them from the world of toy trains, making no appeal to them in the train portion of the catalog.

As if the Chem-Lab did not compete directly enough with A. C. Gilbert's well-known chemistry sets, in 1947 Lionel brought out its Lionel Construction Set, obviously aimed at Gilbert's famous Erector building kits.

Neither the Chem-Lab nor the Construction Set was very successful compared to the trains, and they were soon dropped.

Another attempt at diversification, introduced in 1947, was the Lionel Stock-Watch, a portable device for electrifying a farm's wire fence to keep livestock penned in. It developed its electrical charge through a battery advertised as good for one hundred days. While the chemistry and building sets seemed a reasonable extension of the Lionel line and were marketed through the company's existing channels, the Stock-Watch was an unconventional product for a toy company. It was also too sophisticated for the rural farm market, and did not do well.

Ferris wheels, trucks, and bridges could be built with the Construction Set.

The GG-1 in the 1948 catalog had only its rear pantograph up in true railroad fashion.

Lionel decided to broaden its engine roster of motive power. After all, Cowen prided himself on being an up-to-the-minute railroader, and steam was on its way out. In 1947, he introduced a replica of a massive new electric engine, the Pennsylvania's GG-1, a twenty-wheel monster that took its power from overhead catenary lines. Lionel's could do the same thing using its flexible pantographs. However, most Lionel railroaders left the pantographs up just for show while the GG-1 took its power from the center rail like any other Lionel engine. While a confirmed steam man and a sentimentalist, Cowen still liked electric engines. "They sort of slide along, like a real pretty snake," he said. "I could watch them for hours." Diesels were regarded with more scepticism. "I am not personally an anti-diesel railroad man," he once said. "They make a pretty engine, but they give a dull performance. They lack movement." By dull performance, he meant they were without the exposed piping, flashing driving rods, chuffing smoke, and mournful whistle of his favorite steamers, like the New York Central Hudson. But diesels were the wave of the future. Railroads were already one-third diesel-powered in the late forties, and Lionel Lines was not about to be left waiting in the roundhouse.

When the modern diesel came to Lionel in 1948, it was such a smash hit Cowen must have wondered why he hadn't "modernized" sooner. If any one single item could be said to be responsible for Lionel's phenomenal postwar success, making the company one of the leading toy manufacturers in the world, it was the silver, red, and yellow streamlined Santa Fe twin diesel. The best-selling engine in Lionel's long history, the Santa Fe F-3 was so sleek, its colors so bright in contrast to the sooty black steam engines, it immediately became the highly recognizable symbol of Lionel. Its two motors humming, it moved implacably around the tracks, sounding its nasal air horn, able to pull any number of glistening passenger cars up the steepest toy railroad grade. (The horn was powered by a flashlight battery in the engine, bringing Cowen full circle from his early days at the Acme Electric Company.)

The Santa Fe seemed the very engine grade school readers were always describing when "Tom" and "Nancy" took an overnight train trip to visit their country cousins (leaving their collie, Shep, in the baggage car), eating in the diner, sleeping in berths, and admiring the conductor and engineer. Over two feet long, with headlights and operating couplers at both ends, the Santa Fe was so popular it ran in the Lionel catalog for nineteen years.

A year after its appearance, the diesel was doing better than the steam engine ever had. Salesmen couldn't fill their orders for the new engine. In a reversal of normal practice, store buyers courted salesmen in hopes of being favored with an extra three or four Santa Fe's. Jack Benny built part of a radio show around the engine, and even twenty-five years later the Santa Fe was still being written about as newspaper columnists recalled their childhoods.

While it was Lionel's star diesel, the Santa Fe did not debut alone. Cowen had always felt boys wanted to play with trains that they saw in their own regions of the country. (For that reason he was never very eager to manufacture a foreign locomotive, even though they had more colorful markings than American engines.) The Atchison, Topeka and Santa Fe Railway served the western half of the country, from Los Angeles to Chicago. What of Lionel's customers east of Chicago? Geographic balance was needed.

Lionel was already using the Pennsylvania Railroad's name on its steam turbine locomotive, so it turned to the New York Central for the markings on the companion diesel to the Santa Fe. The New York Central engine had nothing like the colorful graphics of the Santa Fe; the legacy of stern, pinch-penny Commodore Vanderbilt still governed the Central. Its steam locomotives were black, without any splash of color on cab roof or boiler front, and its diesels were a sedate, tasteful two-tone gray with white striping. So Lionel made its New York Central diesel just that way. It looked dull compared to the Santa Fe, but it was very realistic and was popular with serious enthusiasts, staying in the catalog a respectable eight years.

Cowen was aware that putting the name of a railroad on the side of tens of thousands of engines or cars was great advertising for a company. The F-3 was an animated ad. What other media could claim it entered not only literally into the living rooms of American families but into their hearts as well? Lionel trains were treasured for years and passed on to the next generation still bearing the advertiser's message.

Cowen at the new showroom layout with the modernized electromagnetic crane to his left.

Bringing out a new F-3 diesel like the Santa Fe in distinctive road markings, the railroad's name emblazoned boldly on the engine's side, gave Lionel a good opportunity to ask the railroads to contribute toward the cost of the new engine. The Sun Oil Company (Sunoco) paid Lionel an ascending fee of fifteen to twenty-five cents a car up to a yearly total of $15,000 to put its name and yellow diamond emblem on Lionel tank cars. And the Curtiss Candy Company had its Baby Ruth bars not only on the sides of boxcars but on Lionel station placards and miniature roadside billboards.

With broader, flatter surfaces than the traditional curved boilers of steam locomotives, diesel engines gave railroads a real chance to sport special color schemes and symbols. This was even more true for Lionel's miniature engines.

Both the railroads themselves and the diesel's builder, General Motors' Electro-Motive Division, stood to gain from the publicity connected with Lionel's introducing its first modern streamlined diesel engine. With these factors in mind, Lawrence approached General Motors, the Santa Fe, and the New York Central with a scheme for joint financing of the new dies required for the F-3. Each company would put up one-quarter of the cost in exchange for their names being on the new diesel.

The deal was made. The Santa Fe came off best, for while putting up the same amount as the New York Central, it saw substantially more of "its" engines made. On the other hand, General Motors had its emblem on every F-3, whether Santa Fe or New York Central. (And in 1952, when the orange and silver Western Pacific joined the Lionel F-3 fleet, it, too, sported a GM emblem right next to where it said "Built By Lionel.")

In typical though puzzling fashion, the Lionel catalog downplayed the introduction of the F-3 diesel. In fact, in the hectic years just after the war, the catalog seemed always a year behind the line. In 1947, when the new GG-1 electric engine was introduced, it was squeezed into half

THE ATCHISON, TOPEKA & SANTA FE

To have its name put on Lionel's new F-3 diesel, the Santa Fe Railway agreed to pay approximately $7,000 to cover one quarter of the cost of tooling. Lawrence, who approached the railroad, estimated that 16,000 Santa Fe engines would be made in 1948, the first year of production, and more in following years. In fact, at its peak, Lionel was turning out 125 Santa Fe's an *hour,* the engines coming off the assembly line under their own power in a final test of their twin motors.

Ironically, while the 1948 catalog bragged of the diesel's "colorful, accurate markings," it was pictured with drab black markings. Silver would eventually appear on the engine (the catalogs were often drawn up before color schemes were made final on the trains). Lawrence had also promised the railroad that the Santa Fe name would appear on a boxcar. The 1948 catalog showed such a car, but it was not made until the next year.

CARSTENS PUBLICATIONS

The Santa Fe completes the trinity of father, son, and Christmas tree (above) *in a Lionel publicity photo epitomizing the early fifties. Since most children saw little distinction between Lionel and Santa Claus anyway, Lionel put him on the cover of its employee house organ, busily making one of the country's favorite diesel engines.*

The Santa Fe Railway was as proud of its F-3 diesel as Lionel was of its smaller version of the engine that pulled the Super Chief.

JACK BENNY AND THE SANTA FE

Lionel's model of the F-3 diesel in Santa Fe road markings did much to popularize an already legendary railroad. Jack Benny utilized the success of Lionel's engine in a skit on his radio show of December 17, 1950. Announcer Don Wilson set the scene:

> DON: And now, ladies and gentlemen, let's go out to Jack Benny's home in Beverly Hills. At the moment, Jack is out doing his Christmas shopping and Rochester is just leaving to do his.
>
> *(Sound: window closing)*
>
> ROCH: Oh, oh. What's this on the desk? Hm . . . a letter in Mr. Benny's handwriting. "Dear Santa . . . Christmas is almost here and it would make me very happy if you gave me a train." . . . Hee, hee, hee. When Mr. Benny wants a train, he wants a *train*. This letter isn't addressed to Santa *Claus*. It's addressed to Santa Fe. . . . Well, they may send him one; he's mentioned them enough.

The Santa Fe did not send Benny a real train. But its public relations department did send him what many children in the country felt was just as good: a Lionel model of the F-3, which the Santa Fe Railway could buy at a special 50 percent discount price of $21.25. "Rochester" already had his own model, however, for he was a Lionel fan.

a page and shown with the wrong number on the front of the engine, probably because the decision to release it was not made until relatively late in the year. When the Santa Fe and New York Central made their debuts, the catalog cover featured a typically romanticized painting of Lionel's smoking twenty-wheel steam turbine. Whether out of caution or a sentimental attachment to steam, it was not until page twenty of the thirty-six-page catalog that the diesels appeared under a banner headline.

With new engines and cars pouring out of the Lionel shops, a suitable display layout was needed in the New York showroom. The old prewar layout was sadly outdated, even with the added scenic attractions of Niagara Falls and the Grand Canyon; indeed, accessories from as far back as the days of standard gauge were still on the layout. During the summer of 1948 a new layout was built (Lionel called it a panorama). It was approximately sixteen by thirty-two feet and cost $12,000 fully landscaped and equipped. To a young child, his chin just clearing the railing, it contained all the magic a Lionel catalog had ever promised.

There was a four-track main line, just like the fabled New York Central's that ran up the Hudson from New York to Albany. A tiny village perched on a mountain plateau. Some distance away was a two-track below-ground-level station, reminiscent of New York's subway system. Artificial rivers coursed through the layout, spanned by every type of railroad bridge Lionel made. For servicing steam locomotives, there was a roundhouse with a turntable. Stations, water towers, cranes, coal loaders, crossing gates, and signals were scattered with wild abandon. And in the front, in a place of honor, was a hand-built factory named the J.L.C. Manufacturing Co. The control panel had four huge ZW transformers, Lionel's newest, each of which could operate four trains.

The J.L.C. Manufacturing Co. on the showroom layout duplicated the raked windows of the Lionel factory.

MIKE MAROTTA

Cowen delighted in showing the layout off to toy buyers and visiting dignitaries. But like everything else he built, it was not only entertaining but practical as well. For in addition to being a fine way of displaying Lionel's latest trains, it became an attraction in itself. Newspapers and TV newsreels, seeking their annual Christmas story, often ended up at the showroom. The layout became the standard backdrop in photographs of Cowen and Lawrence. Wire service photographs of it were distributed around the country. Lionel had photos of it made up and sent free to hobby and toy magazines, which often used the pictures with their stories on the growing popularity of electric trains. A tremendous draw for the public, the layout also gave Cowen a setting in which to practice his own special brand of incognito market research.

Cowen was mingling with the showroom crowds one Christmas season, eavesdropping as usual without identifying himself, when a man with his son accosted a salesman on the floor.

"I just bought my boy here a new Lionel train set, and when we got it home it didn't work," the man said accusingly.

Cowen, all ears, sidled up to them. "Did you fasten the wires to the clip you attach to the track?" Cowen asked, pretending he was just an interested customer.

"Well, I set the wires under there so they were in contact," the man said.

"Did you attach them or did you just set them there?"

"I set them under there because the weight of the train would make the contact," the man explained.

Cowen scowled up at him. "The reason your trains don't work is because you don't read the instructions, you damn fool!" And with that, Cowen stalked off. The salesman was too embarrassed to inform the customer he had just been told off by Joshua Lionel Cowen himself.

Cowen's irascibility was usually only a thing of the moment. America's premier manufacturer of toy trains seemed to indulge himself in passing tantrums no less than any child for whom his product was intended. But those whom Cowen seemed to respect most didn't accept his outbursts. Lillian Appel Herman was one of them. Lillian, of an old Charleston Jewish fam-

LIONEL GOES FISHING

Cowen with one that didn't get away.

Both Cowen and his son enjoyed fishing. It was through Lawrence's interest in the sport that Lionel acquired its subsidiary company, Airex.

Lawrence was on a fishing trip on the St. Lawrence River when he met Bache Brown, one of the world's leading fresh-water casters. Brown was using a new type of spinning reel manufactured by the Airex Company, with which he was connected. Lawrence was impressed not only at the accuracy and length of Brown's casts, but at the absence of backlash that frequently fouled conventional reels.

Enthusiastic both about the reel and the opportunity to make his mark at Lionel, Lawrence returned to New York and set about acquiring Airex. By January 1948, Lionel had purchased two-thirds of Airex's stock for $15,000 plus future bonuses to the stockowners. Lawrence explained the purchase to Lionel's stockholders by noting that many of Lionel's regular retailers, such as hardware stores, already sold fishing tackle, which would simplify the distribution of Airex.

But it was not until 1953 that Lionel began using the train catalog to promote Airex. The fishing equipment appeared on the back cover, startling children, who wondered what a trout fisherman was doing in their train catalog. Perhaps some of them thought the fisherman was part of a new operating car, a kind of milkman who dangled his line from a passing freight train.

Airex reels, rods, and complete fishing outfits were a profitable sideline for Lionel.

While it was true that probably as many dads as sons read the Lionel catalog and it was therefore a logical place to advertise rods and reels, Airex's appearance was a merchandising blunder. Having an actual piece of adult paraphernalia invade the fantasy world of Lionel Land was shocking. It undermined the carefully-constructed illusion of the catalog, whose magic lay in presenting the toys as if they were real. Showing true adult objects in the catalog exposed the myth.

Airex was Lionel's only significantly profitable attempt at diversification. The company did well until cheaper Japanese imports in the late fifties were able to undersell it.

ily, knew many in Cowen's circle, and was called one evening by Cowen's niece to provide a fourth at bridge. Afterward, Cowen dropped her off at home. "Call me," he said casually before driving away. Naturally, Lillian did nothing of the kind. The next week, when they gathered again for bridge, Cowen asked why he hadn't heard from her. "I have a telephone, too," Lillian parried, indicating it was up to Cowen to call her. He apparently did, because they started seeing each other.

Cowen enthusiastically initiated Lillian into the world of toy trains, taking particular pride in showing her the milkman. Cowen demonstrated it for her. She thought it was cute but not that exciting. How Cowen overlooked this glaring heresy is not known, but on Sunday, November 21, 1948, they were married in New York.

Despite the heightening of international tension brought about by the Soviet blockade of Berlin and the resulting American airlift, or perhaps because they were an antidote to anxiety, toy trains continued to flourish. The real railroads scheduled a Freedom Train to tour the country, a red, white, and blue-striped streamliner pulled by an Alco diesel christened *Spirit of 1776* that exhibited historic documents. Cowen could not quite send his Santa Fe on a nationwide tour carrying Lionel's incorporation papers, but he did create a special train to support the United Nations' Appeal for European Children to raise money for food and clothing. A layout complete with houses, station, and even a

Quonset hut was constructed in the waiting room of Washington's Union Station to inaugurate the fund drive. A Lionel steam turbine pulled a freight train of four automatic coal-dumping cars. As the train went around, people put donations in the open cars. When they passed over a slot in the table, an attendant dumped the money into a receptacle by pushing a remote control button.

Great fanfare attended the inaugurating of Lionel's version of the Freedom Train. Secretary of State George C. Marshall and Attorney General Tom Campbell Clark were on hand along with Cowen and Lawrence to put the first donations into the dump cars. Roz Relin anticipated national publicity for Lionel. All the press was there. TV and movie newsreel cameras were set to roll when it was discovered there wasn't adequate wiring in that part of the station for their high-intensity lights. Relin was crushed. As the camera crews disgustedly started taking apart their equipment, the young publicist flopped down on a bench, sobbing. Despite the dignitaries milling around, Cowen went over and sat beside her. "Stop crying, Roz," he said. "You'll never live to be my age if you carry on like that with every disappointment."

Lionel highballed along in the next five years with all the momentum of its speediest Santa Fe. Trains and accessories rolled from the Irvington factory in abundant variety and number. Sales mounted ever upward: $15.2 million in 1949, $21.5 million in 1950, $28.1 million in 1952, and $32.9 million in 1953, Lionel's peak year for train sales. In addition to having the Lionel name behind them, the trains sold well because Lionel's operating cars and accessories offered so much action. Cowen's dictum that the trains had to do more than just run around in a circle was honored in the extreme in the postwar years. Lawrence explained some of the lure of Lionels to the New York Society of Security Analysts in 1949: "And the reasons for Dad's interest [everyone's dad, not just Cowen] are very understandable. Lionel trains and accessories have an endless variety of nonrepetitive movements, all directed by means of remote

MOOING RIGHT ALONG

The cattle car operated via a vibrating platform that moved the cattle through the car and around the corral. It was similar to those electric table games in which tiny football or hockey players ran up and down the playing field. Opening or closing a door on the rear of the car moved a bar that either kept the cows in the car or let them out into the corral.

How was the cattle car invented? From where came the inspiration that brought joy and fascination to a generation of children? For Frank Pettit, it was all part of the job.

"We had the [nonoperating] stock car," Pettit says, referring to the prewar model, "and I just thought, 'Wouldn't it be good if we could have cattle inside?' So, how do we move them? The vibrator mechanism, we already had used that before. Now, how do you direct them? Little feelers on the bottom of the cows' feet. I'd worked with them; I knew I could use them for direction. So, now I'm inside the car. How do I get the cattle outside? A ramp or a platform. And to guide them around, a corral with adjustable gates."

Press a Remote Control Button—Watch the Cattle Move

Like their real counterparts, Lionel's cattle were often balky. Vaseline on the side of their bases helped them turn the corners of the corral.

controls operated selectively by the user. It is easy to see why Pop is instinctively challenged by the problem; for example: of bringing a train up to a log loader, loading a car with logs, swinging the train through switches and unloading the logs back into the loader. It requires a degree of skill and coordination, and, above all, it is not an automatic cycle brought about by merely pressing a button."

An operating cattle car was introduced in 1948. Its doors flew open at the push of a button, allowing black cattle to troop out into a trackside stock pen where they either could be detained for the imagined slaughter or routed back into the car to take a few more turns around the layout. Complete with car, corral, and nine docile head of cattle, the outfit sold for approximately fifteen dollars.

The orange cattle car never achieved the popularity of the milk car; it was more expensive, and it didn't have that all-important human figure. But it did become one of the more memorable postwar cars. "The milk car was fantastic! What a seller! I could never get enough of them," salesman William Gaston recalled enthusiastically. "The cattle car, that was a good number, too, but fifteen or sixteen dollars was a lot of money for people to spend on one car." Frank Pettit, who had invented much of the car's mechanism, disagreed. So did his son, who was the first on his New Jersey block to have anything new from Lionel. A few months after he had tried his father's cattle car, every kid in the neighborhood was clamoring for one. (Just so there was no chance of the younger Pettit forgetting where his father worked, his bedroom was decorated like the ticket office of a railroad station.)

There was always competition between the members of the outwardly serene Lionel "family." (Although patents of Lionel employees were signed over to the company, there were bonuses and sometimes royalty payments for new designs.) While Pettit filed the first patent on the cattle car, Chief Engineer Joseph Bonanno's name joined his when the full patent with details of the car's operation was filed. This patent was much fuller than the original, running to six pages of drawings alone, and Pettit was unhappy. He felt Bonanno was trying to take credit for "his" invention.

The feud between Pettit and Bonanno went back at least to 1938, when Pettit patented the remote-control operating coupler and Bonanno

Magne-Traction, introduced in 1950, was featured on Lionel's store posters.

patented the special track and push-button controller to go with it. It exemplified in part the New York-New Jersey schism in the company; Pettit had originally come from New York and had close ties to Cowen, while Bonanno was a product of the New Jersey manufacturing side of Lionel.

The cattle and milk cars were the flashiest of Lionel's operating cars. But just as the real railroads did not depend on dairy products for their freight revenues, so Lionel Lines looked to bulk loads like coal, lumber, oil, and scrap metal. Clever new cars were invented that made complete industries possible. Raw materials were carried from source to consumer, loaded and unloaded without the intrusion of human hands. Lionelville (the name on a small-town station that automatically stopped and restarted a passing train) was self-contained. Only the black wires running under the train table and poking up through the green sawdust "grass" gave away the illusion. There was a coal car whose side tilted over with a *snap!* when the distant remote control button was pressed, disgorging its load. Another type of coal car, a hopper, had bottom doors that opened automatically to drop miniature coal through the tracks of a raised coal ramp. A trackside conveyor belt carried the coal back into the cars, although if the power were on too high the coal also spewed out over the tracks and the living room rug.

A logging layout might include a flatbed car with hinged stakes that tilted its logs into a long gray trackside log conveyor. Oil tank cars came with one, two, or three domes on the top, but since the domes couldn't open and no oil could be put in, the cars weren't much fun. A foot-high oil derrick and pump with a Sunoco sign on its top showed yellow "oil" bubbling up out of the ground. (The oil was a bubble-making chemical, the same used in old-fashioned Christmas tree bubble lights.) Scrap metal was still an active

INDUSTRY IN LIONELVILLE

Like many railroads, Lionel Lines depended on coal, lumber, oil, and other heavy industries for its freight. As the automotive and trucking businesses grew, Lionel added cars and loading facilities to accommodate them. Loads unaffected by the weather, like barrels and scrap metal, traveled in open gondolas, but closed boxcars were still Lionel Lines' most ubiquitous freight carriers.

Ore dumping car carried coal. Both it and log car unloaded by remote control.

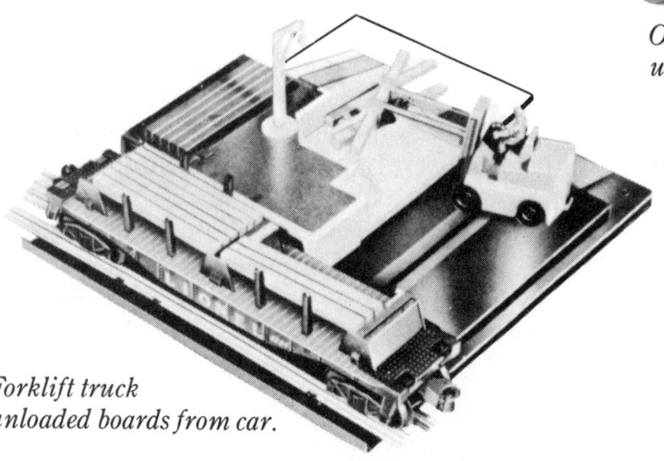

Forklift truck unloaded boards from car.

Caboose brought up rear of every freight train.

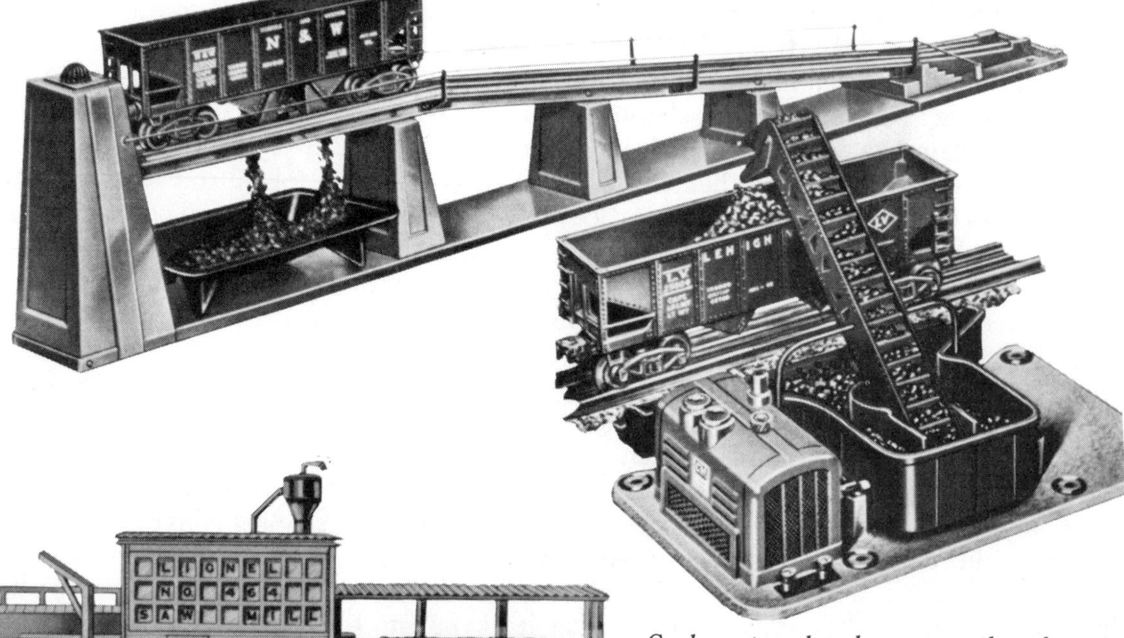

Coal ramp and coal conveyor, though separate accessories, could be used together to load and unload cars.

Logs fed into sawmill came out as planks.

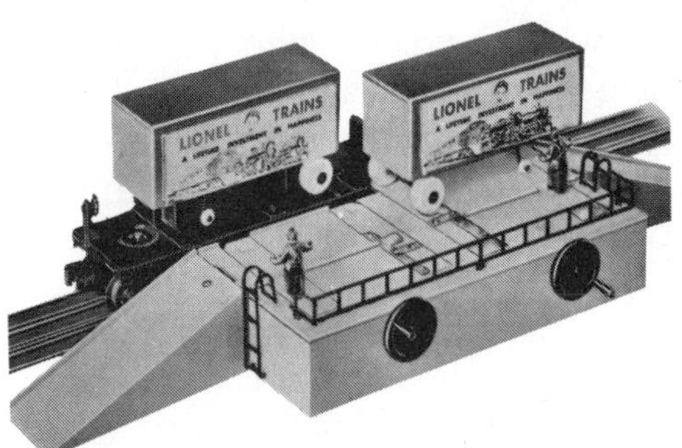

Piggyback set moved trailers from flatcar to platform.

Auto carrier transported four cars.

Oil derrick didn't really fill tank cars, but it bubbled when turned on.

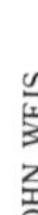
JOHN WEIS

Log loader with chain hoist (right) *took logs from one track and loaded them into car on second track. Log conveyor* (above) *needed only one track on which to receive and load logs.*

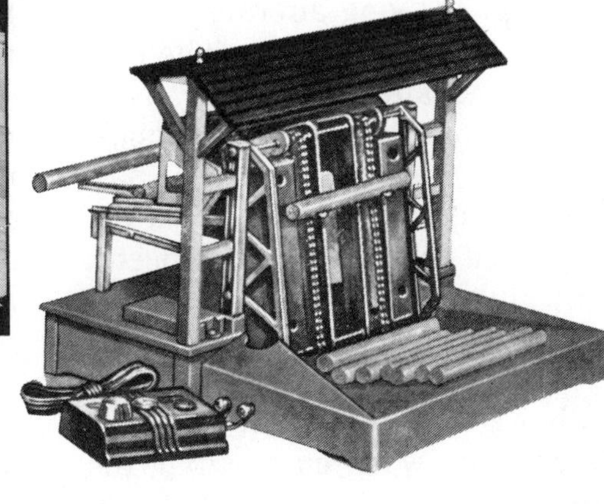

Barrel loader sent barrels up ramp and into waiting gondola.

LIONEL LEADS THE NATION

America's real railroads couldn't compete with Lionel Lines. In 1952 alone, Lionel produced 622,209 engines and 2,460,764 freight and passenger cars (freight outsold passenger by twenty to one), thoroughly eclipsing the nation's railroads, which had a mere 43,000 locomotives and 1.8 million cars in service.

Lionel industry. The look of prewar electromagnetic crane was modernized, but it still picked up old track rails (and, sadistically, an occasional iron toy figure that might come its way) and dropped them into waiting gondolas.

Light towers and searchlight cars of all descriptions were created to illuminate these industrial goings on. One car had a revolving searchlight mounted beside an orange generator. A work caboose, which came with the railroad crane car, had its own searchlight for a few years until it became too expensive to produce. There were floodlight towers and rotating beacons to warn off low-flying aircraft, swiveling yard lights, and metal lampposts. The new passenger cars (named after the nearby New Jersey towns of Chatham, Maplewood, Hillside, and Livingston) were illuminated so that passenger silhouettes stood out in the windows. And the Santa Fe got its own set of magnificent, fifteen-inch-long aluminum streamlined cars that were lit with two bulbs each. Highway crossing signals twinkled red, semaphores and block signals showed red or green warning lights, and the crossing watchman swung his lantern as trains roared past stations, their windows glowing softly. Putting out the room lights made it all magical and mysterious. Kneeling down beside the rails and squinting your eyes made it almost real.

A new group of operating accessories appeared with little Lionel-sized people in them. Lawrence patented an operating switch tower, a quaint, clapboard two-story building to fit in train yards. As the train approached, a dispatcher standing out on the porch automatically moved inside while another man came down a flight of steps with a lantern, presumably bringing orders to the through freight. A barrel loader bore a tiny man who appeared to tip over barrels as they traveled up a conveyor belt and into a waiting gondola (where another man was soon created to receive them). A freight station featured two baggage carts with attendants on them. The carts went into the station and came out loaded with baggage.

New engines were equipped with magnets to give them better traction on hills and more pulling power, and to keep them on the rails at higher speeds. Called Magne-Traction, this improvement on steam, diesel, and electric engines magnetized the driving wheels to grip the rails better. Engines and cars were offered in a rich variety of railroad names and markings: Rock Island, Chesapeake & Ohio, Union Pacific, Lehigh Valley, Erie, Norfolk & Western, Baltimore & Ohio, Great Northern, and Delaware, Lackawanna & Western. Even the Korean War hardly slowed the pace of train sales, although a shortage of certain materials removed Magne-Traction from the 1952 steam engines and they had to spin their driving wheels while chugging up those long mountain grades.

Lionel trains seemed to be everywhere. A Cleveland medical research laboratory used a standard GG-1 electric engine to transport radioactive radon twenty-one feet between storage room and laboratory. The radon capsule rode in a lead-lined container on Lionel's regular production depressed-center flatcar. While scientists originally picked up the capsule with long, radiation-shielded tweezers, they soon used Lionel's ore-dumping car, which dropped the capsule down a chute by remote control. An Indian rajah built an elaborate track system in his palace to serve food to his guests from Lionel flatcars, while in the White House, Ike and Mamie Eisenhower set up Lionels on the floor under the Christmas tree for grandson David.

Coffee shops in various parts of the country ran hamburgers and ice cream sodas up and down their lunch counters on Lionel trains. The train stopped in front of the patron, he removed his order, then the train backed down the track to the kitchen again. An Oregon farmer used a toy train to carry the mail from his highway mailbox to his farmhouse. Military hospitals used fancy train layouts as occupational therapy for disturbed veterans. Playing with the trains helped them to both relax and to learn to make decisions and cooperate with others.

Lionel trains even figured in international relations. To counter the propaganda of an East

The Santa Fe becomes the Hamburger Express at lunch counter.

Berlin World Youth Festival in August 1951, West Berlin Mayor Dr. Ernst Reuter wrote Cowen asking for a set of trains that, with other exhibits, would extol the Western way of life. Cowen, ever the patriot and strongly anti-Communist, responded with four lavish freight and passenger sets, thirty operating accessories including the latest in coal and lumber loaders, the cattle and milk cars, five hundred feet of track, and detailed instructions for creating a fully-landscaped layout. The railroad became the hit of West Berlin's Culture Festival. Thousands of youths deserted the East Berlin event and slipped across the border to watch the trains being operated from an elevated switch tower labeled *Lionel Modellbahn Ausstellung.* To support the show's propaganda effort, the Voice of America interviewed Lawrence and beamed the broadcast over Soviet-controlled territory.

Lionel managed to get involved when a Czechoslovak engineer and train dispatcher hijacked a train with 108 passengers aboard, including their own families, and raced it into the American zone of Germany in 1951. Crashing through the border on an all-but-forgotten railroad spur whose switch they had secretly thrown, the pair wanted to emigate to the United States but had no sponsor in the country. They tried the Brotherhood of Railroad Trainmen, but American railroad workers were out of work and the union could not guarantee jobs. Lawrence Johnson, who had succeeded Roz Relin on the Lionel public relations account, went to Lawrence Cowen and suggested Lionel sponsor them, offering the railroaders jobs manufacturing toy trains in New Jersey.

"That's one heck of a good idea," Lawrence said; he was quicker to grab at public relations stunts than his more conservative father. Johnson went to Germany and brought home the pair and their families. He had hoped to bring back the bell from their locomotive as well, to serve as a Lionel Freedom Bell, but the locomotive had no bell. "How about the whistle, then?" Johnson asked. But the train had already been returned to Czechoslovakia. Lawrence met the group at what was then Idlewild Airport in New York. A two-week, six-city tour was arranged by Johnson, and Lionel received tremendous publicity. Afterward, the pair actually did go to work at the Irvington factory.

It seemed impossible for Lionel *not* to get publicity in those electric train-happy days. That perennial Lionel fan, Joe DiMaggio, appeared in his first television show, the NBC *The Lionel Club House,* every Saturday afternoon. Joltin' Joe, the Yankee Clipper, demonstrated Lionels himself. Lionel was ecstatic to have DiMaggio pushing the trains. "The hero of train-age boys and buying-age fathers!" Lionel told its dealers, sending them DiMaggio posters for their windows. "What a name! What a hero for men and boys (women, too)!" Lionel gushed. DiMaggio was paid $125,000 for the thirteen programs, but he probably enjoyed the trains he received as much as the money.

While DiMaggio was the Yankee Lionel booster, the Dodgers had their own Lionel railroader in star catcher Roy Campanella. Campanella, who was the third black ballplayer to break the major leagues' color bar, got his first Lionel when he was eleven. (Ironically, no black person appeared in the Lionel catalog until the 1970s.) "I always wanted a bicycle," he recalled,

MIKE LIPTON

Night in Lionel Land saw airplane beacon glowing and station lit as passengers peered from illuminated cars.

"but my father wouldn't get me one. Then one morning I looked up and there was a Lionel train. My older sister's boyfriend set it up for me and I've had them ever since." After the pressures of a big ball game, Campanella found it relaxing to sit and tinker with his trains. "In my mind I wanted to make Lionel look like a real train," Campanella said. "I wanted to run ten, twelve cars on my Santa Fe and New York Central. I remember I wanted that signal bridge that was four tracks wide, the one they made before the war. So I went up to the showroom and they introduced me to Mr. Cowen. I knew he was a Yankee fan but I said, 'You have to get over to Ebbets Field [in Brooklyn] some day.' He laughed. Then he told them to look around for those signals and they came up with two. I think they were off of the showroom layout from before the war."

Campanella took his Lionel trains on television in 1953 on Edward R. Murrow's first *Person-to-Person* show. Half the show was an interview with conductor Leopold Stokowski, the other half a tour of Campanella's Glen Cove, Long Island, home that included a look at his train layout. Only it wasn't entirely his layout. When Lionel learned Campanella was going to be the subject of Murrow's first *Person-to-Person* show, it asked if it could set up a special layout in Campanella's basement to advertise the trains. Several of the company's best display men arrived, and within a day Campanella had a dream layout. Publicist Johnson watched the program, waiting for Campanella to mention Lionel by name, but to Johnson's chagrin he never did. It didn't really matter, because *Lionel* had become synonymous with electric trains, a proper noun turned generic like Jell-O or Kleenex or Frigidaire.

Lionel was frequently on television. The trains were so well known their appearance often did as much for the program as for Lionel. One afternoon in Toots Shor's New York restaurant, Johnson met with Jackie Gleason's script writers. They wanted to explore ways of working the trains into a Gleason gag. How could they use them with Gleason's rich-boy, tails-and-top-hat character, Reggie Van Gleason? Johnson quickly suggested a train running on Reggie's bar. The idea expanded: Gleason would push a button and out would come the train, whistling and smoking, carrying a shot glass. Gleason would take a drink, put the glass back, and send the train on its way. Everyone loved it. On the next Sunday night, all went according to the script. The steam engine performed perfectly. Gleason grimaced so the audience would know he was drinking liquor. And as the train chugged off, Gleason ad libbed, "Booze is swell with Lionel."

Johnson was ecstatic at the plug, but he knew how conservative Cowen was. "Holy cow," he thought, "am I going to catch hell for tying Lionel trains in with booze." The next day, Johnson called Lawrence to ask him what he thought of the Gleason show public relations coup. "I think it was terrific," Lawrence said, adding ominously, "but I haven't talked to dad yet about it." A short while later Lawrence phoned Johnson. "Hey, Larry," Lawrence said, "Josh was storming until one of his old buddies called him from the West Coast and told him, 'That was one hell of a plug you got on the Jackie Gleason show,' so you're off the hook." The next time Johnson saw his boss, Cowen grudgingly admitted, "That was pretty good."

Cowen was more protective of the trains than Lawrence. He didn't like seeing them belittled in any way. When Johnson arranged to have a trained chimpanzee run the big showroom layout for newsreel cameras, Lawrence thought it a terrific idea. Cowen didn't like it at all. "J.L. is the father of the baby," a friend said, explaining their differing attitudes. "Larry is simply the pediatrician." Lawrence saw himself as a modern businessman, using up-to-date techniques to improve his father's company and to make it reflect himself. Cowen, having long since made his mark, could afford to take the high road. "I'm in the business of happiness," he said, feeding the public's (and the media's) wish to find more than a practical businessman behind America's number one toy.

Lawrence's attitude was revealed in the stories he chose to tell about himself and the trains. Lawrence once told a writer for *Collier's:* "At the San Francisco Fair in 1939, we ran two of our locomotives twelve hours a day for three months and at the end of that time they were as good as new. Pop was pleased as punch but had I been in his place, I think I would have been a little discouraged. I have a tendency to worry about turnover."

Lionel celebrated its fiftieth anniversary with great fanfare. A huge tent was erected on the factory grounds and a day-long party held in October 1950, fifty years and a month after Cowen and Harry Grant had filed as the Lionel

Dodgers' Roy Campanella (above) *with Lionel's Western Pacific streamlined diesel. Yankees' Joe DiMaggio* (right) *favored the scale Hudson.*

Manufacturing Company. Door prizes provided by the company ranged from watches and TVs to a new Ford and Plymouth. The executive staff presented Cowen with a gold-plated Santa Fe, which became one of the very few trains he displayed at home (the engine also made the cover of *Popular Science* magazine).

Highlight of the afternoon was the presentation to Cowen by his two thousand employees of a bronze plaque inscribed: "To J. Lionel Cowen in commemoration of the fiftieth anniversary of the Lionel Corporation. His fellow workers present this plaque to the company's beloved founder with affection and loyalty. His integrity and ideals and his inspiring leadership shall always guide us unswervingly toward greater accomplishments." A bas relief of Cowen (wearing the glasses he usually removed for photographs) was framed on the plaque by medallions of two engines symbolizing Lionel's history: The old B. & O. No. 5 tunnel engine, last made in 1905, and the Santa Fe.

The staff in New York made its own presentation to Cowen of a clock. The day after he received the gift, Cowen tacked a note on the bulletin board. "Thank you very much," it said. "May I suggest that you start your fund now for my seventy-fifth anniversary?"

In the gold-colored 1950 annual report, Cowen addressed the company's stockholders in a signed letter. He reviewed Lionel's shaky origins, the early distrust of electricity, the competition from foreign toys. "Since the end of the last war the expansion of our business has exceeded my fondest hopes," Cowen wrote. "Today all indications point to an even greater expansion. The population of our country is still increasing rapidly, and our electric trains have come into their own as an educational force and an adult hobby, in addition to being just toys. Naturally, I take great pride in the knowledge that from a small beginning the Lionel Corporation has grown to be the largest manufacturer of miniature electric trains in the world."

Cowen had every reason to be proud. In his seventies, he could say his company was a great success. Not only was it doing well financially but it had become a treasured part of the American scene. Cowen had played the role of patriarch, giving employment to nieces and nephews, brother- and son-in-law, and ultimately to his own son. As he stood under the striped tent on that slightly overcast October Saturday, beside the factory he had built, receiving the homage of those who had livelihoods and careers because of his vision, Cowen could never have guessed that it would all be in a shambles before the end of the decade. How could he know, his hand on the heavy bronze plaque, his son on the podium beside him, that both company and family would crumble, the one losing over a million dollars a year, the other torn by distrust and betrayal? And how could he imagine, on that day of honor and happiness, that it would be he, Cowen himself, who would be the instrument of this incomprehensible debacle?

LIONEL
AIREX
US STEEL
AIREX

7

OFF THE TRACK

1954-1965

Dapper as a banker in his double-breasted gray suit, Joshua Cowen stood in a corner of the bustling Lionel showroom watching a small black boy and his mother. The holiday crowd ebbed and flowed around the mountainous railroad, but the boy remained fixed at one end of the layout, right beside the model of the Best Feed Store. A gleaming silver passenger train, the Pennsylvania Railroad's New York to Washington *Congressional,* streaked by. The boy looked up at his mother. She shook her head. A yellow and blue Virginian diesel clickety-clacked past, pulling a long freight. "That one, mama?" he asked. No, went his mother's head. On an inside track a little red and yellow trolley rolled by. It said "Lionelville Rapid Transit" on its side and had a silver trolley pole on its roof. "Can I have that one?" the boy asked. His mother shook her head for the third time.

Cowen called a salesman over and said something to him. The man returned a few minutes later with a package wrapped in brown paper, which he gave to Cowen. As the boy and his mother walked toward the elevator, Cowen intercepted them. "Here," he said, putting the package in the startled boy's hands, "here's something for you." Then he walked off. Trailing behind Cowen, publicist Lawrence Johnson joked, "Santa's going to bring somebody a trolley car for Christmas, and maybe some track."

"Yeah," Cowen said, sheepish at Johnson's having witnessed his sentimental gesture. "I gave him a transformer, too, but just a cheap one." Then he went back to patrolling the layout.

JOSEPH SADORF/TTOS BULLETIN

Advance catalog for dealers showed new Virginian diesel.

JOHN CUJAS

Forklift lumber loader and talking station on layout.

Despite the heart-warming stories and the flood of new trains and accessories in the showroom, Lionel was about to enter its most difficult period. Net sales had peaked in 1953 at $32.9 million. (In the same year, Cowen's salary plus a bonus on profits had hit a high of $100,464.13.) Sales started to decline then. But the diminishing toy train market and confusion within the company did not effect the line. New inventions continued to fill the catalog every year. The diesels and box cars, culvert loaders and lumber mills were the most varied and clever in toy train history. Yet not even the cleverest of talking dispatch stations could isolate Lionelville from a changing world.

Lionel was essentially a one-product, one-family company, and Cowen was the total antithesis of that faceless, bloodless "man in the gray flannel suit" who was taking over the business world in the mid-fifties. In an era of increasingly impersonal, diversified conglomerates, the marketing techniques and business strategies that had sustained the company for half a century were no longer viable. Lionel tried to keep up with the times. Lawrence attempted to institute modern management methods. But like its reliable locomotives, Lionel stayed unswervingly on the track it knew best until it was too late.

Even before train sales started the long slide that ended with the triumph of the model racing car in the early sixties, Lionel had attempted to diversify. The Stock-Watch—an electric cattle guard produced in the late forties and sold to farmers—was an improbable try at developing a new product. Strange as it seemed for Lionel to market, the Stock-Watch did incorporate electrical elements with which the company was familiar. Another attempt at diversification, the purchase of controlling interest in the Airex company, involved Lionel in the profitable production of fishing reels. In the mid-fifties, Lionel produced a stereo camera, the Linex. But the results in this case were disastrous, costing Lionel hundreds of thousands of dollars.

Lionel got into the stereo camera business

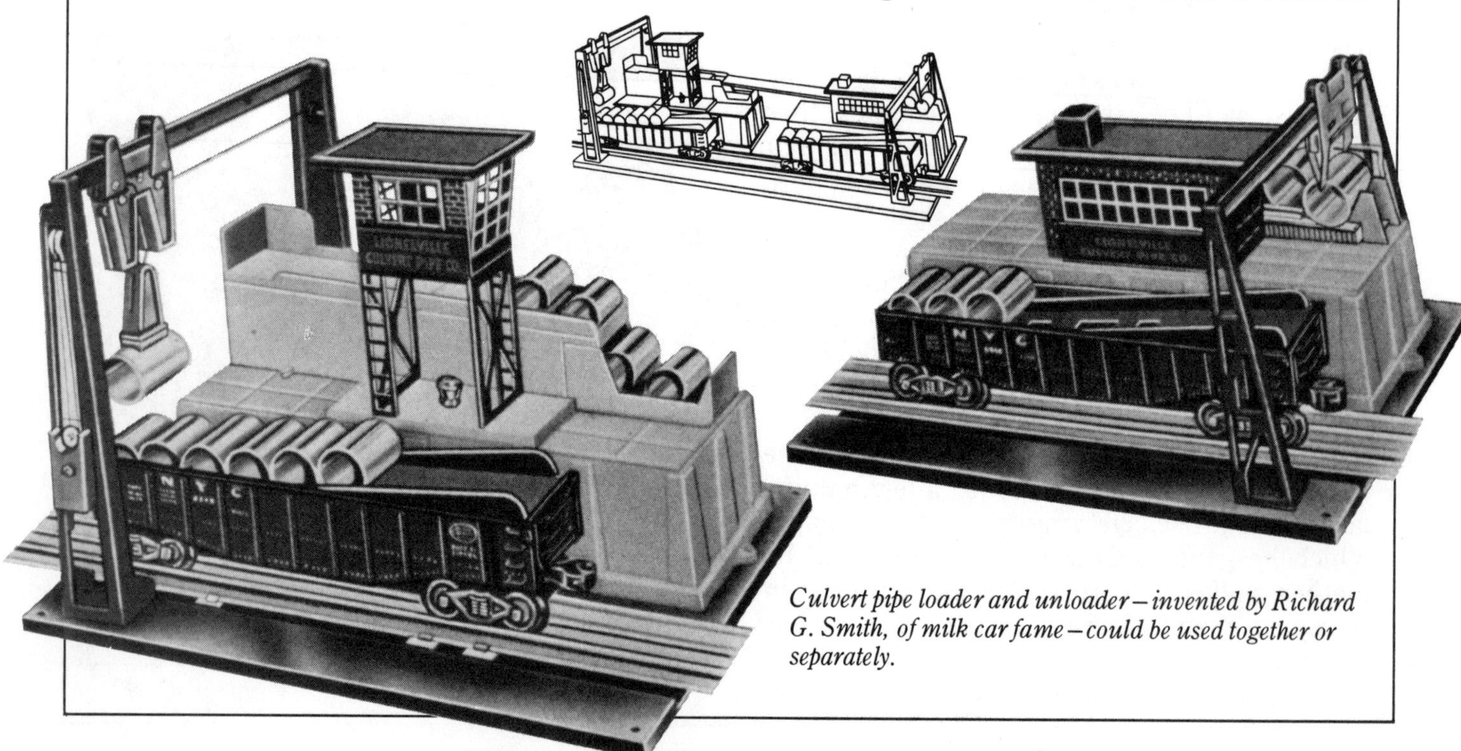

Culvert pipe loader and unloader—invented by Richard G. Smith, of milk car fame—could be used together or separately.

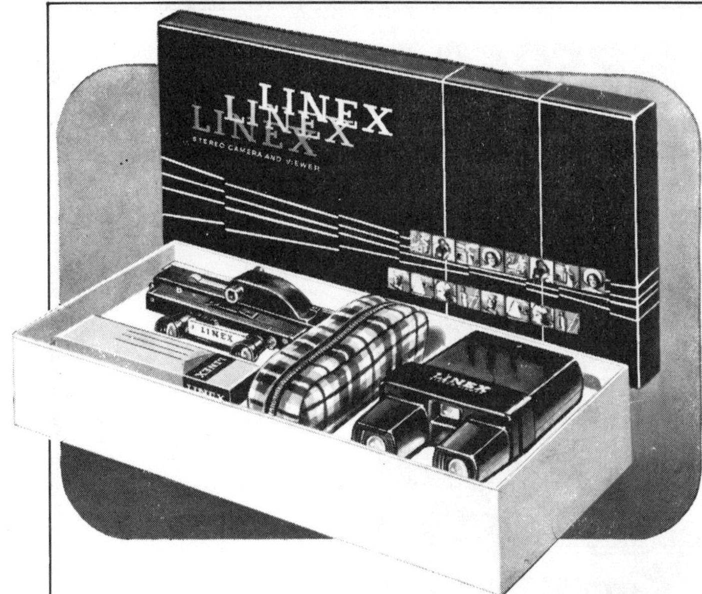

Linex stereo camera set included viewer for slides.

because both Cowen and Lawrence were interested in photography. For Christmas 1949, Lawrence, an avid photographer, had given his father one of the new stereo cameras on the market. The camera had two lenses side by side that produced almost identical slides. When the slides were mounted and put in a special viewer, they created one three-dimensional picture, something like the old stereopticon views once popular as parlor entertainments. Cowen took the camera with him that winter on his trip to Hawaii. He took the usual tourist's snapshots of his wife (Lillian at the monument for the sunken battleship *Arizona;* Lillian in the lobby of their hotel) and came home with a typically blunt assessment of the new camera.

"Too complicated," Cowen decided. "Take the fancy exposure meter and setting: I used one setting all the time regardless of the weather and it worked fine."

From this experience it was decided Lionel would develop a simple fixed focus camera to capture the low end of the then-growing 3-D market. The camera was introduced in 1954 in New York, with limited distribution at first. Echoing his father's sentiments following his Hawaii trip, Lawrence said, "Basically, this is a good-weather camera. That's when most people want to take pictures. And this will give them good ones . . . at a price they can afford." The Linex was priced at $44.50 including viewer and carrying case, less than half the price of the nearest of its five competitors. But those competitors, including major photographic names like Revere, View-Master, and the Stereo Realist, were already well established.

Within two years, Lawrence acknowledged to Lionel stockholders, "The Linex camera and viewer, in common with all other stereo cameras, has had limited public acceptance." Stereo cameras were one more fad of the fickle fifties. They had a brief burst of success, but people soon tired of the cumbersome viewer, which allowed only one person at a time to see the slides.

The merchandising of the electric train was buffeted by forces beyond Lionel's control in the fifties. Discount stores sprang up that sold the trains for less than the prices listed in Lionel's consumer catalog, which undercut the company's traditional retail outlet, the mom and pop hardware/hobby store. This network of small shops with their legendary, smiling proprietors behind the counter, always willing to render immediate first aid to a small boy's balky locomotive, was the heart of Lionel's nationwide repair system. The company sent them reams of technical instruction sheets that explained how to make any possible repair to Lionel trains. These service stations, displaying the famous Lionel *L* in an orange and blue circle, were

COWEN AS REMEMBERED BY . . .

HIS WIDOW

DAVID EISENDRATH

Married to Cowen for the last seventeen years of his life, Lillian Cowen is still proud of the china cabinet Cowen wired to show off their carved coral collection. "If hands could do it, his could, especially if it was electrical," she says, showing the metal strips that cleverly ran up the cabinet's doors, lighting a series of bulbs taken from a Lionel station. A concealed train transformer powers the soft lighting. Cowen enjoyed electrical gimmicks. Working with his daughter, Isabel, he electrified cakes for parties so they lit up when a switch was thrown. Earlier, he created a device for stirring the baby formula for his children.

Except for a Lionel transformer in the china cabinet and an occasional train rigged to pass around hors d'oeuvres at a party, Lillian never had much at home to remind her of Lionel. "Joshie loved the trains but he didn't bring his work home with him," she explains. "He didn't talk too much about the office or keep files at home."

Every winter Cowen and Lillian crossed the country by train, then took a boat to Hawaii, where they stayed for eight or ten weeks before returning in the same stylish manner to New York. The Cowens lived fashionably in New York as well. "He had a box at the opera for years. I don't know how much he liked it, but that's what the women in the family wanted, so he had it. He loved Caruso, though. When we played the 'Pearl Fishers' on the record player, oh, he just was carried away."

Cowen probably enjoyed playing gin rummy with friends more than going to the opera. Besides cards, he also golfed a little and fished. But he had no absorbing passion besides his trains. He did enjoy a fast drive in his chauffeured Rolls-Royce. "We were driving on the New Jersey Turnpike once," Lillian narrates. "Joshie was up front and he's saying, 'Faster, faster.' We were already doing seventy-five. Well, when we got to the tollbooth, they were waiting for us. We had to follow a police car to the justice of the peace at five miles an hour all the way. That was the worst part for Joshie. The fine was only ten dollars, but it was going that slowly that was hardest for him."

Wherever he went, Cowen encountered people who had Lionel trains. "One time he was in San Francisco and a man called at the hotel and said he had one of the first trains Joshie'd ever made. He came up with it. It was just a flat wooden car, old and banged up, but it was one of the very first, with the initials *JLC* scratched in it. Oh, Joshie wanted that car in the worst way. He would have given anything for it. I think he offered him a thousand dollars right there. The man said no, he wouldn't part with it, but he would will it to the company when he died. But he never did."

Lionel's direct link to communities across the country. They gave the company local presence, helping to make a neighborhood pal of a national corporation.

But the fifties introduced aggressive, high-volume, low-profit-per-unit merchandising. Low-overhead discount houses threatened the continued vitality of the Lionel stores. People examined the trains at a hobby shop, received advice about them, and then went to the discount house to buy them for less. Many of the discount houses were located in that phenomenon of the fifties, the suburbs. In simple, unadorned buildings, paying low rents, serving the suburbanite who shopped by car, the discount chains could more than compete with the older downtown stores.

The existence of the suburbs was both a boon and a bane to Lionel. Enshrined in suburbia was that ideal family to which Lionel addressed itself. In the suburbs, dad as pal, mom as nurse, sis as audience, and son as Lionel engineer reached their apotheoses. The suburbs provided finished basements to house electric train empires. And the show of financial success that the suburbs represented called for nothing less than a Santa Fe on Christmas morning. But it was also the suburbs that nurtured the shopping center and the discount house that stole customers away from the traditional electric train shops.

Lionel had always controlled the minimum price of its trains. The Fair Trade Act, in effect in forty-four of the forty-eight states, upheld this right. When a dealer bought from Lionel, he literally signed an agreement not to sell the trains for less. The uniform minimum price across the country indicated that Lionel trains were high quality, not to be marked down or haggled over. Most of Lionel's sales were to middlemen: electrical, hardware, or toy jobbers and distributors who in turn sold to retail stores. With the exception of national chain stores and large department stores, Lionel did not sell directly to retailers.

By the mid-fifties, however, fair trade laws were being ignored by the discount houses. Lionel's efforts to have the laws enforced became enmeshed in a series of court cases challenging the constitutionality of fair trade laws. The major department stores, which did buy directly from Lionel, saw their customers going to the discount houses. Faced with a loss of business, they, too, ignored fair trade and cut their prices.

Lionel sued some of its best and oldest cus-

Lionel's passenger cars were named for New Jersey towns near the factory. A streamlined car was lettered Hillside.

tomers, including Macy's and Gimbels, to have them honor fair trade minimum prices. The department stores claimed Lionel ignored price cutting by the discount houses through the early fifties and only acted when the department stores tried to be competitive. Temporary injunctions were even obtained against the stores, but it was a losing battle. In 1955 Lionel gave up the fair trade fight, even though the statutes remained theoretically in effect.

The tensions of the new decade were felt even closer to home when the 2,500 workers at the Irvington factory went on strike for seventeen days in 1954. The strike by the local of the Playthings, Jewelry and Novelty Workers, C.I.O., came when Lionel proposed a seven-cent-an-hour cut in the workers' average wage of $1.60 an hour. Lionel claimed a drop in sales necessitated the salary reduction. The union countered with a demand for a ten-cent-an-hour raise plus increased fringe benefits.

It was the fourth strike to hit Lionel since the war. Unlike the others, which had been amicable enough to even permit deliveries of raw materials to the plant, labor and management were far apart, and feelings ran high. A settlement might have been reached sooner but the membership rejected union leaders' plans to accept the prestrike status quo. Finally, Lionel dropped its planned wage cut and agreed to an increased Christmas bonus that the union leadership said averaged out to a five-cent-an-hour raise. (In fact, when Christmas came, train sales were off so much the bonus was actually less than it had been the year before.)

The strike clearly proclaimed the end of the Lionel patriarchy. It was a new day, and employees worked not for a founding (and providing) father figure like Cowen but for a company. The solitary entrepreneur and the loyal, grateful workers who followed in his wake were as dated as standard gauge electric trains. Lionel's house organ, *All Aboard,* might continue to extol the "Lionel family." The board of directors might pass resolutions of sympathy when executives' parents died that affirmed, "The Lionel Corporation is a company in which corporate and family life have ever been entwined." But there was no going back to the dream of a company town presided over by an understanding boss. Lawrence was not the founding father (to many, he was still "the old man's boy"). Nor did the modern management methods to which Lawrence aspired call for being a parent to one's workers. There were administrative layers between the president of a company and those on the assembly line. Lawrence did not know all his workers by name like his father; nor did he pretend to. Lionel was a business, not a family. Despite the latest in speedy, Magne-Traction engines, the fifties were overtaking electric trains.

From 1953, Lionel's peak, to 1955, sales dropped by 38 percent. It was an astounding plunge for a company that only two years before could do no wrong. Part of the decline in sales was traceable to Lionel's failure to secure government defense contracts, which had bolstered its earnings during the Korean War. The doomed Linex camera project also sapped the company's strength. But the whisper that was abroad in the land was that interest in toy electric trains sales was waning. (During the same period, American Flyer sales fell by one-third.)

The decline in train sales as the decade progressed (Lionel's sales dropped by more than half by 1959) was also related directly to the decline of the industry that had spawned the electric train: America's railroads. Their renaissance during the war gave railroads a new lease on life, but it was short-lived. Soon, the abandonment of track, reduction in service, deterioration of equipment, and dissolution of whole railroads began that eventually left the country with only a few major freight carriers. That gleaming symbol of the modern passenger railroad, the air-conditioned vista-domed streamliner pulled by a throbbing diesel, lived on in Lionel Land long after its brief time on America's ballasted right-of-way. Transportation news of the late fifties was made by Boeing and TWA, not Baldwin and New York Central. The *oohs* and *ahs* of the public went to DC-6s and Stratocruisers, not to the Pennsylvania's steam turbine locomotive. In 1957, for the first time, airlines carried more passengers than railroads. The federal government didn't help when it transferred the U.S. mail to planes, depriving passenger trains of 30 percent of their revenue. And under President Eisenhower, massive federal funding went to building the interstate highway system and regional airports.

The effect of the railroads' decline on young boys and their passion for electric trains was pronounced. The airport observation deck replaced the local depot (if it still existed) as the hallowed spot for mystic rites of communication

TRAINS FOR THE POPE

Cowen and Lillian, accompanied by other Lionel executives, went to Rome in 1953 to present trains to Pope Pius XII for the poor boys of Italy. Received in a private audience at the Vatican, the group piled the distinctive Lionel boxes on the Vatican's rococo, gold-leafed furniture, making it look like any other home on Christmas morning.

The Pope posed for pictures in front of an unlikely train: A Santa Fe diesel pulling a milk car, a tank car, and the tender from a steam engine (probably because it said "Lionel Lines" on its side) was set up on track on a marble side table. "Use these photographs in any way you wish," the Pope told Cowen.

"Good, let's use them in our advertising," the irrepressible Cowen said to his executives. But cooler heads prevailed and it was decided it would not be in good taste to link Lionels with the Vicar of Christ.

Lillian said she felt a sense of calm in the Pope's presence. But Cowen, noting the beautiful straight lines of buttons down the back of the Pope's white cassock, quipped as they left the audience, "The only thing I'd like to know is, who is his tailor?"

Lionel trains, including the biggest ZW Trainmaster *transformer, were carried past imperturbable Swiss Guards* (above). *Pope Pius XII* (left) *posed with Lionel's most popular engine and operating car in a Vatican reception room.*

Lawrence and Cowen examine vista-dome.

between fathers and sons. Children built wooden airplane models with silver propellers that could be spun with a flick of a finger. Boys no longer aspired to be engineers (*engineer* in the late fifties meant someone with a slide rule, a drawing board, and a good income). The grimy locomotive engineer in his baggy overalls was replaced in the pantheon of boys' heroes by the spotless, tailored airplane captain. The locomotive engineer was a legendary hard-talking, tobacco-chewing maverick who broke speed rules and waved his own distinctive bandanna. The airplane pilot was a bland mechanic with the expressionless voice of a bureaucrat. Interchangeable in his blue company uniform, he was the perfect symbol of the "cool" fifties. He was Lawrence, the administrator, and not Cowen, the entrepreneur; the son and not the father.

Other changes in the country contributed to the decline of the electric train in the fifties. It was the age of television. At the start of the decade, 3.1 million homes had TVs. By 1955, 32 million households had the glowing box, and by decade's end, the average American family watched television six hours a day, seven days a week. That didn't leave much time for toy trains. Families got together on Monday nights in front of *I Love Lucy,* not to crawl around wiring Lionel's new icing station and watching a tiny man push blocks of ice down the roof hatch of a Pacific Fruit Express reefer. (*Reefer* still meant a refrigerated railroad car and not a consciousness-heightening cigarette.)

The late fifties and early sixties were also a time for moving, with the emphasis on getting ahead. National corporations were growing, transferring their executives around the country every two years. Ambitious men climbed the corporate ladder. There was less room for electric trains at each move, less time to set them up in each temporary home, less reason to keep carting them around the country with each transfer.

Fathers and sons found themselves on opposite sides of the track. Dad may have grown up waving to engineers beside his father, but it was not so clear that his son wanted to repeat this ritual. Fathers may have lusted after the newest Lionel in a store window, but their boys were now in Little League, knocking mud off their imagined spikes like fledgling Mickey Mantles. The train catalog, filled with diesels, continued to urge fathers to "pal" with their sons, but children looked increasingly to each other for comraderie. A childhood community developed that was pointedly separated from parents. All that electric trains represented—home and security and family togetherness—was now reason for their rejection. Electric trains, like the men who loved them, were embarrassingly "square" and "dullsville" to a teen-ager obsessed with Elvis Presley and James Dean.

In the unsettled years immediately following World War II, Lionel reflected an image of America that the country wanted to believe. Lionel's advertising and catalog reaffirmed

Lionel's Santa Fe streamliner included a vista-dome; on real railroads, it offered two-level seating.

BURLINGTON ROUTE

Advertising for Lionel grew more sophisticated and clever even as the toy train market declined.

ALBERTA BERNECKER/ROADSIDE AMERICA

Down at the depot on Roadside America Lionel layout in Pennsylvania. Station platforms are by Lionel, depot is homemade.

family and neighborhood. As the fifties wore on, however, that mythic small town of Lionelville, with its spanking white station and dependable trolley car, became too dated even for parents in need of reassurance. There were no teen-age gangs or juvenile delinquents or rebels without causes in Lionelville. TV quiz shows were not fixed by seemingly illustrious college professors. The tensions of McCarthyism and desegregation were absent. The winds did not carry nuclear fallout over Lionelville. In the beginning of the decade, this tiny town reflected back to contented Americans a picture of their idealized selves. But by the end of the fifties, Lionelville only made them feel bad.

The toy that best expressed this change in society was not the miniature railroad, but the model racing car—the mini-hot rod. The keys to the family car, given grudgingly by father to son, provided the means by which the teen-ager escaped from the family altogether. For younger children, the model racing car became the fantasy substitute for the real thing. *New York Times* columnist Russell Baker lamented the passing of the electric train and its replacement by the racing car, noting, "... Children are responding naturally to an automotive world. And no wonder. Most youngsters nowadays have had their first car accident before they ever set foot on a train. They grow up in cities that are being destroyed to accommodate cars and in homes where life moves to the tempo of the internal combustion engine. The train may be part of their folklore, but it is no longer the locomotive that starts long dreams of faraway places and adventure beyond the mountain."

Baker observed that the rise of the racing car coincided with the arrival of the Barbie doll, which he called a "sex kitten" requiring a $250 wardrobe. "The ugly implications of 'Barbie' are clear enough," Baker wrote, "but the racing-car layout seems a deceptively logical development of the old toy train. The cars go around on electrified rails, like the trains, and get nowhere. And yet everything is different.

"The racer is a bomb on wheels. Its only purpose is to dash around the track faster than another toy racer. To break the mindless monotony of the speed, it emits a high-pitched insect whine, satisfying the modern craving for nerve abrasive, and occasionally roars into the plasticene crowds in humdrum little mock disasters.

"The toy train was a beautiful piece of engineering to be savored gently. Hours could be passed deciding whether the box car should be coupled between the gondola and the tank car for best esthetic effect or whether the cattle car could be placed behind the refrigerator car without violating the principles of sound railroading.

"You sent the whole rig up the grades barely moving, because that was the way real freights moved. You exulted in the glow of a headlight creeping through the tunnel, worried about switches, took pride in a skillful piece of coupling and fretted about making the whistle echo off the papier-mache mountains with the proper tone of melancholy.

"The train was a toy to teach a boy to dream. The racing car merely prepares him for the day when he will want to escape from 'Barbie.'... Like the best of modern machinery, it puts dreaming in its proper place and makes life ever so much more practical.

"What are we doing to these children?"

To meet competition, Lionel introduced its own racing car sets, complete with grandstands and service pits.

Dealer display for Lionel HO trains showed only freight sets, although passenger trains were available, too.

Lionel had actually introduced its own racing cars on the market years earlier, but had withdrawn them when they didn't do well. The country was more accepting of speeding automobiles in 1962 than it had been in 1912. Similarly, Lionel had introduced another innovation before the country was ready for it... and was suffering the consequences. For while the sale of toy trains was declining, the popularity of smaller, HO-gauge trains was rising. The HO trains, with track five-eighths of an inch wide, were exactly half Lionel's size, similar to the 00 gauge that Lionel had made before the war and never revived. By the middle of the fifties, the combined production of HO from a number of smaller manufacturers exceeded Lionel's total output of toy trains. HO equipment took up less space than Lionel (although its curves were often broader for the most realistic effect). This was an advantage during a time when people were moving more and railroad hobbyists were confined to smaller spaces than suitable for Lionel or even American Flyer. HO engines and cars were in exact proportion to each other, unlike Lionel's somewhat arbitrary measurements. And detailing was even more exact and realistic than Lionel's. Most HO was bought not by children but by adults who had been weaned on smoke pellets and cattle cars.

Had Lionel maintained its prewar 00-gauge line, it would have been in a commanding position in the small-scale war of the late fifties. (On the other hand, 00 probably would have been a drag on the company through the boom years of toy trains.) As it was, Lionel did not introduce its own HO line until 1957, the last year the company made a profit on the manufacture of electric trains. It had waited too long.

When HO did come to Lionel, its introduction typified the confusion and indecision afflicting the company. The line was manufactured in Italy by an established HO producer to save

HO trains were small enough to fit under trestle set supporting Lionel's new Super-O track, which had extra ties.

Lionel the cost of creating its own dies, much as the prewar tooling had been produced at La Precisa. A good-quality line that carried many familiar Lionel train names, it went into production too late to be included in the regular catalog. Instead, a two-page folder was inserted that bore the name of the Italian manufacturer, Rivarossi, effectively neutralizing the Lionel imprimatur. At the same time, the regular catalog undercut its own HO sales by warning parents, as it had for two years, of the "complicated wiring and extra gadgets" two-rail HO track required. Why buy HO, the catalog implied, when "even a bridge table top is space enough to accommodate a complete Lionel layout."

Nothing Lionel did in HO made sense. It waited too long to get into the field. It had the trains manufactured abroad, and couldn't keep up with the American market. Then it went American but produced a cheap, unreliable train (a fragile rubber belt carried power from the motor to the wheels) for an adult market that demanded quality. Ultimately, it made gimmicky HO trains that shot rockets and blew up, just the opposite of what the HO market required. HO was a complete disaster.

Everything began to converge on Lionel at once. A severe recession hit the economy, causing high unemployment and curtailing the amount of money people had to spend on luxuries like electric trains. That same tight economy produced ferocious competition for the few government contracts available, further cutting Lionel's income. Cheaper Japanese fishing equipment forced Lionel to mark down its Airex tackle, resulting in a $330,000 loss for the company. Then came the announcement from the Soviet news agency, Tass, that a 184-pound radio-transmitting satellite named *Sputnik* ("traveling companion") had been launched and was even now circling the earth. It took a lot to still be interested in old-fashioned electric trains with the space age orbiting overhead.

At Lionel, the management team that might have coped with these crisis conditions was no more. Mario Caruso was long gone, running a construction company in Naples. Arthur Raphael had died in 1952, depriving Lionel of its most creative sales mind. And Cowen was semi-retired, living almost half the year in Palm Beach. At the 1958 stockholders meeting, a disgruntled shareholder grilled Lawrence on how much time his father (absent from the meeting) actually spent in New York. "Does he come to Twenty-Sixth Street?" the stockholder asked. "He most certainly does," Lawrence replied, adding loyally, "If he worked for only six weeks of the year this corporation would be getting a bargain."

"Not at his salary of $82,000 a year," the stockholder shot back.

Whether or not Cowen's absence was the cause, Lionel seemed to have lost its direction

Lawrence and ad manager Joseph Hanson in ad.

"CAN YOU FIX OUR TRAINS?"

While it was usually Cowen who was associated with heart-warming stories about fixing children's trains, his son, Lawrence, had his share of Father Christmas experiences, too. Lawrence lived in Manhattan at 2 Sutton Place, an elegant apartment building overlooking the East River. One Christmas morning at 6:00 A.M., Lawrence was awakened by the persistent ringing of his doorbell. Sleepily opening the door, he found two small boys in pajamas looking up at him.

"Can you fix our trains?" one asked. They explained that Santa Claus had left them electric trains but that they couldn't get them to work.

Lawrence got his bathrobe and followed them upstairs to their apartment, where they thoughtfully tiptoed around to avoid waking the boys' parents. The president of Lionel soon had the trains going. The boys thanked him. Lawrence wished them a merry Christmas and returned to his own apartment, there to greet the holiday at a more adult hour.

Lionel's Norfolk & Western with real prototype.

and focus in the late fifties. With steam all but gone from America's railroads, Lionel offered a beautiful new streamlined steam locomotive with Norfolk & Western markings. Chugging right into a deepening recession, the fifty-dollar Norfolk & Western bullet-nose was the most expensive steam engine Lionel made that year. "Here is dramatic evidence that steam locos can be right up to the minute in power and design," the catalog claimed, sounding a little defensive; Lionel seemed to want to turn back the clock to a simpler steam era.

Of all the merchandising decisions made in the late fifties, however, the introduction of a pastel train for girls, complete with pink locomotive, was proof positive that Lionel had lost its marketing mind. Trying to reach that half of the population it had previously ignored made good business sense. But trying to reach it with a grotesque train set that negated the realism that was the very lure of the electric train made no sense at all. Missing entirely was the understanding that any girl who wanted a train wanted it for the same reasons her brother did: Electric trains looked big and powerful, just like the real thing, and their operators could pretend they were real engineers. "Now She Can Do Anything He Can Do... With Lionel's New Exclusive Pastel Train Set For Girls," the 1957 catalog bragged. "Girls, you wanted it! Here it is... a real Lionel train set in soft, pastel shades. How your friends will envy you when you actually take the throttle of the beautiful, pink frosted steam locomotive and send her on her way."

While most were black, the transformer for the girls' set was white and gold. Boxcars were "robin's egg blue" and "buttercup yellow," while the hopper was "lilac-colored" and the caboose was "sky blue." Advertised as being "in fashion-right colors... with cars to match," the girls' set was at once both bizarre and entirely logical for Lionel, considering the way it had viewed the women of America for fifty years.

Lionel had never marketed trains to girls. The only time it had recognized them as customers was in the early thirties, when it produced the miniature electric range. Girls in Lionel Land were not as invisible as black people, but they were as powerless. When they appeared in the catalogs at all, it was as part of an admiring audience. Girls were never in control; it was brother's hand that rested on the throttle. Girls were secondary to the main action. They were the accessories of Lionel Land—the trackside equipment and not the locomotives. Boys were prepped to become captains of industry, men who would run things, often from a distance,

Girls got dolls, but boys got the train sets.

just as they operated their trains through the highly-touted use of remote control. Women would be in the background, a cheering section, creating entrees to match their men's empires.

Like most everything else Lionel touched in those confused years, the girls' set flopped. Girls did not want an obvious fake. Nor did their fathers, who were still Lionel's principal buyers. A salesman for a small-town Pennsylvania train shop recalled trying to unload the Lady Lionel sets. "I can remember father after father being approached by myself and other salesmen to 'purchase a train for your daughter this Christmas,'" said LaRue Shempp, "and their firm reply with furrowed brow, 'What! Buy my daughter a girl's train with a pink engine! LaRue, you are out of your head!' " On Christmas Eve the three girls' sets were still sitting in the window, and Shempp and the other salesmen took them home.

The girls' set was one more instance of Lionel's clinging to outdated attitudes. In the same year Lionel was selling a pink train for girls, in a New York suburb still bursting with Lionel trains and their outwardly happy families, Betty Friedan was starting work on *The Feminine Mystique,* the seminal work that named a malady never acknowledged in the mythical Lionel family.

The frantic search for another product continued. Lionel started development of an outboard motor in conjunction with an Italian company, the feeling being that the motor could be distributed through the outlets selling the faltering Airex fishing equipment. Some $50,000 were spent on development, but the motor never went into production. Back in train land, *Sputnik*'s beeps were becoming audible even to Lionel. The result was a new train line dominated by the ominous shadow of a detailed rocket launching tower. A flatcar carried glowing red cannisters marked *Radioactive Waste—Danger,* while another transported a condenser and heat exchanger used in nuclear power installations. It was described as "a brand-new car for the Atomic Age."

To go with the rocket launching tower (which came complete with a push-button, count-down firing control panel) there was a flatcar bearing a miniature intercontinental ballistic missile. A radar tower was described as being "just like the real thing used for detecting enemy air-

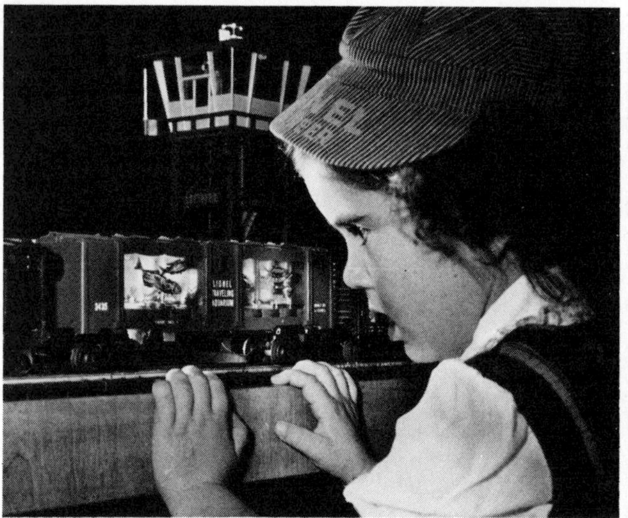

Girls were rarely shown actually touching the trains.

craft," while two military trains replete with tanks, amphibious landing craft, and antiaircraft cannon were also offered. Lionel was trying to be current, but the cheaply-made space and war trains only served to tarnish the Lionel image. Trains had always been a symbol of the "good" things in America. Bristling with guns and rockets and nuclear radiation, their message now was destruction and death.

Perhaps it was the sight of an ICBM on the tinplate tracks that had once carried "Pay As You Enter" trolley cars that drove him to it, but at the end of 1958 Cowen announced his retirement. By Cowen standards, he had been partially retired already, acting more as the elder statesman than as an active co-general manager and chairman of the board. He was at least eighty and even he must have felt his extraordinary energy flagging. At the December 18, 1958, meeting of the board of directors, Cowen's resignation was accepted, effective at the end of the year. With Cowen out of the room, the board voted to designate him Chairman Emeritus. It also retained him as a consultant "to give management advice and suggestions born of his many years of experience" at the generous salary of $30,000 a year plus expenses —which the troubled company could hardly afford.

Cowen got out just in time. Crippled by the recession gripping the country, Lionel's sales fell 23 percent in 1958 to $14.4 million. The company showed a loss of $469,000, its first losing year since the Depression. Stock dividends were cut by more than half to sixty cents a share. The stockholders meeting in spring of 1959 was long and often bitter. No dividends had

LOOK TO THE SKIES

The cleverness and engineering expertise that had once gone into making trains that delivered milk and carried cattle was used to create miniature forerunners of the MX missile system in the late fifties. The trains did reflect Cowen's guiding dictum by offering plenty of action, but they were flimsy and broke easily. Plastic was used in couplers, car steps, and on wheel side frames that were previously all metal. While obviously made to be played with by children (they were hardly realistic enough to appeal to adult model railroaders), Lionel's space trains couldn't absorb childish punishment.

Train layouts that were once landscaped with farms and villages became settings for war games in early sixties.

Rocket fired after remote control countdown of ten seconds.

"Radioactive" canisters and nuclear reactor heat exchangers constituted Lionel's freight in late fifties.

Army missile general John Medaris, who became Lionel's president in 1960, launches missile with president of Lionel's youth club. Behind them in showroom are Cowen's first trains.

1958 catalog with rocket launcher and radar tower.

Lionel wreaked devastation on all fronts with missile-firing train set.

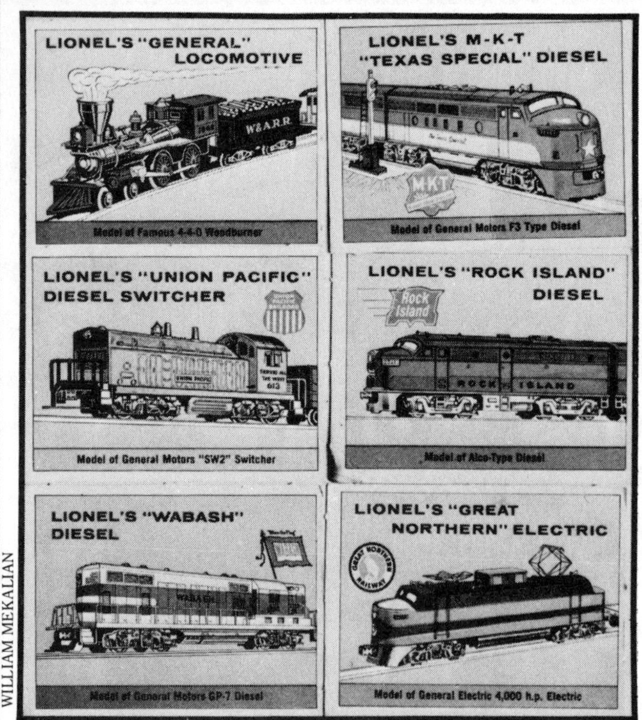

WILLIAM MEKALIAN

Lionel trading cards showed variety of engines.

been paid for the last two quarters and stockholders were worried. Although Cowen was now retired, resentment over the salary that he had received when he was only semi-active continued to surface. A resolution to abolish the vacant office of chairman of the board was defeated, but it received 11 percent of the vote. (The stockholders did not seem aware of Cowen's status as consultant, and Lawrence did not enlighten them.) Some stockholders grumbled that Cowen had stayed on too long and that in the future directors should resign at sixty-five. (In Cowen's case, that would have meant resigning in about 1942.) Others, however, praised him in outbursts that drew applause.

In light of the change in management and the family split that was to occur six months later, it is interesting to note who attended the New York meeting. Cowen, having retired, was not there (nor had he been for several years, to some stockholders' chagrin). His 49,830 shares (Lillian held another 5,600), representing 6.92 percent of the 720,000 shares of outstanding stock, were voted by management by proxy. Lawrence controlled 42,266 shares, or 5.87 percent. However, Lionel's major stockholder was Isabel Brandaleone, Lawrence's sister, and she was at the meeting. In her own name and in trust for her two children, Anthony Otis and Cynthia Saypol, Isabel voted 67,225 shares, equal to 9.34 percent of the company's stock. It was unusual for her to be present and to vote her shares herself rather than deliver her proxy to management, as she had when her father was still chairman of the company. Her attendance was an indication of both her dissatisfaction with declining dividends and her unease at Lawrence's management. In fact, Isabel's presence at the meeting was noted by a share holder who thought she was a member of the board of directors. "Well, I don't quite understand how you figure my sister," said Lawrence. "She is not a director and officer of the Lionel Corporation . . . merely a stockholder."

As the year continued, Lionel's losses mounted. By September, the company was down $583,000; by year's end, $1.2 million. Although sales increased slightly, Lionel had not raised the prices of its trains sufficiently to cover rising costs of material and labor, so the profit margin was far below what it had been in the early fifties. Still attempting to broaden its product line, Lionel acquired through Airex the trademark of the World Wide Sporting Goods Company for $15,000 and began importing baseball gloves and other sporting equipment from Japan. Although the company was in trouble, there was little at the September 17, 1959, board of directors meeting to indicate it would be the last at which Lawrence would have control of the company. The employees' retirement plan was amended so that it would cost the company less money. The outboard motor corporation, Lionel-Italia, was created. The bleak operating statements for Lionel and Airex were examined. The only unusual thing about the meeting was the surprising presence of Cowen himself, there as a guest at the first board of directors meeting he had attended since his retirement nine months earlier. The meeting lasted an hour and a half. Cowen could not have liked what he heard, for five days later, while Lawrence was in the Orient exploring new lines of sporting goods, Cowen and Lillian sold their stock for $825,000 to a group led by Roy Cohn, Cowen's great-nephew. Lionel was no longer a father and son railroad.

This shocking turn of events, which was a repudiation of the rhetoric upon which Lionel was based, had originated a year earlier. At that time, Cohn said later, "two or three family stockholders" came to see him to ask his advice on their holdings. They were worried about Lionel's poor earnings record, Cohn said, and

COWEN BREAKS THE NEWS

Comptroller Edward Zier, with Lionel since 1931, was the first to learn that Cowen had sold out to Roy Cohn. Zier was in his office at about 3:00 P.M. when the telephone rang.

"Eddie, are you busy or what?" It was Cowen's gravelly voice.

"No, why?"

"I'm at the apartment and I want you to come up here."

Zier jumped into a cab and went uptown to Cowen's condominium apartment on Fifth Avenue and Seventy-sixth Street. Cowen was sitting on a silvery gray brocade sofa beneath his portrait, which had been painted in 1948 and had hung in the Lionel offices. There were white mums in a vase on the gold rococo coffee table in front of him. The gray drapes were open, and through the casement windows Zier could see the apartment buildings across Central Park.

"I want to talk to you about something," Cowen said. "Oh, by the way... Roy, oh Roy, come out here." Zier thought he was calling Roy Clark, who worked with Lionel in Canada.

Out of the next room came Roy Cohn. "You know Roy, don't you, Eddie?" Cowen asked. Zier said sure, they had met several times before. They shook hands. There was a moment of silence in the thickly carpeted room. Cowen cleared his throat.

"Eddie," Cowen said, "I wanted you to learn it from me that I have just sold my stock to Roy and a group he represents."

approached him for guidance on how they might change things at the company, perhaps through some merger or acquisition. Cohn, thirty-two, had served as chief counsel to Senator Joseph McCarthy and was practicing law in New York. He was already experienced in corporate maneuverings, having been part of a group that gained control of the American News Company, building it into a profitable newsstand and restaurant concern. (Cohn was a director of American News when the "family stockholders" came to see him.)

Excluding Lawrence and Cowen, the only major family stockholders in Lionel were Isabel and her two grown children, Anthony Otis and Cynthia Saypol. Isabel's 9 percent of stock was roughly divided between herself and the two children. For the ten years prior to 1958, Lionel had paid a dividend of $1.25 or more per share each year. Halving that dividend in 1958 and skipping it entirely in 1959 meant a loss to her of some $85,000. Ronald Saypol, Cynthia's husband, had worked at Lionel since 1951. At the time of the Cohn group takeover, he was assistant to Vice President and General Sales Manager Alan Ginsburg. A change in management backed by his mother-in-law could certainly be expected to improve his position.

It was never completely clear what convinced Cowen to sell, knowing it would certainly mean the end of his son's control of Lionel. Perhaps he truly was dissatisfied with the way the company was being run. Maybe he was concerned, in his retirement years, that his ample holdings would lose their value. Perhaps his daughter and her family influenced him. And who knows what egotistical crosscurrents were at work as he watched the company that bore his name go on without him. In any case, on September 22, five days after he sat in on the board of directors meeting, Cowen agreed to sell his 55,000 shares to the Cohn group for fifteen dollars a share, approximately five dollars over the then-current market price. The next day the group secured another 21,800 shares from an investment company not connected with Lionel, and the deed was all but done.

During these last maneuvers, Lawrence and his wife, Vicki, were in the Orient. Also out of the country at the time was Philip Marfuggi, vice president for industrial relations and a company director. Marfuggi had married a niece of Mario Caruso's and had been with Lionel since 1937. He was in Naples, where the outboard motor was being developed, when he received a transatlantic call from his brother, Rex, who went on to become plant superintendent. "I was awakened about three or four in the morning by the call," Marfuggi recalled later. "It was Rex. He said, 'Phil, do you know Lionel's been taken over?' I said, 'What's the matter with you. You're out of your mind. It's impossible.' But he said, 'Yes, it happened. Believe me what I say.' "

Marfuggi met Lawrence in Rome. "Larry and Vicki came off the plane," Marfuggi said, "and she ran crying into my arms. I said to Larry, 'Is

HELICOPTERS TO THE RESCUE

Lionel achieved one of its major public relations coups in the turbulent months of late 1959, while control of the company was changing hands. Advertising director Jacques Zuccaire, a suave Frenchman, was fascinated with a new flatcar that actually launched a whirling helicopter by remote control. (The helicopter blades were wound by hand, the copter was set on the flatcar, and at the touch of a button, off it went!)

Zuccaire — who knew nothing of the Cohn takeover until he was tipped off that news of it would be in Walter Winchell's column the next day — thought the helicopter had potential for a great feature photo. He went to the plant and asked Joseph Bonanno if four helicopters could be launched at once. Yes, Bonanno said. "Well, could you set off six at one time?" Zuccaire inquired. Yes, came the reply. Zuccaire kept raising the ante until the engineering department figured out a way to launch several hundred Lionel helicopters at the same instant.

Working with freelance photographer Bill Stahl, Zuccaire managed to interest *Life* magazine in possibly using a photo of a mass launching. He hired the gymnasium of Newark College, where a technical crew under his direction set up fifteen parallel tracks running the length of the gym. Some 400 helicopter flatcars were placed on the tracks, and each of the helicopters was wound by hand. Up they went and down they came, as photo after photo was taken to be sure of getting a good one. (It took more than an hour between shots to wind up all the helicopters.) The crew worked into the early morning, but at the end Zuccaire was satisfied.

So was *Life.* Stahl's photo was spread over two complete pages in the popular "Speaking of Pictures" section in the December 21, 1959, issue. "Tiny Fleet in Mass Flight" read the headline that was superimposed over Lionel helicopters filling the air. The caption said it was "a scene that would top any child's dream of toyland" and mentioned Lionel by name. That topped any advertising director's dream of publicity. At the next board of directors meeting, a motion was passed commending Zuccaire "for his splendid work."

it true?' and he said, 'Yes, it's true.' He was pale and in a state of shock that his own father and sister did this to him, that his father could put such a dagger in the shoulder of his own son. Coming back on the plane we decided to put up a fight. After all, they'd have to go through proxies and a stockholders meeting. We decided to meet the next morning at the factory at Irvington."

At the plant the next day, Marfuggi waited for Lawrence with Charles Giaimo, plant superintendent, vice president, and secretary, and Joseph Bonanno, chief engineer and treasurer—men who had been with Lionel for decades and who had helped make it great. Giaimo had invented the whistle. Bonanno had some two hundred train patents to his name. Marfuggi had created the department of personnel. They all felt they had a chance to keep control of the company. But when Lawrence arrived, their hopes died. "Boys," he said, "I have sold my shares and I'd appreciate it if you'd let me have your resignations." Marfuggi said he "almost fell through the floor." Between the time he had returned from Rome and the meeting at the plant, Lawrence had met with the Cohn group. They offered him the same $15 a share they had offered Cowen (although the market price of the stock was now up to $11.75). Perhaps Lawrence was too dispirited to put up a fight, and maybe he was secretly glad to be out of the failing company, but he accepted the offer of $684,990.

A board of directors meeting was called October 8 to formalize the new management. A provision requiring a special meeting of stockholders before new members could be put on the board was simply changed then and there to allow Cohn's election. Lawrence resigned as president and was appointed chairman of the board; provisions were made for his acting as consultant after his chairmanship expired. (In 1962, Lawrence would sue Lionel, claiming he was never paid as consultant.) The old guard directors (Bonanno, Marfuggi, comptroller Edward Zier, and Giaimo) resigned, although Giaimo balked at the last minute and had to be convinced by Cohn that he had no choice. Isabel was elected to the board and appointed secretary of the corporation. Her son-in-law, Ronald Saypol, was elected vice president in charge of administration. His salary was raised to thirty thousand dollars a year plus a five-thousand-dollar expense account. Saypol, along with Cohn and several others, became part of a management advisory committee.

Lawrence's position as chairman was untenable while Cohn was the moving force on the board of directors. On December 7 he resigned the chairmanship in a letter to the corporation: "My experience in this capacity since the New Management took over convinces me that it would be preferable for the corporation to make the position of Chairman an executive officer of the company. It is for this reason that I hereby offer to resign from the position and title of Chairman. . . ." For the first time since Lionel's inception, there was no Cowen at its head. Coincidentally with Lawrence's resignation, a small item appeared in the travel section of *The New York Times:* "On Oct. 1 there were 875 steam locomotives in service on Class I American railroads. This compared with 28,964 in 1949. Since 1954, not one has been built. . . . Many children have never seen one running."

Lionel president John Medaris mulls over a point while chairman Roy Cohn presides at stockholders' meeting.

The takeover of Lionel had many ironic consequences. While it had been motivated in part by the failure of the company to declare its customary dividends, the mismanagement that followed so decimated Lionel that dividends were not paid again until 1977. During the years of Cohn's chairmanship, Lionel lost $13.3 million. Isabel remained as secretary less than two years, when she was succeeded by one of Cohn's original group. Saypol became vice president for operations but left in 1962 as the first of several battles for control of the company raged between Cohn and challenging groups. Whereas before 1959 Lionel had been slow to diversify and acquire new holdings, in the sixties the company added so many new electronic, toy, and manufacturing lines that it was unable to manage them properly, and most recorded huge losses. The number of acquisitions was equaled only by the changes in administration: In 1963 alone, the corporation went through three operating officers. While Cohn paid an inflated price of $15 a share when his group bought the stock during the takeover (and it rose to $18.37 in the following weeks), by the time he sold out in 1963 Lionel stock was worth only $5.25.

Amazingly enough, through all these changes in direction in the company, the trains continued to limp along. Quality was generally poor and the space-age gimmicks were silly, but there was never a year that Lionel did not offer a train line, despite financial disasters.

Within three months of the takeover, Lawrence became chairman and chief executive officer of Schick, Incorporated, manufacturers of electric razors. "I had a couple more offers beside Schick," he said, "but I chose it for two primary reasons. First, there isn't too much difference between electric train motors and shaver motors. Second, Schick has the same merchandising and distributing setup as Lionel, and in a great many instances sells to exactly the same accounts. Most businesses who sell electric razors also sell electric trains." Rem-

COWEN AS REMEMBERED BY...

His Chauffeur

Don Castro joined Cowen as his chauffeur in the early fifties and stayed with him until his death in Palm Beach.

"The boss always rode up in front with me in the Rolls-Royce," Castro recalls. "Even when Miss Lillian [Cowen's wife] was in the car, she sat in the back and the boss sat in the front, dozing. One day I was buying some gas. The boss, he looked like he was asleep even though the pump was ringing up the gas. I filled up and said, 'Boss, you owe me ten dollars.'

"'And how many gallons did you get, Don?'

"'Oh, fifteen,' I said.

"'Like hell you did,' he says to me. 'You only got five.' See, he was listening to the rings of the pump.

"Well, boss, I have to get some money from you. What you pay me, it's crumbs,' I told him. I was making about four thousand dollars. So the boss, he laughs and turns to Miss Lillian.

"'Last week Don complained he got peanuts; Now it's crumbs.' He laughed some more but he gave me the ten dollars."

Much of the badinage between Cowen and Castro involved money. Cowen would give Castro a generous five or even ten dollars for lunch. Castro might spend a dollar-fifty, but when he offered the change to Cowen, his response was, "What are you trying to do, insult me? Keep the change."

"One day Mr. Cowen gave me twenty dollars for lunch," Castro recalls. "Afterwards he says, 'Where's the change?' 'Oh, but you said to keep the change,' I told him. After that he carried smaller bills for my lunch!"

Cowen provided jobs for Castro's son and daughter. "Mr. Cowen told me to send my son to Lionel when he came home from Korea," Castro says. "He told me he would give him a job. My son went in and the office manager told Mr. Cowen, 'I'm sorry, but we have no desk for him.'

"'Hey, did you hear what I said to you,' Mr. Cowen told the manager. 'Find him a place.' But the manager kept questioning him. So finally Mr. Cowen said, 'Okay, well, you give him your desk and you go look for another job.'"

According to Castro, Cowen was "stubborn as a bulldog. Things had to be done his way, or else. He was a good man but you had to understand him. He had his own way of thinking and if you didn't follow it...I'd rather have a man get mad, lose his temper, let go than just fix me with that steely look of his."

iniscent of his days at Lionel, Lawrence immediately announced that Schick was interested in diversifying its product line. But not surprisingly, he could give no specific details.

Cowen retired to his undistinguished white seven-room house in Palm Beach. If he knew that in one of its first economy moves, the Cohn management had sold the antique Lionel trains in the showroom in which he had taken so much pride, Cowen never mentioned it. "He walked out of there and closed the door behind him," Lillian said later. The vine-covered house, its backyard full of foliage, became the center of Cowen's life. He would go for a drive—often to the bank—in the morning in his new black and gold Rolls-Royce, driven by his long-time chauffeur, Don Castro. When he came back he would read the papers or a book in a chaise lounge on the white patio. Often in the afternoons or evenings he played cards with friends. Lillian did petit point that was made into handbags.

They occasionally entertained, but the kitchen in the house was not really large enough for the catering Castro had provided in New York. They were early members of the Palm Beach Country Club, although Cowen no longer played golf. When publicist Lawrence Johnson dropped by for a visit one day, he found Cowen, "bored to death," rambling on about the early days of the company. There was little contact between him and Lawrence. A housekeeper who stayed with him for a year said Cowen talked often about Isabel but never about his son.

Cowen's health declined in his late eighties. He had given up driving several years earlier, when his night vision deteriorated. His memory worsened and he had trouble speaking. He hired a nurse to help him around, as he had difficulty walking. He was not feeling well, and as August 25, 1965 neared (it would have been his eighty-fifth birthday, according to the birth date he had given out for years), he decided to forego his customary birthday party.

"I'm not going to have a birthday party," he told Lillian. "How old am I, anyway?"

"How should I know?" Lillian answered.

"You mean to say you never had the sense to look at my insurance policies?" Cowen railed, showing some of his old spunk. "I'm eighty-eight."

Two weeks later he had a stroke, and on September 8 he died in Palm Beach. His body was flown to New York, and the funeral was held at Campbell's funeral parlor on Madison Avenue and Eighty-first Street. It was only about a mile south of where Cowen had spent part of his boyhood, across from McNally's farm, listening to the steam engines whistle on what was then the Fourth Avenue viaduct. The funeral was understated, conducted by a young rabbi whom Cowen himself had chosen. Family, friends, and some employees from Lionel attended. Two irreverent mourners used the occasion to ask Castro if he now wanted to come to work for them.

Cowen was buried in Brooklyn beside Cecelia at the base of a large stone that said, simply, "Cowen." Next to the plain Cowen plot was the looming mausoleum of Joseph Marcus, Cowen's brother-in-law and Roy Cohn's maternal grandfather. In its long obituary, *The New York Times* called Cowen "the father of the toy electric trains that run on thousands of miles of miniature track in homes throughout the world." Cowen, *The Times* said, had made the Lionel name "the third wing of Christmas along with the evergreen tree and Santa Claus." *The New York Herald Tribune* played up the same theme. "The man who influenced the celebration of American Christmas almost as much as Santa Claus died yesterday," the paper proclaimed.

Cowen's simple gravestone makes no mention of Lionel.

But if the rest of the world made note of Cowen's passing, the corporation that bore his name took no notice of it at all. Lionel was a changed company from the days when the board of directors passed resolutions of sympathy upon the death of the parents of fellow directors. A new administration was now in charge at Lionel, and Cowen was a perhaps unwanted reminder of the company's past greatness. At the Lionel board of directors meeting following Cowen's death, only matters of business were discussed. No reference to Cowen was recorded. Ironically, the new president, Robert Wolfe, pointed out that the toy portion of the business, including electric trains, was continuing to drain profit from Lionel's other operations.

After Cowen's funeral, a plain, flat marker was placed on his grave. It read, "Joshua L. Cowen. Beloved Husband And Father. Departed Sept. 8, 1965." Nowhere on the plot did the name Lionel even appear. Neither through motif nor legend was recognition made of the fact that here lay the creator of dreams for boys of all ages, the founder of America's favorite railroad. But although there was no monument to Lionel Lines, the cemetery was not an entirely inappropriate final resting place for the chief engineer of the world's longest—though smallest—rail system. For there beside it on the Brooklyn-Queens border ran the secondary tracks of the Long Island Railroad. A diesel switching engine trundled freight cars back and forth. The engine was the same one Lionel had made in 1949, the first to have Magne-Traction. The sound of its honking air horn carried over the grave. Joshua Lionel Cowen was in good company.

8

IN THE ROUNDHOUSE

1966-TODAY

Standing at Cowen's unpretentious grave, hearing the throb of the diesel switcher outside the cemetery gates, I realized how late I had come to the story of Lionel. By the time I learned there was indeed a Mr. Lionel, he was gone. So, too, was Lawrence, his plot one over from Cowen's, dead in 1970 of a heart attack at sixty-three, the age at which his incredibly vital and long-lived father was just beginning to prepare Lionel for World War II. Much of the post-Cowen history had already transpired before I began my quest for the roots of that puffing steam locomotive given me by my father on that long-ago Christmas in Brooklyn. Like the track of Lionel Lines, much of the remaining story passes familiar stations.

Jacket patch of contemporary Lionel Railroader Club.

Two years after Cowen's death, Lionel shocked the boys of America and created agonies of divided loyalties by buying American Flyer for $150,000 from the disintegrating A. C. Gilbert Company. It was the final triumph in the saga that had begun in 1929, when Cowen gained control of Ives, the pioneer Connecticut toy company that had regarded Lionel as a brash upstart. Lionel had outlasted them all, never failing to produce a train line even in the financial chaos of the sixties. The ultimate irony for Flyer fans, always so contemptuous of Lionel, came in 1981, when after an absence of fifteen years, American Flyer S-gauge, two-rail trains were available once more—made by licensing agreement with Lionel. Cowen, who himself had outlived both A. C. Gilbert and Gilbert's son, would have relished Lionel's victory.

Among those who advanced in the Cohn takeover of the company in 1959 was Ronald Saypol, Cowen's grandson-in-law. He left after three years, as Lionel was torn by battles over control of the faltering company. Yet in 1968 it was Saypol who headed a group that gained control of Lionel. A former department store

THE LIONEL CORPORATION

Ronald Saypol with modern freight train.

demonstrator of Lionel trains, Saypol was elected president and chief executive officer the same year. Saypol and Cowen's granddaughter, Cynthia, were later divorced, but Saypol stayed at the helm of Lionel, taking it into the eighties as a holding company specializing in—appropriately enough—toy stores. But in the recessionary year of 1982, Lionel hit an unfortunately familiar open switch. Burdened by $165 million in debts, largely from its toy stores, and unable to secure short term bank loans, on February 19 the corporation filed for protection from creditors under Chapter XI of the federal bankruptcy law to gain time to reorganize its finances.

Housed in plush, modern offices overlooking New York's Central Park, Lionel under Saypol is a far cry from the company that had a giant electric train layout as the centerpiece of its reception area. The company that bears his name hardly acknowledges Joshua Lionel Cowen; neither does it manufacture trains.

Ever reflecting their times, Lionel trains today are manufactured by a conglomerate, General Mills, which in addition to breakfast cereals produces Parker Brothers board games, Kenner Star Wars toys, Craft Master paint-by-number kits, and MPC plastic models. When Saypol returned to Lionel, he sensed that while the company name was magic, the trains were not. A marketing survey in 1969 revealed that the Lionel name was known in the leisure field by 70 percent of those queried. Only giant electronics firms like General Electric, RCA, and Zenith were better known. Amazingly, Lionel's nearest "competitor" was Eastman Kodak, recognized by 66 percent of the sample. Yet Kodak made $3 *billion* a year, compared to the $33 million taken in by Lionel during its best year under Cowen.

The Lionel name was too good to jettison. The same was not true of the trains. They were losing money, and Lionel had neither the capital nor the inclination to remain in the manufacturing business. General Mills was acquiring toy lines. In 1969, Saypol leased the Lionel electric train name to the Minneapolis corporation for a 3.5 percent royalty on annual sales. Through 1981, Lionel had received approximately $7 million in royalties from General Mills merely for allowing it to use Joshua Cowen's middle name and the tooling he created.

The trains are actually manufactured by a subsidiary of General Mills with the felicitous name of Fundimensions, located in Mt. Clemens, Michigan, an industrial suburb of Detroit. In 1981, its best year, Fundimensions sold approximately $22 million in Lionel trains and accessories. Since many of the original Lionel dies are used (Fundimensions also has created new cars and engines), the trains are frequently intentional duplicates of Lionel originals from the 1950s. Adult Lionel purists who see the originals as symbols of their childhoods are loathe to admit it, but Lionel by Fundimensions trains have many of the best features of the oldies. Steam locomotives are heavy, die-cast metal; they smoke (a new model of the Norfolk & Western bullet-nose expels smoke from its steam cylinders as well as from the stack); they whistle (though the "whistle" is an electronic microchip sounded through a tiny speaker in the tender); they have Magne-Traction to hold them to the rails at high speeds; and they include the "Mighty Sound of Steam," an eighties version of Cowen's 1930s "chugger" that uses electronic chips to produce the rhythmic *choo-choo* of a steam engine. The indefatigable highway crossing gateman still rushes out of his shack waving his lantern at the approach of a train, and a lift bridge automatically stops trains with a warning bell when it is raised.

In 1974, a girl actually appeared on the catalog cover. Her appearance was the result of a letter Fundimensions received from seven-year-old Caroline Ranald of New York. "Dear Sir," she wrote, "I don't like your new ads. Girls like trains too. I am a girl. I like trains. I have seven locomotives. Your catalog has only boys. Don't you like girls? PS. I love the Metroliner." Caroline's letter prompted a TV ad campaign with the closing line, "Lionel trains: We never said they were only for boys." A mother was shown wrapping a Lionel under the Christmas tree. She recalled that her "very worst Christmas" was when her brother got the Lionel she wanted and wouldn't let her play with it because she was a girl. "That's not going to happen to my little girl," the mother said, putting the last touches on the present. *Ms.* magazine hailed the campaign. More girls and a black boy appeared on the 1977 catalog cover. Lionel had come a long way from the days of the pink Lady Lionel set.

The "new Lionel," Fundimensions, is keenly aware of the merchandising value of associating itself with Joshua Lionel Cowen. For Lionel's seventy-fifth anniversary in 1975, Fundimensions produced an Anniversary Special train, its freight cars gimmicked up with pictures of old Lionel catalogs, Lionel logotypes, and the company's best-known trains going back to Cowen's earliest cars. To observe what Cowen led people to believe would have been his hundredth birthday in 1980, Fundimensions issued a series of six boxcars with historical information about Lionel on their sides. The last was called The Man and said somewhat blandly, "Joshua Lionel Cowen was an individual with many talents... as he entered the business world he filled the varied roles of inventor, engineer, manufacturer and salesman." A seventh car, with the same 1950 portrait of Cowen on its side that appeared with his *New York Times* obituary, was given to major buyers at the 1980 Toy Fair. Even in death, Cowen was selling toy trains.

"Not Just A Toy, A Tradition," is the slogan Fundimensions uses to establish its links with the past. Ironically, one of its major customers is The Lionel Corporation through its Lionel Leisure toy store operation. Some seventy-five Lionel Leisure toy supermarkets buy Lionel trains from Fundimensions, which was owed $827,000 when Lionel filed Chapter XI. Fundimensions' trains are excellent. In some ways, they are even better than the originals (the painting and striping is more elaborate than anything attempted by Cowen). They carry the Lionel name (though in modern typeface). But something is missing. The new catalogs make them look like pieces of hardware. They are photographed against plain paper backdrops, lifeless lumps of metal and plastic. No longer are they pictured roaring through idealized farmlands and country towns where children wave and look to distant horizons. Ads refer to old Lionel ("a tradition"), not to the world of real railroads and commerce. No more do the catalogs claim that dad obtained his early training for the job he holds today by playing with a Lionel train. The trains are "product," so many to the shipping carton, so much in freight charges. They are no longer a source of dreams.

Like many other adult train collectors, I thought (or fooled myself into believing) it was solely the trains I sought when I began visiting old Lionel train stores, wanting a Berkshire locomotive because I had grown up with the steam turbine, a milk car because I was weaned on the cattle car, a log loader because I had been given the coal conveyor. I found I was not alone. I joined the Train Collectors Association (TCA), one of several nation-wide groups, and my membership number was 12,384. I attended Sunday-morning train "meets" in crowded, smoky social halls where collectors hovered over tables filled with wonders I had never imagined: standard gauge State Sets and Power Stations; postwar engines in color combinations never shown in the catalog; freight cars to complete the perfect railroad whose manifest I carried in my head.

Lionel's catalog cover for 1973.

One of four buildings at Train Collectors Association's semiannual toy train meet at York, Pennsylvania.

I learned a new language. Glowing catalog descriptions were reduced to the numbers on a computer print-out. We spoke not of the "scale Hudson" but of the "700E." Trains were evaluated by whether they were "mint-in-the-box" (new as when they came from the store), "prototypes" (one-of-a-kind original models), or in early or late-production color schemes. The bubbling joy of playing with trains turned into the serious business of collecting.

I made my first of what has become a twice-annual pilgrimage to York, Pennsylvania, where the largest regularly scheduled toy train meet in the world is held by the TCA in four cavernous state fair buildings. Over 7,000 collectors from as far as Hawaii and England buy and sell at 1,600 crammed tables. I was staggered not only by the trains but by the specialization. Some collectors do not collect at all but manufacture rare parts for early engines. Others, "paper" collectors, deal only in catalogs, instruction sheets, and other train-related memorabilia. Some concentrate on train boxes, seeking every Lionel (or American Flyer) cardboard container. One collector displayed X-rays of his trains in their original, sealed cartons so that anyone buying the trains would not have to break the seals but could keep them in their virginal condition. In this way, an electromagnetic crane passed through the hands of several collectors without ever being opened.

The obsession of collecting—and the cash deals that go with it—attempt to legitimize our preoccupation with the toys of our childhood.

There is even a genuine body of scholarship in collectors' journals, as serious as any in anthropological texts, which includes counts of rivets on plastic boxcars and measuresments of couplers' lengths. Variations in shades of color and in locomotive trim are meticulously noted. But the lure of the trains resides only superficially in these details. For whether extolling the grimy locomotive engineer as American hero or equating a gift of electric trains with fatherly love, Lionel provided beguilingly easy solutions to complex social problems. So deeply did Lionel plant the vision of a simpler world, so great is the desire to reconstruct a perfect childhood, that today grown men vie to own a single outstanding locomotive, as if its possession could solve the vagaries of adult life. I do not think I believe this, and yet I, too, pursue these elusive symbols.

For things didn't work out the way Cowen promised they would if we played with his trains, not for us and not for him. (Finally, despite all the propaganda, Cowen himself was the father who "never knew his own son.") Most of us never grew up to be engineers, to say nothing of railroad presidents or builders of empires. We never had the idealized relationships with our fathers that existed in Lionel Land. The family iconized by Cowen is even less real in the 1980s than it was in his time—if it ever existed at all except in Cowen's imagination. There have been divorces and remarriages. Friends have died fighting in wars and fighting against them. And yet we all had Lionels.

Still, we collect the trains in hopes of trying again. Maybe this time we will rub the totems in the right way, take proper care of the talismans, and have those mythologically perfect relationships we—and Cowen—never had. Once Lionel offered the promise of a fulfilled childhood. Now it holds the possibility of something better than eternal life—the illusion of starting over. Maybe with enough new trains, we can go back and make it right. The most desirable trains today are the ones that have never been run. They help us to believe, even if just for a moment, that we are eight again, opening the boxes for the first time—ourselves as new and unscratched as the trains, as pure as Lionel Land.

When I started to pursue the vanishing marker lights of the Lionel Limited, I thought I was writing about electric trains. But they turned out to be only part of the story, and the simplest part, at that. Behind the trains was the company, and behind the company, the man. Then I thought I was writing about a man, but I found I was writing about a father and a son. And that made me think about all sons, and thus about myself. Although I was drawn to them, I learned myths could be lived only in Lionel Land. I knew I loved my father even though he wasn't the perfect Lionel dad, and I wasn't the perfect Lionel son. I found that remote control worked fine on train layouts, but in life you had to be involved if you wanted something back. I discovered a world unlike Cowen's Lionelville, where women were partners and not just an audience. And I realized I didn't have to be an engineer to be a real man.

Having learned all this, I still cherish my Lionels. For to run Lionel over its defiantly three-rail track is to leaf through a treasured photo album, to see America and my early self, the images only slightly faded, the captions written in a familiar hand. Though it may be years since I rode the Lionel Express, for a part of me, Lionel City will always be home.

In an age of space exploration, Fundimensions' ads still portray boyhood dreams of steam locomotives.

LIONEL TRAINS
NEW YORK, N.Y.

INDEX

A

B

D

E

F

G

H

I

J

K

L

M

N

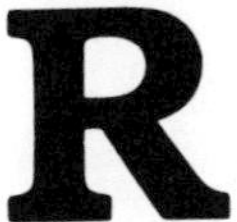

U

V

Z

IN GRATITUDE

In gratitude to those authors on toy trains who have come before: James Burke, Jr., Harold Carstens, Donald Fraley, Howard Godel, Bruce Greenberg, Frank Hare, Louis Hertz, Ward Kimball, Case Kowal, Allen Levy, Eric Matzke, Tom McComas, James Sattler, Guy Williams, Stephen Wolken, and the many contributors to the *Train Collectors Association Quarterly* and the *Toy Train Operating Society Bulletin*...and with encouragement to those who will come after.

WITH THANKS

With thanks for special support to Paul Hilzen, Nancy Kramer, Alan Shanel, the group, and especially to Pat Berens of The Sterling Lord Agency — a true daughter of the Santa Fe — who believed from the start.

The following members of the Cowen family, Lionel employees, train collectors, and general public gave their time, recollections, mementos, and photographs to make this book possible:

Al Anderson, Hal Ashley, Anthony Astrachan, Roland Baker, Jr., Tom Barker, Jean Basecq, Fred Beach, John Belock, Jr., Sam Belser, Edward Bernard, Alberta Bernecker, Richard Besser, Louis Bohn, Elizabeth Bonanno, William Bostelman, Isabel Brandaleone, Robert Brannon, Eric Buckley, Jr., James Burke, Jack Caffrey, Roy Campanella, Joel Cane, Anthony Caprio, Harold Carstens of *Railroad Model Craftsman,* Mario Caruso, Don Castro, Graham Claytor, James Coakley of Time-Life Books, Sam Coggins, Irving Cohen, Paul Conte, Sr., Martha Cooper, Kenneth Couch, Lillian Cowen, John Cujas, John Daniel, Lenny Dean, Maurice Demers, Don Denlinger, Terence Dodson, David Eisendrath, John Felber, Roy Fischer, Daniel Focht, John Foskett, Arthur Fritsche; at Fundimensions: Jim Boosales, John Brady, Dan Cooney, Bill Diss, Dan Johns, Pete Sappenfield; William Gaston, David Gauer, David Genszler, Edward Gerson, Francis Glasser, Norman Glasser, Betty Goad, Howard Godel, Phyllis Goldblatt, Bertram Goodman, Jean Greenbaum, Mary Lee Grisanti, Thomas Groff, John Hafner, John Haher, Frank Hare, William Harry, Robert Hauser, Lesley Hazleton, Richard Higgins, Larry Hollander, Marshall Hollander, Bruce Hudzik, Henry Jensen, John Johnson, Jr., Lawrence Johnson, Philip Kaplan, Lois Kenney, Natasha Kern-Heitman, Ward Kimball, Philip Klopp, Max Knoecklein, Emmi Kosak, Stanley Kramer, Anthony Kukal, Hector Labarca, Russell Larson of *Model Railroader,* Hillel Lazarus, Samuel Lenhart, Alvin Levin; at Lionel: George Padgett, Ronald Saypol, Richard Schilling, Liz Smith, Robert Stein, Michael Vastola, office staff; Mike Lipton, Franklin Loveland, William Maier, Cam Mann, Fanny Mann, Bruce Manson of Toy Train Museum, Joemine Marfuggi, Rex Marfuggi, Mike Marotta, John Marron, Mario Mazzone, Joseph Mead, Jr., William Mekalian, Thomas Michels, Charles Miller, Frank Miller, Rudolph Miller, Frederick Minchella, Daniel Mordell, Robert Morgan, Ron Morris, Morris Moses, George Muller, Richard Nappi, Estelle Newman, Robbie Nielsen, Nikon (Ehrenreich Photo-Optical), Larry Novy, Michael Ocilka, Quentin O'Sullivan of Allis-Chalmers, Dave Otth of *Toy Train Operating Society Bulletin*, Tom Pagano, Louis Park, Dominick Perella, Frank Pettit, Mollie Pollack, Marie Quaid, Ernest Raab, Virginia Ranck, Richard Rasmussen, Lou Redman, Irene Relin, Roz Relin, Ignazio Rizzuto, Juanita Robertson, Harvey Roe, Maurice Romer, Vincent Rosa, Ken Rosenberger, Joseph Rudley, Joseph Sadorf, Phil Sayer, Cathy Saypol, Cynthia Saypol, Ruth Schwarzkopf, Thomas Sefton, Robert Selig, Thomas Senior, Philip Shelly, LaRue Shempp, Robert Shepard, Ron Shumate of the Association of American Railroads, Carl Shaw, Lou Shur, Don Simonini, Duane Skokut, Elliott Smith, Ralph Spielman, Richard Stafford, Alvin Staufer, Emmert Stouffer, Dan Stupek of Bucyrus-Erie, Peter Tilp, John Tilsch of Santa Fe, Fred Tucker, William Vagell, Martin Vehstedt, Bruce Walthers, Ed Weidner, John Weis, Rodney White of Norfolk & Western, George Yohe, Frank Zachary of *Town & Country*, Tom Zaebst, Gordon Zern, Dorothy Zier, Robert Zier, Ron Zier, Jacques Zuccaire, and in memory of Joseph Bonanno, Philip Marfuggi, and Edward Zier who contributed greatly to *All Aboard!* but who did not live to see it.

I would also like to thank the following staff members at Workman Publishing: Kay Evans, Louise Gikow, Donna Gould, Paul Hanson, Jan Hersh, Sallie Jackson, Sally Kovalchick, Wayne Kirn, Gabrielle Maubrie, Julienne McNeer, Wendy Palitz, Richard Rew, Jennifer Rogers, Maureen Salter, Bert Snyder, Geoffrey Stevens, Joanne Strauss, Ludvik Tomazic, Peter Workman.

REPRODUCTION CATALOGS CONSULTED

Reproductions of toy train catalogs used in preparing *All Aboard!* include those published by: E. A. Basse Jr., Lester Gordon, Greenberg Publishing, House of Heeg, Iron Horse Productions, Max Knoecklein, Jerry Rubenstein, Robert Schnitzer, William Vagell.

PHOTO CREDITS

AAR: Association of American Railroads
Bettmann: The Bettmann Archive
TCA: Train Collectors Association
TTOS: Toy Train Operating Society

Photos not credited are by the author or from his collection. Every effort has been made to credit photo sources. Any omissions are regretted.

AUTHOR'S NOTE

I welcome hearing from readers who want more information about their trains, or who have Lionel and other trains for sale. Research continues, and I also look forward to talking with former Lionel employees and others who have memories and memorabilia of America's favorite railroad.

Ron Hollander
562 West End Avenue
New York, N.Y. 10024
Telephone 212-877-3832